LANGUAGE, THOUGHT, AND CULTURE: *Advances in the Study of Cognition*

Under the Editorship of: E. A. HAMMEL

DEPARTMENT OF ANTHROPOLOGY
UNIVERSITY OF CALIFORNIA
BERKELEY

SYMBOL AS SENSE

New Approaches to
the Analysis of Meaning

SYMBOL AS SENSE

New Approaches to
the Analysis of Meaning

EDITED BY

MARY LECRON FOSTER

STANLEY H. BRANDES

Department of Anthropology
University of California, Berkeley
Berkeley, California

ACADEMIC PRESS

A Subsidiary of Harcourt Brace Jovanovich, Publishers

New York   London   Toronto   Sydney   San Francisco

ACADEMIC PRESS, INC.
111 Fifth Avenue, New York, New York 10003

United Kingdom Edition published by
ACADEMIC PRESS, INC. (LONDON) LTD.
24/28 Oval Road, London NW1 7DX

Library of Congress Cataloging in Publication Data
Main entry under title:

Symbol as sense.

(Language, thought, and culture)
Includes bibliographies and index.
1. Symbolism. 2. Communication. I. Foster, Mary
LeCron, Date II. Brandes, Stanley H.
CB475.S96   302.2   79−8542
ISBN 0−12−262680−X

PRINTED IN THE UNITED STATES OF AMERICA

80 81 82 83   9 8 7 6 5 4 3 2 1

Contents

v

20. Symbolism, Canalization, and *P*-Structure 323

CHARLES D. LAUGHLIN, JR. AND CHRISTOPHER D. STEPHENS

VI. SYMBOLIC UNIVERSALS

21. Introduction 367

MARY LECRON FOSTER AND STANLEY H. BRANDES

22. The Growth of Symbolism in Culture 371

MARY LECRON FOSTER

List of Contributors

Numbers in parentheses indicate the pages on which the authors' contributions begin.

EDWIN ARDENER (301), *St. Johns College, Oxford OX2 6PF, England*

MAURICE BLOCH (93), *Department of Anthropology, London School of Economics, London WC2A 2AE, England*

DWIGHT BOLINGER (9), *2718 Ramona Street, Palo Alto, California 94306*

MELISSA BOWERMAN (277), *Department of Linguistics and Bureau of Child Research, University of Kansas, Lawrence, Kansas 66045*

STANLEY H. BRANDES (3, 71, 77, 125, 203, 271, 367), *Department of Anthropology, University of California, Berkeley, Berkeley, California 94720*

NEIL CHALMERS (131), *Department of Biology, Open University, Milton Keynes MK7 GAA, England*

COLIN CHERRY* (249), *Department of Electrical Engineering, Imperial College, London SW7 2BT, England*

PERCY S. COHEN (45), *Department of Sociology, London School of Economics, London WC2A 2AE, England*

MARGARET W. CONKEY (225), *Department of Anthropology, State University of New York at Binghamton, Binghamton, New York 13901*

MARSHALL DURBIN (103), *Department of Anthropology, Washington University, St. Louis, Missouri 63130*

MARY LeCRON FOSTER (3, 71, 125, 203, 271, 367, 371), *Department of Anthropology, University of California, Berkeley, Berkeley, California 94720*

HOWARD GARDNER (175), *Harvard Project Zero, Harvard University, Cambridge, Massachusetts 02138*

* Deceased.

JEAN KITAHARA-FRISCH (211), *Life Sciences Institute, Sophia University, Kioicho 7, Chiyoda-ku, Tokyo 102, Japan*

JOHN T. LAMENDELLA (147), *Linguistics Program, San Jose State University, San Jose, California 95192*

CHARLES D. LAUGHLIN, JR. (323), *Department of Sociology and Anthropology, Carleton University, Ottawa, Ontario, Canada K15 5B6*

JENNIFER M. SHOTWELL (175), *Harvard Project Zero, Harvard University, Cambridge, Massachusetts 02138*

DAN SPERBER (25), *Centre National de la Recherche Scientific, 33 Rue Croulebarbe, 75013 Paris, France*

CHRISTOPHER D. STEPHENS (323), *Department of Sociology and Anthropology, Carleton University, Ottawa, Ontario, Canada K1S 5B6*

DENNIE WOLF (175), *Harvard Project Zero, Harvard University, Cambridge, Massachusetts 02138*

Colin Cherry, a valued contributor to *Symbol as Sense,* died on November 23, 1979, after a long illness. His quiet insistence on a high standard of logic in debate curtailed our more flagrant rhetorical excesses, while his profound insight into the role of modern technology in shaping symbolic transformations bridged the evolutionary space between our industrially conditioned, symbolizing selves and our technologically less saturated, symbolizing ancestors. That we could profitably extend our consideration of symbolizing from Paleolithic beginnings into the present and future owes a great deal to the perspicacity of Colin Cherry.

Preface

Symbolism, as a theme, has implications not only for anthropologists, but also for biologists, psychologists, sociologists, linguists, and students of other communication systems, and for those involved in the analysis of any kind of aesthetic or humanistic endeavor. All these fields have contributed to our understanding of symbols, but progress is slowed by lack of interdisciplinary communication. In order to promote this kind of communication and to explore the possibilities of symbolism as a unifying topic for anthropology, Mary LeCron Foster organized an international symposium that included representatives of many of these disciplines. The symposium, under the auspices and support of the Wenner-Gren Foundation, took place July 16–24, 1977, in Burg Wartenstein, Austria.

Participants were drawn from the four major fields of anthropology (archaeology, physical anthropology, sociocultural anthropology, linguistic anthropology) and from sociology, ethology, linguistics, communication technology, developmental psychology, and psycholinguistics. Since a number of the participants were capable of wearing more than one intellectual hat, the topical coverage was even greater than this list implies.

The ensuing interaction resulted in what Lita Osmundsen, director of research of Wenner-Gren and a valuable *ex officio* participant, termed "a clash of epistemologies." We gradually became aware that this clash resulted from important disciplinary differences in methodology, model building, hypothesis testing, and focus. Because of the clash we were forced to rethink and reevaluate the categories and assumptions implicit in our own disciplines, which we had long taken for granted. This implicit categorization, accompanied by what we termed "the aha reaction," was itself deeply symbolic. We believe that all of us had many of these reactions, and those of the editors are incorporated in the introductions to the different parts of this book.

It seems safe to say that the symposium participants tended to emerge from epistemological clashes with somewhat the same feeling that social anthropologists have after overcoming the initial culture shock induced by the field experience: a respect for the fact that each different world view legitimately calls for a different type of solution. As we discovered the reasons for these disciplinarily induced, disparate world views, we gained respect for differing methodologies and modes of explanation. Although we did not necessarily change our own mental biases, we at least gained new insights from our differences. Some of our problems stemmed from such things as differences in time scale, ranging from the thousands or millions of years in the Pleistocene to the months, or even days, of ethological or developmental psychological analysis; differences in use of inductive or deductive methods of analysis, of experimentation versus observation; and terminological confusions that required clarification. A certain amount of difficulty also arose over the degree to which participants were intellectually committed to causal models with verifiable determinants and easily replicable results.

Each contributed chapter contains its own unique theoretical merit, and the controversial issues that permeated the conference discussions provide the book with a variety of novel approaches to major problems combined with a multifaceted interweaving of methodological solutions to common problems. Our editorial aim was to organize the material in such a way that a consecutive reading of the contributed chapters and editorial introductions might convey some of the epistemological challenge and excitement engendered by the conference itself.

Inevitably, our organization of materials coupled with our interpretations has introduced something of a personal bias. However, that bias was induced first by the interaction of the conference itself, then by postconference focus on issues stimulated by reading revised versions of the papers, by discussion of key issues in person or by mail with contributors and with one another, and by review of some of the taped discussions. While the editorial conclusions in the introductions are our own, our fellow participants will recognize the special insights that each contributed.

The book, then, is an effort to formulate a symbolic theory from a wide variety of interpretations. It builds thematically by stages, using each chapter as a building block in deriving general formulations that are given depth by the extraordinary range of data that inform them.

The title *Symbol as Sense* results from our conviction that the central problem of symbolism is meaning and that, although much that is symbolic makes no sense whatsoever in terms of rationality, symbolism makes very good sense indeed in terms of its functional adaptivity for mankind—the only species to organize its social activities in terms of this kind of cognitive model and, by so doing, to surmount many environmental constraints to freedom of action that have greatly limited the behavioral potential of other species.

As editors, we adopt the terms *symbol* and *symbolize* as cover terms for all of human behavior that is systematically organized, whether for social or individual purposes. Authors of some of the chapters in this book exclude from the meaning of *symbol* those aspects that are primarily referential. We do not, because we believe that there is a human behavioral continuum ranging from the referential (denotative) to the figurative (connotative), mediated by intentionality (affect, motive, or mood). Important as it is to differentiate the two poles and to indicate dominance of one or the other, we feel that theory is ill served by making a complete dichotomy, or either–or situation, from the fact of two interrelated manifestations. Furthermore, we believe that it is primarily the figurative dimension that separates the behavior of *Homo sapiens* from that of other species capable of a considerable referential ability and with probably as wide a range of affectivity and motivation as ourselves.

As we attempt to isolate the meaning of symbols, we are confronted with a tripartite semantic problem that has to do with the relationships among (*a*) reference, or the conveyance of "pure" information; (*b*) connotation, or the conveyance of commonly held associations to that information; and (*c*) intentionality, or the conveyance of the motives and mood of the purveyor of that information. Reference and connotation are on a continuum, with any symbolic message containing one or the other to a greater or lesser degree. Intentionality, or at least the degree of affect determining the intentionality, seems more characteristic of connotation than of denotation. Even a heavily denotative system such as language allows a paralinguistic intentionality through devices like intonation, rhythm, and selective manipulation of words and phrases. Although ritual is primarily connotative, repetitive familiarity may reduce its affective impact.

Our thesis is that each of these symbolic dimensions is present to some degree in every symbolic act, whether individual or social. Proportions vary, but no act is entirely devoid of any of these aspects. Of the three, denotation is the most rule-bound and content-specific (i.e., the least ambiguous); figuration is the most open to multiple interpretations. Motivation must be present if any act at all is to occur or be interpreted.

Denotation and connotation thus form a behavioral continuum with intentionality as the human energy required for its activation. Each of these manifestations operates within the context of a particular set of rules. Those of motivation have to do with style, those of denotation with reduction of ambiguity, and those of figuration with interpretational freedom, which increases ambiguity but is constrained by the *value system* (motivation) of the culture in which the behavior occurs. Because emotion is universal, there will be similarities of motivational influence (i.e., style) between quite disparate cultures, making myth, for example, or art, appealing even when nothing is known of the cultural systems in which it is embedded.

The first part of this book, Sense and Non-Sense, presents these three major symbolic dimensions and illustrates them. The second part, Cohesion and Continuity, illustrates the way in which they are interwoven in ritual and aesthetic activities in three cultures removed from one another in space or time. Nature and Structure introduces the biological implications for symbolism of ontogeny, phylogeny, and interspecies homologies. Transmission and Transformation is concerned with the problem of change in the formation of the symbolic act. Technology as Transformer shows ways in which increase in the complexity of skills influences the course of cultural events. The Growth of Symbolism in Culture considers a spectrum of symbolic universals reflected in specific behaviors anchored in time and space. We conclude with a discussion of symbolic universals, not simply as a recapitulation, but as a theory of process with implications for both the past and the future.

Acknowledgments

As editors, our debts are many: to the Wenner-Gren Foundation for financial support and gracious hospitality; to its director, Lita Osmundsen, for her loyal and creative endeavors on our behalf, for the many insights she contributed, and for the special quality with which she imbues a Burg Wartenstein event; to our fellow participants who, each in his or her own way, contributed a special dimension to our understanding and an individual style of friendship and cooperation; and finally, to our families for moral support and for serving as sounding boards, advisers, and patient bystanders as we struggled through the many difficult and time-consuming activities associated with any enterprise of this type.

I
SENSE AND NON-SENSE

1
Introduction

MARY LeCRON FOSTER
STANLEY H. BRANDES

In Part I we plunge headlong into the heart of the symbolic problem: the meaning of symbols. Although we may vary individually in our evaluation of the *kind* of sense conveyed by particular symbols—good sense or utter nonsense—we cannot but agree that to their users every symbol makes some kind of sense or it would neither come into use nor be perpetuated.

To recapitulate our introductory formulation: Symbolic meaning is of three types, or has three components: denotation (or reference), connotation (or figuration), intentionality (or motivation). The three chapters in this section introduce some of the problems that are involved in the analysis of these intersecting systems.

Bolinger focuses on an important motivational system, by means of which the sender of a symbolic message indicates his own intentionality. Sperber shows that denotation and figuration serve separate functions, require different systems of interpretation and description, and complement or supplement one another in human activities; he argues for the priority of rationality (i.e., reference) over figuration ("evocational" systems). Cohen interrelates motivation and figuration as a dynamic, unconscious process that culturally builds upon human, biologically based drives.

Part I introduces yet another important premise: Symbolism is not merely representation but is a representational *process* that depends both for its creation and for its replication on human interaction within a culturally defined social setting. This makes social context of crucial importance in determining and interpreting symbols.

SYMBOL AS SENSE

To understand meaning it is necessary to take context into account because as Bolinger puts it, "the culture inserts a sign and gets back a symbol" (p. 10). He feels that the use of *only* linguistic context to discover meaning is circular because, "A dependence on context has to assume that we know everything except the one item in question, but if we do not know that item, and context is a string of interdependencies, then we cannot be sure that we know the context either" [Bolinger, 1968:246].

Unlike many linguists, anthropologists and psychologists are concerned with language as more than a referential system. Utilizing different perspectives, they look outside language for aids in understanding the formation of linguistic meaning. Anthropologists look to the formalized stereotypy of social occasions for clues (for a particularly cogent approach see Bloch, 1975). Psychologists look at more particularized personal interactions in order to hypothesize the nature of internalized meanings (see Bowerman, this volume, for one such point of view).

To quote Bolinger once again:

> Linguists are sensitive to reputations. It has been so cozy inside the formal system, with everything ticketed and orderly, that they have been reluctant to allow any rowdy element on the premises. Meaning, as we have seen, is an exceedingly ill-assorted fellow. One can scarcely invite him into the house without admitting at the same time one or more of his drunken friends. The technique has been either to lock him out or to demand a password and slam the door shut the moment the legitimate guest is inside, which not infrequently has cost him part of an arm or a leg . . . . In theory—though not always in practice—American linguists of the past thirty years have kept their investment in meaning as low as possible by dealing with it in one of two ways: admitting only a well-defined minimum of it or not admitting it at all and pretending it was already there—that is, carrying on with its ghost [1968:243–244].

Language is often defined as the symbol system *par excellence*, differentiating the human from other species. If symbolization is defined as the representation of one thing by another, at least the first part of this categorization of language would seem to hold. Experiments in teaching chimpanzees representational systems based on language throw some doubt on the second part. Linguists often follow the usage of Saussure, the founder of modern structural linguistics, in defining language as a 'sign' rather than a 'symbol' system. The linguistic sign, according to this position, unites a *signifier* (word or morpheme) with a *signified* (a conceptualized object, activity, or function). Since the signifier and the signified bear no physical resemblance to one another, for Saussure the term *symbol* was inappropriate to the linguistic situation (Saussure, 1959: 66–67). Unlike a symbol, a sign is arbitrary.

Bolinger uses this definition as the point of departure for his chapter in this book, which establishes the fact that intonational universals show a degree of nonarbitrariness not found in phonology. Intentionality seeps through and affects the interpretation of denotational messages by differentiation of pitch level, the forcefulness with which syllables are uttered, and the rhythm with which linguistic units are temporally spaced. The speaker thus inserts himself and his feelings about events into the *sense* of the message that he is purveying. This invasion is neither *sense* as 'rationality,' nor *nonsense* as 'lack of meaning.' Like the syntax of denotational meaning it is formalized (i.e., rules for intonational usage usually form a minor but necessary part of grammars) rather than random. It is affectively rather than referentially evocative, and the way that the message is produced or interpreted is dependent upon real or imagined relationships between speaker, listener, and the context of situation. The listener reacts to the connotations of the inflection at the same time that he or she is attending to the denotative meaning of the sentence that is being heard, which the connotative message sometimes contradicts.

Bolinger, then, is more conscious than many linguists of the fact that language is more than a denotational system. He would undoubtedly agree with Silverstein that while "all of our analytic techniques and formal descriptive machinery have been designed for referential signs . . . the sign modes of most of what goes on in the majority of speech events are not referential" [Silverstein, 1976:15].

Sperber and Cohen are anthropologists who have investigated social systems as well as ritualized interactions. Sperber's view as to the inadequacy of transferring a structural model derived from linguistics to description of nonlinguistic systems closely parallels that of Silverstein, so that Sperber's and Bolinger's positions are actually closer to one another than would perhaps be apparent from their respective chapters in this book. Sperber sets out to demolish the common assumption that "prerational" thinking is either primary or prior to rational thinking in which denotation and close attention to event-related causalities determine behavior. If we look for homologies in the behavior of man's closest primate relative, the chimpanzee, we must agree.

Chimpanzee "language" learning in the studies of the Gardners (1969), Premack (1976), and Rumbaugh (1977) corresponds to the causality implicit in stimulus–response behaviorist theories. Behavior (i.e., production of signs) is learned only in response to the expectation of some reward. These studies have definitively demonstrated that apes are capable of producing quite complex denotative communications as well as of extending denotative classes (e.g., Washoe's designation of other scented things as "flower," Gardner and Gardner [1969]; van Lawick-Goodall's [1971] observation of the substitution of a kerosene can for a tree branch in an otherwise typical aggressive display).

More important from the standpoint of Sperber's theory is the fact that instead of substituting behavior based on "symbolic" thinking when serious ambiguities present themselves, chimpanzees apparently continue to press for rational solutions. Gill (1977) describes deliberate efforts to confront Lana with ambiguity by not supplying her with the food that she had requested and always previously received upon request, or asking if she wanted some refreshment previously supplied only at another time of day. Her responses were all denotative attempts to correct the ambiguity or refusal to converse if frustration became too extreme. Small children, on the other hand, learn language not through reward but through experimentation (see Bowerman, this volume) in interpersonal situations and in fantasy situations of their own devising. The ambiguity of messages is resolved through mediation of the dynamic unconscious, greatly assisted by such cultural devices as fairytales (Bettelheim, 1976) or through various means of fantasy "acting-out."

Freud establishes the importance of fantasy in structuring the covert cognitive processing of the human individual. What is less clear, and has been a stumbling block for anthropology, is the relationship of such processing to culture. This is the issue to which Cohen addresses himself in this volume, arguing that other than adopting some form of the Freudian view (which he would modify for the purpose) anthropologists have no way of explaining either the invention or the reuse of cultural symbols. Bolinger's position converges with Cohen's in that both are concerned with the role of affect in determining symbolic meaning. Sperber and Cohen converge in their view that primary process, or *symbolic* cognition, plays a greater role in some cultural systems than in others, and that understanding this mode of thought (which is not rational thought) is the key to understanding ritual and mythic symbolism. They perhaps part company on the issue of psychoanalysis and the role of the dynamic unconscious in producing and interpreting cultural symbolism, and the value of structuralism in this endeavor. Although, with Sperber, we may reject too strict a reliance on linguistic descriptive methodology in the formulation of behavioral rules, as Cohen demonstrates, structuralism can still show how the *manifest content* (i.e., overt realization of such systems as myth and ritual and the interpretation of their *deep structure or latent content*) may reflect the motivation behind at least some forms of social behavior.

Like Bolinger, both Sperber and Cohen define *symbol* connotatively. For Sperber and Cohen this usage equates with Freud's "primary process" manipulation of meaning. Both stress the lack of rationality that characterizes this cognitive mode, which, in Sperber's view, comes into play when rational ways of making sense out of events are exhausted. Somewhat similarly, Cohen views symbolism as an escape from anxieties that a more rational (i.e., secondary process) approach may generate. Thus it would seem that for both of these authors the symbolizing process is something of an inevitable makeshift that arises from rational inadequacy. As we will see later, some other authors take a more optimistic view of the kind of sense that connotative symbols make.

Sperber emphasizes the creative individuality that comes to the surface when connotative symbols are richly evocative. One may assume from this that much of the depth and diversity of cultures derives from imaginative interpretation of inevitable anomalies. Cohen calls attention to the fact that the explanatory predicaments that arise produce an elaborate hierarchy of creative solutions, building from "natural" to "cultural" symbols as a means of resolution. The hierarchical nature of symbolism as predominate characteristic will be elaborated in later chapters.

References

Bettelheim, Bruno
  1976 *The uses of enchantment.* New York: Knopf.
Bloch, Maurice (ed.)
  1975 *Political language and oratory in traditional society.* London: Academic Press.
Bolinger, Dwight
  1968 *Aspects of language.* New York: Harcourt.
Gardner, R. Allen, and Beatrice T. Gardner
  1969 Teaching sign language to a chimpanzee. *Science* **165,** 664–672.
Gill, Timothy
  1977 Talking to Lana: The question of conversation. In *Program in ape research,* edited by G. H. Bourne. New York: Academic Press. Pp. 125–132.
Premack, D.
  1976 *Intelligence in ape and man.* Hillsdale, New Jersey: Laurence Erlbaum.
Rumbaugh, Duane M. (ed.)
  1977 *Language learning by a chimpanzee.* New York: Academic Press.
Saussure, Ferdinand de
  1959 *Course in general linguistics.* New York: Philosophical Library.
Silverstein, Michael
  1976 Shifters, linguistic categories and cultural description. In *Meaning in Anthropology,* edited by K. H. Basso and H. A. Selby. Albuquerque: Univ. of New Mexico Press. Pp. 11–55.
van Lawick-Goodall, Jane
  1971 *In the shadow of man.* Boston, Massachusetts: Houghton.

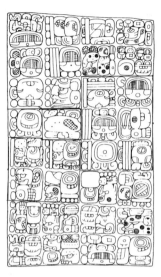

2
Intonation and "Nature"
DWIGHT BOLINGER

Introduction

Why, if the whole of culture communicates, is language such a tempting model? Is it adequate? If not fully adequate, is there some part of it that bears a closer relationship than the rest to nonlinguistic communication?

Edwin Ardener answers the first question: "Among the behavior uttered is linguistic utterance—nesting like a small detailed replica of the whole, and yet purporting to represent acoustically an image of some of the whole. It is not surprising that to some it seems easiest to see it all as an excrescence of language in the first place" [this volume]. Or at least to see *in* language the refinement of all the phenomena to be studied, served up in a form most accessible to study.

Yet language is a refinement that is specialized away from the full range of symbolic phenomena, and therefore—to answer the second question—of rather dubious adequacy. It is the chief part of that "formalization of behavior for the ancillary function of information transmission between organisms" [Laughlin, 1977:10], a system in which *signs* take over from *symbols*. In its bulk—and the bulk is lexicon—language is not the best image of the vast range of communicative behavior, where the typical conveyers of meaning are symbols.

Nevertheless there are a number of residues, and among these one stands out for its coherence and high degree of nonarbitrariness. *Intonation* is the affirmative answer to the third question. Of all the systems within language

SYMBOL AS SENSE

it is the most highly symbolic—the least arbitrary, most appropriate in its sound-to-sense relationships, and most obviously motivated by the physical and mental impressions it conveys. The subjective evidence for this lies in our inner sensations. The objective evidence comes by way of comparing languages and discovering similarities too great to be the result of chance convergence or diffusion. If we find that languages widely separated in space and with no genetic affiliation nevertheless share specific patterns of intonation that are similar in both form and meaning, we can only conclude that the form and the meaning must correspond in some natural way. Though the evidence from numerous languages varies widely in scope and quality, most of it points to just such a natural correspondence. It is mostly with such comparative evidence that this chapter is concerned.

Language strikes a balance between the arbitrary sign and the nonarbitrary symbol. The classical distinction is stated by Turner (1977): "In symbols there is always some kind of likeness (metaphoric–metonymic) posited by the framing culture between signifier (symbol–vehicle) and signified(s); in signs there need be no likeness" [p. 77]. Signs are arbitrary. Arbitrariness was the gift of Babel—its origins have been stated by Hockett and Ascher (1964) to lie in the prehistoric buildup of an unmanageable number of symbols, each of which may have represented more or less faithfully some thing or concept and had to be executed independently of all other symbols. The only way to relieve the burden on the symbolizing medium (whether speech or gesture) was to resort to combinations, to bring more than one symbolic element into correspondence with a single concept. As Chafe (1970:24–29) points out, this resulted in a divorce between meaning and form, setting them free to evolve independently. Without an anchor in representational meaning, the forms used in different geographical areas drifted apart. Formal systems changed with little drag from semantics, and even onomatopoetic expressions took on a separate cast depending on what set of distinctive elements was used in them: English *bow-wow*, French *oua-oua*, Japanese *wan-wan*, Greek *au-au*, Russian *am-am*, Chinese *wang-wang*, Turkish *hav-hav*—but the doubling for repetition lived on (Hornos, 1976).

Arbitrariness never fully carried the day. With meaning, it was mostly in individual *words* that speakers accepted a fundamental arbitrariness. Even there it is softened to the extent that once an arbitrary word-sign is established, the sound–meaning correspondence seems as "natural" as if it really were phonosemic (Wescott, 1971), and may go on to precipitate clusters of like-sound, like-meaning words; an example is *jamboree, shivaree, corroboree, jubilee, massacree, shooterie* (Bolinger, 1950). The culture inserts a sign and gets back a symbol. Elsewhere—in syntax to a large degree, and in the organization of discourse—appropriateness and arbitrariness are intertangled and intershaded. *Dog* and *bite* may each be arbitrary, but *dogbite* is not an arbitrary combination. *He stumbled* and *He fell* may be arbitrary sentences with an arbitrary sequence of subject and verb, but *He stumbled and fell* corresponds to the order of events.

These grammatical and other manifestations of appropriateness, while abundant, are fragmentary. Intonation remains the part of language with closest and most systematic ties to symbolism. The symbolic source is the nature of the human organism—its emotional and attitudinal states; and the symbolic medium is the fundamental pitch of the voice—"la vive voix" (Fónagy, 1976). The connection is both spontaneous (as when sudden fright or anger narrows or expands the range of pitch) and controlled (as when anger is simulated, or any one of a number of half-grammaticized attitudinal fluctuations is produced). To the extent that intonation is symbolic, the resemblances between languages are more numerous than the differences—and even many of the differences can be put down to the cultural adoption of attitudes (for example, deference) which have natural correlates in intonation. To the extent that it is arbitrary, it represents the rational choice—the decision to *use* a pattern, say, for a grammatical purpose—that Sperber (this volume) argues must underlie even symbolic processing.

Intonation and Grammar

The grammatical uses of intonation have been the main door through which intonation has entered linguistic descriptions. There is a fairly high correlation between certain types of sentences and certain modulations of pitch, particularly those occurring at the ends of utterances. Questions and statements are the classical examples. Structural linguists (and their transformational–generative followers, who have innovated very little in this field) have tried to pare the distinctive uses of intonation to a minimum, usually in some form of so-called juncture, wherein the pitch rises, falls, or remains level—with degrees of one or the other and overlap between them dismissed as irrelevant to grammar. But two points have been consistently overlooked: To the extent that correlation between sentence types and intonation is a fact, the underlying symbolism of the intonation is still there; and to the extent that it is not a fact, the explanation is to be found in that same underlying symbolism.

There is no necessary connection between the grammatical class of a sentence and its intonation (unless intonation is used circularly to define the class). Statements may rise at the end, questions may fall; the intonation can always be manipulated independently of the syntax. Accordingly, intonation has to be seen somewhat dimly through the foreground of all the other speech activities that play before it, including some, such as the use by tone languages of the fundamental pitch in other, more arbitrary ways, which drastically reduce its freedom.

Comparative Intonation

Comparing intonation cross-linguistically requires first a separation and then a dissection. The separation is to exclude the segmental uses of pitch, which do not count intonationally. Their function is *distinctive*. Tone languages are of two kinds: In one, a tone or tonal pattern has the same status as a phoneme (like a distinctive consonant or vowel); in the other it has the status of a morpheme—for example, as a sign for verbal aspect. Since the voice is incapable of producing more than one fundamental frequency at a time, the presence of distinctive tone complicates the analysis, but when the two are disentangled they are found to ride different waves.

The dissection is made within intonation. The controlled uses of intonation are likewise of two kinds: accentual and melodic. Melody is the musical patterning whereby speech is segmented, whether through melodic configuration alone (there is a recognizable tune with a recognizable end-point) or through configuration plus pause. Accent is the highlighting of certain elements for their importance. A given word (or phrase, or sentence) has a key syllable that is obtruded above (sometimes below, in nontonal languages) the melodic line. This is usually referred to as *stress*, but it is better to reserve that term to designate the particular syllable of a word that receives an accent when the speaker decides to confer one. Thus in answer to *Why did he deposit the money on Friday?* one may say

```
            told
    I

        him
          to deposit it then.
```

—the word *deposit* is not accented, and the lexically stressed syllable -*pos*- has no pitch obtrusion; but in answer to *What are you going to do with that money?* one may say

```
                    pos
        I'm going to de    it
                        it.
```

with the stressed -*pos*- now accented. An accented syllable is almost always a stressed syllable, but a stressed syllable is not accented unless the speaker intentionally highlights the element in which it occurs. Besides pitch obtrusion, two other phonetic correlates of accent are length and intensity. The three usually coincide, but intensity contributes least. Length can be viewed as a necessary timing device for the perception of the pitch turn.

Accent

First, let us look at accent and its reflection in the stress systems of languages. If stress is the lexical means of predicting where an accent will occur when a segment is highlighted, then we may expect certain regularities in the location of stressed syllables in a word; they will be in those positions that best serve the needs of accentual prominence. Hyman's survey (1975) points to four syllabic positions within the word as most frequently stressed: first, second, next-to-last, and last, with next-to-last a slight favorite (in my own smaller count of 23 languages [Bolinger, 1978:481–482], it is a heavy favorite). The preference for the next-to-last syllable can be explained by the mechanics of pitch obtrusion if we assume one additional factor, namely a tendency to put the accent as close as possible to the end of the utterance (this assumption is justified in the next paragraph). To be prominent, a syllable must stand out *in relation to* other syllables. The most effective contrast is achieved when the prominent syllable is flanked on both sides by subdued ones. There is also a melodic factor: The most important turns of pitch occur at the end. Having a final syllable without accent provides the means for the upward or downward movement that marks the end of most melodic patterns. So stress position, while arbitrary in the sense that it sometimes makes a difference in the meaning of words—for example, *undertáking* (enterprise) and *úndertaking* (business of conducting funerals)—tends to be the place that naturally "works best" when a word is accented in final position.

The effectiveness of end position for accentual prominence seems to respond directly to psychological principles of emphasis. The closer to the end a major accent occurs, the more impact it carries. I term this process *climax*, and it is found in languages of every description. It functions not only passively in the frozen forms of words that favor stresses at or near the end, but also actively in the behavior of speakers when they are being very emphatic. The end-shifting of stress for emphasis is described as a regular feature of languages as diverse as Chontal (Mexico; Waterhouse, 1962), Kunimaipa (New Guinea; Pence, 1964), Tagalog (Philippines; Dacanay, 1963), and Western Desert (Australia; Douglas, 1964). Some languages embody it as a rule for emphatic sentence types; it is often used for the imperative. In English we find it occurring sporadically under conditions of excitement. The commonest manifestation is merely that of putting an accent in the normal position within a word, but seeing to it that that accented word occurs finally. In answer to *Why didn't you do as I asked?* one may reply *Because I knów better* or *Because I know bétter!* At a further extreme, speakers may put an accent on a normally unstressed syllable, especially if it contains a full vowel. One may occasionally hear the word *enthusiasm*—itself a word with a certain emotional impact—accented *enthusiásm* when phrase-final. A number of words in English have a kind of level stress that permits either one of two syllables to be accented fairly regularly: *I was óutraged* conveys less emotion that *I was outráged. Máybe* expresses less skepticism than *maybé*. In Buenos Aires Spanish, there are two intimate forms of address, using the pronouns *tú* and *vos*. In the imperative, the *vos* form is preferred for extra emphasis; it has terminal stress—*comé* 'eat' instead of *cóme* (Fontanella and Lavandera, 1975).

Why this tendency to associate terminal accent with extra force? The psychological principle is perhaps that of recency—what is said last remains most vivid in the speaker's mind. It is also what is farthest from the "old stuff" that has gone before—which is to say that it fits the thematic organization of the utterance. The topic of a sentence normally ties in with preceding context and tends to stand close to it; the comment, containing the least predictable elements, is pushed toward the end—but what is unpredictable tends to be more exciting. The logical structure and the climactic buildup are made for each other.

The evidence for climax as a universal phenomenon is overwhelming. Another similar phenomenon is scarcely recorded at all, but I suspect that it may be just as natural and widespread. It is a more or less controlled use of a primitively uncontrolled outburst, and is manifested by a shifting of the major accent leftward rather than rightward. The speaker is (or pretends to be) so carried away in reacting to some thing or some trait of something as to be unable to resist coming out with it well before the end of the utterance. Its effect is to wipe out the normal comment-accent (the one associated with the new information in a sentence). The words on which the exclamatory accent falls are typically exclamations and intensifying modifiers. An example of the latter:

TER
It was
ri
ble that he should have been permitted to get away with that!

Mark Twain gives an example of this using an exclamation. A Western miner meets Bret Harte for the first time, and is so overcome that he greets him with outstretched hand exclaiming *Són of a bitch! Put it there!* (Twain, 1940) The normal position for the main accent is of course on *bitch*. Exclamatory accent is probably the French *accent d'insistance*, and is also found in the morphology of intensifying adverbs in Hungarian.

It was pointed out earlier that accents are usually manifested by upward obtrusions. If we view an accent as being prompted by the semantic importance of a segment—it is "something to get excited about"—it is easy to find a nonarbitrary significance in the rise of pitch: Excitement and tension are obviously related, and pitch rise answers to increased tension on the vocal cords. But this would not be a very strong argument were it not for the possibility of *downward* obtrusions with an opposite meaning. A tension–excitement theory would predict that an accent manifested by a pitch lower than the surrounding pitches ought to mean something like *restraint* or *inhibition,* and this is exactly what we find. Compare the excessively restrained

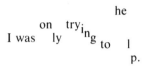

containing "reverse" accents on *on-, try-,* and *help,* with the excessively assertive

he
on try_in_g
I was   ly   to   l
p.

containing the normal upward obtrusions. (A great variety of shadings can be achieved by balancing upward and downward obtrusions—the varying effects depend not only on the gradient size of the obtrusion but also on which obtrusion comes first; note the contrast between the following two

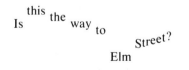

with the opposite sequence of down-up, up-down on *on-* and *help.*)

Reverse accents are rarely mentioned in linguistic descriptions, but when they are, they are assigned meanings that accord with toning-down. In Western Desert, a reverse accent is used as a sign of deference (Douglas, 1964); compare this with the identical use in English when one asks a question of a complete stranger:

this the
Is   way to
Street?
Elm

—the main accent on *Elm* being reversed. The same is true of Kunimaipa (Pence, 1964). No references to reverse accents have turned up in descriptions of tone languages. It is understandable that they should be less usual in systems where even the normal upward obtrusion introduces complications in the interrelationships of the tones. The fact that a resource is available does not always mean that it is convenient to exploit it.

Melody

The melodic part of intonation consists of those controlled movements of the fundamental pitch that are not meant to highlight the individual elements of an utterance. Most important are the overall direction (up, down, or level) of the utterance and the direction (again up, down, or level) of the terminal— typically the syllable or syllables after the final accent.

Here we encounter the most widely observed and discussed phenomenon in intonation: the tendency to go down toward or at the end. The downmotion may be smooth from beginning to end, or it may be interrupted by one or more jumps back to a higher pitch; but if jumps occur, the usual thing then is for each jump to be a little lower than the preceding one. The jumps may correspond to tone in a tone language or to accents in a nontonal language. So in English we have

$$\text{I} \quad \overset{\text{hope}}{} \quad \text{you're} \quad \overset{\text{not}}{} \quad \text{going to be} \quad \overset{\text{ma}}{} \quad \text{d.}$$

where the overall motion is downward and the tangent to the accents on *hope, not,* and *mad* is likewise downward.

The downmotion, of course, is associated with "being finished." The nonarbitrary basis is pretty obvious, and Lieberman (1967) makes it the keystone of his theory of the "innate referential breath group," which he believes is an automatic result of an initial buildup of subglottal air pressure that decreases gradually up to the end of expiration and then falls abruptly. Although this is doubtless a factor, the pitch drop can also be attributed to the relaxation of nervous tension as the speaker discharges "what he was keyed up about." In either case, the falling pitch at the end becomes a controllable signal for "being through," "having nothing more to say," and, by extension, for being positive (we can even use the words *There is nothing more to be said* to convey logical rather than physical finality).

The terminal fall is not only present in an absolute sense (fall rather than rise or level), but is also graded: the lower or steeper the fall, the greater the finality. All the sentences in a monologue may end with a fall, but the last sentence will probably have the deepest fall. Gradience of this kind is of course evidence of a nonarbitrary basis. The gradience is found both intra- and interlinguistically. The latter possibility is exemplified by Chamorro, which differs from most other languages in that sentences have to be especially *final* (e.g., arguing or scolding) to end with a fall, but discourse-final sentences normally have the fall (Topping, 1969). Tone languages may not only have the overall downdrift but, as with Telefol, there may also be a discourse-terminal particle that carries a fall (Healey, 1966).

The gradience between falls extends to nonfalls, which are best observed at some juncture within an utterance, usually at the end of a clause. The speaker is not completely through and therefore does not go down all the way—and, furthermore, is free to symbolize the degree of nonthroughness by either cropping the fall or replacing it with a level or a rise; the rise in turn may be graded for degrees of incompleteness: A high rise means "definitely more to be said." "Internal open juncture with mid or high pitch" is a phenomenon that has been observed almost as widely as terminal fall. It is reported for virtually all nontonal languages and, in my sample, for about a fourth of the tone languages (7 of 27) (Bolinger, 1978:495–497).

This brings us to questions, one variety of which, the so-called yes–no question, is associated in most traditional grammars with a terminal high pitch. But what appeared in traditional grammars as an odd coincidence—the use of the same intonations for internal clause breaks (internal open juncture) and for interrogative terminals—can be seen by discourse grammar as merely two aspects of the same thing, incompleteness. A nonfinal clause awaits the concluding clause of the sentence. A question awaits an answer. The two are often syntactically the same as well. For example, English conditional clauses can be essentially analyzed as questions (the same *if* that introduces a condition also introduces an indirect question: *He asked me if I knew her*), and questions may substitute for them; they differ from ordinary questions only in that the same person asking the question also supplies the response:

> Did he complain? They fired him. Did he bring charges? They had him beaten up. Did he seek work elsewhere? They blacklisted him. (= If he complained, they fired him, etc.)

In most Western languages the usual intonation of the conditional clause is also the same as that of the yes–no question.

Three surveys (Hermann, 1942; Ultan, 1969; Bolinger, 1978), covering about 250 languages in all, have revealed that questions of all types have either a rising (or high) terminal or a higher overall pitch than nonquestions, with rising terminals accounting for about 70% of the languages examined. There is clearly some prevailing opposition here between questions and nonquestions (for convenience, we will call these *statements*), and it is fair to ask whether the fact that questions tend to rise may reflect merely a formal opposition between the two inclusive sentence types. That is, statements go down, for whatever reason, and questions go up because, grammatically, they have to be differentiated from statements. But the fact is that unless a question really asks (that is, unless the speaker is really curious and expresses the feeling intonationally), the syntactic markers of interrogation may remain but the intonation will not be the one supposedly typical of questions. Thus, in a series of questions that cover a subject exhaustively, the last question, which "closes the issue," goes down. This is also the basis for alternative questions—one of the alternatives supposedly has to be chosen, and such questions normally have rises on all but the last alternative. WH questions (those introduced by interrogative words—*how, where, when,* etc.) quite readily take a terminal fall; they are, of course, questions that contain presuppositions, and are not purely interrogative: *Why did you do it?* assumes that you did it. The high or rising pitch therefore represents more than a formal opposition. It is the antithesis of the fall-for-completion. If we go down as an indication of relaxation, we go up or stay up as an indication of tension, of not being through. However fully the speaker may control this resource as part of the design of language, it nevertheless rests on a nonarbitrary foundation. It is only one step closer to full arbitrariness than affecting a sob when one feels no grief.

When we get down to the details of intonational patterns and their correspondence to traditional grammatical categories such as question and statement, the uniformities between languages are too great to be the result of coincidence, and yet the claim that they are universal and necessary is too strong. Even something so nearly universal as the tendency for statements to end in a fall has its exceptions. All the same, on close examination the exceptions turn out not to be very strong counterevidence. We have already seen how Chamorro merely shifts the terminal fall from end-of-utterance to end-of-discourse. Belfast English reportedly has a terminal rise on statements as well as questions—but the rises on statements do not go up very far, so the same relative contrast is maintained (Jarman and Cruttenden, n.d.). It is significant that differences of this kind can be found as readily between dialects of the same language as between two different languages, with the result that Dialect A of Language L may resemble Dialect A' of Language L' more than it resembles another dialect of L. This suggests that features highly susceptible to social variation are involved. It is not that the intonations *mean* something different, but that the *manners* of the group are different—using an intonation that implies positiveness may get the same reception that is bestowed on aggressive body language. Such sensitivity is documented in at least one case, that of a series of tests conducted with young speakers of Black English. The experimenters concluded at first that the terminal rise on yes–no questions common in most dialects of American English was absent in Black English (Loman, 1967; Tarone, 1971). But then one experimenter (Tarone, 1973) repeated the tests making sure that the test setting was completely relaxed, with none of the formality that had been present before. The terminal rises magically reappeared. The children had been using the positive terminal downmotion as a defense against what they took to be threatening behavior.

Kindred Patterns in Diverse Languages

Thus far we have looked at the generalities of intonation. The picture would not be complete without a sketch of resemblances in more specific terms—particular intonation *patterns* that can be found from language to language.

An excellent source for comparison with a non-Indo-European language is the Swahili textbook by E. O. Ashton (1947). The similarities to English are striking: Both have terminal fall for imperative, terminal vocatives and similar elements on low-pitched intonational tail, reverse accents with same meaning as in English, and rise–fall–rise as an option in place of simple rise at internal clause breaks (same option as in American English). The most surprising parallel is in the two kinds of statement contours, one for statements in answer to questions and one for other statements. English has the same contrast. For example, in answer to the question *Why did you do that?* we may have

$$\text{I}\quad\begin{array}{c}\text{did}\end{array}\text{ it because I}\quad\begin{array}{c}\text{want}\\\text{ed to}_{.}\end{array}$$

—the highest pitch being toward the end. An example of a statement that does not answer a question is one that begins a story:

$$\begin{array}{c}\text{Once upon a time there was a little boy named }\text{Al}\\\text{fr}_{ed}\ .\ .\ .\end{array}$$

—the highest pitch being toward the beginning.

WH questions in Swahili reveal one of the reasons why two languages can have essentially the same intonations and yet seem to be very different. The Swahili question does regularly what the English one does occasionally; it puts the interrogative word at the end:

$$\text{They}\quad\begin{array}{c}\text{did it ho}\\\text{w}_{?}\end{array}$$

rather than

$$\text{How did they}\quad\begin{array}{c}\text{do}\\\text{i}_{t_{?}}\end{array}$$

Here it is the interference of a syntactic rule that causes the usual intonation of WH questions to sound so different in the two languages.

The parallels in other non-Indo-European languages are equally impressive. Pintupi uses the same device that English uses for reiterated emphasis: Each syllable of a word is given a separate accent (Hansen, 1969); compare *golly* pronounced *góllée!* Kunimaipa has the same fall-rise-fall for "deep feeling" (Pence, 1964):

It was

a^w ful!

Huastec expresses disgust in the same way as English, with a rapid down-glide (Larsen and Pike, 1949):

Who
^{eat}s h$_{or}$s$_{e?_!}$

Compare *What do I care? Mind your own business,* and so on, uttered on this same contour of disparagement.

Ontogenesis

The development of intonation in the human individual is still a great mystery. Are babies born programmed *with* intonation, or only with a special capacity to *learn* intonation, or both? This is a burning question to the whole field of language-learning, but it has special significance for intonation, which seems to be so closely tied to innate reactions of the organism.

All studies of child language that touch on intonation agree that it is the first linguistic subsystem that a child learns to use. Patterns of intonation that we associate with adult speech are heard as early as the babbling stage (Menn, 1976:182), starting at 7 or 8 months (Peters, 1974:212; Weeks, 1974:9). An as early as 1 year of age, differences in intonation were heard between infants in a Japanese-speaking and an English-speaking environment (Nakazima, 1966). So children are either born equipped with innate vocalizations that correspond to intonational patterns, or they are born equipped to learn such patterns with relative ease. At present one can only theorize that the infant whine is the basis of rising intonations and their observed association with a desire for something (Menn, 1976:193). As for the falling intonation and Lieberman's "innate referential breath group," two studies agree that a falling intonation is the easiest to learn (Delack and Fowlow, 1975; Li and Thompson, 1976)—this in spite of the fact that the child hears far more rises than falls from parents and other adults (Garnica, 1974; Pike, 1949). At least one aspect of pitch that would have to be learned from experience—but would be learned at practically the very first contact with the world—is the relationship that high and low bear to size and power: Menn (1976) surmises that there is "probably some innate component of the association of high pitch with weakness and low pitch with power" [p. 220]. But low pitches are not only those emitted by the (usually) larger, rougher, and more powerful of the two parents, but they are also the ones emitted in general by large objects in vibration; and they correspond to frequencies that are felt by the body as well as heard by the ear. It is also no accident that probably all languages have a synesthetic tie between size and second-formant frequency—the higher frequency tends to symbolize smaller, closer things (*near–far; wee–large; chip–chop; keen–dull*). Though all we can do at this stage is speculate, it seems that instinctive cries and environmental sounds are both involved in the child's very early acquisition of intonation. A limiting factor of another kind is the delay in the development of the supralaryngeal mechanisms that are required for producing articulate sounds (vowels and consonants)—the apparatus for producing pitch is present in neonates. The physical equipment and the environmental inducements conspire to the same effect: an early skill in the use of intonation. And this is not only essential for the carrying of the first messages of desire, complaint, inquisitiveness, and contentment, but is also essential as a receptacle for all else that comes later. Intonation is both directive (in its illocutionary instructions on "how to interpret" an utterance) and integrating, in the patterns that organize speech and mark its divisions. The latter function is indispensable for the child learner; it would be very hard for a child to induce a syntactic pattern if the model sentences produced by adults were not set off with unmistakable boundaries. Therein we have the explanation of the exaggerated intonational contrasts that parents use with young children—and this becomes not merely a support for the learning of words and syntax, but one more push toward the early and complete control of intonation.

References

Ashton, Ethel O.
   1947   *Swahili grammar*. London: Longman.
Bolinger, Dwight
   1950   *Shivaree* and the phonestheme. *American Speech* **25**, 134–135.
   1978   Intonation across languages. In *Universals of human language*, vol. 2, edited by J. H. Greenberg. California: Stanford Univ. Press.
Chafe, Wallace
   1970   *Meaning and the structure of language*. Chicago: Univ. of Chicago Press.
Dacanay, Fe R.
   1963   *Techniques and procedures in second language teaching*. Quezon City, Philippines: Phoenix.
Delack, John B., and Patricia J. Fowlow
   1975   The ontogenesis of differential vocalization: Development of prosodic contrastivity during the first year of life. [Preprint.]
Douglas, Wilfred H.
   1964   An introduction to the Western Desert language. *Oceania Linguistics Monograph No. 4*, rev. ed. Australia: Univ. of Sydney.
Fónagy, Ivan
   1976   La vive voix: Dynamique et changement. *Journal de Psychologie* (No. 3–4), 273–304.

Fontanella de Weinberg, Maria B., and Beatriz R. Lavandera
   1975   Variant or morpheme? Negative commands in Buenos Aires Spanish. Paper presented at New Ways of Analyzing Variation (NWave), Georgetown University, 25 October 1975.

Garnica, Olga
   1974   Some prosodic characteristics of speech to young children. Unpublished Ph.D. dissertation, Stanford University.

Hansen, Kenneth C., and Lesly E. Hansen
   1969   Pintupi phonology. *Oceanic Linguistics* **8**, 153–170.

Healey, Phyllis, M.
   1966   Levels and chaining in Telefol sentences. *Linguistic Circle of Canberra Publications,* B. ser. 4.

Hermann, Eduard
   1942   Probleme der Frage. *Nachrichten von der Akademie der Wissenschaften in Gottingen.* Philologisch-Historische Klasse, Nr. 3, 4.

Hockett, Charles F., and Robert Ascher
   1964   The human revolution. *Current Anthropology* **5**, 135–147.

Hornos, Axel
   1976   *Ouch!* he said in Japanese. *Verbatim* **3**, 1, 4, 5.

Hyman, Larry M.
   1975   On the nature of linguistic stresses. In *studies on stress and accent,* edited by Larry M. Hyman. Los Angeles, California: Univ. of Southern California Press, 1975. Pp. 37–82.

Jarman, Eric, and Alan Cruttenden
   n.d.   Belfast intonation and the myth of the fall. In preparation.

Larsen, Raymond S., and E. V. Pike
   1949   Huasteco intonations and phonemes. *Language* **25**, 268–277.

Li, Charles N., and Sandra Thompson
   1976   Tone perception and production: evidence from tone acquisition. Paper presented at Child Language Research Forum, Stanford University, 3 April.

Lieberman, Philip
   1967   *Intonation, perception, and language.* Cambridge, Massachusetts: MIT Press.

Loman, Bengt
   1967   *Conversations in a Negro American Dialect.* Washington, D.C.: Center for Applied Linguistics.

Menn, Lise
   1976   Pattern, control, and contrast in beginning speech: A case study in the development of word form and word function. Unpublished Ph.D. dissertation, University of Illinois.

Nakazima, Sei
   1966   A comparative study of the speech developments of Japanese and American English in childhood (2)—the acquisition of speech. *Studia Phonologica* **4**, 38–55.

Pence, Alan
   1964   Intonation in Kunimaipa. In *Intonation,* edited by D. Bolinger. Harmondsworth, England: Penguin. Pp. 325–336.

Peters, Ann M.
   1974   Progress report. *Papers and Reports on Child Language Development* (Stanford University) **8**, 212.

Pike, Evelyn
   1949   Controlled infant intonation. *Language Learning* **2**, 21–24.

Tarone, Elaine E.
   1971   Unpublished pilot study for Tarone, 1973.
   1973   Aspects of intonation in Black English. *American Speech* **48**, 29–36.

Topping, Donald M.
    1969   A restatement of Chamorro phonology. *Anthropological Linguistics* **2**, 62–78.
Turner, Victor
    1977   Process, system, and symbol: A new anthropological synthesis. *Daedalus* **1**, 61–80.
Twain, Mark
    1940   *Mark Twain in eruption*. New York: Grosset, P. 272.
Ultan, Russell
    1969   Some general characteristics of interrogative systems. *Working Papers on Language Universals* (Stanford University) **1**, 41–63.
Waterhouse, Viola
    1962   The grammatical structure of Oaxaca Chontal. *International Journal of American Linguistics* **28**, Pub. 19 of Indiana University Research Center in Anthropology, Folklore, and Linguistics.
Weeks, Thelma E.
    1974   *The slow speech development of a bright child*. Massachusetts: Lexington Books (Heath).
Wescott, Roger W.
    1971   Labio-velarity and derogation in English: A study in phonosemic correlation. *American Speech* **43**, 123–137.

3

Is Symbolic Thought Prerational?

DAN SPERBER

The Issue

Many philosophers, psychologists, and anthropologists have assumed that so-called symbolic thought processes are primary, primitive, or prerational. More recently it has been recognized (by Piaget and Lévi-Strauss for instance) that symbolic and rational thought processes are intermingled. This has sometimes been pushed to the point of rejecting the symbolic–rational distinction altogether and of extending the notion of symbolism so as to include all aspects of conceptual thinking. I have criticized this extension in Sperber (1974). Here I wish to argue both against the view that symbolism is prerational and against the view that symbolic and rational thought processes are indistinguishable. In attempting to outline the structure of interaction between the two types of thought processes, I also hope to shed light on some important aspects of symbolic interpretation.

In his survey of cognitive psychology, Ulric Neisser (1967) remarked:

> Historically, psychology has long recognized the existence of two different forms of mental organization. The distinction has been given many names: "rational" vs. "intuitive," "constrained" vs. "creative," "logical" vs. "prelogical," "realistic" vs. "autistic," "secondary process" vs. "primary process." To list them together casually may be misleading. . . . Nevertheless, a common thread runs through all the dichotomies. Some thinking and remembering is deliberate, efficient, and obviously goal-directed; it is usually experienced as self-directed as well. Other mental activity is rich, chaotic and in-

efficient; it tends to be experienced as involuntary, it just "happens." It often seems to be motivated, but not in the same way as directed thought; it seems not so much directed towards a goal as associated with an emotion [p. 297].

An equally vague and very similar distinction has been made in anthropology under many different names: e.g., *logical* versus *prelogical, scientific* versus *magical,* and today, usually *rational* versus *symbolic.* Modern anthropologists would not dispute the fact that rational thought is, on the whole, deliberate, efficient, and goal-directed. But as for symbolic thought, they have tried to show that it may be less chaotic and inefficient than would seem. Rather than contrasting *rational* and *symbolic* as *consistent* versus *chaotic* and *efficient* versus *inefficient,* they would prefer *directly consistent* versus *indirectly consistent* and *directly efficient* versus *indirectly efficient.* These interesting qualifications on the part of anthropologists do not eliminate the similarity in psychologists' and their basic distinction between two different modes of thought. This distinction should be clarified in two ways: (*a*) Since it is essentially a psychological distinction, even when made by anthropologists, the mental mechanisms and processes involved should be more explicitly characterized; (*b*) The distinction has been and still is closely linked with the view that symbolic thought is in some sense prerational; this view should be either developed and justified or reconsidered and possibly abandoned.

The view that symbolic thought is prerational actually consists of three distinct assumptions:

1. A phylogenetic assumption according to which rational thought is a later development in the history of the human species, following a first stage where all thought was symbolic. Lucien Lévy-Bruhl (1910, 1922, etc.), with his notion of a *pre-logical* stage, was the most cogent exponent of this view which, in spite of numerous criticisms, notably those of Claude Lévi-Strauss in *The Savage Mind* (1966), is still commonly held.

2. An ontogenetic assumption, according to which conceptual rationality is a late acquisition in the history of the organism, the child having first to go (in the terms of Piaget, 1968) through a stage characterized by *preconceptual* and *symbolic* representations.

3. A cognitive assumption about the genesis of individual thoughts, according to which rational thought is a more directed, more attentive development and exploitation of symbolic thought. In Neisser's terms:

Rational thought is "secondary" in the sense that it works with objects already formed by a "primary process." If these objects receive no secondary elaboration, as in some dreams and disorganized mental states, we experience them in the fleeting and imprecise way of iconic memory. However, the same multiple processes that produce these shadowy and impalpable experiences are also essential preliminaries to directed thinking [Neisser, 1967: 302].

Although these three assumptions are generally bundled together in one form or another, they are in fact mutually independent, and there is no logical reason to adopt them all simultaneously. On the other hand they could all three be refuted together if it were shown that the reverse of the third assumption were true: If one assumes that symbolic thought is necessarily built on some prior rational processing, symbolism could not have preceded rationality either in the history of humankind or in that of the individual. This is the rather paradoxical assumption I wish to defend. The argument will essentially bear on models in cognitive psychology. However, the choice of such a model may have important implications for both developmental psychology and anthropology.

Something seen, heard, smelt, felt—in other words a stimulus—can undergo several types of mental processing. To begin with, the stimulus can be identified, recognized as falling under a given conceptual category. For instance on hearing a specific sound one may build the corresponding elementary proposition: "This is the sound of a doorbell." Such processing is usually called *perceptual*.

Second, the identified stimulus may evoke other mental representations. For instance, an unexpected doorbell ring may evoke the idea of someone one wishes would come. Such processing has been described in terms of association of ideas, of connotation, of symbolic meaning. Here, I shall use the theoretically more neutral phrase *symbolic evocation*.

Third, the identification of a stimulus may be used as a premise in a logical argument. For instance, from the identification of a doorbell ring, one may infer that someone wants the door opened. Such processing is at the basis of *rational* thought.

Let us term *device* the set of mental operations that are part of the same type of processing. Let us term *perceptual device* a device that accepts as input the information provided by external stimuli, and that yields as output elementary identifying propositions. Let us term *symbolic device* a device that accepts as input propositions (from the perceptual device or from other sources) and that yields as output further propositions *evoked* by the input and retrieved from (or constructed on the basis of) long-term memory (LTM). Let us term *rational device* a device that accepts as input propositions and that yields as output further propositions *logically inferred* from the input (and other premises available in memory).

These notions will permit the characterization of three elementary hypotheses about symbolic and rational thought processes mutually incompatible but each compatible with the most general kind of evidence. Indeed, no obvious evidence precludes considering that the information yielded by the perceptual device is first symbolically and then rationally processed, or is simultaneously processed in both ways or is first rationally and then symbolically processed.

The first hypothesis (Figure 1a) is the most commonly accepted: The output of the perceptual device is fed into the symbolic device; the output of the symbolic device can be fed into the rational device (both devices feed from and into memory). This hypothesis fits general intuitions: If no intellectual effort is made or if there is no cause for alertness, evocation tends to be the normal activity of the mind. A variety of loosely connected ideas follow either external stimuli or each other in a seemingly disorderly manner. On the other hand, it takes a certain effort to think rationally, for example, to construct or understand a logical argument. In that case, fewer closely connected ideas are processed in an orderly manner. There appears to be a positive correlation between the energy expended, the selectivity of recall, and the degree of organization of thought. It seems commonsensical to assume that a higher degree of organization, typical of rational processing, develops from a lower degree of organization typical of symbolic processing, rather than the other way around.

The second hypothesis (Figure 1b) is the weakest and the least interesting one: The output of the perceptual device is fed both into the symbolic and into the rational devices. As part of this second hypothesis, it is assumed that according to the level of attention either the symbolic device or the rational device does the greatest part of the overall processing.

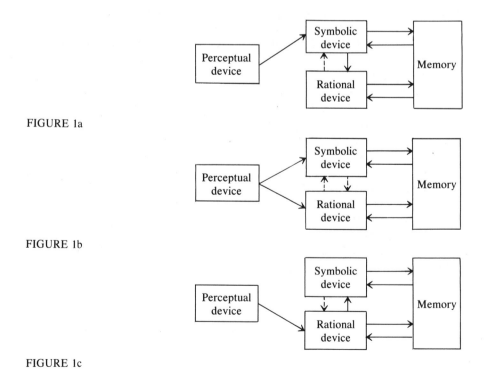

FIGURE 1a

FIGURE 1b

FIGURE 1c

The third hypothesis (Figure 1c) is the most paradoxical: The output of the perceptual device is fed into the rational device, and the output of the rational device can be fed into the symbolic device. It is assumed that if enough energy is spent on rational processing, symbolic processing need not take place at all. On the other hand, if rational processing is not carried out sufficiently, symbolic processing then takes over. When rational processing is minimal, the overall processing is mostly symbolic and may even give a false impression of being wholly symbolic.

These three hypotheses are compatible with simple introspective evidence. So are three slightly more complex hypotheses that can be constructed from the previous ones by allowing for feedback paths (dotted arrows on Figures 1a, 1b, and 1c) and cyclical processing between the symbolic and the rational device. It seems likely that the processing of most information involves such interaction. But even when this element of complexity is incorporated into the model, the problem remains: In this interaction, which kind of processing initiates the cycle? Which device is directly fed the output of the perceptual device? The symbolic one? The rational one? Both simultaneously? The three possible models are still in competition.

There are neither commonsensical nor obvious phylogenetic or ontogenetic grounds to decide between these three models. The issue is rather to determine what kind of further evidence is needed to make a well-grounded selection. For example, relevant evidence would show that rational processing requires at least some prior symbolic processing or that symbolic processing requires at least some prior rational processing, or that neither of these requirements obtains, thereby favoring either the first, the third, or the second hypothesis, respectively. First I shall argue that some rational processing does not require any prior symbolic processing, and second that all symbolic processing does require some prior rational processing. If this argument is accepted, then the cyclical version of the third hypothesis (Figure 1c) is to be preferred.

The Symbolic Contribution to Rational Processing

The rational device can be seen as deriving conclusions from premises. Some of these premises are the output of the perceptual device, others are taken from memory. To give just two simplified examples of rational processing:

There is the sound of a bell [premise from the perceptual device].

When there is the sound of a bell, someone is ringing one [premise from memory].

Someone is ringing a bell [conclusion]. (1)

Peter is nodding [premise from the perceptual device].

Whoever nods is answering positively to whatever question he or she has been asked just before [premise from long-term memory].

Peter has just been asked whether he wanted some more coffee [premise from short-term memory].

Peter has answered positively the question as to whether he wanted more coffee [conclusion].　　　　(2)

Symbolic processing could contribute (or even be necessary) to rational processing as a means of retrieving propositions from LTM that can then be used as logical premises. There is little reason to doubt that such contributions occur and even play a crucial role in creative thinking. For instance, it makes sense to describe one of the processes involved in scientific discovery as follows: Sometimes the scientist "lets his mind wander" around and about the problem at hand; in other words, the problem is being symbolically processed. It may happen that the considerations thus evoked, however far-fetched they may seem at first, will provide crucial premises for a new—rational—treatment of the problem. More trivially, discovering a knot in one's handkerchief triggers a symbolic evocation which, if successful, will provide the additional premises to explain the knot rationally. In both cases a fairly free search of memory provides information which, when combined with propositions that are in the focus of attention, enhances rational understanding: Some symbolic processing is required for full rational processing.

These two typical examples are compatible not only with the "symbolism first" hypothesis, but also (and I would say even more so) with the cyclical versions of the second and third hypotheses. Intuitively, in the preceding cases, symbolic evocation occurs not before rational understanding but between two of its stages. Evocation serves as a kind of heuristic to retrieve from memory information too loosely specified for directed recall, or in Tulving and Pearlstone's terms (1966), information that is *available* but not quite *accessible*. The need for that information, the loose specification of it, the internally generated probe, one might say, is best understood as the outcome of a prior, initial stage of rational processing. For instance the knot example could be described (in a simplified way) as follows:

There is a knot in my handkerchief [premise from the perceptual device].

When there is a knot in my handkerchief it is because I made one in order to be reminded of something when I look at the knot [premise from LTM].

When I made this knot I wanted to be reminded of something [conclusion].

What did I want to be reminded of? [question raised by the conclusion].　　　　(3)

Having reached this stage, either the information in working memory will provide the answer to the question or there is no logical algorithm, no manageable sequential procedure that will make it rapidly accessible. The best way then is to try and recreate the state of mind one had at the time one made the knot. In order to do this, several cues, chronological, analogical, and otherwise, have to be followed; varied connections have to be explored; vague suggestions tested. In other words, symbolic evocation is the appropriate approach. If this description is a fair approximation, then, in this example at least, symbolic processing *must* follow upon some prior rational processing and *may*, if successful, trigger some further rational processing.

Consider, on the other hand, cases where all the information needed for the rational processing of the input is already present in working memory. This is typically the case when the input matches prior expectations so that all the pertinent premises needed to derive relevant conclusions from the input are already accessible and no symbolic evocation is needed. Example (2) is a case in point: When one asks a yes–no question, one expects a behavior that standardly expresses a positive or negative answer. One knows in advance the relevant consequences of such a behavior, and no extra search in LTM is needed to decide, for instance, to pour some coffee for someone who nodded when asked whether he or she wanted some.

Similarly, when an experience is familiar (matches standard "schemata"— see Bartlett 1932; Neisser 1967, 1976; and Norman and Rumelhardt 1975 for various developments of this notion), no symbolic evocation is necessary. Identifying the stimulus already brings to working memory whatever background information is needed for rational processing. Example (1) is a case in point: Recognizing the sound of one's doorbell makes immediately accessible the required premises that bells ring when triggered by someone, that whoever rings a bell wants the door opened. A fairly elaborate deduction process may ensue without ever requiring any loose, evocative, symbolic processing.

In short, there are cases where symbolic evocation provides crucial premises to rational processing. However, this could be a feedback phenomenon rather than a prerational one. There are also cases where the memorized information needed for rational processing is directly accessible and where, therefore, no symbolic evocation is a prerequisite to either the inception or the development of rational processing. In other words, on the one hand no evidence points unequivocally or even strongly towards the view that symbolic processing is a precondition for rational processing. On the other hand there is evidence that *some* rational processing requires *no* prior symbolic processing.

Evocation and Association

I want to argue that *any* symbolic processing requires *some* prior rational processing, and as a first step I shall try to show why accounts that do not make and develop such an assumption fail to match some very general evidence. As a second step, I shall defend an account based on this assumption.

Any account of symbolism must answer two fundamental questions: (*a*) *Which stimuli get symbolic processing, under which conditions?* (henceforth the *which stimuli?* question); and (*b*) *Which evocation gets triggered by which stimulus, under which conditions?* (henceforth the *which evocation?* question).

Hypothetical answers to these two questions are constrained by various kinds of evidence from anthropology and psychology.

Anthropologists interested in symbolism have tended more or less explicitly to adopt a classical associationistic approach (see Lévi-Strauss, 1963: 90; Turner, 1967: 28). They assumed that ideas are associated by similarity or contiguity, that associated ideas tend to evoke each other, and that an idea with a great many associates is especially likely both to be evocative and to be evoked. Similar assumptions have been rejected or modified beyond recognition in experimental psychology (see Anderson and Bower, 1973, for a review and a defense). Since this rejection has not been accompanied by any alternative theory to account for oneiric, poetic, or cultural associations, it is not surprising that psychoanalysts, rhetoricians, and anthropologists should persist in using associationistic principles. Hence it may be appropriate to show that the very data they intend to account for is the best evidence against these principles.

The psychological import of the anthropological evidence I shall adduce to counter associationistic principles is usually not considered. Most humans in most societies spend a share of their time, energy, and sometimes wealth in setting up simple or complex rites. In most cases, whatever effects these rites have derive from the triggering of a process of symbolic evocation in the minds of the beholders and of the participants. Even those anthropologists who think that indirect effects on social status, societal cohesion, economic exploitation, etc. are the crucial factors in explaining rites must base their sociological explanations on an implicit assumption of psychological efficaciousness. This in turn is based on two properties ascribed to cultural symbolism, its *selectivity* and its *directionality*. *Selectivity* means that out of the infinite range of available stimuli, a small, finite, but nevertheless quite varied set is selected to serve ritual purposes. Presumably the stimuli selected have a greater symbolic potential (i.e., a greater likelihood to trigger a rich evocation). *Directionality* means that different stimuli are carefully chosen for different rites. The expressed purposes of these rites (e.g., induce a rainfall) are usually not achievable by the chosen means. However one may assume that different rites achieve different symbolic evocations. If this is so, then at least the direction of the evocation (the part of LTM to be searched), if not its exact content, is somewhat determined by the properties of the stimulus.

Although these two points—selectivity and directionality—may be phrased otherwise or left implicit, all anthropologists dealing with ritual take them for granted. They are, if not sufficient, at least quite necessary to explain ritual action (and for that matter all forms of symbolic communication—i.e., communication through the triggering of an evocation in the receiver—ritual being just the most compelling case).

Given this, the answer to the "which stimuli?" question cannot be expressed only in terms of the degree of intellectual alertness (a looser attention to ritual stimuli does not increase their symbolic import—if anything the opposite seems to be the case). Rather, it must specify a class of stimuli (or a class of paired stimuli—conditions) as being systematically symbolic. The answer to the "which evocation?" question cannot limit itself to individual idiosyncratic factors (such as interest); rather, it must specify some systematic relationship between the stimulus and the content or at least the direction of the evocation.

These constraints rule out any account of symbolic evocation in terms of association based on contiguity or similarity because this would entail two predictions: (a) that a very frequent or a very trivial stimulus should, since it enters into many more relations of contiguity and similarity, be much more evocative than a rare or unusual stimulus; and (b) that the representations a stimulus is most likely to evoke are either those that co-occur most often with it or those that are most similar to it. Both these predictions are patently falsified by cultural symbolism. For example, according to the first prediction odd animals such as the pangolin (Douglas, 1957) or the cassowary (Bulmer, 1967) should be poor symbolic stimuli as compared to ordinary mammals and birds. On the contrary, they are highly symbolic (see Sperber, 1975a for a discussion). A lion is both more often found with and more similar to a lioness than to a brave warrior; yet, contrary to the second prediction, the latter and not the former is evoked in most cultures in which the symbol is used. In other words, having a great many associates in terms of either contiguity or similarity is neither necessary nor sufficient to be a powerful symbolic stimulus. Close association to a stimulus is neither necessary nor sufficient for a representation to be evoked.

Whereas classical associationists may have underrated the selectivity and directionality of evocation, anthropologists are prone to overestimate them and to neglect some of the points suggested by experimental and introspective evidence: for instance, that any stimulus may trigger an evocation, given appropriate conditions, and that any representation can be evoked by any stimulus, given appropriate conditions. The first point is evidenced by free association: A sufficient condition for any stimulus to trigger an evocation is the simple decision to associate freely. The second point is evidenced by the success of mnemonic techniques based on deliberate association: A subject is instructed to associate two arbitrary stimuli in an image or in a story.

Later, the use of one of the stimuli as a cue will facilitate the retrieval of the other (see, for example, Miller, Galanter, and Pribram, 1960: Chapter 10). Even without instruction, many subjects tend spontaneously to build associations as a mnemonic prop.

Between the idiosyncratic and occasional evocations of free association or cued recall and the more widely shared and more regular associations of ritual symbolism a continuum of intermediate states can be found (e.g., in poetry or the arts).

Beside this varying degree of idiosyncrasy, there is no empirical argument to suggest that cultural symbolism and individual evocation are based on different mental mechanisms; and anthropologists should reject models of symbolism not compatible with experimental evidence on associations. This puts important constraints on any view of symbolism otherwise based on anthropological evidence. In particular, it rules out from the start any so-called grammar of symbolism; that is, any explicit account of symbolism as a kind of language.

The idea of a grammar of symbolism is appealing because it immediately provides a frame to answer the "which stimuli?" and "which evocation?" questions.

By definition and in principle, it should be possible to formalize a grammar of symbolism so that it would generate, on the basis of a finite set of axioms and rules, finite or infinite set of pairs, where the first element would be the representation of a stimulus and the second element the representation of an evocation. The general answer to the "which stimuli?" question would thus be: A stimulus gets symbolic processing if and only if it corresponds to the first element in one of the grammatical pairs. The general answer to the "which evocation?" question would be: The evocation triggered by a given stimulus is specified by the second element of the appropriate grammatical pair. When a stimulus is represented in several such pairs, several evocations would be possible. Then, answering more specifically the two fundamental questions and making detailed predictions would amount to writing the appropriate grammar.

However, since any stimulus can be evocative, all the possible psychological stimuli should be generated as first elements of the pairs; and since any representation can be evoked by any stimulus, there should be for each stimulus at least as many pairs as there are representations in the memory of the subject(s) considered. This is sheer absurdity. It would take more than elaboration and qualifications to redeem the notion of a grammar of symbolism from its purely metaphorical, not to say misleading, character.

Anthropologists have developed various versions of what could be called *cultural associationism* rather than a truly grammatical model (whose formal constraints have not always been grasped). Cultural associationists assert or imply three ssumptions: first, that humans have the general ability to build associations on the basis of either contiguity or similarity, and to use them in retrieval, as described by classical associationists; second, that a finite subset of these associations is learned as part of the acquisition of the culture; third, that the subjects learn to give preference to these cultural associations whenever the proper stimulus is presented, that is, mainly on cultural occasions. In other words, a restricted and shared subpart of the overall individual associative network is used in prescribed cultural contexts. The answers to the "which stimuli?" and the "which evocation?" questions are provided by the cultural group itself and learned by the individuals who are socialized in the group.

This cultural associationism shares neither the pitfalls of the simple kind of associationism considered in the preceding (which fails to account for the selectivity and the directionality of evocation), nor the pitfalls of pseudo-grammatical views (which could never handle the fact that any stimulus may be evocative and may evoke any representation). However, cultural associationism makes (and cannot but make) heavy and unwarranted assumptions about the learning of symbolism. For instance, Turner (1967, 1969) assumes, first, that the kind of exegesis that is sometimes taught in some societies provides the right associations to "make sense" of cultural symbols, and second, that when exegesis is absent, the way the symbols are talked about or handled contributes to learning just as exegesis would. It is hard to see how a cultural associationist would dispense with these or similar assumptions. However, I have argued at length (Sperber, 1974) that not only is exegesis rare and fragmentary but it also is as much in need of being "made sense" of as the symbols themselves. I have further argued that the only way in which rules for the use of symbols (and other peripheral data) can be considered as equivalent to exegesis is that they too need to be "made sense" of. Exegesis and other types of data are stimuli for evocation rather than representations to be evoked. In short, only a small part of cultural symbolism is the object of teaching, and that teaching is itself quite symbolic. The only form of learning that then remains available in this associationistic framework is the building and strengthening of associations on the basis of contiguity and similarity. The cultural associationists will assume that specific associations are fostered in a cultural context by creating the right contiguities and pointing out the right similarities. However, once again, no amount of cultural contrivance will reverse the fact that a lion is both more generally contiguous and more similar to a lioness or to a lion cub than to a brave warrior. There is no way, in this account, of avoiding the prediction that the closest associates of a stimulus in terms of contiguity or similarity will be the most likely to be evoked. When that prediction can be checked against experimental or introspective evidence, it is often falsified. When it cannot be checked and is assumed to be valid, it usually fails to "make sense" of the cultural phenomena it was meant to explain in the first place.

To sum up this section, the answer to the "which stimuli?" question must accomodate both the fact that any stimulus can sometimes trigger an evocation and the fact that some stimuli nearly always trigger one. The answer to the "which evocation?" question must accomodate both the fact that any representation may be evoked by any stimulus and the fact that different stimuli differ as to the representation they are most likely to evoke.

It might have been thought at first that these requirements call precisely for the kind of probabilistic treatment that the notion of strength of association provides. But it turns out not to be so. Inasmuch as predictions can be made at all on the basis of number and strength of associations, they fail to be borne out by the evidence. Although the assumption of a cultural fostering of selected associations might draw attention to interesting facts, it does not radically improve the quality of predictions. To generalize the argument: Knowledge of prior associations is not sufficient to predict which stimulus is likely to get symbolic processing; and knowledge of both a stimulus and prior associations is not sufficient to predict which evocations are likely to be triggered.

Contextual Constraints on Evocation

What more than the stimulus and prior associations should one know to be able to predict which evocations (if any) are likely to be triggered? Even associationists would agree that evocation is a function not only of the stimulus and of prior associations, but also of the context. What is needed is knowledge of the context. However, references to it are generally a way of sweeping various pending questions under the rug, and the study of symbolism is no exception. How important are the questions thus disposed of?

If on the basis of prior associations a restricted class of possible evocations could be paired with a given stimulus and if the job of the context was just to permit a final selection, then indeed a vague reference to the context might do for the time being. But I have tried to show that in no way can prior associations restrict the class of possible evocations. If this is correct, the contextual selection is made out of the whole range of evocations available in memory, and association strength plays at best an ancillary role. In other words, what is being swept under the rug is the central problem, and what is being diligently studied is a side issue.

Why do students of symbolism hardly ever do more than mention in passing the relevance of the context, and never attempt to make explicit the psychological mechanisms involved in contextual selection? At least part of the answer is clear enough: By talking vaguely—and misleadingly—of "the role of the context," one minimizes the problem and postpones the challenge to basic assumptions that the study of contextual selection would involve. Indeed, properly speaking, not the context, but the intellectual *representation of* the context, can have a direct effect on symbolic processing.

The intellectual representation of the context is not a matter of simple perception, but involves the integration into a logically consistent whole of various perceptual identifications with prior knowledge and expectations. In other words, the only way the context ever appears in conceptual processes such as the symbolic one is through the synthesis of diverse information by the rational device. But acknowledging the role of context and really trying to make it explicit would amount to admitting that rational processing is a prerequisite for symbolic evocation. This seems to be something that both classical associationists and cultural associationists do not want to do because their basic assumption is that symbolic evocation is prior to rational understanding. All the shortcomings that I have tried to point out are linked to this basic assumption and to the concomitant refusal or inability to consider seriously the role of rational thought in the contextual selection of evocations. I believe that the repeated failure of generations of scholars to build a reasonably explicit theory of symbolism on the basis of that assumption is a sufficient reason to try and dispense with it.

Compare:

(a) Wine referred to as "wine"
(b) Blood referred to as "blood"
(c) Wine referred to as "blood" (4)

(a) Lighting a cigar with a match
(b) Buying a cigar with a dollar bill
(c) Lighting a cigar with a dollar bill (5)

(a) A cackling hen
(b) A crowing cock
(c) A crowing hen (6)

(a) The issue number 1247 of a periodical
(b) A $1000 price tag on a second-hand car
(c) The issue number 1000 of a periodical (7)

In the four examples, the (c) cases tend to be more symbolic (more likely to trigger a rich evocation) than the (a) and (b) cases. The stimulus or the symbol is present in the (b) cases but it becomes properly symbolic only when put in an (a)-type context. Innumerable examples such as these can be found, or coined at will. What do they have in common? There is something that could be described as incongruous, paradoxical, or striking in the relationship of one specific item with its given context. Notice that the relationship need not be especially unlikely: The issue number 1000 is not less likely than the issue number 1247. Nor need it be unexpected: Hearing wine called "blood" during the Mass is highly expected. Nor need it be mysterious: The newly rich are rather obvious when and if they light a cigar with a dollar bill. Nor need it be *meant* to strike you: The crowing hen is guileless.

All one can say is that in each example an extra intellectual problem is raised by the (c) cases as opposed to the (a) and (b) cases. Even if you expect wine to be called "blood" at the Mass, you also have a much more general and practical assumption that words are used according to their meaning, and that assumption is challenged. The careful carelessness of the newly rich is hard to interpret as the unintended behavior it is intended to be seen as. A crowing hen challenges zoological common sense. Example 7, although very ordinary, is also subtler: The number of an issue is somewhat like a proper name with a semantic element in it expressing order of issue. It is not meant to express a quantity. To grasp the quantity expressed by a number such as "1247," an effort of arithmetical analysis would have to be made and usually is not when the number is used ordinally. When the number "1247" is seen on the cover of the periodical, the information grasped is precisely the relevant one and nothing more: It indicates the issue following number 1246 and preceding number 1248. However when the number is "1000," it is hard *not* to grasp the quantity expressed. We have an unanalyzed (although, of course, analyzable) concept of "a thousand" but not of "a thousand two hundred and forty seven." When verbal (or numerical) information is given to us orally or in writing, our rational processing consists of establishing its relevance (see Sperber and Wilson, forthcoming). In this case, attaching relevance to the unwittingly grasped quantity is a challenge.

Thus in the four (c) cases the load on the rational device will tend to be much higher than in the (a) and (b) cases. I propose that this can be generalized to answer the "which stimuli?" question: *Whenever the perceptual representation of an additional stimulus in a given context cannot be fully processed on the basis of the resources accessible to the rational device at that moment, symbolic processing will occur.*

Put differently, when the rational device cannot reach a satisfactory synthesis on the basis of information provided by the perceptual device on the one hand, and directly accessible memorized information on the other, then a nonsequential search is made in LTM for additional premises. It is this search that is intuitively grasped as an evocation: an awareness more of the activity of research than of the information actually parsed.

This proposition permits several general predictions. Indeed, if it is correct, then two factors will affect the likelihood of an evocation: The first involves the compatibility of the information to be processed with the frameworks or schemata of rational interpretation available to the individual; the second involves the intellectual resources actually mobilized or accessible at the time when the information is presented. Predictions are:

1. When some information challenges basic assumptions of a cognitive system, it will be symbolically processed, whatever the degree of intellectual alertness.

I would argue that this first prediction is borne out by most of cultural symbolism. Supernaturalism, mystical causality, and religious mysteries challenge basic cognitive assumptions and thus are sure to be processed symbolically. To consider things the other way round: If the assumption that overloading the rational device triggers a symbolic processing is right, then it is not surprising that this psychological liability should have been exploited sociologically in the surest possible way, by systematic irrationality. The selectivity of cultural symbolism should be explained along such lines.

2. When the degree of intellectual alertness is very low, most information processed tends to overload the rational device and thus to trigger a symbolic evocation.

This prediction might be borne out by "some dreams and other disorganized mental states" such as the hypnagogic states studied by Silberer (1909). Less dramatically this prediction offers an alternative to the usual explanation of the introspective evidence that the lesser the intellectual alertness, the greater the symbolic character of the thought process. This evidence is usually considered crucial to justify the view that symbolic processing must be primary and prior to rational processing. However, it corroborates as well if not better the opposite view defended here: If symbolic processing is triggered by an overload of the rational device, then the less the rational device can process at a given moment, the more the symbolic device will have to process.

3. Mastery of rational, culturally adapted schemata will proportionately limit the occasions on which symbolic interpretations must necessarily occur.

Again this prediction provides an alternative account of the assumed importance of symbolism both in technologically primitive societies and in children. The development of science and technology multiplies the possibilities of rational interpretation of, and rational dealings with, the environment and diminishes the chances that environmental facts will overload the rational device and be symbolically interpreted. However, this historical process is a very slow and marginal one. More dramatic is the case of children. They rapidly internalize a large number of adapted schemata, facilitating the rational processing of information and thereby diminishing the chances of overload and the probability of symbolic processing.

According to the traditional view, in the history of either humankind or of the individual, rationality was progressively acquired and tends to take the place of symbolic thought processes. According to the view advanced here, not rationality but only knowledge is acquired. It is organized in schemata for rational processing, and thereby enables the individual to process a greater load of information with the rational device he or she possessed from the start. The range of stimuli that are automatically processed symbolically is reduced accordingly. However, it need not decrease the overall use of symbolic thought since this depends also on other factors such as the level of attention or individual and cultural interests. The development of rational schemes makes this decrease possible, but not necessary.

There is no a priori reason to prefer the classical empiricist view or the rationalist one presented here; only empirical considerations such as the validity of predictions should decide. I have tried to show that concerning the "which stimuli?" question, whatever valid predictions are implied by the empiricist view are also implied by the rationalist one, that further invalid predictions are implied by the empiricist view only, and that further valid predictions are implied by the rationalist view only, thus favoring the latter. I will now attempt to show that the same situation obtains regarding the "which evocation?" question.

During the Mass when the wine is referred to as "blood," neither the close associates of wine nor those of blood, nor their common associates (such as other reddish liquids) are likely to be evoked. What is likely to be evoked (among other possibilities) is a transcendent order of reality where the evidence of the senses would cease to be reliable, where a superior power would be able and willing to transmute substances. In other words, a set of supplementary premises is evoked. Within the framework provided by these premises, it makes sense to refer to wine as "blood."

When someone lights a cigar with a dollar bill, what is likely to be evoked is such an extreme degree of wealth and such a complete indifference to the concerns of ordinary people, that the use of a dollar bill as a matchstick might deserve no more notice than the use of a matchstick as a toothpick. In other words, this striking use of a dollar bill evokes supplementary premises such that, within the framework they provide, the only striking thing that remains is that one should have been struck in the first place.

The crowing hen may not evoke much to the modern academic, but it was very evocative to traditional European peasants. Judging from the native commentaries compiled by Sébillot (1906: vol. III, pp. 222–223), this anomaly was likely to evoke misfortunes or anomalies with which it was related either causally or analogically, or in both ways at the same time: The hen had copulated with a reptile, in its eggs were snakes, or the owner of the house was dominated by his wife, or husband and wife would quarrel, or someone would die (in the latter case the analogy should be: What the crowing cock is to life, the crowing hen is to death). Surely beside and beyond these traditional exegeses further representations could be arrived at; but the direction is fairly clear: What is evoked is a set of supplementary premises such that the isolated and unexpected crowing of the hen becomes part of a chain of expectations.

The thousandth issue of a periodical is likely to evoke the amount of time spent, paper printed, work done, as if part of the aim had been to achieve this precise quantity, as if an objective threshold were thereby passed. Thus, supplementary premises are evoked that would make the irrelevant but noticeable quantity incidentally expressed by an ordinal number become relevant. Notice that, conversely, to render a cardinal number symbolic, one way is to make it ordinally noticeable, for example, *"The Thousand and One Nights,"* a title that evokes an important thousand-and-first night in a way neither "the thousand nights" nor "the thousand-two-hundred-and forty-seven nights" would do.

What the four cases have in common can be, I would argue, generalized to answer the "which evocation?" question: *When the rational device is overloaded, the symbolic processing thus triggered consists of a searching on the basis of information available in long-term memory for supplementary premises that, had they been accessible in the first place, would have permitted a fully rational processing of the initial input.*

According to this view, at least three factors contribute to determine the content of the evocation: the input to the symbolic device, the state of the rational device, and the content and organization of LTM.

So far I have considered only one major type of input to the rational device, perceptually processed information about a stimulus-in-context. Two other types of input should also be considered: first, the grammar-based decoding of sound waves (or other types of linguistic signals), where the input to the rational device is a semantic representation (see Sperber, 1975b; and Sperber and Wilson, forthcoming); second, the feedback of the symbolic device, i.e., the additional assumptions symbolically evoked that are fed into the rational device and that may in turn raise a new challenge and call for further evocation (I have suggested [Sperber, 1974] that such cyclical evocation may be crucial in understanding both cultural and dream symbolism).

Whatever the inputs to the rational device, be they perceptual, linguistic, or endogenous, the outputs of the rational device capable of becoming inputs to the symbolic device are always of the same nature: The symbolic device is fed defective conceptual representations resulting from an incomplete rational processing of challenging inputs.

Beside the input to the rational device, the second factor determining evocation is the state of that device. Depending on the assumptions accessible to it at the time, the input will either get full rational processing or not, and if not, the search for additional premises will take specific directions. The direction of the evocation will depend on the nature of the intellectual challenge. When this is a challenge to the most basic cognitive assumptions, as in much cultural symbolism, the direction of evocation is fairly predictable. This is one more consideration when explaining the selectivity and directionality of cultural symbolism. When, on the other hand, the challenge is due to cognitive idiosyncrasies or to intellectual fatigue, the direction of evocation is much less predictable; this kind of susceptibility to symbolism is culturally exploited (as in some initiation rituals) or encouraged (as in many art forms) only by societies who favor a high degree of individuality.

Even when the directionality of symbolism is strong or, in other words, the focalization of evocation narrow, the exact content of the evocation is still not predictable. Indeed, beside the initial input to the rational device and the state of that device, a third factor is crucial in determining the evocation: the content of long-term memory. Supplementary premises have to be retrieved or constructed from the information available in LTM, and this always comprises a high level of idiosyncrasy. In the present account, the most pointed kind of cultural symbolism cannot elicit a standard response. Evocation is an individually creative use of memory and can be manipulated to some extent only in its direction, not in its actual content.

The easy acceptance by humans of odd and sundry symbolic systems according to their milieu of birth has repeatedly been taken as an argument for the malleability of the human mind. However, if the present account is correct, these symbolic representations are internalized not as ordinary knowledge but, so to speak, "in quotation marks"; not as thoughts, but as starting points of evocations, as food for thought. Members of the same social group may take in the same so-called beliefs, but it does not follow that they think the same thoughts. Reports starting with "The so-and-so think that . . . " should be reconsidered. Cultural symbolism, often construed as an argument for a behavioristic, manipulative view of humankind, is better understood as based on the ability to search one's memory in a creative way, open only to limited and uncertain manipulations.

In addition to these three factors—symbolic input, state of the rational device, content of LTM—it is arguable that a fourth factor plays a role, namely, the associative network. It is possible that once a probe has been specified as a result of the shortcomings of the rational device, once a range of information in LTM has been focalized, then, within that range, associative paths are followed in priority. However, even if the present account is extended so as to include such associationistic considerations, it would still yield predictions fundamentally different from the classical associationistic ones.

Associationists predict that between a stimulus and its evocation there is an associative path. Even more than psychologists or anthropologists, rhetoricians have devoted themselves since the time of Aristotle to corroborating this view. However, this is trivially true: Not only between the representation of a stimulus and the representation evoked, but between any two representations whatsoever, there are always several relationships of contiguity or similarity or both. This might cease to be the case if strong constraints were put on the notions of contiguity and of similarity (for instance, by considering these relations to be nontransitive). But to my knowledge no constraints that would redeem the associationistic predictions from triviality without falsifying them have ever been proposed. Not an oversight but an impossibility, one imagines.

Still, it is hard to see how associationists could dispense with making at least one more prediction, implied by their whole approach, namely, that the stronger the contiguity or the similarity, the stronger the association and the greater the likelihood of mutual evocation. I have argued that this prediction is trivially false.

Whereas the associationist should predict that the stronger associates of a stimulus are its most likely evocations and that, among these, contextual factors may effect a final selection, I have proposed here a rationalist view that is the other way round. Contextually relevant representations are the most likely to be evoked; among these it may be that strength of association to the stimulus contributes to the final selection. But contextually relevant representations may include only very weak associates of the stimulus. Therefore the two types of predictions are quite different. The rationalist prediction is not subject to the objections raised against the associationistic ones. It is neither trivially true nor trivially false, and should therefore be preferred.

Conclusion

The fact that under appropriate conditions any stimulus can evoke any representation precludes any grammar or grammar-like model of symbolism. On the other hand, the selectivity and directionality of symbolism cannot be accounted for in simple associationistic terms. When an attempt is made, as in cultural associationism, to find a middle way between the too strong constraints of a grammatical model and the too weak ones of an associationistic model, it turns out that not just the strength of the constraints but also their nature has to be reassessed. Symbolic interpretation does not consist of recalling or reconstructing a strong or weak connection between a signal and a sense; it is rather a particularly creative form of problem solving. The main constraint on any problem solving lies in the problem itself; the main source of constraint is whatever specifies the problem to be solved. In the present instance, the problem is, generally speaking, one of retrieving of imagining supplementary premises that should make it possible to process fully some challenging input information. The specification of these problems has to be done by a device capable of synthesizing various input data, of evaluating these against accessible schemata, and, if this is not sufficient, of specifying what kind of supplementary assumptions are to be looked for. These abilities are characteristic of the rational device. There is no reason to assume that they are duplicated in the symbolic device, when it is much simpler to assume that some rational processing takes place before any symbolic processing. In other words, the constraints on symbolic evocation are typically those a rational device would put; the problems dealt with are those a rational device would raise. Therefore, in thought processes, the cycle of interaction between symbolic and rational processing should be considered as initiated by the latter. If so, then neither phylogenetically nor ontogenetically, nor in any other sense, can symbolic thought be prerational.

References

Anderson, J. R., and Gordon H. Bower
    1973 *Human associative memory.* Washington, D.C.: Halsted Press.
Bartlett, Frederic C.
    1932 *Remembering.* London and New York: Cambridge Univ. Press.
Bulmer, Ralph
    1967 Why is the cassowary not a bird? A problem of zoological taxonomy among the Karam of New Guinea Highlands. *Man* 2(1), 5–25.
Douglas, Mary
    1957 Animals in Lele religious thought. *Africa* 27(1), 46–58.
Lévi-Strauss, Claude
    1963 *Totemism.* Boston, Massachusettes: Beacon Press.
    1966 *The savage mind.* Illinois: Univ. of Chicago Press.
Lévy-Bruhl, Lucien
    1910 *Les fonctions mentales dans les sociétés inférieures.* Paris: Alcan.
    1922 *La mentalité primitive.* Paris: Alcan.
Miller, George A., Eugene Galanter, and Karl H. Pribram
    1960 *Plans and the structure of behaviour.* New York: Holt.
Neisser, Ulric
    1967 *Cognitive psychology.* New York: Appleton.
    1976 *Cognition and reality.* San Francisco, California: Freeman.
Norman, Donald A., David E. Rumelhart, and the LNR Research Group
    1975 *Explorations in Cognition.* San Francisco, California: Freeman.
Piaget, Jean
    1968 *La formation du symbole chez l'Enfant.* Neuchatel: Delachaux et Niestlé.
Sébillot, Paul
    1906 *Le folklore de france* (Vol 3.). Paris: Maisonneuve et Larose.
Silberer, Herbert
    1909 Bericht über eine methode, gewisse symbolische halluzinations—Ersheinungen hervorzurufen und zu beobachten. *Jahrbuch für psychoanalytische und psychopathologische Forschungen* 1, 513.
Sperber, Dan
    1974 *Le symbolisme en général.* Paris: Hermann. (English translation: *Rethinking symbolism.* London and New York: Cambridge Univ. Press, 1975.)
    1975a Pourquoi les animaux parfaits, les hybrides et les monstres sont-ils bon à penser symboliquement? *L'Homme* XV(2), 5–24.
    1975b Rudiments de rhétorique cognitive. *Poétique* 23, 389–415.
Sperber, Dan and Deirdre Wilson
    n.d. *Language and relevance.* (In press).
Tulving, Endel and Z. Pearlstone
    1966 Availability versus accessibility of information in memory for words. *Journal of Verbal Learning and Verbal Behaviour* 5, 381–391.
Turner, Victor
    1967 *The forest of symbols.* Ithaca, New York: Cornell Univ. Press.
    1969 *The ritual process.* London: Routledge and Kegan Paul.

4

Psychoanalysis and Cultural Symbolization

PERCY S. COHEN

Introduction

There is no obvious problem in explaining symbols whose referents are evident: provided one accepts that the referents are what they are said to be; and provided that one acknowledges the fact that explanation, going further than linking one symbol to one referent, also involves looking at a number of symbols and referents—not necessarily an equal number of both—as a system or as part of one. The obvious problems arise where the stated connection between symbol and referent(s) is considered to be an unsatisfactory explanation of that symbol and, even more so, where there are no obvious referents at all to link to a symbol. Where the stated connection is not fully credited by the investigator, he or she needs a theory that both generates further referents and also explains why there is more to the symbol than meets the eye. However, where there are no referents whatsoever provided by a text or none of which an informant is consciously aware, the investigator needs a body of theory that tells him not only what referents to attach to a symbol but that also enables him to justify his assumption that what he is dealing with *is* a symbol or a set of symbols.[1]

If the issues are stated in this way, then it becomes clear that much of the

[1] This is not to overlook the fact that theories are also used to explain the meaning of a symbol to which the referents come attached and to which no other referents are added; but that theory is usually trivial and taken for granted; consequently, the investigator is seldom aware of its use or of his or her need for it.

SYMBOL AS SENSE

anthropological discussion of symbolism is about different and, therefore, separable problems that may also be interconnected. But much and, until recently, most of this discussion shows no recognition of these issues; moreover, it uses a number of assumptions about what is permissible and nonpermissible in the investigation of cultural symbolism that are neither questioned nor, for that matter, fully stated and scrutinized. This partly results from the great indebtedness of the anthropological study of cultural symbols to Durkheimian sociology; but it results no less from the way in which the elements of that doctrine were detached from a wider body of ideas that Durkheim formulated on the subject and that were then constituted in such a way as to encourage only certain modes of symbolic analysis without providing adequate justification for doing so.[2]

Of late the near-hegemony of neo-Durkheimianism has been not only challenged but largely undermined.[3] This has produced a renewed respect for the sort of theory of culture that, in the United States, never fully gave way to Durkheimianism. It has also been associated with an even newer Durkheimianism that also owes something to Wittgenstein. But, above all, it has been consequent upon the structuralist and semiotic attempts to treat symbolism as a phenomenon *sui generis*.

In view of all these changed circumstances, including the fact that the whole theoretical question of the attribution of referents to cultural symbols can still be seen as problematic—since the Durkheimian assumptions that enable one to identify cultural symbols and their referents can no longer be taken for granted—the time has come to reconsider the theoretical arguments for, as well as those against, the applicability of psychoanalysis to the explanation of cultural symbols. One good reason for this is that psychoanalysis, like the original Durkheimian doctrine, does have a comprehensive general theory of symbolization, as such, a derived (or partially derived) specific theory of cultural symbolization, as well as a number of subsidiary ones about particular forms of symbolism. A second reason is that psychoanalysis can explain *some aspects* of cultural symbolism that are

---

[2] Of course, no one could deny that this rather dogmatic and narrow interpretation of the Durkheimian tradition produced results that were not only impressive but were, for the most part, far more impressive than those produced by other modes of analysis. There were several reasons for this, but the most important was that neo-Durkheimian sociologism did constitute a clear set of prescriptions and prohibitions that came sufficiently close to the mark to be valuable and fruitful, provided it was used, in the circumstances then existing, in a fairly singleminded fashion. For the alternatives had either been dismissed as illegitimate—for example, intellectualism and various forms of psychological reductionism, including psychoanalysis—or they were like American culturalism, no match for this tough and determined opponent.

[3] This has been due less to an initial and acknowledged dissatisfaction with Durkheimian sociologism and its principal, earlier rivals than to a change in intellectual fashion that has produced new rivals whose existence has helped to create dissatisfaction with older modes of thought.

not readily explicable by any existing rival theory; and it is a good principle that *any* theory that answers a particular question or kind of question is better than none.

Objections to Psychoanalytic Interpretations of Culture

In the past, it was not only the hegemony of Durkheimianism but also the imperialist ideology of psychoanalysis itself that stood in the way of a reasonable assessment of psychoanalytic ideas of cultural symbolism. If the former asserts that only sociology can explain social facts, the latter claims that only psychology—and, what is more, a particular psychology—can explain the products of the human mind; and, if the first asserts that cultural symbols are social and are, therefore, the domain of sociology alone, the second asserts that all symbols are mental phenomena and are, therefore, the domain of psychology alone.

Most anthropologists have tended to reject psychoanalytical imperialism. The grounds for this objection are often very general and relate to any attempt to reduce social and cultural phenomena to so-called psychological laws. But these need not concern us here. What should concern us are the specific grounds that relate only to the matter at hand. Here the minimalist— and, one would argue, the strongest—grounds for rejecting psychoanalytic imperialism are as follows: that while psychoanalysis may well explain the formation of personal symbols in terms of the more or less endogenous, spontaneous internal conflicts and other processes that occur both unconsciously and consciously in the individual human mind, it can not explain cultural symbols in this way because these are not generated independently, spontaneously, and endogenously in each human mind but are, rather, presented as more or less finished products to those minds. By this view the individual human mind needs to do no more processing than is required for the adoption of those cultural symbols, along with the referents that are attached to them.

Additional objections to psychoanalysis are as follows: that commonly both symbols and referents are consciously communicated to social members who consciously adopt them; and that where only some of the referents—or none of them—are consciously communicated and adopted, all that is required by an observer who wishes to impute certain referents to social members is the assumption that those members share certain tacit or covert understandings concerning the nature of their social and physical world that enable them, unconsciously, to experience the referents that the symbols imply; so that there is no need for the observer to assume that even referents that are not consciously communicated and adopted—to say nothing of those that are—are created by each individual by the workings of the so-called dynamic unconscious.[4]

But even if one is ready to embrace psychological theories of cultural symbolism, one is still left with a number of further objections to psychoanalysis itself. The first is that it is unscientific. This objection is commonly made by some anthropologists who do not, however, question the scientific credentials of other theories of symbols with this degree of scrupulousness and who, in any case, either choose to ignore or are genuinely ignorant of the following considerations: that some philosophers of science, of some distinction, consider certain methodological objections to psychoanalysis to be either disingenuous or misconceived (see Lakatos, 1974; Wisdom, 1956); that, to the credit of psychoanalysis as a research program, many of its hypotheses have been subjected to independent tests and that a number have, by the relevant criteria, done quite well (see Fisher and Greenberg, 1977); that a great deal of clinical psychoanalytic evidence is strengthened by the experience of clinical nonpsychoanalytic evidence and is, itself, not quite as suspect—in the sense of being created by its own theoretical expectations—as is commonly thought; that the fact that clinical psychoanalytic evidence—and, for that matter, much experimental evidence—relies for its value on certain theoretical assumptions no more invalidates such evidence than does the same condition invalidate that of the natural sciences (see Lakatos, 1970); that psychoanalysis is no more damned for having a metatheory that is, for the most part, nontestable than are other sciences, provided that that metatheory is suggestive of theories that are more testable (see Agassi, 1964; Watkins, 1958).

The strongest defence of psychoanalysis is that, to date, it can explain a great deal that has not been otherwise better explained. Provided it is used without the arrogance of intellectual imperialism and absolutism, psychoanalysis has at least as much claim to be considered a body of "scientific" ideas as do most others that are used by anthropologists in the study of symbolism.

The second objection that anthropologists raise against psychoanalysis is that is unnecessary in that all that is needed to explain the use of cultural symbols is that they are there. But if that objection holds good, then it applies to other theories of cultural symbolism such as those of Mary Douglas, Lévi-Strauss, and Edmund Leach to say nothing of those of Durkheim and of the post-Durkheimians.

---

[4] The concept of the dynamic unconscious as used in psychoanalytic theory will be explained later in the text. But this particular term is used here because few anthropologists would deny that some kind of unconscious process occurs in the adoption and use of cultural symbols where only some or even none of the referents are consciously communicated along with them. What they might well deny is that the unconscious process is dynamic in the specifically psychoanalytic sense.

The third objection, that psychoanalysis justifies itself by imputing referents to symbols of which symbol users are unaware, can easily be disposed of: for the same objection applies to almost any theory of social and cultural symbolism. If such theories did not do this, they would all be, more or less, the same theory, which would state that symbols mean what informants or texts tell us they mean. This argument does not justify theories that attribute referents to symbols of which their users are unaware; it merely states that double standards should not be used when assessing their relative merits.

The fourth objection—that the psychoanalytic attribution of referents is arbitrary—is linked to the third. A high degree of arbitrariness was characteristic of early psychoanalytic attempts to interpret cultural symbols. The assumption was dogmatically made that, although the cultural world may present a large number of symbols, these could be related to a relatively small number of referents. In fact, it was almost assumed that one could use psychoanalytic theory to provide a manual of symbolic interpretation. But that sort of practice is no longer even characteristic of dream interpretation, and is certainly not encouraged in the interpretation of cultural and other symbols. This is not a denial of the view that there are certain universal themes that are taken up in dreams or, for that matter, in myths. But the assumptions used are the following: that dream symbols condense a number of different meanings; that the particular combination of referents must, to some extent, be taken as a whole; that a pattern of referents may, in some respects, be personally idiosyncratic; and that such patterns should not be treated so much as keys to an individual's personality but, rather, as a product of it that can only be understood when other aspects of the personality are understood.

The final objection is that the use of unconscious referents to symbols—and, what is more, the use of additional assumptions about unconscious mental processes—does not require the use of psychoanalysis. This objection is, of itself, valid; the recognition of unconscious mental processes is not, of itself, a recognition of psychoanalytic assumptions. For example, Durkheim clearly did not think that aboriginal men were conscious of the processes whereby they invented symbols, such as totems, to express their otherwise inexpressible dependence upon society and its external, coercive influence on their conduct; in fact, he thought the inexpressible to be either imperfectly apprehended by consciousness or, even more, to be not part of it. Nor can it be said of the post-Durkheimians that, in making their interpretations of ritual symbolism—especially those expressing reversals—that they were claiming to have found their informants conscious of how and why they used symbols in the way in which they did. Nor can it even be said of the neo-Durkheimians, such as Mary Douglas, that they insist that their informants are fully conscious of the meanings that are attributed to their symbolic usages. As for Lévi-Strauss, he not only admits that he is assuming much about unconscious mental processes, he even takes pride in doing so; since he holds that without such enquiry into unconscious processes there can be no true structural examination of symbolic systems.

But none of these modes of symbolic analysis owes very much to psychoanalysis; their use of the term *unconscious* is very different from the psychoanalytic use. Consequently, one cannot argue that a commitment to explanation in terms of unconscious symbolic referents is, in any way, a commitment to psychoanalysis. Furthermore, if one wishes to show that psychoanalysis does make some contribution to the explanation of cultural symbolism, one has to show that there is some way of applying its own ideas about unconscious mental processes and that there is also some justification in doing so.

The Dynamic Unconscious and the Freudian Theory of Symbolism

In discussing psychoanalytic ideas I refer in this chapter to Freudian psychoanalysis. I do not deny that Jungian psychoanalysis is often rich in the suggestive but specific insights that it offers in the understanding of symbolism; but I find it rather poor in theory, since it seems often to take for granted that which most needs explanation.

But, by Freudian psychoanalytic theory I do not mean one well-integrated body of propositions of one man or even of one codifier of Freud's writings; nor do I mean one well-integrated or codified body of propositions of Freud and of his successors; rather, I refer to a rather loose assembly of ideas, formulated by Freud and by two generations of his followers, which includes some important modifications of and even deviations from his own ideas.[5]

[5] These are a number of different sorts. The most important, for our purposes and for others, are the following: the development of "ego theory" in England by Anna Freud and her followers and, in the United States, by Heinz Hartmann and his associates and followers; the exploration of personality formation in very early childhood by Melanie Klein and her followers, by D. W. Winnicott and his, and by Michael Balint; the general exploration of object relations by those already mentioned as well as by a number of others; and, finally, the general discussion of the nature of unconscious fantasy. In addition one should mention the singular contribution of Erik H. Erickson who has, of all living psychoanalysts, done most to use its ideas with sufficient flexibility, to say nothing of creative ingenuity, to make them of greater use to sociology and anthropology. Erikson has also taken the lead from earlier psychoanalytic writers in developing certain ideas which have direct relevance for the psychoanalytic study of symbolism: First, he has stressed how the psychological modalities associated with specific infantile stages of development may carry over from one stage to the next thereby affecting the manner in which the subsequent modality may form; second, he has thereby shown how the specific referents of symbols that appear to derive from, say, a later stage of development, may have attached to them referents that derive also from an earlier one.

In stressing the importance of these various schools and contributions I am not, thereby, accepting all of their contributions at their face value: Thus, for example, while I consider the

These modifications have enabled psychoanalytic thought to do at least two very different things: on the one hand, to put greater emphasis on the relative autonomy of the processes making for rationality and for reality-testing; on the other hand, to put greater emphasis on the importance of fantasy in the mental construction of man's experience of the world. The first reminds us that, for certain purposes, conduct is strongly influenced by an external social (to say nothing of natural) reality to which the mind must adapt even though it does so in terms of certain inner expectations, dispositions, and so on; the second reminds us that, for certain purposes, the objects of the external world can only be treated as inner objects to the extent that they have been constructed within the fantasies of the inner world.

In all psychoanalytic writing, two distinctions are made that are both fundamental to psychoanalytic thinking and of direct relevance to our discussion of symbolism. The first is the distinction between the *descriptive* and the *dynamic* unconscious. The second is the distinction between two types of thinking: *primary process* and *secondary process*.

Freud himself pointed out that the term *unconscious* could have a simple and obvious descriptive significance: It could simply refer to mental processes of which the individual is not conscious (see Freud, 1949). This descriptive use of the term *unconscious* has been equated by many psychoanalysts with Freud's term *preconscious*, which he used to refer to those things that can, more or less easily, be brought to consciousness. However, this equation is unfortunate since there are many unconscious mental processes that do not fall into this category: Freud himself points out that instincts affect us unconsciously in the sense that, though we may become conscious of their effects on our behavior, we are not conscious of the source from which instinctual promptings derive. One could add that a multitude of cognitive and affective processes also derive from areas of mental functioning of which we are not at all necessarily conscious in order for them to be effective.

What is common to all descriptively unconscious phenomena is that they may express themselves directly; whereas, what is common to all those dynamically unconscious mental phenomena is that they can not. The reason for this is that the so-called dynamic unconscious is created, according to Freud (and to all of his followers, whatever else they may agree or not agree

---

contribution of Melanie Klein to have been considerable I do not necessarily accept her own formulation of it which, in the judgment of other psychoanalysts and of academic psychologists, is in many respects quite inconsistent with what is known to be possible at certain stages of infantile development. The same criticism applies, though perhaps to a lesser extent, to the writings of other psychoanalytic theorists who have dealt with the very earliest stages of infantile development. The chief criticism made of them is that the best evidence that they adduce is not direct evidence of the stages referred to but is evidence filtered through the mental experience of older children or even of adults with their very different kinds of mental equipment. (See Balint, 1968; Erikson, 1953; Anna Freud, 1954; Hartmann, 1958; Klein, 1948; Winnicott, 1965.)

upon) through the process of repression. Consequently, wishes that stem from the so-called dynamic unconscious cannot, normally, express themselves directly; they must either be so strongly repressed that it becomes obvious to a trained observer that something is struggling to emerge, or they must be disguised, denied, or sublimated. Thus, the important difference between the descriptive and the dynamic unconscious is as follows. The first concept refers to mental resources that are stored until use is made of them—if use is made of them at all—and of which the user is not consciously aware; it also refers to any part of a mental apparatus of which one is not at all conscious but that structures one's mental processes and one's conduct. The second concept refers to all those complexes of wishes, thoughts, and feelings that one has repressed because their earlier occurrence has been accompanied either by a real external prohibition or by an instinctive or near-instinctive inner fear of "retaliation." The first concept refers to unconscious processes that are assumed to express themselves directly in mental activity and conduct; the second refers to processes that only express themselves in disguised form. Freud used the term *dynamic* because he assumed a constant process of conflict between unconscious wishes and the mechanisms of control that either prohibit their expression or that permit their expression only in some more acceptable form.

The distinction made by Freud and the Freudians between primary and secondary process is not a very clear one and is based on a number of assumptions about the cognitive aspects of infantile mental processes that are, in some respects, and at worst, inaccurate and misleading. Let us begin, since it is easier to do so, with secondary process. It is assumed that, as individuals mature, they will come in the ordinary business of their lives to depend more and more on the use of more or less correct but, perhaps, simple rules of logic and on reality-testing. However, all adults are also, to some extent—and more so in some circumstances than in others—affected by more "primitive" forms of thought and ways of perceiving the world. It is these latter that are called primary process and that are thought to dominate the thinking of infants, though less so as they mature. In primary process, things are brought together in the mind not because they are observed together in the external world but because there is an inner motivation and an inner fantasy life that links them; furthermore, there are either no real rules of reasoning or those which are used defy the correct rules of logic.

We all more or less understand what psychoanalysts mean when they refer to secondary process thinking: They mean the kind of thinking that, in its most sophisticated forms, becomes science. But, although the distinction between primary and secondary process is one that is made in other systems of thought and although there is no doubting that such a distinction can and should be made between the ideal, polar extremes of infantile and adult human thought, there are still some difficulties with the characterization of primary process. The reasons for this are: that pure primary process is almost inaccessible to direct investigation; that its study is often carried out with children whose thought has already been influenced by what are acknowledged to be early forms of secondary process; that those who do the investigating can only do it by way of secondary process thinking and can not, therefore, present their discussion in other than secondary process terms; and, finally, that much that is presented as primary process thinking appears to be, at least in part, secondary process thinking.

A psychoanalytic response to this could be to acknowledge that we can seldom witness pure primary process, which is characteristic of a very early stage of development in which fantasy can link things together, because feeling alone dictates these links. And this answer is directly related to the theory of symbolism: for symbolization, according to psychoanalysis, develops out of this early tendency to equate things. In fact, the very earliest phase of primary process thinking does not, itself, involve symbolization; for, at that stage no clear distinction is made between the things that are equated with one another. Later, primary process is still dominant but the infant can now distinguish one thing from another that might, previously, have been treated as though it were the other; but even here the one is still treated as almost equal to the other because the secondary process, which enables the identification of the separate object to be made, still tends, because of the great affective charge that is attached to the experience of the object, to be crowded out by primary process; this equation, or near-equation, of one object with another is a very early or primitive form of symbolization, or it is, if one prefers, the basic symbolizing process. At a still later stage, one object is actually *selected to represent another* but is not consciously or unconsciously equated with it: At this stage, primary process continues to dominate in certain areas of mental activity but is now more strongly opposed by secondary process; consequently, although there is an unconscious need to replace one object by another, there is, also, and unconscious recognition that this is a protective device and that the two objects are not identical.

Psychoanalytic theory is not altogether clear as to whether the earliest phase of true symbolizing is simply a cognitive–perceptual error guided by a powerful affect that seeks and makes equivalents, or whether these processes of early symbolizing are, themselves, functional in creating defences against anxiety. However, the theory is clear in its assertion that whether symbolizing does or does not start with this defensive function it comes to acquire it very early on: Thus, the unconscious selection of one object to represent another is motivated by the wish to avoid—or even to evade— the anxiety aroused by the affects that attach to the object that is so replaced.

However, whatever psychoanalysts do think concerning the precise ontogenesis of symbolization, they are agreed that once the defensive function emerges it becomes an essential part of all symbolization of a particular kind:

Thus, it considers that a particular kind of symbolization is always a process of displacement from an original object to another in which there is a number of condensed and ambivalent associations or evocations linked with the original object; it also considers that, owing to its displacement–condensation–defensive functions, symbolization thereby orders the internal world and serves to create a sense of holding the self together by constraining inner, destructive feelings (see Milner, 1955).

The use of the term *symbolization of a particular kind* could be said to render this statement partly or wholly tautologous; but it is not necessarily so if we explain why we have used the qualification, "of a particular kind." For, while it might be absurd to argue that every form of symbolism—such as the use of natural languages, of mathematics, and of musical notation—has the functions that psychoanalysis attributes to the symbolizing process, it does not appear absurd to attribute these functions and characteristics to other forms of symbolism—of myth, ritual, or poetry, to take some obvious examples—that, following Sperber (this volume), we might term *evocational*. However, while it might be absurd to attribute certain characteristics to nonevocational but not to evocational symbols, it is still debatable as to whether all evocational symbols do have the characteristics that psychoanalysts attribute to dream symbolism. Thus, while it might even be argued that some or even all evocational symbols are influenced by unconscious beliefs and associations, it does not follow that all or even any cultural symbols of this kind are influenced by the defensive–displacement–condensation process. But the psychoanalytic contribution to the study of evocational symbols is, of necessity, an assertion of the influence of this process. Thus, several theories of cultural symbolism not only emphasize unconscious mental processes, but also emphasize some of the very areas of unconscious mental activity—for example, sexuality and other matters relating to human anatomy and physiology—that are also emphasized by psychoanalysis; they may even stress the importance of mental processes that are similar to those that psychoanalysts refer to as primary process thinking; but what such theories do not usually do is to emphasize or even to consider the kinds of dynamic unconscious processes whose description and explanation is central to psychoanalysis.

There are two principal ways in which psychoanalytic theory can explain or contribute to the explanation of cultural symbols and to the social process of cultural symbolization: One way is to assert that certain processes of unconscious splitting, displacement, and condensation and the accompanying ones of defense will, as they occur in the individual, also quite spontaneously manifest themselves in shared cultural forms, such as myth and ritual; the second, very different way is to assert that certain processes of cultural symbolization will always or sometimes activate and/or make use of certain dynamic unconscious sources—perhaps one should refer to them as resources—that give such symbols part of their character or provide them with some of the meanings that are condensed in them.

If one favors the first way, then one is usually committed to a number of additional assumptions that justifies that mode of analysis of cultural symbolization: first, that its cognitive–perceptual style is predominantly that of primary process; second, that affect, especially unconscious and ambivalent affect, is the driving force behind it; third, that the socially accepted cultural forms—mythical beliefs and ritual acts—exist largely as ways of disguising the so-called dynamic unconscious processes that underlie them, just as the manifest content of dreams is an elaborately disguised expression of their latent content; fourth, that all forms of cultural symbolization are inventions whose unconscious functions are those of sublimation and of public expression and sharing, both of which are means of making unconscious conflicts more tolerable and, perhaps, less disruptive, both personally and socially.

This first way was the one adopted by Freud and by his first disciples as well as by a number of their immediate followers. It was first proposed both in order to solve genuine theoretical problems and in order to demonstrate that if the truths of psychoanalysis were confirmed in the public as well in the private domain of the human psyche then they must, indeed, be indisputable even though they were found implausible and, indeed, unpalatable to so much of the world of science and scholarship. So one had not only Freud's own attempts to explain the origins of human culture and the nature of ritual and of other forms of cultural symbolism but also a large number of subsequent attempts to take on almost any specific or general question of this kind; and almost all of the latter—there were some exceptions even among those trained in psychoanalysis itself—were fairly stereotypical applications of the whole set of Freud's ideas on the subject, regardless of the fact that some of them—such as his attempted reconstruction of the origins of human society and culture—were not altogether necessary parts of the intellectual exercise.[6] But the world of anthropology paid little attention to these exercises.[7]

The orthodox, psychoanalytic program for explaining cultural symbols is unacceptable. For, to assume that symbols simply seep through from the dynamic unconscious into social activity, mediated only by certain of the circumstances of social life, is to beg two great questions: Are those unconscious processes not themselves affected by social and cultural influences? And, is that so-called process of mediation not, itself, something that

[6] See, for example, Rank, 1952; Reik, 1931; and Roheim, 1969, 1971.

As Kroeber has shown—and as is, indeed fairly obvious—it is unnecessary to cite Freud's ideographic speculations concerning the primal, patricidal horde in order to show that there are parallels between, say, obsessional and ritual conduct. (See Kroeber, 1920, 1939).

[7] This is, of course, an exaggeration. Among noted anthropologists who did, quite early on, pay serious attention to psychoanalysis were Kroeber, Seligman, and, of course, Malinowski.

requires investigation.[8] Furthermore, to explain some of the obvious functions of cultural symbolism, per se, as well as some of the correlations to be found between forms of symbolism and forms of society, requires the assumption that some rather complex cognitive processes are at work that bear a greater resemblance to secondary then they do to primary process thinking. To deal with all of these objections in an orthodox, Freudian manner would require an extremely cumbersome and questionable set of assumptions concerning processes of social and cultural evolution, the nature of earlier states of primitive societies, and the characteristics of the thought processes of infants and of adults in a whole range of societies.

There is, however, another approach that requires that, in the first place, we abandon the assumption that evocational cultural symbolization—to say nothing of nonevocational signals for formal, artificial languages—is, predominantly or primarily, an expression of primary process thinking. The second assumption to be dropped is that the manifest content of cultural symbols is to be treated as merely concealing and possibly even disguising a latent content that provides their true referents: This assumption as applied even to dreams, themselves, has been seriously questioned (see Fisher and Greenberg, 1977: 30–46); as applied to myths, ritual, witchcraft, and to other uses of cultural symbolization, it is a positive obstacle to an explanation of their cognitive and even affective significance in social life. The third obstructive assumption concerns the variety of levels at which the dynamic unconscious influences those of cultural symbolization.

In place of these assumptions I would propose a different set that not only acknowledges the autonomy of social and cultural processes, but that also shows how such processes may relate to those of the dynamic unconscious.

The first is that the kind of thinking that characterizes social and cultural symbolization is very much, but not exclusively, that which Freud terms *secondary process*.

The second is that we *do* need to treat the manifest content of cultural symbols very seriously indeed: This is not only because the symbolic statement, or expression itself, has a structure and even a particular content that tells one something about the way social or some other experience is conceptualized; but also because the fairly obvious associations—which may be, to some extent, culturally standardized by certain tacit rules—that social members attach to certain symbols do, themselves, tell us much about the

---

[8] These two questions were, in fact, dealt with directly by Malinowski (1927). They also gave rise to theoretical and field research in *basic personality* and to the slightly different kind of study of the "culture–personality" and "culture–character–structure" schools of psychological anthropology. (See, for example, Bateson and Mead, 1942; Kardiner, 1945). Malinowski, Kardiner, Bateson, Mead, and others did take psychoanalytic anthropology very seriously, though they did not, unlike Freud's direct followers, mistakenly attempt a simple, psychoanalytic reductionism in the explanation of cultural symbols; however, they did not provide a satisfactory anthropological theory of cultural symbolization that could show how use could be made of psychoanalysis in a nonreductionist manner.

internal connections between symbols and about the relationships between these connections and certain areas of social and cultural experience. As a supplement to this second assumption, we might add that enquiry should always, initially, be directed to tacit and covert thoughts and feelings that are culturally shared and that are not deeply unconscious. And we add the additional supplement *that the form attributed to dynamic unconscious processes is also to be found at this other, more accessible, subliminal level.* This amounts to saying that psychoanalyic assumptions can be incorporated into a structuralist mode of symbolic analysis and that the latter can deal not only with cognition but also with affect.

The third assumption is that though it may be to some extent, in some respects, and in some instances the case that the dynamic unconscious simply forces its way into the area of cultural symbolization, it is far more likely to be the case that what actually happens is the reverse process: It is the relatively autonomous process of cultural symbolization that, to a greater or lesser extent—depending on the nature of that process—*mobilizes or activates certain processes of the dynamic unconscious and uses them as a resource in the fashioning of cultural symbols.* It is this formulation that is made almost fully explicit by Edmund Leach and that is, I think, implicit in the statements of certain other anthropologists, such as Meyer Fortes (see Leach, 1958; compare with Fortes, 1966).

This is less a chicken–egg assertion that the social and cultural processes of symbol formation are somehow followed by the mobilization of the resources of the dynamic unconscious, than an assertion as to how one should state the relationship between the two sets of factors. Thus, what is rejected is the assertion that the dynamic unconscious simply erupts into social life, here and there, because "it will out." What is proposed is that, far from being permitted to erupt, indiscriminately, the resources of the dynamic unconscious are subliminally selected as appropriate to the exigencies of social and cultural life. However, this formulation does not rule out interaction between the two sets of factors. Thus, existing social and cultural forms may be the product of past interactions; consequently, existing exigencies of social and cultural life may, themselves, reveal the past influence of the dynamic unconscious.

The great advantages of these assumptions, especially the third one, are: that they do not tie one down to the notion that all forms of cultural symbolization are affected, to the same extent, either in general or in particular ways, by the processes of the dynamic unconscious; they do not require the belief that societies or sections of them can be treated as though they were simply individuals written large; they enable one to explain why some processes of the dynamic unconscious, and not others, are linked with some areas of cultural symbolization and not with others; and they may even enable one to explain why some processes of cultural symbolization do not seem to draw much, or even at all, on the dynamic unconscious.

But we have dwelt enough on theoretical matters and must now turn our attention to some examples.

Symbols of Social Rank

I choose, as my first example, the cultural notions of high and low, or upper and lower, as applied to social rank; and I take this example because it does not seem to have aroused the curiosity of sociologists and anthropologists, because it is not easily explained in Durkheimian and post-Durkheimian terms, (though it may, perhaps, be explained in some other ways that differ from the explanation offered here), because most commonsense explanations are unsatisfactory and because an answer seems to be very obvious. The explanandum is simply this: Why do we refer to those who are richer, more powerful, or more prestigious as being members of an upper class, or of a higher status group, or as having higher rank than those who are poorer, less powerful, or less prestigious, who are referred to as members of a lower class, of a lower status group, or as having a lower rank?

A crude Durkheimian would assert that our spatial categories are determined or, at least, are strongly influenced by the structure of society. But how would that theory help us here? If our vertical–spatial categories are influenced by our experience of social rank, then how does a vertical–spatial metaphor come, in the first place, to refer to social rank?

If we turn to the commonsense assumption, that vertical–spatial categories are simply applied to social experience, then two questions still remain: Why are they? And, if they are, why are the poorer, the less powerful, and the less prestigious not referred to as higher? Why is higher, in other words, superior? And why, for what matter, does the word *superior*—or its equivalent in some other languages—also mean *higher* and *not lower*? To this, the commonsense replies tend to be of the following sort: People look up (skyward) to seek that which is more powerful than themselves; or they tend to believe that *super*natural powers are located above them. But even if these answers are correct—and, as universal statements they are not, but let that not bother us—the question remains: Why do they?

The simple answer to this question concerning social rank is this: All men have experienced childhood; and all children have experienced adults as more powerful, more prestigious, and more advantaged than they are; all children have also experienced adults as higher than they are and have come to recognize or, at least, to suppose that greater height has much to do with greater advantage (see Brandes, this volume, for an example). The fact that this is a simple answer does not make it true; but it does make it better than any others that have yet been thought of; what also makes it better is that it explains a great deal more than the mere use of a spatial metaphor.

An immediate objection to this explanation is that not all societies refer to distinctions of social rank in terms of vertical–spatial language. But we might, at least, ask whether there are any societies in which the more powerful, the richer, or the more prestigious are not at least thought of as greater, if not higher, than others. We might also ask whether there are many, or even any societies, in which the more powerful, rich, or prestigious are conventionally thought of, or are referred to, as lower than others, except in those circumstances in which others are clearly expressing strong contempt and are, therefore, denying that those who profess to be their superiors are, in fact, doing so legitimately. One example of using a term related to *lowness*, rather than to *highness*, to refer noncontemptuously to someone of great prestige, wealth, and power is the one-time Russian use of the term *Little Father* to refer to the czar. But one should note that the czar was not referred to as *Little Man, Little Fellow, Little Chap*, or *Little Brother*, but as *Little Father*: so that the term of reference that emphasizes that his subjects are his "children" may well also permit those "children" to express the czar's dependence on them by the use of the protective *little*. The czar remains the one symbolic adult to all of his children; consequently, the use of the diminutive does not constitute a strong counterexample to our hypothesis.

The sorts of encounter that children, at different stages of their development, have of adults are those of being supine and experiencing adults hovering over them and ministering to them; of being able to crawl and observing adults and older children able to walk and to tower over them; of struggling to walk and finding adults able to walk effortlessly; and of being able to walk and of adults being able to do so more effectively. Together with these sorts of encounters children are aware, as they grow up, that being taller, or "more grown *up*," means having more self-governing access to things and services and more power to control and to withhold, as well as to give, in their dealings with those who are less "grown up."

To assert that the uses of the terms *high, low,* and *middle* to refer to rank are metaphoric, in that they refer to the visual and other forms of childhood experience of power and advantage is *not* to assert that those experiences are among the causes of ranking in human societies or that they are among the determinants of particular structures of ranking. All that is asserted is that the development of forms of ranking activates or mobilizes particular, unconscious psychological resources that may be used either to define the qualities of rank or to symbolize them. And, insofar as this is the case, use is made of certain complexes of thought and affect that are evoked by symbols of rank. Thus, in systems of ranking in which cultural differences between ranks are emphasized, it is almost invariably the case that the higher ranks are considered cleaner than the lower.[9] It is not that the lower ranks

---

[9] Maurice Bloch has drawn my attention to an exception to this rule (and there may be others) to be found among some Malagasy societies that previously had slavery. In these societies the descendants of slaves tend to consider the descendants of the slave-owning class as dirtier than

are considered lower because they are, or are thought to be, dirtier. What is important is that the greater dirtiness of lower social ranks is either emphasized or even invented. The sources of this emphasis are twofold and linked: It is the physically less mature who are more in contact than the more mature with their dirt, such as feces, and who are less restrained, initially, in maintaining contact with it, in showing curiosity in it, and, above all, who are relatively incontinent in producing it when prompted to do so; but also it is the lower part of the body that is dirtiest and smelliest. Thus an "equation" develops between being less privileged in rank, being closer to dirty habits, and being closer to dirty parts. The use of such an equation is characteristic of some types of class structure, expecially at certain stages of their history, of some forms of racial and ethnic ranking, and of caste.

It would be wrong to suggest that all dirtiness is linked only with the lower part of the body and, there, only with the anus and with defecation. In many cultures—and some far more than in others—dirt is associated not only with feces but also with the oral ejection of food—vomiting—and with ideas of taking in food that is bad, smelly, harmful, or even poisonous. Furthermore, any form of ejection or incorporation whether oral, anal, or genital, that has to be disciplined—in the case of sexual acitivity not just because it is an ejection from or incorporation into the body—is, thereby, associated with activities about which feelings of guilt or shame can be easily aroused and therefore also comes to be experienced as potentially unclean.

Another quality that is commonly associated with those of lower social rank is that of being more overtly aggressive or even violent or, at least, of being less disciplined in restraining aggressiveness. Again, this kind of stereotyping may well be fairly "realistic"; but what is important is that this characteristic is emphasized to show that, in yet another major respect, those of lower rank are "irresponsible" and not capable of curbing the less acceptable impulses or "instincts" of so-called human nature.

Most systems of social stratification are governed by inequalities of wealth and/or other kinds of power and by differentials of prestige; and the more privileged ranks in them may make use of certain characterizations of the ranks lower than themselves that refer to their dirtiness and to their aggression. But it is only in caste systems that the actual determinants, as well as other associated criteria of rank, are those relating to varying degree of

themselves. The explanation that he gives for this is that the first group considers the marriage rules of the latter to permit unions that, in their view, are incestuous. No psychoanalyst would be surprised to find that those accused of practicing incest are also thought of as dirty; and would not, therefore, be surprised to find that that factor may outweigh another in categorizing another group as dirtier or as cleaner than one's own. But one would really like to know more about these thoughtways: Did the slaves, in the past, think of their masters as dirtier than themselves, or did the masters think of the slaves as dirtier? Or is it only now, when the heirs of masters think of themselves as the superiors of the descendants of slaves, but where the slaves do not acknowledge much substance or legitimacy to this claim, that one group openly or secretly rejects the other's claim by referring to them as dirty by virtue of being incestuous?

purity and pollution that attach, in the first instance, to different caste occupations and, in turn, to a variety of practices permitted to certain castes
and prohibited to others: Thus certain occupations are more polluting than
others because they involve contact with substances that are dirty; others
are more polluting because they involve acts that are destructive. Thus, if
one belongs to a caste whose traditional occupation is highly polluting, one
is still polluting even if one does not practice the caste occupation. Members
of higher castes should keep those of lower caste at their distance, should
not eat with them, nor have sexual relations with them, lest they be polluted
by such contacts. But, if there are to be sexual relations, or even marriage,
between members of different castes, then it is better that the male be a
member of the higher caste and the woman of a lower caste: because a
woman of higher caste is internally polluted by a man of lower caste, while
a man of higher caste is only externally polluted by a woman of lower caste.

Hindu beliefs and practices relating to caste constitute the most extreme
case of stratification mobilizing certain unconscious ideas and feelings concerning "lowness" and "highness" and building them into the very criteria
that determine rank. Why caste does so is not a question that can easily be
answered: But an appropriate answer is not one that starts with these unconscious mental processes but, rather, one that starts with the development
of certain social and cultural processes that, in turn, are accompanied by
a particular symbolizing process that makes use of the material of the dynamic unconscious. For, can one doubt that these ideas linking various degrees of restraint on aggression, on contact with either excreta or other
substances that are treated like them, on sexual intercourse as a more or
less polluting activity, and on the eating of food that can be more or less
polluting (depending on the polluting qualities of the cook) are the very
substance of dynamic unconscious processes that are revealed in psychoanalysis?

Another feature of some systems of inequality is the tendency for those
of higher rank to address those of lower rank in terms that are demeaning:
For example, servants may be referred to or addressed by their personal
names or surnames without the use of titles like Mr., Mrs., or Miss; or a
servant woman may be called a *maid* even though she is old enough to be
considered a *matron*. In societies that are racially stratified and even in some
racially homogeneous, class-stratified societies, a man of lower status may
be referred to or addressed as a *boy* and a woman as a *girl*. These terms
imply that occupying a lower status is similar to being a child in relation to
an adult; and this, in turn, evokes associations between lower status and
immaturity and irresponsibility, thereby indicating that those of low social
rank can be entitled to few claims on resources, power, and social consideration.

The use of such terms may have an additional and, perhaps, secondary
significance. It is quite commonly the case that men and women of lower

social rank become objects of unconscious or even conscious sexual fantasy on the part of those of higher social rank. The explanation for this may be that those of lower social rank are considered sexually freer or less disciplined, or self-restrained, as children might be thought to be. In fact, the sexual activities of men of higher social rank often do occur with women of lower social rank; but sexual relations between men of low and women of higher social rank are considered totally impermissible and perhaps even unmentionable. The use of terms that imply immaturity on the part of those of lower social rank enables those of higher rank to "deny" either that such sexual relations are possible or that, if they do occur, they are of any social importance.

It must be emphasized, yet again, that psychoanalysis can not claim to explain much about social stratification. It can not even, by itself, explain certain differences between systems of stratification in the ways in which they make use of certain unconscious resources: For example, it cannot explain why, in a caste system, it is considered polluting for members of higher castes to eat food prepared by members of lower castes while in racially stratified societies it is not only permitted, but even considered desirable for those of higher rank to accept food cooked by members of a lower rank, provided those of lower rank are employed as cooks; nor can it explain why, despite *these* differences, *both* types of society either forbid or strongly discourage commensality between members of different ranks. Rather, what psychoanalysis can do is to explain why, given certain social conditions, the process by which they are symbolized may also evoke certain corresponding processes of the dynamic unconscious. Thus, for example, a system of caste is much more an ideational system than are systems of rank that are intrinsically those of domination and/or exploitation; consequently, in a caste system, mental processes are almost permitted to run wild in drawing on unconscious resources relating to pollution and purity. However, other forms of ranking—which may, of course, co-exist with caste, thereby introducing certain contradictions that have to be reconciled or papered over—do, for the most part, rest on differential advantage in acquiring and maintaining power, wealth, and prestige: Consequently, although the social processes whereby such systems are created and maintained also draw, for their symbolic representation, on mental resources related to cleanliness, they are unlikely to "run wild" in doing so; and, certainly given the importance attached to physical power in some such systems, it would be strange if all forms of destructiveness were to be characterized as altogether connected with low-status irresponsibility.

Animal Symbols of Aggression and Restraint

The second example, which I treat very briefly, is Dan Sperber's (1975) discussion of animal symbolism among the Dorze of Ethiopia. These comments relate specifically to the way in which the symbolic assertions, which his analysis reveals, make use of the resources of the dynamic unconscious.

The Dorze—that is, presumably, those who speak for them—claim to be Christian. They know that they were originally converted to Christianity in the fifteenth century but that they lapsed into paganism and, only recently, became Christians again. Being Christian links them to the central culture of the wider society and state; but their recent Christianization makes them latecomers and, therefore, fairly low in cultural rank.

Dorze think of Christianity as representing a high level of culture that, in turn, is linked with the virtue of restraint, on which the Dorze, in everyday life, put great emphasis: Thus, they commend eating in moderation; they seem to welcome constipation; and they find erotic pleasure in seminal retention. (In linking Christianity or, at least, civilization, with restraint, they are not unlike a number of Western social theorists).

The Dorze think of leopards as Christians: For, what they know of leopards is that they kill more than they eat; what they use this knowledge for is to suggest that leopards are restrained in their intake of food and are not gluttons. They also seem to use it to show that even the good have to kill but not for purposes of gluttony.

By contrast, hyenas eat more than they kill, by eating carrion or by eating dying animals that may be eaten even before they are dead: Thus hyenas are gluttons, they know no restraint, and they are not thought of as Christians.

But, to think of hyenas as gluttons and as not being Christians is not the end of the matter. For, just as leopards are humanized by "being Christian," so some men are dehumanized by "being" hyenas; they are in fact werehyenas and are of course evil. Perhaps the most terrible act that were-hyenas can inflict is to kill their victims by coming to devour their guts—in stages: And their victims are aware of what is happening to them.

Let us start by agreeing with Sperber that, for this purpose, the symbolic use of leopards and hyenas is a statement of sorts about the Dorze dilemma concerning their moral qualities and their social and cultural identity: Are they or are they not Christians? Are they or are they not virtuous and restrained? Are they or are they not better than pagans? Are they or are they not fully entitled to be acknowledged as part of the central, imperial culture? The Dorze would like the answers to all of these questions to affirm their favorable self-image; but they also have grave doubts, knowing that they are still, to some extent, pagans, and that, much as they would like the fact to be forgotten, suppressed, or eliminated, they did lapse from Christianity for a long time and are, therefore, really not-so-Christian. They could affirm their Chirstianity by contrasting themselves with distant tribes who are still (obviously pagan and unrestrained) blood-drinkers: But to do so would only be to damn themselves with very faint praise. So what they do is to contrast themselves with their neighbors, who were also recently and partly Christianized but, perhaps, less so than themselves. They do this by referring to particular neighbors, the Gamo, as gluttons. But the Gamo, not by chance, are also thought to produce were-hyenas who, however, do their work among the Dorze!

The Dorze conflict concerning their status as Christians or pagans is resolved as it were, by the use of animal symbolism: But the resolution is only of a magical sort—why, otherwise, refer to animals and not directly and literally to themselves?—because it does not end the doubting but merely enables the doubters to apprehend it, to "get a fix on it."

The first stage in this process is that of denying their paganism and lack of restraint: This denial is probably neither altogether conscious nor deeply unconscious, but does make use of the devices of displacement, condensation, projection, and splitting. Thus a number of characteristics are condensed into the leopard and hyena symbols; the use of encyclopedic knowledge about animals is a displacement from the characteristics of Christianity and paganism; and the attribution of good Dorze characteristics to leopards and of bad ones to hyenas is a process of projection and splitting. All of these are dynamic devices that are commonly discussed by psychoanalysts as belonging only to the deep unconscious.

In considering the question of their Christianity and their paganism, Dorze are also, in a more general way and, perhaps, at a deeper level, considering the question of their "goodness" and "badness." Referring to themselves as Christians is one thing; but to refer to the Gamo as gluttons and as the source of were-hyenas is quite another. The first reference is an idealization; but the latter is the complementary projection achieved through yet another split: The Gamo are bad Dorze, for they are, after all, not only close neighbors but also very similar to the Dorze in culture and in their cultural predicament; and they are also the source of that which does its evil work among the Dorze.

The opposition between leopards and hyenas—or, better still, between humanized, Christian leopards and dehumanized, pagan were-hyenas—represents a conflict that the Dorze, or some of them, internalize as part of their cultural predicament. There is no difficulty in reconciling killing, by itself, with Christianity and restraint: All men, even Christians, are permitted some "legitimate" destructiveness. But there is a difficulty in coming to terms with the connection between destructive aggressiveness and greed; it is this connection that the Dorze deny and that they seem to equate with paganism and with lack of restraint. They can idealize their self-restraining qualities by affirming their commitment to restraint, to Christianity, and to being like leopards; furthermore, they can deny their complementary destructive gluttony—their malevolence—by displacing and projecting it elsewhere, so that they are not like hyenas though their close neighbors are. But they can not, in all reality, doubt that some Dorze behave very badly—more like pagans than like Christians; they are Christians who lapse into paganism—and that all Dorze are capable of doing so if they do not maintain their restraint; so they characterize bad Dorze and, for that matter, the bad Dorze feelings that are normally restrained, as not being really Dorze.

Finally, to be bad and unrestrained must be to invite punishment; for, if not, then virtue is not its own reward; and the most fitting punishment for unrestrained, gluttonous destructiveness is retaliatory destructiveness that goes direct to the repository of one's gluttony; so it is that one becomes ill and that the were-hyena comes, in stages, to tear out one's guts until one dies.

What I am suggesting is that the symbolization of the Dorze cultural predicament makes use of natural symbols as devices in themselves. But I am also suggesting that it does so in this way because the manner in which the cultural conflict is experienced draws on those unconscious mental processes that best lend themselves to the task at hand. In this instance we can see that at least one of these unconscious resources—the concern with restraint in everyday life (offset by permitted forms of expenditure and excess)—is used in a number of different ways by the Dorze. Why this should be so is a question that is not easily answered: The Dorze may have certain common personality traits or a shared cultural code that patterns the process of cultural symbolization; but, alternatively, they may experience their symbolic systems as interrelated and may therefore repeat the same moral and aesthetic themes, at a variety of levels, in a number of different spheres in which the symbolic apprehension of social, cultural, and common existential predicaments is called for.

The Dynamic Unconscious in Culture

I have emphasized—perhaps to excess—that psychoanalytic theories do not explain the process of cultural symbolization but that they may be called upon to explain how and why that process draws upon, and therefore creates a certain kind of evocational field. I have sought to show that some forms of cultural symbolization exhibit features that are very familiar to psychoanalysts and that are explicable in terms of their own theories; and I have done so without simply reducing those processes to processes of the dynamic unconscious. What I have not done is to try to explain why it is that some forms of cultural symbolization appear, far more than others, to lend themselves to the kind of treatment that I have discussed and illustrated here.

The explanation that I would offer consists of the following two propositions: that, where the process of symbolization is not that of simple and direct representation—serving mnemonic or other such "technical," cognitive purposes—but is rather that of apprehending certain social and cultural predicaments or quandaries, one might expect evocational symbols and a process of symbolization that draw on the referential resources of the dynamic unconscious; and that in societies in which people are closer to nature and to natural processes—and therefore to their own bodies and to the fantasies that develop around their bodies, around the relationship of their bodies to their selves, to other bodies, and to other selves—there will be a greater and more obvious tendency for certain processes of cultural symbolization to call upon the resources of the dynamic unconscious (see Kroeber, 1940).

A number of arguments can be marshalled in support of this second proposition. The first is that the process of civilization not only removes people from contact with nature but also requires a greater degree of repression of certain "natural" drives or impulses. The second is that the process of civilization creates increasingly more elaborate cultural forms that intervene between the need to gratify certain "natural" wants and the actual process of their gratification, so that being "spontaneously natural" either becomes disallowed or it becomes, along with nature itself, either idealized or objectified (see Elias, 1969; Freud, 1946). The third is that continuous cultural development, or accumulation, is characterized not only by the creation of an increasing quantity of culture but also by the imposition of new cultural forms onto older ones. The fourth, fifth, and sixth arguments, which follow either from the first three alone or, in addition, from one another, are as follows: The growing dissociation from the natural world tends to result in symbolization being directed increasingly to culture itself, rather than to nature, as though certain levels of culture were, themselves, natural; cultural accumulation and cultural complexity create predicaments and quandaries that become more and more remote from "natural" realities; consequently, there is an increasing tendency for the referents of cultural symbols to be other cultural symbols, so that a hierarchy of symbolization occurs, with the highest levels either resembling nonevocational symbols and referents that are, themselves, the products of a history of symbolic accretion.

These buttressing arguments of the second proposition make it very plausible: No doubt, there are some such tendencies at work. But it should also not be forgotten that in some less civilized societies there are systems of symbols that seem to be rather remote from "natural" reality while in some more civilized societies there are some that come rather close to it. It should also not be forgotten that there are marked differences between societies and cultures in the extent to which they make great use of elaborate forms of evocational, cultural symbols.

Parts of the first proposition, which links the resolution of cultural predicaments, or *contradictions*, to the processes of the dynamic unconscious, can be justified as follows: The process of symbolization that seeks to resolve such inner, cultural conflicts makes use of certain mechanisms of defence, such as denial; this tends to create inner links with other mental processes in which the same or similar mechanisms of defence are at work; and this, in turn, results in the drawing in of material that can be assimilated to the processes occurring at a higher level and that thereby strengthen the latter.

Clearly, parts of this second proposition are either not testable at all or are certainly not testable by reference to the substance of cultural symbolism; but other parts are. Such tests may well show that it is not always clear that certain forms of symbolic apprehension of cultural predicaments, quandaries, and contradictions are affected by the processes of symbolization that are thought to be characteristic of the dynamic unconscious. But it is only when that empirical task has been undertaken that it will be worth modifying our explanations.

Acknowledgments

In preparing this essay I was greatly helped by comments from participants at the conference held at Burg Wartenstein. In particular, I want to thank Mary LeCron Foster for her most valuable appraisal of my paper and for her suggestions regarding this final version of it. I am also indebted to my good friend Professor William Shack of the University of California, Berkeley, for his pertinent comments and valued encouragement.

References

Agassi, Joseph
  1964   Scientific problems and their roots in metaphysics. In *The critical approach to science and philosophy*, edited by Mario Bunge. London: The Free Press of Glencoe, Collier-Macmillan Ltd.
Balint, Michael
  1968   *The basic fault: Therapeutic aspects of regression*. London: Tavistock.
Bateson, Gregory and Margaret Mead
  1942   Balinese character: A photographic analysis. *Special Publications of the New York Academy of Sciences, 2*.
Elias, Norbert
  1969   *Ueber den prozess der zivilization*, 2nd ed. Bern: Francke Verlag.
Erikson, Erik H.
  1953   *Childhood and society*. London: Imago.
Fisher, Seymour and Roger P. Greenberg
  1977   *The scientific credibility of Freud's theories*. New York: Basic Books.
Fortes, Meyer
  1966   Totem and Taboo. *Proceedings of the Royal Anthropological Institute*. Pp. 5–22.
Freud, Anna
  1954   *The ego and the mechanisms of defence* translated by Cecil Baines. London: Hogarth.
Freud, Sigmund
  1946   *Civilisation and its discontents*. London, England: Hogarth Press.
  1949   Consciousness and the unconscious. In *The ego and the id*. London: Hogarth.
Hartmann, Heinz
  1958   *Ego psychology and the problem of adaptation*, translated by David Rappaport. New York: International Universities Press.
Kardiner, Abraham and associates
  1945   *The psychological frontiers of society*, New York: Columbia Univ. Press.

Klein, Melanie
Contributions to psychoanalysis 1921–1945. London: Hogarth.
Kroeber, Alfred L.
1920 Totem and taboo: An ethnological psychoanalysis. *American Anthropologist* **22**, 48–55.
Kroeber, Alfred L.
1939 Totem and taboo in retrospect. *American Journal of Sociology* **45**, 446–451.
1940 Psychosis or social sanction. *Character and Personality* **8**, 204–215.
Lakatos, Imre
1970 Methodology of scientific research programmes. In *Criticism and the growth of knowledge*, edited by Imre Lakatos and Alan Musgrave. London and New York: Cambridge Univ. Press.
1974 Popper on demarcation and induction. In *The philosophy of Karl Popper*, edited by Paul Arthur Schilpp. Illinois: Open Court, La Salle.
Leach, Edmund R.
1958 Magical hair. *Journal of the Royal Anthropological Institute* **88**, 147–164.
Malinowski, Bronislaw
1927 *Sex and repression in savage society*. London: Routledge and Kegan Paul.
Milner, Marion
1955 The role of illusion in symbol formation. In *New directions in psychoanalysis*, edited by Melanie Klein *et al*. London: Tavistock.
Rank, Otto
1952 *The myth of the birth of the hero*, translated by Robbins and Jeliffe. New York: Robert Brunner.
Reik, Theodor
1931 *Ritual: Psychoanalytic studies*, translated by Douglas Bryan. London: Hogarth.
Roheim, Geza
1931 *Psycoanalysis and anthropology*. New York: International Universities Press.
1971 *The origin and function of culture*. New York: Doubleday.
Sperber, Dan
1975 *Rethinking symbolism*, translated by Alice L. Morton. New York and London: Cambridge Univ. Press.
Watkins, John W.
1958 Influential and confirmable metaphysics. *Mind*, n.s. **67**, 344–365.
Winnicott, Donald Woods
1965 *The maturational process and the facilitating environment*. London: Hogarth.
Wisdom, John O.
1956 Psychoanalytic technology. *The British Journal for the Philosophy of Science* (Sigmund Freud Centenary) **7** (25).

II
COHESION AND CONTINUITY

5
Introduction

MARY LeCRON FOSTER
STANLEY H. BRANDES

Symbolization, by means of its three, meaning-bearing, interactive processes—denotation, figuration, and motivation—maintains itself over time as a strongly cohesive force. Temporal continuity is provided by the meanings activated by each process and is strengthened through the repetition or replication of symbolic representations. The chapters in this section provide specific examples of integrating representations from three cultures widely separated in space and time. Two of the chapters concern rituals, and the other, a visual representation with social and ritual implications. The first two are at the figurative end of the figuration–reference continuum; the other binds together figuration and reference in single representations but is also more figurative than referential. As such, the three examples are, as we can conclude from Sperber's discussion, highly—and probably ambiguously—evocative. According to Bott (1972), "The ambiguity of myths and ceremonies is part of their point. It gives individuals some leeway to play with experience, to make culture their own possession" (p. 232).

Reference, in rituals such as those described by Bloch and Brandes in their respective chapters, is very similar to what Freud (1931), in discussing dreams, called *manifest content. Manifest structure* might be a better term, since referentially the structure must be taken only at face value; it is referentially literal, having no denotative meaning outside of itself. One might compare it to a nonsense language in which the whole of the denotative meaning is nothing but the structure of articulation.

As with dream, the manifest structure of ritual derives its deeper, or *latent,* content from its relational equivalences to other, implied events. We must either accept the fact of indirectly implied content or conclude that ritual is meaningless. Sperber will apparently accept only highly individualized interpretations, which would leave ritual with only a very weak integrational potential as a cultural force. Cohen grants it a dynamic potential in calling up similar culturally and socially induced responses to repressed material in individual members of the same social milieu; some of these responses may be universal. Brandes's interpretation is similar to that of Cohen, but is, perhaps, closer still to that of Bott (1972):

> In the course of trying to understand and interpret the kava ceremony it has repeatedly occurred to me that a ceremony has much in common with a dream. A dream is a condensed and disguised representation of unconscious thoughts and wishes. A ceremony is a condensed and partially disguised representation of certain aspects of social life. A dream and a ceremony both communicate dangerous thoughts and emotions; but at the same time they disguise and transform them so that the element of danger is contained and to some extent dealt with. An effective ceremony protects society from destructive forms of conflict, an effective dream protects the sleeper from anxiety [pp. 205–206].

In comparing analysis of ritual to that of dream, Bott (1972:214–215) likens social context, spontaneous remarks, and answers to questions about the structure of ceremonies to the use of a psychoanalyst's previous knowledge of the life situation of the patient and the associations that he makes to his dreams as a means toward discovery of deeper meanings. Both Bloch and Brandes use these techniques as well as the structure of the event in the effort to discover the function of the ritual. Leach (1972), in a discussion of Bott's analysis, finds it illuminating in some ways but feels that it would be enhanced—made less "intuitive"—by a closer adherence to the structure of the event: "the distinctive characteristic of structuralist procedure is that the analyst tries to avoid making symbolic substitutions which are not already quite overtly specified in the evidence" [p. 240]. What this boils down to is that the relationships that the interpretation uncovers should be present in the manifest content. What he does not say, but what is evident in his interpretations is that the interpreted (i.e., latent) meanings are much more abstract than those of the manifest content, which are both concrete and condensed.

Both Bloch and Brandes makes use of structural oppositions to good advantage. Those employed by Brandes are, largely, those discussed by Cohen, above, as having probably universal validity as a function of childhood associations of greater size or height with greater power. The monumental art described by Durbin also exploits this connotative resource.

The ceremony that Bott describes has in common with those discussed by both Brandes and Bloch that it expresses a fundamental contradiction stemming from a hierarchical imbalance such that "In everyday life these people can be expected to harbour feelings of jealousy and resentment about their differential privileges" [Bott, 1972:225]. Bloch quite clearly considers the Merina marriage ritual to be a sop to the losing side in a hierarchical imbalance. Brandes speaks of the provision of goodies during the San Blas parade as a sop to the working class from the elite. G. Foster (1972) has discussed sop behavior as a reaction to fear of envy in a fair degree of detail, but without reference to complexly integrated rituals of the kind considered here that seem designed to perpetuate existing social imbalances by creating a climate suggesting some degree of equality.

The Mayan stelae described by Durbin are, on the other hand, forceful reminders of the grandeur and social impeccability of a powerful elite. Here there is no equalizing dialectic. Perhaps such a dialectic is only possible in ritual and cannot be, or can less well be, conveyed through art. According to Bloch the fantasy world portrayed through ritual serves to mystify and hide the real situation. The stelae message cloaks the real situation in idealism; only certain kinds of information are referentially alluded to in the stelae hieroglyphs. Bloch (1975) called attention to a formal stereotypy in language used by the elite in addressing the masses. In the hieroglyphic messages described by Durbin, the information is greatly simplified to include only the most favorable highlights in the ruler's life history. The real is thus masked through the ideal.

This brings us to the question of intentionality. If we know who is the sender of the message and to whom it is addressed, we will be closer to the intentionality: what the message is intended to accomplish. Durbin's material is illuminating here. He discusses two kinds of messages, the structures of which differ greatly for two kinds of audiences. The sender of one type—the most referentially informative and least stylized—is the elite priest–ruler class, while the recipient is of that same class. The sender of the other type is presumed to be of that same elite, while the receivers for whom the message is formalized are the common people. The message in the first type is highly referential, that in the second type is figurative.

The major message in Bloch's material is sent by the bride's family to the family of the groom. The intent is quite clearly to redress a status imbalance with the losing party addressing the winning party. Here the language of the losing party is free and irreverent. That of the winning party formal and stereotyped. The irreverence is a put-down that allows the bride's family to move into a higher position. In Bloch's interpretation, it is lower because economically unproductive; religiously, it is higher because spiritually productive.

The message in Brandes's material is a condensed dialectic, with neither side clearly the victor. Nothing is settled through this ritual. The elite is still the elite, producing an elitist message of calm and grandeur, with a sop to the masses; but the lower class is still threatening through reference to its vigor and greater numbers that can always be reinforced through unrestrained sexuality. The masses listen to the elite—in the sense that it is they who primarily attend the ritual and receive the sop. The elite (at least in this introductory ritual) fails to respond, but the threat still remains.

The fact that the parade described by Brandes is considered a very minor ritual by the citizens of San Blas brings up a point that is rarely considered: What is the meaning of a ceremony that involves only a small portion of the populace, that is considered nonserious and relatively unimportant but is nonetheless continued? To continue the analogy that we have established between ritual and dream, one is reminded of the portions of the dream that the dreamer either omits to mention or remembers only later. According to Freud (1924:146–147), the central, latent foci of dreams are less clearly defined or often omitted when the dream is first told. At the present time we have no way of knowing whether this is true of ritual, but the analogy is suggestive. Some rituals, such as stocking hanging at Christmas or egg hunts at Easter in the United States (see M. Foster, 1978 n.d.), can be assumed to be important to the socialization of the child. Brandes's ritual seems to have a similar function for children and young adults.

In anthropologists' analyses of particular societies, the models provided by men loom large. According to Ardener (1972), "Men's models of society are expressed at a metalevel which purports to define women. Only at the level of the analysis of belief can the voiceless masses be restored to speech. Not only women, but (a task to be attempted later) inarticulate classes of men, young people, and children. We are all lay figures in someone else's play" [p. 153]. We might add to this that not only anthropologists' analyses but also many community rituals express not only the views of men, but predominately the views of the males of the elite. To obtain an undistorted picture of world view we would also need to look at lesser rituals, participated in by only a limited group or deprecated by social leaders.

Leach (1961:132–136) discussed ritualized role reversal—costuming, masking, unrestrained behavior—as a function of sacred, or time-out-of-time, stretches associated with rites of passage. The mocking behavior of the Merina marriage ritual discussed by Bloch would seem to be an example of this and is associated with a status change for both families with regard to one another. The unrestrained masking behavior discussed by Brandes seems to have little to do either with role reversal or rites of passage, unless further analysis should show the whole festival to be, in some sense, a rite of passage for young, working class males. The reversal in Bloch's ritual would seem to be closely related to the type of mythic transformation discussed by Lévi-Strauss (1963), in which a hierarchical imbalance is redressed (see also M. Foster, 1974). Neither ritual seems to be a case of the liminality and communitas that Turner (1969) associates with rites of passage. Careful studies such as those of Bloch and Brandes help to clarify the role of abnormal behavior in rituals that make different kinds of statements. One aspect of the ritual use of such behavior that seems to become increasingly clear is that it serves to de-emphasize social oppositions by symbolically redressing hierarchical imbalances. Its uses seem to be more diverse than the literature on the subject implies.

In the manifest content of ritualized figurative symbolism, symbols are highly condensed, providing a high degree of simultaneity in contrast to language with a strong temporal or spatial sequentiality and only the simultaneity of intonational and articulatory features. In some kinds of figurative schemata, ritual and myth in particular, content is based on ideal ways of resolving or averting potential conflict induced by differential access to power and the goods or good that are the prerogatives of such power. To say this is not to assert a "Band-Aid" adhesive bandage relationship of the kind that Dolgin *et al.* (1977:34–36) deplore: a therapeutic purpose that seems to consider social and economic forms as more "basic" or prior to ritual. We believe as strongly as they that no cultural system is more basic than any other and that all are symbolic. Systems interact because they are mutually consistent and sustaining, or else interlock to create and sustain such consistency. The three chapters included in Part II effectively illustrate this point.

References

Ardener, Edwin
  1972 Belief and the problem of women. In *The interpretation of ritual,* edited by J. S. LaFontaine. London: Tavistock. Pp. 135–158.
Bloch, Maurice (ed.)
  1975 *Political language and oratory in traditional society.* New York: Academic Press.
Bott, Elizabeth
  1972 Psychoanalysis and ceremony. In *The interpretation of ritual,* edited by J. S. La-Fontaine. London: Tavistock. Pp. 205–237.
Dolgin, Janet, David S. Kemnitzer, and David M. Schneider (eds.)
  1977 *Symbolic anthropology: A reader in the study of symbols and meanings.* New York: Columbia Univ. Press.
Foster, George
  1972 The anatomy of envy: A study in symbolic behavior. *Current Anthropology* **13,** 165–186.
Foster, Mary LeCron
  1974 Deep structure in symbolic anthropology. *Ethos,* **2,** 334–355.
  n.d. Deciphering Santa: A structural study of American values. Unpublished manuscript.
  1978 Decoding culture. Paper delivered at the Xth International Congress of Anthropological and Ethnological Sciences, New Delhi, India. December 10–16.
Freud, Sigmund
  1924 *A general introduction to psychoanalysis.* New York: Permabooks.
  1931 *The interpretation of dreams.* New York: Carlton House.
Leach, Edmund
  1961 *Rethinking anthropology.* London and New York: Oxford Univ. Press (Athlone).
  1972 The structure of symbolism. In *The interpretation of ritual,* edited by J. S. LaFontaine. London: Tavistock. Pp. 239–275.
Lévi-Strauss, Claude
  1963 *Structural anthropology.* New York: Basic Books.
Turner, Victor W.
  1969 *The ritual process: Structure and anti-structure.* Chicago, Illinois: Aldine.

6

Giants and Big-Heads: An Andalusian Metaphor[1]

STANLEY H. BRANDES

Introduction

Every year on September 16 in San Blas, a town of some 10,000 inhabitants in southeastern Spain, thére occurs a brief parade of costumed figures known as Giants (*Gigantes*) and Big-Heads (*Cabezudos*). The event, which lasts barely an hour, is only one of several occasions included in the most important celebration of the town's ritual calendar: the festival in honor of the *Santísimo Señor del Consuelo,* the Most Holy Lord of Consolation, who is the object of deep and widespread devotion in the town and surrounding countryside. Throughout the 4 days of festivities, San Blas swells with outsiders and pulses with activity, including an impressive evening fireworks display, a solemn religious procession, and a steady flow of dances and entertainment. To the untutored eye, the parade of Giants and Big-Heads, which precedes the truly grand ritual spectacles, seems rather pale and insignificant. Yet I hope to show how this event can be viewed as a metaphor, a concrete expression, and projection of critical aspects of San Blas society and culture. Like the Balinese cockfight described by Geertz (1973), the parade of Giants and Big-Heads is, at least to certain segments of the San Blas populace, "A story they tell about themselves" (p. 448). It is an interpretive, humanistic display of both collective and personal experience.

[1] I must express appreciation to the National Institute of Child Health and Human Development and to the American Council of Learned Societies for awarding me generous grants, which supported the research upon which this article is based. San Blas is a pseudonym.

If we were to apply the language of symbolic anthropology to Giants and Big-Heads, we might say that they are, above all *elaborating* symbols, in Sherry Ortner's use of the term (1973: 1340; see Foster, this volume, for a further discussion of Ortner). In and of themselves, these figures are in no sense objects of reverence or deep emotion as the flag, the cross, or other *summarizing* symbols are. Rather, they are best seen as unconscious vehicles that the people of San Blas draw upon "for sorting out complex feelings and ideas" (Ortner, 1973: 1340). As elaborating symbols, Giants and Big-Heads not only enable the people themselves to express some of the most salient features of their society and culture, but also provide us—the anthropologists—with a key to the native conceptualization of experience. In San Blas, the outside observer, unlike the townspeople under investigation, may hope to ascertain in what way the parade of Giants and Big-Heads provides a reenactment of the most psychologically and socially important aspects of town life. For, if we judge by informant statements alone, the parade simply occasions an enjoyable, mirthful break from ordinary routine.

As a concrete projection of feelings and experience, the parade of Giants and Big-Heads is probably best understood as representing the issue of social domination and control, with which the people of San Blas are preoccupied. I intend to demonstrate that the Giants operate as an unconscious metaphor for parents, that the Big-Heads act as metaphoric children, and that the entire parade is a dramatic enactment of power relationships not only within the nuclear family, but also within society generally. The costumed figures, in both form and behavior, suggest a collective, vicarious rebellion against authority and control. The rebellion is most graphically portrayed at the family level, with the children displaying unharnessed aggression. But there is evidence, too, that this hostility becomes generalized, so that it is directed against all the major forces of control and containment with which people, both as individuals and as members of groups, have to contend.

To develop my thesis, I wish first to give a stark description of the parade. I shall go on to provide relevant ethnographic background, and then conclude with an analysis of the parade's symbolic significance. I should caution that the present study refers specifically to Giants and Big-Heads in contemporary San Blas. These figures, particularly the Giants, have a long history and widespread distribution throughout Western Europe. René Meurant (1960, 1967, 1969) and Klaus Beitl (1961) have devoted years of investigation to the enormously variegated manifestations of Giant figures, past and present. It seems that bona-fide processional Giants first appeared in early fifteenth-century Flanders (Meurant, 1967:123), and shortly thereafter diffused to the Iberian peninsula (van Gennep, 1935, I:168). We know that Giants and Big heads have existed in Spain throughout the past 400 years, during which time they have usually been associated with Corpus Cristi and pre-Lenten *Carnaval* celebrations (Almerich, 1944:54–52; Caro Baroja, 1965;

Gómez-Tabanera, 1968:188–193; Plá Cargol, 1947:291–296). What we lack from virtually all accounts however, is the combination of detailed description and extensive local ethnography, which might explain the phenomenon from a symbolic, structural, or other point of view.

Belgian folklorist Albert Marinus is the one investigator to have posited more than merely an historical or diffusionist explanation for the existence of processional Giants. He suggests that these figures "must be considered as manifestations of the need for the masses to translate in a concrete and conspicuous fashion their ideas or abstract feelings, particularly in the domain of the supernatural and the extraordinary" [Marinus, 1951, III:281; my translation]. Elsewhere, he indicates that the Giants reveal a sort of "collective conscience" [1951, II: 232]. These universalistic statements may point in the right direction, but they fail to account for variations in the types and numbers of Giants, or for the persistence of these figures in some regions and not others. Nor can such analyses explain the absence or presence of Big-Heads, or other similar masked characters. These are all complex issues for which adequate comparative data are at present unavailable. The most we can hope for at this stage is a thorough examination of a single occurrence of Giants and Big-Heads, whose meaning may be interpreted in terms of the immediate social environment in which they appear. It is now appropriate to turn to this significant event in San Blas.

The Parade of Giants and Big-Heads

We may begin our analysis with a simple description of the parade of Giants and Big-Heads. At noon, amidst the loud, incessant ringing of church-bells, the Giants emerge from the town hall, located just off the main square. There are two of them, a man and a woman, known as the King and the Queen, dressed with crowns and simple tunics reminiscent of the garb of medieval monarchs. Each figure is about 12 feet tall, its clothing and molded papier-mâché head suspended from a wooden frame that is borne by a man. The man's identity remains anonymous, for his entire body from the knees up is enveloped and hidden by the flowing gown of the towering image.

Immediately following the Giants appear 14 Big-Heads, whose oversized papier-mâché heads and necks each rest directly on the shoulders of young townsmen. In the case of the Big-Heads, the human body becomes part of the figure itself. However, because of the baggy, flamboyant costumes and especially the false heads themselves, the actors' identities remain completely disguised. No two Big-Heads are the same. Some, like Popeye, the Devil, a Witch, a Chinese, and a Black African, are easily recognizable. Others, like the Ape and the Cow–Goat, two anthropomorphic figures, are the grotesque products of fantasy. A number of the Big-Heads obviously represent men, both young and old, but there is one with clean-shaven face and medium long hair whose sex is ambiguous. The Witch, Devil, and Ape wear specially designed costumes appropriate to their images. The others wear the loud, brightly colored garb of jesters or clowns. Aside from the Witch with her broom and the Devil with his blunt wooden spear, the Big-Heads all carry white, sausage-shaped cloths that are about a foot long, stuffed stiff with sawdust and attached loosely to a short stick.

For about 45 minutes the Giants and Big-Heads wind their way through the most important, centrally located streets and plazas of San Blas, with a crowd of children following behind. The Giants, tall and domineering, walk together at a slow, even, dignified pace. The Big-Heads swarm around them, skipping, running, and jumping erratically; they seem intrusive and disruptive, a chaotic element when compared with the stately Giants. The Big-Heads pause at the several plazas where townspeople are gathered, and rush around in unpredictable directions, bopping people with their stuffed cloths. The Devil and Witch use their spear and broom for the same purpose. Adults and teenagers find the scene amusing and they laugh, but young children become frightened and cling to their older brothers and sisters. And no wonder, for in many San Blas homes, children are scared into eating or going to sleep with the threat that the Big-Heads will otherwise come to take them away.

Meanwhile, a large crowd has gathered in the main plaza, which is known as the *Huevo*, or Egg, from its shape. From a second-story window of the town hall, small skyrockets laden with candy and minature toys are sent up and out over the Huevo. The rockets explode in midair with a loud crack, causing the candy and toys to shower down on the people below. Explosions take place at intervals of 2 or 3 minutes, and with every blast the spectators compete furiously for the spoils. Teenaged boys, because of their size and aggressiveness, as much as because they attend the event in the greatest numbers, catch most of the flying objects. But they are usually content merely to have won the contest, and distribute the goods to the unsuccessful girls and young children, who would otherwise remain disappointed. The skyrockets make the Huevo the center of action, and it is here too that the Giants and Big-Heads stop for 15 minutes at the end of their tour. By 1:00 P.M. the churchbells and cannonfire have ceased, the Giants and Big-Heads have reentered the town hall, and the crowds have dispersed.

To understand the metaphoric imagery of this parade, more information is needed about who particpates in it, as actors and audience. This will tell us for whom the parade is designed, to whom its symbolism would most likely appeal, and consequently of which social entity—the town as a whole or only certain segments of it—the event may be said to supply an inside view. The status of the performers can be described easily enough; they are all young working-class men, who are selected on a first-come, first-served basis. Since there is competition for the posts, many sign up several days in advance to assure themselves of a part. Informants claim that no woman, regardless of age or social background, has ever acted in the parade. It is said that the Giants' frames are too heavy and awkward for a woman to carry and that the Big-Heads play a role that would be shameful for any female to assume. The people of San Blas find it impossible even to imagine how a woman might act in the parade. Similarly, no upper-class man would taint his own or his family's dignified image by dressing up in a silly costume and behaving like a fool. The roles of Giants and Big-Heads are definitively set aside for male working-class youth.

To define the audience is more difficult, because even though some towns-people claim that "everyone" attends, it is clear that certain segments of the community are more heavily represented than others. The spectators are overwhelmingly children and teenagers,[2] with perhaps a quarter of the onlookers—a third at most—being mature or elderly adults. Males of all ages vastly outnumber females. This disproportion is especially evident among young children, because many little girls voluntarily avoid the event or are prevented by their parents from attending. Small girls tend to be afraid of the costumed figures and, if they are incautious, they can be trampled in the scramble for toys that occurs in the Huevo. Of the females in attendance, most are teenagers, with a smattering of young mothers accompanying their children. There is, finally, a class component of the audience. Young people from all socioeconomic segments of the populace come to watch the parade. But, of those spectators past the teenaged years, vitually all come from among the workers. Members of the elite consider themselves too sophisticated to waste their time on a frivolous, rowdy event like the parade of Giants and Big-Heads.

It is on the basis of the social composition of performers and audience alike that I shall claim that the parade is of paramount importance to the following segments of the San Blas populace: children of all ages and socioeconomic strata and men of the working class. The social composition of the actors, in particular, gives the parade a distinctly male, lower-class aspect. This, by the way, is why an outsider like myself, witnessing the pageant for the first time, views it as rather poorly attended and insignificant when compared with other festival occasions, for large portions of the community are absent from the parade. For the purposes of discussion, then, we may assume that those who participate and attend are the people for whom the parade has meaning. It is from this point of view that we shall analyze Giant and Big-Head imagery. First, however, we should indroduce some critical features of society in San Blas.

[2] That the parade of Giants and Big-Heads is a special significance to young people is also substantiated by the fact that these same figures inaugurate the sporadically held *Fiestas de la Juventud,* or Youth Festivals. The Youth Festivals are held some years in late spring, at no fixed date, and consist largely of dances and sports events. Most recently they were given in 1974 and 1977. In 1976, the only year in which I spent the spring in San Blas, they were suspended, so I have never witnessed them, and therefore know little about them.

Dominance and Submission in San Blas

To understand the parade of Giants and Big-Heads, it is necessary to realize that San Blas is a typical Andalusian agro-town. Unlike the small, egalitarian, corporate communities of northern Spain (see, for example, Aceves, 1971; Brandes, 1975; Freeman, 1970; Kenny, 1966), the agro-towns of the south are deeply divided by conflict between classes, as well as between the sexes. In San Blas, as in most such communities (Gilmore, 1975, 1976; Moreno Navarro, 1972), power relationships are uppermost in people's minds, and provide one of the most pervasive themes of interaction. No matter what a person's status, the tendency is to feel dominated and controlled by those of the opposing group. Among everyone, from all segments of society, there is a perpetual yearning for personal autonomy, which is perceived as being somehow seriously limited or threatened. The hatred and fear of allegedly powerful elements in society can only be described as immediate and pressing.

To these specific features of Andalusian society, we must add the ubiquitous conflict between the generations. In San Blas, as everywhere else in the world, children must learn to develop mechanisms of self-control. During this process, parents are the initial agents of suppression and domination; later, of course, their role is incorporated within the self, so that each person gradually becomes master or mistress of his or her own behavior, and in this sense becomes his or her own parent. In San Blas, whether we speak of class, sex, or generational conflict, it is the concern with restrictions on personal freedom that dominates people's thoughts and emotions. The class and generational dimensions, in particular, emerge in the parade of Giants and Big-Heads; they therefore merit a brief discussion.

Let us turn first to class. People usually distinguish between two socioeconomic groups in San Blas: a small, landed, educated elite, on the one hand, and the mass of illiterate or semiliterate workers who earn their living by daily wage labor, on the other. Workers deeply resent the landed elite, upon whom they depend for their livelihood. They claim that the elite exploits and cheats them by taking advantage of their economically precarious position and that the elite controls the town government so as to divert public funds to its own benefit. Above all, workers are convinced that the elite has done and will do everything possible to prevent the economic advancement of the poorer segment of the community. The elite, they state bitterly, is accustomed to having "slaves" at its disposal, and wants nothing less than to suppress the poor completely, thereby keeping them at the continual mercy of the rich.

Members of the elite themselves, however, feel far from omnipotent. They remember the Civil War years (1936–1939), when the Communists overturned the town government and workers' committees seized their land, converted the churches into granaries, and distributed the harvest to all families equally. They recall with anguish that extensive and valuable family libraries were burned as fuel and that landowners were imprisoned, executed, or put to work building roads. And they desperately fear the resurgence of these events. The hatred and distrust between the classes in San Blas is intense. And the single greatest source of class conflict is the real or presumed threat of domination. Each group believes that the other has more power than it deserves and that this power has been and will be used as a tool of exploitation and destruction.

An even deeper, and certainly more universal, point of conflict represented in San Blas is the opposition between the generations. We know from psychoanalytic research that young children develop a profound resentment and hostility toward their parents as a reaction to restrictions placed on their freedom of action and bodily function. In San Blas, as in other parts of the Hispanic world (Brandes, 1974), the youngest child in a family is lavishly indulged; but once a new infant is born, the displaced child becomes subject to ridicule and corporal punishment in case of misbehavior, accidents of bowel or bladder, or other transgressions. Even teenagers can expect thrashings, especially when their misconduct is carried out in public and might endanger the family's reputation. Children naturally develop a strong emotional attachment to and dependence on their parents, but this dependence in no way negates the anger and resentment they simultaneously feel towards them.

At least for the men of San Blas, submission to an older generation persists throughout life and becomes a nagging source of anxiety. Increasingly throughout the middle years and into old age, a man's wife becomes like a mother to him. The wife, in addition to feeding and clothing her husband, just as his mother did, chides him for drinking too much or staying out too late. She controls the purse and doles out money. In short, she is a source of maternal-like security, but also a cause of irritating restrictions on personal freedom. In San Blas, the role of child—whether enacted in chronological childhood or in adulthood—requires submission to a dominant power-holder, whose rules and regulations seem irrational and unnecessarily confining. The child, in this context, feels as threatened and oppressed as do members of the two classes in their relations with one another.

Giants and Big-Heads as Social Metaphors

To place the parade in its social context, let us begin by simply listing the formal characteristics of Giants and Big-Heads, as revealed in their appearance and demeanor during the pageant. Here we are struck by a series of binary oppositions, which also characterize contrasting dyads of generation and class in San Blas.

Giants	Big-Heads
few	many
tall	short
dignified	foolish
haughty	familiar
graceful	clumsy
unified	disorganized
controlled	spontaneous
dominant	subordinate

Other contrasting features also come to mind, but even this short list presents seemingly inconsistent traits for each of our costumed figures, which will have to be explained; the list certainly provides an adequate basis for discussion.

Drawing upon these binary oppositions and keeping the perspective of performers and audience in mind, we may postulate an association between Giants and Big-Heads, on the one hand, and particular groups in San Blas society, on the other. The evidence for the generational analogy is clear. The two giants, crowned male and female figures, stand tall and erect and move smoothly through the crowds, exhibiting complete bodily control, a self-control that to anthropologist Mary Douglas would indicate conformity to the demands imposed by the wider society (Douglas, 1973:99–100). Within the family, of course, it is the parents who exhibit this type of behavior, while the children, still incompletely socialized, manifest spontaneous, unpredictable, and clumsy movements, which are also characteristic of the Big-Heads. There could be no clearer example of Douglas's contention (1973) that "the social body constrains the way the physical body is perceived" (p. 93). "Socialization," she says, "teaches the child to bring organic processes under control" (p. 101). In our case, it is the graceful Giants of this parade who have already grown up, while the erratic, playful Big-Heads are still immature.

Of course, the appearance and number of Giants in relation to Big-Heads also conforms to the image as parents and children. First there is the matter of relative height; though the Big-Heads' costumes make them some 7 feet tall, they are still a good deal shorter than the Giants, who loom upwards of 12 or 13 feet. Then, too, the Big-Heads, like natural children, have heads that are much larger in proportion to their bodies than are those of adults.[3] It is in this aspect that the Big-Heads contrast with the Giants, whose heads and bodies are proportionately like those of adult humans. And finally, Big-

[3] Philippe Aries's influential historical study of family life (1962) points out that in Western society children were until recently considered as little adults. Perhaps this is why their heads were represented artistically as small in proportion to their bodies. It was no doubt after children came to be thought of as different from adults that their heads were drawn true to size. I am indebted to Howard Gardner for reminding me of Aries's analysis.

Heads, like the children in most families of traditional Andalusia, are considerably more numerous than their Giant–parent counterparts.

More than anything, however, Figure 1, reproduced from the official program notes for the 1975 parade, demonstrates the popular conception of Giants and Big-Heads as representing a human family. The drawing is all the more striking if we consider that I have never heard anyone in San Blas articulate conscious recognition of these figures as family symbols. Here, there is significant distortion from the actual figures; in reality, the two Giant figures are of about equal height, while the drawing shows the female markedly shorter than the male. In the drawing, too, the Big-Heads are much smaller proportionately to the Giants than they should be. The relative size of the figures in the drawing indisputably demonstrates that people conceive of Giants and Big-Heads as parents and children. And in the drawing, as in the parade itself, the stiff, controlled, dignified bearing of the parents contrasts markedly with the free-flowing, unbridled spirit of the children.

The element of self-control is also essential to an understanding of Giants and Big-Heads as symbols of social class. Here once again we can turn to Mary Douglas for assistance in interpretation:

> A complex social system devises for itself ways of behaving that suggest that human intercourse is disembodied compared with that of animal creation. It uses different degrees of disembodiment to express the social hierarchy. The more refinement, the less smacking of the lips when eating, the less mastication, the less the sound of breathing and walking, the more carefully modulated the laughter, the more controlled the signs of anger, the clearer comes the priestly–aristocratic image [Douglas, 1973:101–102].

Thus, in San Blas we may compare the relatively hushed, sedate atmosphere that prevails in the bars most heavily frequented by upper-class members

Dia 16

A las 12, Inauguración Oficial de Festejos con disparo de cohetes y fuegos

japoneses, repique general de campanas y desfile de

GIGANTES Y CABEZUDOS

acompañados por la Banda Local de Música.

A las 12 de la noche en la Plaza de Santa María, se quemará una vistosa coleccion de

Fuegos Artificiales

confeccionados por la Pirotécnica «Ntra. Sra. de Fátima», de Martos, y subvencionados por el Excmo. Ayuntamiento.

FIGURE 1. Drawing of Giants and Big-Heads reproduced from the official program notes for the 1975 parade.

of the community with the noisy, boisterous, and fully demonstrative setting characteristic of lower-class bars. Upper-class people claim that they can identify lower-class people by their awkward, gawky posture and gait. At the same time, those of the lower class assume a certain defensive pride in the fact that they are unfettered by the excess *etiqueta* of the elite; unlike those of the upper class, these commoners claim, they can use the same utensils throughout several courses of a meal, or even on occasion eat with their hands or share a single platter or bowl among all members of the family. In reality, of course, lower-class people have internalized the image that the upper class holds of them. They feel awkward and graceless, loud and crass, and generally untutored in the social amenities as practiced by the elite. They are, in this important respect, like children—imperfectly or only partially socialized.

The Giant figures, of course, specifically represent King and Queen, the supreme rulers of society. Their aloof, dignified bearing accords perfectly with the lower-class image of monarchs as well as of the social elite (see Durbin, this volume, for a similar iconic representation of royalty). As with most graphic representations, however, the Giants are an exaggerated portrayal. The Giant as a social being is so divorced from and independent of the Giant as physical being that the Giant's body is actually invisible, for it will be recalled that the figure's simple garb reaches to the feet of the human bearer, thereby obscuring him completely from sight. This cloaking may be construed as an indication that the Giants, like the elite, are fully socialized, free from the chaotic passions and whims of the human organism.[4]

Not so with the Big-Heads, whose entirely human bodies bounce and twist as if purposefully to mimic the awkward, foolish, uncontrolled demeanor of the workers. The Giants stand taut and rigid, their faces peering out from a great height over and away from the Big-Heads and the human crowd below. The Big-Heads interact closely with that crowd, mingling with it, standing level with it, and relating to it by touch. "Greater space means more formality, nearness means intimacy," Douglas reminds us (1973:101). By this measure, too, Giants and Big-Heads conform to the social images of elite and worker.

There are other, more obvious, but equally important ways in which the socioeconomic division is represented by our figures. Again, the relative size and number of Giants and Big-Heads have to be taken into account. To

---

[4] One of the San Blas priests, upon hearing my interpretation of Giants and Big-Heads as representing parents and children, agreed with me, and then spontaneously offered the suggestion that the figures symbolize social classes as well. I had already come to this conclusion on my own, but decided, before telling him so, to listen to his reasoning. In Torredonjimeno, the town where he grew up, Giants and Big-Heads are also part of an annual festival. There, however, the Giants are actually given names: Don Jimeno and Doña Leonor. The titles Don and Doña are awarded to the social elite in Andalusian agro-towns, a circumstance that evoked for this priest the class dimension to the costumed figures.

the people of San Blas, economic position is associated with physical size, so that the elite is often referred to collectively as *los grandes,* "the large ones." With this sort of conceptual correlation between the economic and the organic spheres, it is understandable that the relatively huge Giants should symbolize the elite, and the Big-Heads the workers. Like the Giants, the elite are relatively few in number. "Our land is superabundant and rich," say the workers. "The only problem is that it is divided among only a handful of people (*cuatro personas*). The rest of us have nothing."

The Giants and Big-Heads also undoubtedly speak to the specific fears of dominance and submission characteristic of the workers. It is likely that Big-Heads, from the workers' point of view, reflect their own individualism and disorganization. Strength comes from unity, say the workers, who chastise themselves for their inability to organize and cooperate with each other. The Giants, who march at a slow, even pace alongside each other, convey an impression of indestructible cohesion, a cohesion that the workers in San Blas (erroneously) attribute to the elite.

The metaphoric relationships between Giants and Big-Heads, on the one hand, and social classes, on the other, is certainly not as explicit as is the relationship between these costumed figures and their generational counterparts. But the class analogy is still strikingly evident. Moreover, if we accept Percy Cohen's analysis (this volume), it is likely that human beings tend to think of dominance relationships within society in terms that derive from their own childhood experiences (which, as he points out, is not the same as saying that these relationships actually derive from those experiences). Cohen argues that we tend to represent or symbolize social class distinctions as if they were differences between parents and children. One of the major generational distinctions is that adults are not only invariably much taller than infants, but continue to be taller than children at least until these children reach adolescence. From this obvious but all too often ignored fact, Cohen believes that we can explain the linquistic reference in English to *high* and *low* classes. He concludes that the uses of these terms to refer to rank are not only metaphoric but symbolic, in that they represent the unconscious, adult reference to visual and other forms of childhold experience of power and advantage.

In San Blas, we may say, Giants and Big-Heads are fundamentally a visual representation of powerful, large people in juxtaposition with weak, small ones. Like the English usage of the terms *high* and *low,* the Andalusian costumed figures, while referring to all sorts of societal distinctions, are fundamentally modeled on childhood perceptions of power relationships within the family. It is no wonder, then, that the parade has a special appeal to children, for it effectively communicates its wider social message by couching its representations of class in generational terms. The parade not only symbolizes critical social divisions within San Blas, but also through subtle means teaches children about these divisions. Moreover, because the pageant communicates unilaterally, as Cherry (this volume) would say, its message is all the more potent. It is an effective agent of socialization.

The Parade as Fantasy

We have seen how the parade of Giants and Big-Heads juxtaposes a dominant, organized, emotionally controlled group against one characterized by subordination, disorganization, and emotional abandon. Now it remains to explain the activity, the performance, of the Giants and Big-Heads. Here I am particularly interested in exploring two aspects of the parade: Big-Head clowning, and the skyrockets.

Big-Heads, as we already know, spend the entire course of the parade in typical clowning behavior. Perhaps the most essential part of their act is the wielding of the sausage-shaped stuffed cloth, known in Spanish as a *porra*, or "club." Aside from this object's physical similarity to the penis, there is the fact that the term *porra* and its derivatives are colloquially used in San Blas to refer to the male organ.[5] The phallic symbolism of the object is inescapable. When Big-Heads attack the crowd with the porra, they are not only symbolically exposing the penis but are also asserting their masculinity through the penis's aggressive activity.

This is evident not only in the way Big-Heads use the porra, but also in their general antics, their skipping, hopping, jumping, and sliding. The Big-Heads are essentially clowns, and as Martha Wolfenstein has point out, "most clowns and comic characters are male. . . . What is funny in the man is the unpredictable behavior of the penis. This is functional rather than structural, and so readily translatable into comic action. Thus we get the characteristic gambits of the clown or comedian with his unexpected movements, his alternate collapses and surprising hyperactivity" [Wolfenstein, 1954:136–137].

In San Blas, the word *cabeza* ("head") is also associated linguistically with the male organ. The foreskin, for example, is called the "head of the penis" (*cabeza del pijo*). And men also jokingly state that "We men have two heads; when the lower one gets erect, you lose the one above!" (¡*Cuando se endurece la de abajo, se pierde la de arriba!*"). One cannot help but

---

[5] The term *porra* is not among the most commonly used words to refer to the penis in San Blas. But *porra*, meaning 'club,' is the name for a baton-type toy that men occasionally fashion from wild grasses in the surrounding hills and that they say could be put to good use by widows and other "needy" women. The phallic symbolism of the object does not escape them. Moreover, in every religious procession in San Blas there are two men who are dressed in Renaissance garb and who are armed with large wooden maces. Irreverently, the people of San Blas refer to these men as *momporros*, a word obviously derived from the term *porra*, and one that refers specifically to the workers on horse-breeding farms who are charged with guiding the stallion's exhausted phallus into the desired location.

postulate that the Big-Heads represent the "heads" in this saying who are trying to become erect and assert their potency.

This genital imagery is reinforced by the fact that it is the young unmarried men, and not those from other segments of society, who play and (unlike the Giants) actually enjoy the role of Big-Heads. Teenaged boys are sexually aware and potent, but their sexuality has not yet been harnessed and brought under control through the bond of marriage. Big-Head clowning may be viewed as a means by which San Blas society at once highlights the chaotic impulses of these men and permits these impulses to be expressed safely on a symbolic plane. Both actors and audience experience a libidinal release, through the representational enactment of aggressive and sexual feelings; at the same time the social order remains stable and unthreatened, because the parade is a regular, predictable event, in which all participants behave in a fully expectable manner. Big-Head antics are thus no mere reversal of behavioral norms, as some analysts would say. Clowning enables young men to act out an exaggerated version of their normal, legitimate social role as the sexually rampant members of the town.

But the parade speaks not only to adolescent men but also to the dominant segment of the audience, the young children. The parade refers, in this respect, to each child's battle to incorporate within himself all the rules that his parents lay down for him, as much his efforts to control bladder and bowels as to conform to appropriate regulations of social interaction. The child, like the Big-Head, wants to burst out of the straitjacket of conformity, and, watching the parade, he can identify with his costumed counterparts and do just that. The parade provides an occasion when children can vicariously express aggression toward and release from constricting rules. And to the extent that people of both sexes and all ages are engaged in the constant battle to overcome the surging irrational passions within them, Big-Head behavior can perform the same cathartic release for them as it does for children. In the parade, we are presented with an almost classic visual representation of the struggle of the Id against the Superego, of the forces of emotional release battling against those of constraint and containment.

The skyrockets set off over the Huevo must be seen as consonant with the masculine imagery of the costumed figures. The term for skyrocket in San Blas, as throughout the Spanish-speaking world, is *cohete*. The most popular euphemism in San Blas to refer to the male role in sexual intercourse is to *echar un cohete*, literally "to launch a skyrocket." Given his association of terms, it is reasonable to assume that the incessant bursting of skyrockets is unconsciously equated with ejaculation. (We should also remember that the skyrockets are set off within the plaza known as the Huevo, and that *huevo*, or "egg," is the most universal and commonly employed word to refer to testicle.) Just as ejaculation is at least potentially productive, so too the launching of skyrockets produces small toys—including plastic dolls—and packages of candy. These objects, like the skyrockets themselves, are paid for by the San Blas government. Significantly, the place from which these goodies are distributed is the town hall, the locus of municipal government, whose officeholders are almost exclusively drawn from the social elite.

All things considered, this scenario may be understood as the symbolic means through which the governing powerholders provide the commoners of their town with a sop. Men of the working class, who attend this event in great numbers, join with the child and adolescent spectators in trying to capture the toys and candy. Everyone in the audience is thus treated implicitly by the governing elite in the same way: as potentially threatening members of society, who must be placated through the token redistribution of wealth. In this fashion, the parade of Giants and Big-Heads operates to reinforce extant social relationships.

In the final analysis, I expect, the parade is a metaphoric statement of potential social chaos, of the threat both to the individual and to society if the forces of order and control are not permitted to prevail. Paradoxically, by institutionalizing an annual occasion like this, during which disorder reigns, the people of San Blas demonstrate to themselves the advantages of predictability in social life and some of the ways in which predictability can be attained. The parade is evocative, in Sperber's sense (this volume), largely because the costumed figures are able simultaneously to represent contrasting features of society and the individual alike. Here we must call to mind Ernest Jones's contention that "a given symbol may have two or occasionally even more meanings" (Jones, 1949:97). Thus, a man observing or enacting the pageant of Giants and Big-Heads may easily identify with both types of figures, for each of them embodies an essential aspect of himself. Even working-class men are powerholders to some extent, if only in their role as family leader; in this capacity, they may identify with the Giants. To the degree that they feel powerless and oppressed, however, they may project themselves into the Big-Heads, who lash out in a hostile, assertive burst of activity, as if to protest their subordinate position. It is this multiple imagery, I believe, that infuses the parade with highly charged symbolic meaning, and that therefore keeps the event alive in an epoch that has witnessed the progressive erosion of local customs such as this throughout Spain.

Acknowledgments

In writing this chapter, I have especially benefited from the comments of Mary LeCron Foster and Percy S. Cohen. My colleague Alan Dundes has also been of enormous assistance in helping me to formulate my ideas. None of these people bears any responsibility for the accuracy of my data or interpretations. The material in this chapter appears in my forthcoming volume, *Metaphors of Masculinity: Sex and Status in Andalusian Folklore*, a joint publication of the American Folklore Society and the University of Pennsylvania Press, scheduled for 1980.

References

Aceves, Joseph
    1971 *Social change in a Spanish village.* Cambridge, Massachussets: Schenkman.
Almerich, Luis
    1944 Tradiciones, fiestas y costumbres populares de Barcelona. Barcelona: Librería Millá.
Ariès, Philippe
    1962 *Centuries of childhood: A social history of family life.* Translated by Robert Bladick. New York: Vintage.
Beitl, Klaus
    1961 *Die Umgangsriesen.* Vienna: Verlag Notring der Wissenschaftlichen Verbonde.
Brandes, Stanley
    1974 Crianza infantil y comportamiento relativo a roles familiaries en México. *Ethnica* **8,** 33–47.
    1975 *Migration, kinship, and community: Tradition and transition in a Spanish village.* New York: Academic Press.
Caro Baroja, Julio
    1965 *El carnaval.* Madrid: Taurus.
Douglas, Mary
    1973 *Natural symbols: Explorations in cosmology.* New York: Vintage.
Freeman, Susan Tax
    1970 *Neighbors: The social contract in a Castilian hamlet.* Illinois: Univ. of Chicago Press.
Geertz, Clifford
    1973 Deep play: Notes on the Balinese cockfight. In *The interpretation of cultures,* edited by Clifford Geertz. New York: Basic Books, Pp. 412–453.
Gilmore, David
    1975 *Carnaval* in Fuenmayor: Class conflict and social cohesion in an Andalusian town. *Journal of Anthropological Research* **31** (4), 331–349.
    1976 Class, culture, and community size in Spain: The relevance of models. *Anthropological Quarterly* **49** (2), 89–106.
Gómez-Tabanera, José Manuel
    1968 Fiestas populares y festejos tradicionales. In *El folklore español,* edited by J. M. Gómez-Tabanera. Madrid: Instituto Español de la Antropología Aplicada, Pp. 149–216.
Jones, Ernest
    1949 *Papers on psycho-analysis.* Baltimore, Maryland: Williams & Wilkins.
Kenny, Michael
    1966 *A Spanish tapestry: Town and country in Castile.* New York: Harper.
Marinus, Albert
    1951 Le folklore Belge, 3 vols. Brussels: Les Editions Historiques.
Meurant, René
    1960 Géants et monstres d'osier. *Bulletin de la Societé Royale Belge d'Anthropologie et de Préhistoire* **71,** 120–155.
    1967 Contribution a l'étude des géants processionnels et de cortège dans le nord de la France, la Belgique et les Pays-Bas. *Arts et Traditions Populaires* **15** (2), 119–160.
    1969 Morphologie, montage et mode d'animation des géants d'Ath. *Revista de Etnografía* (Lima) **12** (1), 41–58.
Moreno Navarro, Isidoro
    1972 *Propiedad, clases sociales, y hermandades en la Baja Andalucía.* Madrid: Siglo Veintiuno.
Ortner, Sherry B.
    1973 On key symbols. *American Anthropologist* **75** (5), 1338–1346.

Plá Cargol, Joaquín
  1947 *Tradiciones, santuarios y tipismo de las comarcas gerundenses.* Gerona and Madrid: Dalmau Carles.
van Gennep, Arnold
  1935 *Le folklore de la Flandre et du Hainaut Francais (departement du Nord),* 2 vols. Paris: Maisonneuve.
Wolfenstein, Martha
  1954 *Children's Humor.* Glencoe, Illinois: Free Press.

7

Ritual Symbolism and the Nonrepresentation of Society

MAURICE BLOCH

Introduction

The purpose of this chapter is to show by way of example some of the features that characterize the use of symbolism in human ritual. By symbolism I do not mean the whole range of human signification; I use the term in a narrower way, following anthropological practice, which contrasts to the way the word is used in psychology or linguistics. I contrast signification, the process that lies at the back of ordinary language, with symbolism, which, in Turner's words, is the "smallest unit of ritual which still retains the specific properties of ritual behaviour" (Turner, 1967:19). Symbols are therefore a special kind of signification; this point is particularly important for the contrast between symbolism, on the one hand, and the way language in general carries meaning, on the other. Indeed, Sperber (1974) and I (1974b) have both argued that studies of symbolism are misled by the simple assumption that symbols carry meaning in the way words are thought to carry meaning in the lexicon. Because symbols occur in ritualized, that is, formalized, communication, their relation to the world is of a totally different nature from the relation to the world of the units of informal communication. In everyday language, the syntactic mechanism enables a complex and fluid recombination of the meaningful units. The character of these units derives from their continual recombination. In ritualized–formalized language, however, the potential for recombination, the *creativity* of language, is impaired to such an extent that the use of language and indeed all communication in ritual becomes as much a matter of repeating as of creating. This makes the units of ritual symbols ambiguous; it also makes the discourse in which they occur largely unchallengeable. You cannot argue with a song, and songs are one of the most typical uses of language in ritual. Formalized–ritualized communication therefore does not bear direct relation to events; new experience neither modifies nor contradicts its content directly because its form rules out such modification and contradiction.

Ritual is therefore able to carry messages that seem to go against those of nonritual discourse without being open to challenge by nonritual discourse. It creates a disconnected fantasy world that runs right against everyday experience. Furthermore we find that the fantasy world serves to mystify and hide the real situation (Bloch, 1977). This chapter, then, deals with a transformation beyond that studied by, for example, Bowerman (this volume). She is concerned with how concepts are formed. I am concerned with how, once formed, they are denatured and reformed by ritual so that they can serve to build an alternative phantasmagoric world.

I wish also to show in this chapter how the representation of social relations acted out in ritual are totally different from those existing outside ritual. This contrasts with studies of animal behavior that seem to show that "ritualized" behavior is a device for emphasizing and defining roles in such activities as dominance or sexual attraction (see Chalmers, this volume). Ritual among humans stands in a subtle dialectic with the nonritual world. Rituals do not emphasize the social world, but are more likely to contradict or deny that world in a number of highly complex ways. In this way, human rituals are totally different from animal rituals. Human rituals are an alternative, exceptional mode of communication used to carry messages that run against the grain of ordinary communication, whereas what has been called *ritual* in many animal species is the only communication they have.

Merina Hierarchy and Equality

To illustrate the above points I wish to consider the rituals surrounding marriage among the Merina of Madagascar. The Merina are an amorphous group of people whose identity is linked with the growth of a large state in the nineteenth century. Their basic kinship unit is an endogamous group, the deme, whose members are considered descended from the same ancestors. In Merina thought, deme members should all be equal and should marry within the deme in order to regroup inheritance; indeed, nearly all Merina marriages occur between close kin. This causes a problem, because marriage in such a society involves the gain by one side of a woman and her children and the loss by the other side of a daughter. Although in the long run it can be said, as has been pointed out by Lévi-Strauss, that all marriage exchanges in such a system equal out, in the short run a marriage involves two local families in an unequal exchange (local families being a kind of localized extended family). Now the implication of unequal exchange in Madagascar, as everywhere, is hierarchy. This is especially so among the Merina who see the wife-takers as superior; in fact, in the past whenever there was an exception to endogamy, as was the case for high ranking demes close to the sovereign, the wife-takers always belonged to the higher group and the wife-givers to the lower groups.

There thus exists a contradiction in Merina kinship: Members of the deme should all be equal, but marriage involves them in relations that imply inequality. This is dealt with most of the time by simply ignoring marriage and alliance and talking of all relationships as though they were consanguinal. Nonetheless, there are times when the contradiction cannot be ignored. Above all, at the marriage ceremony itself the two contradictory principles, equality between constituent families of the deme and the inequality between wife-takers and wife-givers, become concurrently prominent. How this contradiction is dealt with in the ceremony itself is what concerns us in the following section.

Merina Marriage Ceremonies

The Merina marriage ritual is well known and has been described, although often sketchily, many times. Versions, models, and manuals for the performance of the speech that is essential to this ritual—especially the compilation of an Anglican clergyman, Rasamuel (1928, 1948)—can be bought at every market stall in Imerina. In 1971, I gave ethnographic descriptions of this in *Placing the Dead,* and Elinor Keenan (1975) supplied further accounts, again focusing on the central speech. Since so much has already been published, I shall only briefly describe the ethnographic background before turning to the ceremony that the Merina have no hesitation in considering central. It is the ceremony of the giving of the *vody ondry.* To verify if two people are married the question to ask is "Has the *vody ondry* already gone?" (*"Efa lasa ve, ny vody ondry?"*)

The *vody ondry* is the sum of money given by the groom to his bride's father. It is a small sum by Merina standards, usually worth around $2, and it is contrasted by the Merina as being very different from the bride price given by other Malagasy people (especially the Marofotsy and the Tsimihety) whom they contemptuously see as buying women. *Vody ondry* means 'the hindquarters of a sheep' (the gift is said to have been, in the past, literally that). The giving of the hindquarters of an animal has in Imerina a clearly expressed meaning: obeisance to a superior. Thus a son who kills any animal gives its hindquarters to his father, as does any junior to the head of a local family. Similarly, in the past the hindquarters of any slaughtered bull had to be given to the monarch; not to do so was open treason (Callet, 1908:101, 368).

To give the hindquarters of an animal is therefore an act of submission, but the sheep itself is also significant. Three animals in Merina culture are given away as gifts: (*a*) bulls given to kings; (*b*) sheep given to fathers-in-law; and (*c*) chickens given to fathers. To say that a man gives the hindquarters of a chicken to an elder is a way of saying that he recognizes a particular local family head (however, he would also give the hindquarters of a sheep or any other animal in normal circumstances to the same person). To say that a man gives the hindquarters of a bull to a lord shows that he submits to the lord's jurisdiction. When a son-in-law gives the hindquarters of a sheep, he therefore acts towards his wife's father in a filial way, but not just in a filial way, but in a *superfilial* way, a little as he would to a lord. This *superfilial* element, as we shall see, is a theme repeated throughout the ceremony. After the ceremony, the son-in-law will, in fact, behave towards his father-in-law, when he is in his father-in-law's village, as he would towards his own father, giving him the hindquarters of any animal he kills, including the hindquarters of a chicken. This is especially important, for a son-in-law must visit his father-in-law on numerous occasions.

Marriage for the Merina follows from this initial public performance of superfilial behavior by a son-in-law towards his wife's father; that is, the handing over of the *vody ondry*. This is a complicated matter. The participants are divided into two groups—the wife-givers and the wife-takers. The ceremony takes place in the house of the bride's parents where all the senior men and women of her local family and their head, who may also be the father of the girl, are gathered. In one corner is piled up what I called the *dowry* but which, I think, might better be called the *trousseau*, since it consists of the movables that will furnish the house of the newly married pair in the groom's village. The other party of people, that of the groom, I called in *Placing the Dead* the *Mpaka*, 'the takers'.[1] The takers represent a fairly equivalent group to that of the bride with two significant differences. First, they contain a stranger, nonfamily member who is there as a professional speechmaker and is paid for his services. He is an expert, often a minister of the church; he is never a close relative of the groom. Second, the head of the local family of the groom and/or the father play no special role (in the case of demes of higher status, he is not allowed to be there at all). These two differences exist because the whole ritual involves the groom behaving as a son to another man. This makes the presence of the groom's father an embarrassment. Indeed it is a deliberate humiliation for him and for the family he represents. By replacing the head of the family of the groom by an actor,

---

[1] In her (1975) article, Elinor Keenan called them the *Mpangataka*, 'the askers'. The difference is significant and is due to the fact that when I was giving the description of Merina marriage, I had in mind an occasion when I was associated with the groom's family, whereas it is clear from Elinor Keenan's account that she was associated with the family of the bride. The difference between the two words clearly reveals the status problem in the marriage.

the shame is, as it were, sidetracked and need not be fully faced by the groom's family head (Callet, 1908:334).

The ceremony of the giving of the *vody ondry* begins with the humiliation of the groom's family. They have been told to come several hours too early and are made to wait outside. They must knock three times before they are let in. Then after a period of salutation a speechmaker makes a move to make the speech that will be the central part of the ritual (Andrizmanzato, 1957; Keenan, 1975). At this stage a process, which will carry on throughout, begins. The speechmaker is criticized for the way he has begun and is fined for being rude. After that he can at last really begin. The form of these speeches is typical of all formal Merina speeches, including royal speeches, speeches of elders addressing village councils, and harangues by heads of families against their juniors (Bloch, 1971b, 1975b). They are very long and highly structured. They follow certain set sections and are endlessly decorated by scriptural and proverbial examples. The marriage speech has all those features, only more so. It is very boring; coming to the point—offering the *vody ondry* and asking for the girl—is relegated to an almost insignificant section. What really makes this speech special and different from all others is that it is continually interrupted and criticized by members of the family of the bride, who complain on any grounds they can think of. They may say that it is too abstract, or too long-winded, that it is obscene (it might mention the name of the girl and the boy in the same sentence), that the proverbs are too many or too few. It is too old-fashioned. It is too modern. The point is that one cannot be right. The family of the bride laugh at the speechmaker and fine him for his "mistakes" until he is quite literally rendered speechless and he just puts down the *vody ondry* in front of the head of the local family of the girl who, however, will only pick it up when certain demands have been met by the family of the groom. There are, first of all, demands for money on the part of the relatives of the girl, in compensation for the services they lose. Grandma, for example, will ask to be compensated for the loss of "the pulling out of the white hairs," a service that girls perform for older women. Also, certain conditions of the marriage regarding possible divorce and the disposition of the children and common property are specified. As for himself, the father of the girl just states the duties of the groom. These are to help him in arduous tasks, especially cleaning irrigation channels, to come whenever he is called, to contribute to his, the bride's father's, tomb and *famadihanas* (secondary funerals), duties that are those of an exemplary son. Only when all this has been agreed to by the groom's party will the father of the bride accept the *vody ondry* and will the marriage be official. It is at this stage that the girl is produced and all the parties give good advice to the newlyweds. The couple are then blessed by the older members of the girl's family as though they were both their children. In other words, the new couple, or the potential household, is treated as though it was an accretion to the family of the bride, and this is often quite explicit said in a phrase reminiscent of the one often used at English marriages: "We have not lost a daughter, we have gained a son" (Callet, 1908:617).

This is followed by a new stage that involves the taking away of the girl, one of the most total takeovers of a person I have ever seen. The women of the groom's party strip the girl of her old clothing and throw it away. They untie the little tresses of her hair, reclothe her in clothes and finery brought by the groom, and fix her hair in a different style. As they take her to the groom's house they sing a bawdy song promising alternative pleasures to those of being with "mum." Although several other ceremonies follow this, especially a ceremony at the house of the groom that is very similar to the integration rites that finish the *vody ondry* ceremony, it is the *vody ondry* ceremony that creates the marriage bond.

The central point of the *vody ondry* ceremony is the demonstration of the filial status of the groom towards his father-in-law. By performing the ceremony, the son-in-law puts himself at the beck and call of his father-in-law, receives ancestral blessings from the father-in-law's kin, and will contribute to his father-in-law's tomb expenses, which in Madagascar is the most important sign of affiliation. It should, however, be noted that he does not just become a new son, he becomes a new *superson,* something that is implied by the very action of the giving of the hindquarters of a sheep. He does not just contribute to the tomb expenses like a son, he contributes even more than a son. He does not just help his father-in-law in agricultural tasks, he "rushes" to perform for him before anything, even before the bidding of his own father. He does not just give the *vody akoho,* the hindquarters of a chicken, he gives the *vody ondry*.

One of the aspects of son-hood, and, therefore, all the more of superson-hood, is that it is a condition of unconditional inferiority. Within the parental family this has no meaning as regards the status of a group since both father and son belong to the same set of groups, but as soon as we are dealing with marriage the implication is much more complicated, because during the marriage ceremony the principal actors belong to different groups. The whole ceremony puts the family of the groom in an inferior status to that of the bride. This is not just marked by the giving of the *vody ondry* itself but by the whole marriage speech performance. To understand the significance of this speech it needs to be considered along with ordinary *kabary* or 'formal speeches' that occur in a more normal context.

The central fact about such *kabarys* is that they are the authoritative words of a superior, couched in an authoritative code (Bloch, 1975). They are the acts of ancestors, kings, elders, and fathers. Merina history and law largely takes the form of remembered royal speeches. It follows from this that the proper way to listen to a *kabary* is collective silence. There are, however, rare occasions when this is not so (Bloch, 1971b).

One such occasion arises when the status of the superior, in this case an elder, is challenged or not accepted by the hearers. When a person sets himself up as an elder but his status is refused by his audience, instead of being listened to in reverent silence, he is mocked and ridiculed, a process that means a total denial of his presumptuous claim to high status. If we think back to the marriage speech, as described above, we see that a parallel process is at work. The head (albeit the pseudohead) of the groom's party takes on the role of a superior, that is, a speechmaker, but like the young man who thought he might succeed in behaving like an elder, he is ridiculed and shamed. In other words, what can be said to happen during the ritual is that at the beginning the family of the boy is set up as the superior—only to be knocked down by institutionalized ridicule and, once down, must seal the loss of status towards the listeners, the family of the bride, by giving the token of inferiority, the *vody ondry*. The whole process can be represented in the following diagram:

Status at beginning of ceremony   *Status at end of ceremony*

Wife-takers ⟶ Wife-givers
Wife-givers ⟶ Wife-takers

The ritual is, therefore, one of rank inversion between wife-takers and wife-givers. There is, however, more to this than a simple change of rank. The ranking at the beginning of the ceremony is, as we noted in the preceding, the generally accepted one, that is, that wife-takers are gainers and superior; but the ritual denies this and creates a ritual order where the wife-givers are superior to the wife-takers. Now, if we turn back to the original problem, we saw that the difficulty posed by marriage was that at the deme level and in the long term, wife-givers and wife-takers should be equal, but that the actual marriage involves them in a nonreciprocal and therefore hierarchical relation. At first sight the reversal of the hierarchy through ritual does not solve the problem. The long-term ultimate effect of marriage should be to keep a careful balance necessary in and for the marriage of equals.

In actual fact, the groom takes his bride away to live with his father and, in theory, gains two out of three subsequent children. This blatant fact, obvious to all, is not mentioned in the ritual. It takes place, but that is all there is to it. On the other hand, what is stressed in the ritual is the reverse journey, the coming of the groom to become a member of the family, to become a son, a superson, of his bride's father, accepting his authority in domestic and religious duties. However, by contrast to the real incorporation of the bride in her husband's family, this incorporation of the groom into his wife's family, most of the time, is invisible and immaterial. In other words, in the natural material world, the groom's family are the gainers and therefore superior, but in the world of ritual, the situation is reversed. Since the aim of the ceremony is ultimately to produce equals, it is as though this double inequality in two different worlds produces the sought-after equality where neither gains nor loses. It is as though one real woman equals one unreal superman and, the exchange having been made equal, the final status is one of equality. This can be represented in the following diagram.

Affinal status	*Social status*	*Ritual status*
Wife-takers		Wife-givers
Wife-givers		Wife-takers

From this perspective it becomes clear why the *vody ondry* is not performed in the rare cases of uxorilocal marriage (although at first sight it might appear that the uxorilocal husband was readily taking on the status of son). By giving the *vody ondry* in such a case, the family of the groom would not *only* gain a son, but also a superson. The ceremony would then only heighten the imbalance of the relationship, an imbalance that in a marriage like this is such an embarrassment in the first place that the family of the groom is likely to totally ignore him until he, perhaps ultimately, makes amends by bringing his wife back to his parental village or by a really massive contribution of superson to his *own* parent's tomb ceremonies.

There still remains one problem in the casuistic solution brought about by the ceremony. Being a son is an exclusive status, yet Merina marriage asks the young man to be son to two people at once. This has practical problems, and I was told that the reason why intermarriage in the same village was discouraged was because the newlyweds would not know who to give the *vody akoho* to, in other words, would not know which head of local family to acknowledge. This dilemma is normally avoided by keeping the two conflicting statuses (being a son to one's own father or to one's wife's father) as separate and localized in different places at different times. At the village of his father, where he will be most of the time, the son will give his father the *vody akoho*; at the village of his father-in-law, where the groom will be only occasionally, usually for ritual, he will give his wife's father the *vody akoho*. Here again, however, this segregation cannot be maintained during the actual ceremony since it brings together both sides to witness a highly dramatic giving of the *vody ondry*. It is this problem that explains the presence of the professional speechmaker at the marriage. The ceremony is a time when the groom is asked to behave as a son towards his father-in-law, in front of his real father. This involves the son in behavior that is tantamount to renouncing his father to his face. The whole process is made much easier for everybody by having a stand-in, a paid outsider. It is not the real father who is humiliated and deprived but an actor who does not *really* embody the principle of his actions. If this were not so, the fine equilibrating of status between two equal descendants of the ancestors that is achieved by the ritual would fail through overcorrection, leaving the bride's father superior.

The same problem also occurs for the bride, but in this case we are much more familiar with it. Marriage requires her, too, to act as a daughter to two different sets of persons. This problem is resolved by segregating the two incompatible roles to two different places. For her, too, the marriage ceremony is a difficult exception to this segregation. This would seem to be the explanation of the violence with which she is stripped of her clothing by the family of the groom as a sign of the division of her status in the two places and the awkwardness of the juxtaposing that occurs during the ceremony. However, it is interesting to note that this part of the ritual is unritualized, so to speak, in that it does not involve set formulae or carefully set-apart actions. In other words, this part of the marriage, the actual journey as opposed to the pseudo-journey of the giving of the *vody ondry*, occurs in a sharply contrasted type of discourse, which has none of the characteristics of formalized communication, which I discussed at the beginning. Indeed, for this journey, there is no need to disconnect with reality as seen outside the ritual. In this reality women actually do become juniors of the husband's family.

Summary and Conclusion

To conclude, I would like to return to the general points that I stressed at the beginning of this chapter. The gist was that ritual could not be seen as acting out or emphasizing the basic cultural or social principles of the socieites concerned. In the example we have considered, the *opposite* of the situation that is seen to exist between affines is acted out in the ritual world. In the ritual world wife-takers are superior; in the nonritual world they are inferior, while the final position is one where neither are superior. This result seems to be the product of a complex dialectic between the ritual and the nonritual situations.

A second point concerns the nature of ritual communication and how this produces so-called symbols. I argued earlier and elsewhere that formalization removes ritual statements from the ordinary world so that another picture can be given which neither corresponds to the nonritual world nor is open to challenge from it. I have also argued that ritual and formalization are intimately linked with hierarchy and institutionalized power. State ritual or formalized speechmaking becomes a tool of traditional authority in the Weberian sense, in that it places the hierarchical order beyond challenge (Bloch, 1975b). In this case, however, we have a variation on this theme. The ritual starts like other Merina rituals with a formalized speech from a superior to an inferior delivered in the manner appropriate to kings and elders. However, the speechmaker is not heard in silence; the power of ritual speechmaking is broken by unritualized interruptions, that is, by the criticisms of the bride-takers, and has the effect of totally destroying their hierarchical superiority.

In a sense, therefore, the power of ritual is denied, but the ceremony remains a "play" on the other Merina rituals as well as on ritual in general.

This is the sort of complex situation we can expect in human ceremony, which is so much beyond, or, indeed, opposed to, the phenomena that have been discussed among animals and are equally distant from the processes by which meaning is achieved in more everyday situations.

References

Andriamanzato, R.
   1957 *Le tsiny et le tody dans le pensée malgache.* Paris: Présence Africain.
Bloch, M.
   1971a *Placing the dead: Tombs, ancestral villages and kinship organisation among the Merina of Madagascar.* London and New York: Seminar Press.
   1971b Decision making in councils in Madagascar. In *Councils in action,* edited by A. Richards and A. Kuper. Cambridge Papers in Social Anthropology, no. 6. London and New York: Cambridge Univ. Press.
   1974a Madagascar seen from Roti: A comment. *Bijdragen Tot de Taal-, Land-en Volerkumde* **130,** 348–352.
   1974b Symbols, song, dance and features of articulation. *European Journal of Sociology* **25,** 55–81.
   1975a Property and the end of affinity. In *Marxist analyses and social anthropology* edited by M. Bloch. Association of Social Anthropologists of the British Commonwealth Study, no. 2. London: Malaby. Pp. 203–228.
   1975b Introduction. In *Political language and oratory in traditional society,* edited by M. Bloch. New York: Academic Press. Pp. 1–18.
   1977 The past and the present in the present.*Man The Journal The Royal Anthropological Institute,* **12**(No 2), 278–292.
Callet, R. P.
   1908 *Tantaran ny andriana eto Madagascar.* Vol. 1. Tananarive: Académie Malgache.
Keenan, E.
   1975a Norm-makers, norm-breakers: Uses of speech by men and women in a Malagasy community. In *Explorations in the ethnography of speaking,* edited by R. Bauman and J. Sherzer. New York and London: Cambridge Univ. Press. Pp. 125–143.
   1975b A sliding sense of obligatoriness: The polystructure of Malagasy oratory. In *Political language and oratory in traditional society,* edited by M. Bloch. New York: Academic Press. Pp. 93–112.
Pitt-Rivers, J.
   1960 The egalitarian society, Actes due VIᵉ Congrés International des Sciences Anthropologiques et Ethnologiques. Vol. 2. Paris, France.
Rakoto, I.
   1965 Le Fafy est-il une simple levée des empechements au mariage. *Cahiers du Centre d'Etudes des Coutumes.* Tananarive: Université de Madagascar.
   1971 *Parenté et mariage en droit traditionel malgache.* Paris: Presses Universitaires de France.
Rasamuel, M.
   1928 Kabary am-panabadiana. Translated by M. Colancon. *Bulletin de l'Académie Malgache* (Vol. 9).
   1948 *Kabary.* Tananarive: Académie Malgache.
Sperber, D.
   1974 *Le symbolisme en général.* Paris: Hermann.
Turner, V. W.
   1967 *The forest of symbols: Aspects of Ndembu ritual.* Ithaca, New York: Cornell Univ. Press.

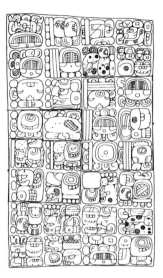

8

Some Aspects of Symbolism in Classic Maya Stelae Texts

MARSHALL DURBIN

Introduction

The Mayan inscriptions available today are found in a limited number of environments. On both the inside and the outside of ceremonial edifices, hieroglyphs accompany the pictorial representations painted and sculpted on the wall panels. Monumental stone sculptures (stelae) stand outside such edifices. Personages depicted on these monuments are accompanied by hieroglyphic texts. Of the many perishable manuscripts that must have once existed, only a few texts painted on fig-bark paper have survived.

The monumental art of wall panels and stelae constrasts with the fig-bark manuscripts in both style and purpose, and the two seem to have been directed toward different audiences. Wall panels and stelae seem to have been intended as commemoratives, either of events or of personalities responsible for events, while fig-bark codices served to preserve traditions of astronomical, mathematical, calendrical, and astrological purport.

Of these three glyphic modes, the stone stelae are the most stylized. The simple messages that they convey mask the elaborateness of the intellectual and political traditions that motivated them. Anyone with a minimal understanding of Mayan calendrical counting and its symbolic depiction can readily grasp the referential meaning even with little or no knowledge of the Mayan language used by makers of these stelae. One can assume that the information that they were designed to convey was of great importance to whole populations and not just to a specialized few. The structure and connotative meaning of these monuments will be explored in this chapter. Hypotheses related to perpetuation of power and authority in cultures with a strong central state will be formulated from underlying structural principles by means of which differing communicative systems can be equated.

Monumental Art in the New World

Among New World cultures that achieved monumental art of high quality, the most notable are in Mesoamerica and the Andean area of South America. Stone sculpture and monumental architecture abound in both areas; paintings also abound in the former, while the only known paintings in the latter are on ceramics. (Andean culture also produced metallurgy, largely unknown in Mesoamerica.) The symbolic content of Mesoamerican art is better understood than that of North and South America, with the exception of the ceramics of eastern Ecuador (Whitten, 1976) and Maquiritare architecture (Arvelo-Jimenez, 1971). Data on Mesoamerican symbolism was collected at or immediately after the Conquest, and some of the symbols are still in use today (see, for example, Andrews, 1970).

Mesoamerican Plastic Art

Monumental art in Mesoamerica dates from at least 1500 B.C. with the Olmec on the Gulf Coast (e.g., San Lorenzo, La Venta, and Tres Zapotes). Monumental architecture, sculpture, and painting (Chalcatzingo) were exemplary, with lapidary work, ceramics, small stonework, and painting also being extant. A rudimentary understanding of the symbolism of this work is only now being reached (Joralemon, 1970). While Olmec symbolism has no known predecessors, its iconographic descendents are found throughout Mesoamerica (Joralemon, 1970).

Concurrent with the Olmec are examples of monumental art in the Oaxaca area, particularly at Monte Alban. Here monumental architecture and sculpture are found; and during this time period, picture or ideographic writing appears in the form of hieroglyphs that seem to be the forerunner of all later hieroglyphic styles in Mesoamerica (Marcus, 1976). Later monumental architecture and painting appear in the Valley of Mexico, though hieroglyphic writing comes later.

Later developments in monumental architecture, sculpture, and painting are found on the Pacific Coast (Izapa), the Maya Highlands (Kaminaljuyu), and the Maya Lowlands (see Figures 1 and 2). All these later developments appear to derive some iconographic elements from the Olmec (e.g., flaming eyebrows, serpent mouth), hieroglyphic elements from Oaxaca, and many

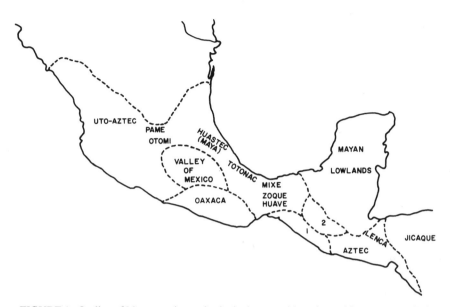

FIGURE 1. Outline of Mesoamerica and principal areas with native writing systems. Code: 1 = Pacific Coast, 2 = Western Highland area.

stylistic features from the Valley of Mexico. The problems of origin and diffusion are extremely complex and cannot be discussed here.

With the three early horizons (Olmec, Oaxaca, and Valley of Mexico) and their mixed progeny on the Pacific Coast and in the Maya Highlands and Lowlands, we can discern a number of features that characterize Mesoamerica, though not necessarily found throughout each region: (a) monumental architecture that has a religious, astronomical (hence intellectual), sociopolitical, and individual or personal significance (all areas except Pacific Coast); (b) monumental sculptures (including portrait sculptures) that have a religious, astronomical, political, and personal significance; (c) monumental paintings (rare along the Pacific Coast); (d) a stelae cult (wood and stone with sculpture and painting) that is lacking only in the Maya Highlands; (e) numerical, calendrical, and astronomical information painted and sculptured in bas-relief on buildings and stelae, and painted on folded books (perhaps lacking from the Olmec area);(f) the recording of personal names, birth and death dates, marriage dates, accession to power dates, and other sociopolitical information (e.g., victory dates, capture dates, spouse and offspring vital statistics) that is possibly not found in the Olmec area; and (g) the use of a hieroglyphic writing system that ranges from pure pictographic to ideographic to a phonetic writing system (least apparent in the Olmec area).

Figures 1 and 2 show the geographical relationships of these areas.

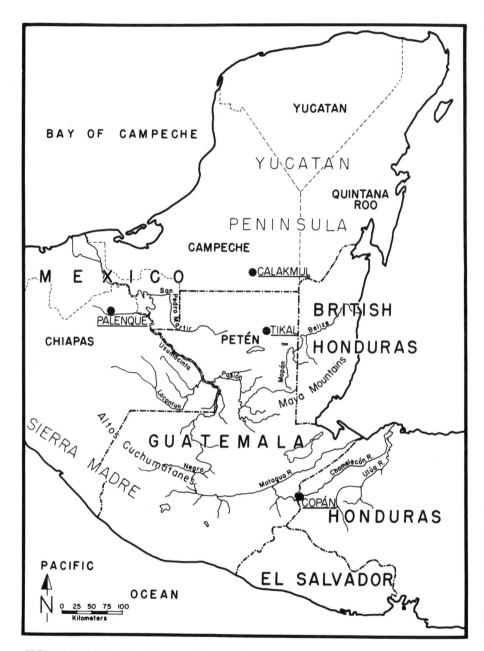

FIGURE 2. Outline of the Maya-speaking area (except Huastec; see Figure 1) with principal geographic and political boundaries. (Adapted from Marcus, 1976).

Lowland Maya Monumental Art Styles

All of the preceding symbols are found together in one time span in only one Mesoamerican area: that of the Lowland Maya. Convergence of these features occurred at a late date (approximately A.D. 250) and is confined to sites occupied by peoples speaking several Mayan languages. Probably not all Mayan-speaking Lowland groups possessed all of these symbolic resources. There are 10 distinct areas in the Maya Lowlands and adjacent hill country in which all features are found, although they are stylistically unique. These areas are shown in Figure 3.

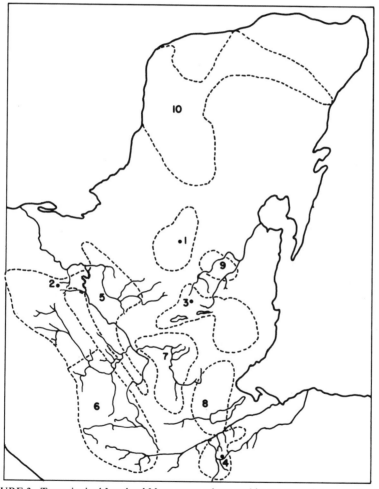

FIGURE 3. Ten principal Lowland Maya areas where architecture, sculpture, and painting are used in conjunction with hieroglyphic writing and the stele cult. Code: 1 = Calakmul, 2 = Palenque, 3 = Tikal, 4 = Copan, 5 = Usjumacinta, 6 = Comitan, 7 = Pasion-Machaquila. (Adapted from Marcus, 1976).

Hieroglyphic writing is routinely found on Mayan monuments. Panels on both the inside and outside walls of buildings are often decorated with portraits of individuals accompanied by an explanatory text. These are painted on the stucco plaster that coats the building. These buildings functioned as personal symbols (as the tomb found at Palenque), religious symbols, astronomical observatories (as at Caracol and Chichen Itzá), and sociopolitical symbols. Outside of the decipherable symbolism of the glyphs, most of the content of the architectural symbolism has been lost.

Clusters of stelae stood outside the buildings. These were sculptured, painted, or both, and ranged from a height of 3–35 feet. They were covered with portraits and glyphs, and conveyed political, personal, social, religious, astronomical, and calendrical information. The information on sculpted stelae has survived while that of the painted stelae has perished, but this can be surmised to parallel that of the sculpted counterparts.

Major sites at which hieroglyphic writing occurs are shown in Figure 4.

Codices versus Stelae

The ancient Mayans painted hieroglyphs and other figures on fig-bark paper manuscripts as well as on walls and stelae, but the manuscripts seem to have served a different purpose; unlike the paintings and sculpture, they contained very little information of a political or personal nature. Instead, their principal symbolic use seems to have been astronomical, calendrical, and prognosticatory in a general rather than a specific sense, with the manuscripts serving as a kind of almanac for an elite, intellectual group to use as a guide in influencing events. In contrast, the monumental arts were expected to be viewed and interpreted by the entire community. Today only three (possibly four) such codices still exist. Unlike painted manuscripts from other parts of Mesoamerica and unlike the hieroglyphs of monumental art, the Mayan codices apparently utilized a syllabic system of writing in addition to the conventional pictographs and ideographs.

Among Mayan hieroglyphic scholars there has always been an interesting division of labor between those—usually artists, art historians, mathematicians, and astronomers—who have been drawn to the codices, while architects, engineers, archaeologists, and other scholars who deal with material culture have been especially attracted to the sculpted material. Only two serious scholars have studied both: the late Sir J. E. S. Thompson and David Kelley.

The two basic camps have engaged in a long-standing debate about the nature of hieroglyphic writing. The issue argued is whether Mayan writing is phonetic or only ideographic or pictographic. Those who work exclusively on the three surviving codices (but principally the Dresden) tend to believe that Mayan hieroglyphic writing is phonetic (e.g., Y. Knorosov, F. G.

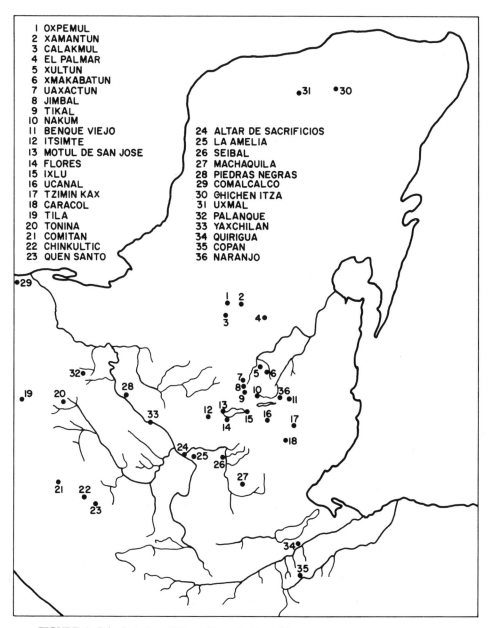

FIGURE 4. Principal sites of Maya hieroglyphic writing. (Adapted from Marcus, 1976).

The legend in the figure reads:

1 OXPEMUL
2 XAMANTUN
3 CALAKMUL
4 EL PALMAR
5 XULTUN
6 XMAKABATUN
7 UAXACTUN
8 JIMBAL
9 TIKAL
10 NAKUM
11 BENQUE VIEJO
12 ITSIMTE
13 MOTUL DE SAN JOSE
14 FLORES
15 IXLU
16 UCANAL
17 TZIMIN KAX
18 CARACOL
19 TILA
20 TONINA
21 COMITAN
22 CHINKULTIC
23 QUEN SANTO

24 ALTAR DE SACRIFICIOS
25 LA AMELIA
26 SEIBAL
27 MACHAQUILA
28 PIEDRAS NEGRAS
29 COMALCALCO
30 CHICHEN ITZA
31 UXMAL
32 PALANQUE
33 YAXCHILAN
34 QUIRIGUA
35 COPAN
36 NARANJO

Loundsbury, and previously B. L. Whorf). Those who are involved with the stelae believe that the system is not phonetic and does not have a valid language base. Of those who have studied both stelae and codices, Thompson took a strong stand against phoneticism while Kelley is strongly in favor of it.

Lounsbury (1973:100) who works principally with long texts believes that Knorosov's general hypotheses of the existence, within the inventory of Mayan signs, of a subset of phonetic signs for open syllables is one of Knorosov's most important discoveries about Mayan writing.

Proskouriakoff, who has worked with the stelae exclusively for about half a century, says: "Linguistic values assigned to hieroglyphs on monuments of the Classic Period have been little more than guesses that command no consensus [Proskouriakoff, 1973:165]." Similarly, Kubler, who has for the most part worked on architectural and stelae data, says: "Students of Classic Maya writing still are not sure about its nature as a system. Is it ideographic, homophonic, logographic, pictographic, phonetic, or syllabic? [Kubler, 1973:145]." Kubler himself does not believe that the system is phonetic but that it is an abbreviated, pictorial and ideographic aid to memory:

> Whole phrases, words, and ideas, rather than single sounds are conveyed by these pictorial glyphs of humans, animals and objects. . . . Their compactness, and the fewness of their parts support the belief that they are aids to memory rather than phonetic equivalents of speech [Kulber, 1973:159].

I am inclined to agree with portions of this argument. First, it must be pointed out that very little is known of the glyphic material in the codices. The texts are much longer than those on stelae and a wider variety of glyphs are used in the codices. There appears to be no portraiture of actual personages but only of deieties with anthropomorphic and zoomorphic features. Almost nothing in these codical texts is understood that is not numerical, computational, and astronomical information, and much of this meaning was determined over 100 years ago.

On the other hand, we know a great deal about the content of stelae. First, the texts are not long and only a few kinds of glyphs are used in each stele. The portraits on stelae appear to represent actual or former rulers. All stelae appear to contain approximately the same kind of information: the placement of a local ruler in time, the enumeration of his ancestry, his titles, his deeds, his marriages, his offspring, and sometimes his victories and his death. Only a few stelae do not convey such information and deal solely with numerical and astronomical data (e.g., all the stelae at Altar de Sacrificios). Historical information occupies anywhere from a half to a whole stele. It seems safe to say that we can interpret three-fourths of all stelae data. Furthermore, we need no knowledge of any Mayan language in order to understand it. Because of this, Thompson (1950) wrote:

> The interchangeability under certain circumstances of the position of affixes

shows, I think, that the arrangement of glyphs and elements which comprise them did not always correspond to the order of the spoken word . . . so one can perhaps conclude that the order of the glyphs is not supposed to correspond without deviation to the spoken sentence, but that all the essential parts are given so that the reader could arrange them and supplement them with speech particles . . . not represented in the text, to correspond to the spoken word, whether the reader was a Yucatec, Chol, Tzeltal, or Chontal priest [p. 51].

I would add that even a monolingual English or Spanish epigrapher can also grasp their basic meaning.

Who, then, were the readers of these stelae? Kubler (1973) suggests that "the original purpose of the Maya scholars who composed them was perhaps to make the meaning clear to the farmer from the fields regardless of dialect [p. 162]." This would mean that historical information was presented by a sophisticated elite to a lay audience. The sophisiticated systems that allowed their elite to compose and read painted codices, were little used when simplified texts were presented to the general public. A codex at that time would have probably been as incomprehensible to a lay reader as they are to us today. This dual system of communication is not dissimilar to our political broadsides or to modern-day Chinese wall posters that present historical and political information in a simplified style manipulated by an intellectual elite group.

Considerable evidence can thus be marshaled to support the contention that the stelae dealt with historical and political information in a simplified visual style intended for a lay audience of any dialect or language provided the reader had access to certain Mesoamerican cultural information. Portraits, ideographs, and numerical and calendrical symbols are included. The rulers and events communicated were probably already familiar to the lay readers to whom they were directed and, as Kubler stated in the preceding quotation, stelae served as mnemonic devices.

On the other hand, the message of codices is occult, and the texts and pictures seem to be directed to a highly specialized audience, probably a noble and priestly class that used the documents to perpetuate cultural traditions that they were trained to administer. This is similar to the uses of books and illuminated manuscripts of the Middle Ages when such texts were composed and read exclusively by a group of intellectuals who interpreted them to the masses. While it seems quite obvious that a more complex form of writing was used in the codices than on monumental art forms, its phonetic nature is not yet completely understood but seems to be at least partially syllabic.

Structure and Referential Content of Stelae

Stelae are customarily large, ranging in size to a height of approximately 35 feet. They are constructed of stone that usually has been brought to the site from some distance, and in bas-relief depict an elaborately accoutred male figure around whom hieroglyphs are arranged in rows, or only rows of glyphs without a figure may be present. A personage typically portrayed wears an elaborate headdress and is girdled with a loincloth with a flap over the pelvic area decorated with a grotesque facial image or mask. He holds a bar or staff and is provided with various animal adornments, especially parts or wholes of snakes, jaguars, deer, and large birds. Figure 5 shows such a depiction. Here a deer hoof projects over the face, and a snake-like protrusion emerges from the rear of the feathered headdress. A large bird decorates the chest, and eagle claws adorn the feet.

Glyphs are arranged into well-defined segments that Kubler (1973) called *clauses:*

1. Initial Series (IS) of glyphs appears on stelae; this consists of an Introductory Glyph (ISIG), usually occupying two glyph blocks, as shown in Figure 6 at position AB1. This glyph depicts the deity that governs the month and is normally followed by an IS date in a five-block sequence that includes a Baktun (period of 400 years) number, a Katun (period of 20 years) number, a Tun (period of 360 days) number, a month (period of 20 days) number, and a day (period of 24 hours) number. In Figure 6, the Baktun is 9, the Katun is 15, the Tun is 10, and the month and day are both 0. This marks the time that has passed since the data of August 19, 3114 B.C., arriving at the day 3 Ahau, which is also the third day in the month of Mol. This date may be that of an important birth or initiation ceremony early in life or some other event. A lay reader who could interpret this date must have known how to count by reading the bar and dot system and must have understood a calendrical system based on a month of 20 days, 18 months equaling a year, 20 years equaling a Katun, 20 Katuns equaling 1 Baktun and that after 13 Baktuns the earth would be cataclysmically destroyed. The reader must also have been capable of mentally manipulating a mathematical system with a vigesimal base. This does not seem unlikely since we are fairly sure that the vigesimal system was widely used by merchants and traders throughout Mesoamerica. Also we must assume that the lay reader knew the day-names and the month-names in their proper order and was able to calculate mentally a few days backward and forward from a given day.

2. On many stelae the next series of glyphs is the Nocturnal Series (NS); this series simply states which one of Nine Lords of the Night rules that day (Figure 7, B4). Its determination involves a simple mathematical calculation that again could have easily been performed by anyone.

3. The third series is the Lunar Series (LS); this gives various kinds of information such as the age of the moon, the length of the present lunar month, and the month of the moon semester (see Figure 7, A5–B6). Again, it is quite conceivable that a lay reader could have captured at least part of

FIGURE 5. Aquateca, Stele 2. (Graham, 1967).

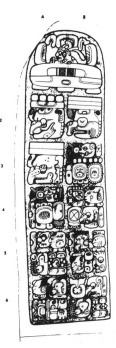

FIGURE 6. Machaquila, Stele II. (Graham, 1967).

the information since many of the Lunar Series glyphs have numerical coefficients.

4. The Secondary Series (SS) (Figure 7) may or may not have its own Introductory Glyph. This series instructs the reader to count forward or backward (usually forward) a certain period of time from the Initial Series date. There may be as many as 15 of these SS dates that are preceded or followed by action glyphs that mark events in history.

Throughout the text, names of persons and places appear, usually after the action glyph. Some place emblems are shown in Figure 8. Since stelae were often erected at 5-year intervals, we presume that most people would not witness the erection of more than 10–15 in a lifetime at a site such as Piedras Negras. At other sites, the erection occurred at 10-year intervals, and at still other sites at 20-year intervals. Thus the events, personages, and places depicted on newly erected stelae only repeat what is already known. Since rarely more than three or four persons were mentioned on a stele, we can assume that the reader could recognize the names of these important personages as well as the name of his hometown and perhaps a few other cities. More than four cities are rarely mentioned in a text.

Finally, the stele usually ended with an SS number that led to a Dedicatory Date (DD) indicating the date of its erection.

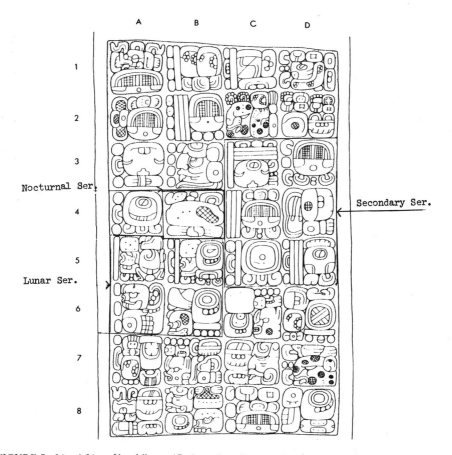

FIGURE 7. Lintel 21, Yaxchilan. (Graham, Ian, *Corpus of Maya Hieroglyphic Inscriptions*, vol. 3, part 1. Peabody Museum of Archaeology and Ethnology. Copyright 1977 by the President and Fellows of Harvard College.)

The amount of new or unfamiliar information needed for members of Mayan groups to interpret a stele was minimal but modern-day epigraphers are less fortunate since, while characteristics of individuals portrayed can be determined, names cannot be phonetically interpreted. Similarly, place names and their geographic coordinates, as illustrated in Figure 8, can be recognized, but we cannot pronounce them. We can infer the pronunciation of the action glyphs of birth, death, accession, and capture from modern languages, but in many cases we are surely mistaken.

Overall, the system was relatively simple even though drastically different from anything we know. I would expect that there must have been nearly monolingual Nahuatl speakers who could read the stelae as effectively as a Maya speaker since interpretation did not require knowledge of a particular language but only of certain cultural characteristics.

Yaxchilán   Palenque   Quiriguá   Copán   Naranjo

Piedras Negras   Calakmul (?)   Yaxchilán   Toniná

Motul de San José (?)   Seibal   Tikal

FIGURE 8. Emblem glyphs from some principal sites. (Marcus, 1976).

Over time, as more SS were introduced and more and more historical information was incorporated onto the stelae, a kind of truncation occurred. The IS and the ISIG were reduced to the day of the month and the day-name with its coefficient as seen in Figure 7. The Lunar and the Nocturnal Series were often completely eliminated. The day and month (Calendar Round, CR) would be followed by event glyphs and a SS date. Thus, a great deal of space could be saved and much more information could be projected. Finally at the end of the classic period, there was a degeneration of the system such that a personage was portrayed but the accompanying text, even though composed of Mayan features, makes no apparent sense. One can perhaps assume that such a simplification was possible because the form and structure were so familiar that a stele could be interpreted even when some elements were omitted or curtailed.

Each element in this structure must serve some referential purpose. The accouterments of the person portrayed undoubtedly identify him as a ruler (see Figure 5). The hieroglyphic messages refer to specific dates. Referentially the total message is simple, but the connotations of the message are inevitably far more complex, as we will see in the next section.

Connotational Conclusions

One function of a symbol is that it serves as a referential sign. The Mayan glyphs found on stelae, probably unlike many in the codices, are largely iconic, which makes a part of their referential meaning relatively easy to interpret. Other referential information is conveyed syntactically; that is, by relative position of a given sign within a total text. Some cultural knowledge is required before the referential meanings of the signs can be understood on either level. A great deal of connotative meaning can be extracted from structure itself (see, for example, Conkey's analysis of Upper Paleolithic art, this volume). Much of the evocative power of symbols seems to be connotative rather than denotative (see Sperber and Bloch, this volume). We can assume that this is true of those found in Mayan monumental art, including the monument itself.

While a sign, such as a linguistic sign, is usually arbitrary in the Saussurian (1959:68–69) sense that articulatory production does not determine meaning, its occurrence as an element in a total structural context is nonarbitrary and determines connotative meaning, which is global rather than specific in that it cannot be tied to a single symbolic component but is conferred upon the whole by virtue of the relationship between parts (for further discussion of this point, see Foster, this volume).

To abstract the structural information needed to interpret Mayan stelae connotatively we can start with the fact that these monuments *are* monumental (see Cohen and Brandes, this volume, for discussion of *size* symbolism) and that they are also *public,* that is, positioned so that they may be viewed and interpreted by large numbers of people. Further, they are referentially designed, as we have seen, so that they can be interpreted with a minimum of specialized knowledge, that is, they are culturally simplified in accordance with an easily replicable design. Depiction of male personages (*personage* rather than *person* is conveyed both through monumentality and elaboration of apparel and other attributes) is accompanied by vital statistics relating to marriage, kinship, dates of birth and (possibly) death, and other key events. Since the dates are real dates, corresponding to the epoch in which the monuments were erected, it can be assumed that the personages were themselves real rather than mythical. Real personages (as contrasted with persons) tend to be those in a position of power, that is, rulers.

Since monuments depicting rulers are familiar to us from many other cultures including our own, much of this would seem to be obvious. It is spelled out here only to show that the knowledge of meaning derives from structure. It is also worth pointing out that, although monuments of this type are found in many cultures, they are not found in *all* cultures, but only in those where power is concentrated in the hands of a central authority. They characterize the cultures that we call *civilized.* Monumental art and civilization go hand in glove; in fact, monumental art can be seen to *connote* civilization, the centralization of power in the state, and its duly constituted rulers.

For rulers must be "duly constituted" if they are to rule, and much of this depends upon the will of those who *are* ruled. In the Mayan case, those who viewed and interpreted stelae were those who must have sanctioned the rulers' power, that is, the masses who had little or no special knowledge of the kind possessed by those who must have authorized the erection of the stelae. The purpose of these monuments must, then, have been the maintenance of the kind of authority that they represented. They were used to persuade and it will be useful to examine the means by which they accomplished this goal.

The most obvious persuasive technique is the use of monumentality itself. The stelae are not only large and elaborately carved, providing the depicted ruler with a profusion of special attributes, but they are solid and *durable,* constructed as they are of a virtually indestructible material, suggesting a like durability for the ruling class. Not just an individual, but a *class* is connoted, for another striking feature of the stelae is their replicability. Just as one stele can succeed another after a determined interval, so one ruler, scarely distinguishable from the last, can replace another. This replicability has a cyclic quality that is echoed in the extensive use of cyclic calendrical information in the glyphic texts. All of this builds to a connotative message that is almost inescapable: The power of this line of rulers is massive, divinely sanctioned (as witness the Introductory Glyph, top of Figure 6), and eternal (as witness the cyclicity and endless replicability). Blood lines (as witness information about marriage and kinship conveyed by the glyphs) also imply both continuity and replicability of ruling traits.

More is implied. The stelae are phallic in shape, they mostly depict male rulers, and these males are portrayed with many masculine power attributes such as an elongated ceremonial rod of some kind, body parts of horned creatures or snakes, and a mythical face adorning a girdle or loincloth. The connotative message is unmistakable here because extensively redundant: Power is male, and masculinity implies power. Neither can be alienated from the other. One can assume that this message is not lost on the female component of the masses to whom the message is addressed.

The difference between the denotative and connotative functions of symbols may not be obvious. Culturally used objects are referentially defined both by form and use. For example, a chair, in our culture, is defined by its form as a free-standing and flattened object with a raised horizontal surface at knee height from which a flattened vertical surface of roughly the same height rises from one quarter of the horizontal base. The dictionary calls these two planes *seat* and *back,* but this definition is based on the use of a chair for a single person (with a single back) to sit upon. Connotations of furniture are quite different from this kind of denotative description.

For example, the materials and spatial arrangement of furnishings in Western society provide a great deal of connotative meaning if one is familiar with the system. Carpeting, sofa, style of desk, and artwork of the office of an executive allow one to infer the kind and degree of power and authority that he or she maintains. In America the bathroom is another powerful symbol of authority. Access to an executive washroom may be only by a key possessed by those authorized to use it, that is, those in a position of power. Other keys may separate the paying public from the public at large, or separate one racial caste from another. Even without a key, labeling according to race or sex and the presence or absence of various internal accouterments will effectively restrict its use to members of a single group. The denotative meaning of a bathroom is defined by its human uses for elimination and cleanliness. The connotative meaning is defined by the user. Because we have some familiarity with the cultural system of which the bathroom is one element, a little introspection will lead to a good deal of accurate connotative interpretation. This kind of introspection is clearly not available to the archaeologist, and yet the kinds of clues that lead to interpretation are very similar. The difference is that behavioral enactment is missing, and the archaeologist must rely solely on the form and distribution of material remains. The ethnologist, like the archaeologist, cannot use introspection as a method of determining meaning. He (or she) may ask questions, but this is more likely to elicit denotative rather than connotative replies. Members of a culture do not necessarily have conscious access to connotative meanings even when they behave in complete accordance with implicit connotative rules. These rules can only be discovered by concentrating attention on the relationships between elements in the structure, especially as these are replicated from event to event. If we consider Maya stelae as separate events, both formal relationships and replication is available, and much connotative information is forthcoming, as we have seen.

The medium—or the structure of the medium—is quite clearly the message. Either rulers erected their own monuments, both to aggrandize themselves and the state they represented, or it was done for them by others after their deaths. The permanence of the monuments reflected the permanence of the authority that each ruler in turn embodied. Since the erection of stelae was not sporadic but was governed by regular intervals of 5, 10, or 20 years at most sites, historical information could be selectively utilized and a certain amount of revisionism could occur. After 5 years, memories dull, and they can be permanently changed and fixed by means of a permanent, semireligious record. We can assume a certain amount of revisionism since no stele now known indicates any derogatory or unfavorable information about the ruler portrayed. Coupled with astronomy and astrology, history produces an interesting web over time. We have seen similar revisionism in our own day during the Watergate crisis in the United States and in the shifts in focus of Chinese wall posters as allegiance to particular individuals or policies waxes and wanes.

We can assume that the rulers were not disinterested in self-aggrandizement, but they were also elements in a hierarchical system and it was important to the system that it be maintained, with maintenance depending upon freedom from obvious weakness and emphasis on moral and physical strength. Rulers must be thought to rule well, to serve the community, and to be on the side of the gods, or they will be overthrown. The Maya, like other peoples before and after, understood that power must be sanctioned by the public, and they used the means at their disposal to create and sustain favorable public opinion.

In comparison with the fig-bark codices, the stelae used a restricted code (see Bernstein, 1967). The formalized messages that they provided were so simplified that speakers of many languages, sharing only a modicum of cultural presuppositions, were able to interpret them. Formalization increased over time in such a way that historical details diminished in importance. Formal reductionism in speech leads, according to Bloch (1975), to a restriction of options and a lack of specificity that limits communicational potential. This is the speech form used by those in positions of authority. Rather than using a wide range of comparison and cross reference, illustrations are limited and stereotyped; often they are presented oratorically as proverbs or scriptures. Thus, specific events are merged to those thought to be preexistent:

> The most important social effect of this merging of the specific into the eternal and fixed, is that it moves the communication to a level where disagreement is ruled out since one cannot disagree with the right order. The move towards the formalised therefore becomes a move in the direction of unity [Bloch, 1975:16].

Formalization of the messages of the stelae serves the same purposes as political oratory in Bloch's description. Use of a common code by wide numbers of peoples is only possible if it is greatly restricted. Common usage provides a sense of belonging that is necessary if the authority of the state is to be maintained. Stelae were the Mayan equivalent of mass communication, defined by Cherry (this volume) as unilateral in that recipients of the message are in no position to respond. According to Cherry, the very unilaterality of modern communicational systems serves to increase the dominance of authority. This would seem to be just as true of Mayan stelae communication as it is of television and radio in the modern world. Technology may change, but structurally and symbolically it would seem that in a broad sense there is nothing new under the sun. The convergence that characterizes the human species in contradistinction to the divergence of other creatures (see, for example, Kitahara-Frisch, this volume) is an ongoing phenomenon that is served by a variety of communicational technologies through history. Adaptive strategies for social and political continuity came into being with the advent of *Homo sapiens,* and have yet to be transformed.

Acknowledgments

I am extremely grateful to Margaret Conkey, Stanley Brandes, and especially Mary Foster for very substantive comments on this paper. If it had not been for her help, this paper would not have been able to appear. Naturally, I take all responsibility for its content.

References

Andrews, E. Wyllys, IV
   1970   *Balankanche, throne of the tiger priest.* Middle American Research Institute, publ. 32. New Orleans: Tulane Univ.
Arvelo-Jimenez, Nelly
   1971   *De'cuana social structure and political organization.* Ithaca, New York: Cornell University Press.
Bernstein, Basil
   1967   Elaborated and restricted codes: An outline. In *Explorations in sociolinguistics,* edited by Stanley Lieberson. *International Journal of American Linguistics* 33(4), 126–13.
Bloch, Maurice (ed.)
   1975   Political language and oratory in traditional society. New York: Academic Press.
Graham, Ian
   1967   *Archaeological exploration in El Peten, Guatemala.* Middle American Research Institute, publ. 33. New Orleans: Tulane Univ.
   1977   *Yaxchilan.* Vol. 3, Part 1 of *Corpus of Maya hieroglyphic inscriptions.* Cambridge, Massachusetts: Peabody Museum, Harvard Univ.
Joralemon, Peter David
   1970   *The features of Olmec art.* Washington, D.C.: Dumbarton Oaks Research Library and Collections.
Kubler, George
   1973   The clauses of classic Maya inscriptions. In *Mesoamerican writing systems,* edited by E. P. Benson. Washington, D.C.: Dumbarton Oaks Research Library and Collections, pp. 145–164.
Lounsbury, Floyd G.
   1973   On the derivation and reading of the "Ben-Ich" prefix. In *Mesoamerican writing systems,* edited by E. P. Benson. Washington, D.C.: Dumbarton Oaks Research Library and Collections, pp. 99–144.
Marcus, Joyce
   1976   *Emblem and state in the classic Maya lowlands.* Washington, D.C.: Dumbarton Oaks Research Library and Collections.
Proskouriakoff, Tatiana
   1973   The hand-grasping-fish and associated glyphs on classic Maya monuments. In *Mesoamerican writing systems,* edited by E. P. Benson. Washington, D.C.: Dumbarton Oaks Research Library and Collections, pp. 165–178.
Saussure, Ferdinand de
   1959   *Course in general linguistics.* New York: Philosophical Library.
Thompson, J. Eric S.
   1950   *Maya hieroglyphic writing: An introduction.* Norman: Univ. of Oklahoma Press.
Whitten, Norman
   1976   Sacha Runa: Ethnicity and adaptation of Ecuadorian jungle Quichua. Urbana: Univ. of Illinois Press.

III
NATURE AND
STRUCTURE

9
Introduction

MARY LeCRON FOSTER
STANLEY H. BRANDES

The "nature" of *Homo sapiens,* unlike that of other sentient creatures, is to create and maintain complex representational structures, in which denotative, connotative, and motivative features are integrated. If connotation is present in other mammals, it has, so far, not been detected in their behavior. Through experiments in which chimpanzees are taught language-based systems (Gardner and Gardner, 1971; Premack, 1976; Rumbaugh, 1977), the important discovery has been made that simple denotative systems are possible for at least some lower mammals to learn, and this faculty includes the ability to construct grammatical and even *novel* sentences in which selections are made from a limited number of syntactically appropriate paradigms. So far, motivation in these experiments has been limited to expectation of sensory reward, to be produced upon completion of the required behavioral sequence.

As Mounin (1976) points out, the apes in these experiments were taught to respond to rather than initiate communication. Responses were conditioned by expectation of reward. It is impossible to ascertain from these data the extent to which unprogramed gesturing might arise from a totally different set of motivations. Certainly, studies like those of van Lawick-Goodall (1971, 1973) indicate that chimpanzees exhibit a large range of gestural interaction, most of these gestures either directly or iconically related to the immediate situation. The iconic gestural capacities of chimpanzees were exploited only in the code-learning experiments of the Gardners (1971), based on American sign language, and their animal, Washoe, was observed in some spontaneous signing to dogs, other chimpanzees, and, introspectively, to herself. As Chalmers points out (in this volume), apes and monkeys integrate experience through manipulation, a characteristic that extends to the human experience and is clearly seen in the play activities of young children as analyzed in the study by Shotwell, Wolf, and Gardner (this volume).

Apes, like children (see Bowerman, this volume), have the capacity to extend categories, either by creating new words through compounding of old (Washoe's "water-bird" for "duck") or by blanketing in new objects as exemplary of a previously learned form (Washoe's extension of "baby" to include all small creatures). They are also capable of the type of cross-modal transfer required in translating a three-dimensional visual representation into two-dimensional form in recognition of known objects pictorially displayed. These examples show a capacity to use analogy creatively, which is a prerequisite for connotative competence.

Since processing information analogically is required for both primarily denotative and primarily connotative representation, one might assume that the same neurological structures would be involved in the two behaviors. However, a far greater degree of cross-modal transfer is required for figuration than for reference. *Arbitrary* use of a symbol transfers the analogy from qualities of the symbol to interactive relationships. If we were to say, "Let this ashtray represent Rommel's army and this notebook the opposing forces," there is analogic appropriateness only in the fact that two units interrelate in the context of a behavioral act. It has been hypothesized that the *arbitrariness* of phonology in the linguistic sign arose in much the same way (Foster, 1978, and this volume).

Lamendella (this volume) speaks of evocation as involving an evocative field localized within the appetitive or affective levels of the limbic system. He also postulates a bipartite associative field consisting of knowledge structures processed in posterior portions of the neopallium. (Sperber's *evocation* does not seem to differentiate these two types of association.) It would seem that Lamendella's evocation is at the most highly intentional pole and his association at the least motivated extreme. Triggering of intense emotion and its behavioral discharge through the degree of intentionality of the figurative act would depend upon a neurological process that does not seem to have been worked out but is necessary to the biosocial understanding of figurative affectivity in myth and ritual and the dynamic unconscious.

It is natural to assume that if connotative operations are possible for monkeys and apes, play is an appropriate place to look for them since fantasy operations begin in the play of human children at a fairly early age—slightly over 1 year. Yet Chalmers (this volume), using the careful methodology of ethological observation and analysis, warns us that play is by no means a unitary class of behavior and that we should not uncritically accept this category, given to us, as it is, ready-made by our language. This is a useful methodological warning for social scientists observing human behavior and often carrying unanalyzed, stereotyped categories from their own culture into their research.

If the fantasy-like operations that underlie figuration are present to any degree in the behavior of lower primates, they should be revealed through the careful analyses of behavioral sequences made by ethologists and physical anthropologists working with primates. To what extent these creatures can act "as if" is still very much an open question as Chalmers shows us. Most mammals seem to display "as if" behavior in playful wrestling in which no one is injured, or in hunting-like practice operations performed on inedible objects. Female chimpanzees play "as if" they were carrying babies. Male chimps brandish branches, "as if" warding off an aggressor. All of these acts seem to show the faint beginnings of figuration. This kind of study and experimentation needs to be developed and synthesized.

While open-minded, observational building of categories such as that used by Chalmers has an important place in constructing theory, end-state models can also be exceedingly helpful. If we are to look, as Chalmers urges, for homologous behaviors across species in order to understand human phylogeny, it is important to know what we are looking for. Lamendella provides us with a complex end-state model in which the painstaking observation and experimentation that underlie its assumptions are very little evident. It is an ambitious end-state model-in-progress.

Chalmers and Lamendella disagree on the extent to which ontogenetic studies are helpful in constructing phylogenetic hypotheses. Developmental psychologists, such as Shotwell et al., and linguists with developmental interests, like Lamendella, are likely to accept Piaget's (1970:13) thesis that since the phylogenetic formation of mental systems is not available to us, we should do the next best thing and turn to ontogenesis for an understanding of how systems of thought develop. Social development is, of course, different from neurological development and, in particular, different from the biological development of the fetus. However, Gould (1977) has fruitfully reopened the issue of the interrelationship of phylogeny and ontogeny, and it is apparent that Lamendella's equation of the two is based upon reasoning similar to that of Gould: that phylogenetic mutations occur ontogenetically because of adaptive variants in the gene pool and that these mutations become built into the ontogenetic biological structures of succeeding generations, later (i.e., ontogenetically) producing the appropriate behavior at the time that those structures are maturationally capable of allowing it. This is consistent with Piaget's discovery that children are incapable of performing certain cognitive operations until the appropriate age for them is reached.

The detailed observations of a small population sample made by Shotwell et al. are very similar in methodology to those carried out by Chalmers. In view of this, we can appreciate the statement of Blurton Jones (1976:429) that the meeting between ethology and developmental psychology is virtually complete. However, he goes on to say that the categorizations presented by our cultures are only beginning to be tested. Chalmers and Shotwell *et al.* test the category of *play* with detailed caution, one from a single monkey species and one from the American human standpoint. In their study, Shotwell *et al.* discover *style*. Ontogenetic styles of dealing with play materials are not standardized from child to child, and stylistic differences seem to persist into adulthood. Apparently, Chalmers did not discover stylistic differences in the monkeys he observed, although it may be that lack of communicative interaction between observer and subjects makes this kind of phenomenon more difficult to detect.

The styles described by Shotwell and associates are reminiscent of those postulated by R. Cohen (1969), who characterized schoolchildren's styles of organizing experience as *concrete* and *abstract,* a characterization that would seem to ally each to one of the two thought modes discussed by Sperber in the preceding, and to the cultural styles posited by Gladwin (1964) as *concrete* and *abstract.* Yet the fit between these models is not clear-cut. Shotwell and associates' styles do not contrast figurative and nonfigurative usages but the extent to which social interaction features in representational learning and the development of figuration. The "patterners" of Shotwell *et al.* are bemused by the potential variation in relationships, while the "dramatists" are caught up in acting these out and thereby testing their efficacy. Both seem to use denotative and connotative processes to the same degree but in very different ways.

Since style is an individualized variant, closely tied to emotional states and socially determined value systems reflected in dominant patterns of culture, work of the kind that Gardner and his associates are carrying out would seem to have particular importance for anthropologists and to be much in need of cross-cultural replication.

Questions of style will be pursued in greater detail in the following two sections. Here we would like to raise the phylogenetic question of whether the stylistic developments in *Homo sapiens'* behavior do not indicate a far greater degree of variability in the human gene pool than in that of any other species, leading to more rapid evolutionary mutations and a greater adaptability that results directly from the human figurative cognition capacity. Piaget's end-state model is concerned entirely with the ability to perform logical operations. While these seem to require more operational denotation than connotation, the cross-modal transfer required in perception of relationships seems to require a connotative analogic leap as well. Studies like those of Shotwell *et al.,* which are based on a *symbolic* (i.e., primarily figurative) rather than the *rational* (i.e., primarily denotative) end-state of Piaget, are bound to throw light on this issue, as well as on the related one of whether the kind of connotation required by fantasy is the same as that required for logical abstractions; for, according to Piaget (1970), "the roots of logical thought are not to be found in language alone, even though language coordinations are important but are to be found more generally in the co-ordination of actions, which are the basis of reflective abstraction'' (p. 19).

In the light of the phylogeny–ontogeny equivalences drawn by Lamendella, certain interesting inferences may be drawn by comparison of the Chalmers and Shotwell chapters:

1. Monkeys, like children, have little problem in mastering arbitrary reference. However, for children, the reward seems to be the mastery itself, while monkeys take a more pragmatic approach. Reward, for monkeys, need not be immediate but may be preceded by an interim "token."

2. Unlike human children, monkeys use antithesis as a classificatory mechanism only in yes–no choices. Humans give it indirect classificatory significance very early on.

3. Monkey use of materials (including their own bodies) is direct and referential from the start, except in the "as if" behavior of mock battles and threats. In contrast, children test materials in a variety of "as if" situations well before they are used referentially (*typically,* in the terminology of Shotwell *et al.*). Both monkeys and children test materials in the exploration of spatial relationships, but that of children shows a focus on *pattern.*

Homo sapiens is the only creature to use materials to any great extent without some essentially pragmatic goal, and the only creature to exploit technology innovatively for both pragmatic and nonpragmatic reasons. Part IV will focus on these uniquely human characteristics.

References

Blurton Jones, N. G.
  1976 Growing points in human ethology: Another link between ethology and the social sciences? In *Growing points in ethology,* edited by P. P. G. Bateson and R. A. Hinde. London and New York: Cambridge Univ. Press. Pp. 427–450.
Cohen, Rosalie A.
  1969 Conceptual styles, culture conflict, and nonverbal tests of intelligence. *American Anthropologist* 7, 828–856.
Foster, Mary LeCron
  1978 The symbolic structure of primordial language. In *Human evolution: Biosocial perspectives,* edited by S. L. Washburn and E. R. McCown. Menlo Park, California: Benjamin/Cummings. Pp. 77–121.
Gardner, Beatrice T., and R. Allen Gardner
  1971 Two-way communications with an infant chimpanzee. In *Behavior of nonhuman primates.* Vol. IV, edited by A. M. Schrier and F. Stollnitz. New York: Academic Press. Pp. 117–185.
Gladwin, Thomas
  1964 Culture and logical process. In *Explorations in cultural anthropology,* edited by W. H. Goodenough. New York: McGraw-Hill. Pp. 167–177.

Gould, Stephen Jay
  1977 *Ontogeny and phylogeny.* Cambridge, Massachusetts: Harvard Univ. Press (Belknap).
Moulin, Georges
  1976 Language, communication, chimpanzees. *Current Anthropology* **17**, 1–22.
Piaget, Jean
  1970 *Genetic epistemology.* New York: Columbia Univ. Press.
Premack, David
  1976 *Intelligence in ape and man.* Hillsdale, New Jersey: Laurence Erlbaum.
Rumbaugh, Duane M. (ed.)
  1977 *Language learning by a chimpanzee: The Lana project.* New York: Academic Press.
van Lawick-Goodall, Jane
  1971 *In the shadow of man.* Boston, Massachusetts: Houghton.
  1973 Cultural elements in a chimpanzee community. Symposia of the Fourth International
         Congress of Primatology. Vol. 1. Basel: Kargar. Pp. 144–184.

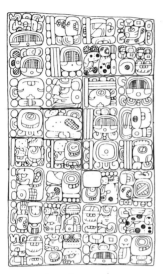

10

Can a Study of Nonhuman Primate Social Behavior Contribute to a Greater Understanding of Symbolism?

NEIL CHALMERS

Introduction

Since symbols figure so prominently in human societies, it is natural to ask whether their use is unique to human beings or whether they are used by any other members of the animal kingdom. Even if it turns out that symbols are unique to human societies, it is still pertinent to ask whether any other animals possess abilities similar to or foreshadowing those that human beings require in order to be able to deal with symbols in their daily life. The animals to which one most readily turns in a search for such *protosymbolic* abilities are the apes and monkeys, for these are our closest living relatives within the animal kingdom. This chapter discusses some of the behavioral capacities found in monkeys and apes that seem to resemble certain human behavioral capacities, and that seem to be relevant to a discussion of symbolism.

Before coming to these behavioral capacities, however, it is important to discuss some of the difficulties of comparing behavioral data from monkeys and apes with behavioral data from human beings. There are two major problems that face any attempt to apply knowledge gained from the study of monkeys and apes to human behavior. First, the major limitation that faces scientists investigating primate social behavior is that they are restricted to dealing with what can be objectively observed. For example, if two animals approach each other, it is possible to record their movements, gestures, calls, and reactions to one another; and from this, it is possible to make inferences about what mechanisms must be operating inside the animals' bodies to be controlling this behavior. Given sufficiently sophisticated equipment, it is possible, in certain cases, to record the electrical activity of the brain accompanying this behavior, the hormonal levels in the blood stream, and so on. If one animal snarls and gestures at another who then backs away, the human observer can interpret the first animal's behavior as a threat, and can judge what it has communicated by the recipient's reactions. The threat is defined as a threat, not by virtue of any emotion or intention imputed to the threatening animal, but on the basis of its observed behavior and the other animal's reactions. In short, those who study animal behavior deal in operational definitions of behavior, and look for their underlying physiological correlates. Their approach is very similar to the Peircean approach to the analysis of communication outlined by Colin Cherry (this volume). Given that the scientific analysis of animal behavior is limited to those aspects of an animal's behavior and their physiological correlates that can be objectively observed, it follows that many aspects of an animal's behavior are quite inaccessible to such scientific analysis. In particular, it is not possible to discover by scientific analysis whether an animal is aware of its own behavior, whether it perceives its own motives, or appreciates the rationality or otherwise of its own goal-directed behavior.

One major area of debate on symbolism is whether in any sense symbolism can be considered to be prior to rational behavior (see Sperber, this volume). Human behavior is usually recognized as rational not only by the fact that it is goal-directed, but also by the fact that the performer is in some way *consciously* directing his or her behavior towards the goal.

It is tempting to look at nonhuman animals for examples of symbolic and rational behavior in the hope of discovering whether symbolic behavior is indeed prerational. However, since it is impossible to know whether an animal is consciously directing its behavior towards a goal, one of the main criteria for identifying rational behavior cannot be applied to animals. Hence, animal studies can give very little information about nonhuman homologues of human rational thought.

What animal studies do show is that goal-directed behavior can be achieved by extremely simple organisms. Flatworms, single-cell organisms such as *Paramecium*, and many others can respond in a goal-directed way towards a feature of the environment (such as light intensity, humidity, acidity, etc.) by simple changes in the characteristics of their movements. The mechanisms controlling their behavior must be extremely simple, and most probably direct the organisms' behavior according to a set of elementary rules. (A fuller treatment of goal-directedness in animal behavior, relevant to the present discussion is found in Dawkins, 1976.) The fact that an animal's behavior is goal-directed and appears rational to the human observer is no guarantee, therefore, that the behavior is being directed by human-like, rational mental processes. Indeed, one of the most striking features that emerges from the study of animal behavior is how elaborate, goal-directed behavior can be achieved by relatively simple behavioral mechanisms.

The second major problem that arises when comparing data on the social behavior of human and nonhuman primates is to decide what significance any similarities that emerge between human and nonhuman primates might have. This can be illustrated by a trivial example. Maurice Bloch (this volume) shows how the ceremony of presenting the hindquarters of a sheep in Merina society is an act of self-abasement. Nonhuman primates also gesture submissively by presenting their hindquarters to their fellows. This similarity provokes, or should provoke, the response, "So what?" for it is not at all obvious that it has any significance. It also raises the question of how one should decide whether any similarities between human and nonhuman primate behavior are significant, and if so, what this significance might be.

A detailed discussion of this problem is inappropriate here, and is dealt with more fully elsewhere (Chalmers, 1979). Three main points need to be made here. First, if one hopes to gain insights into the evolutionary history of human behavior by studying the behavior of present-day nonhuman primates, then it is vital to survey as many aspects of social behavior as possible over as many human societies and over as many nonhuman primate species as possible. It is all too easy, by selecting isolated facets of behavior from one or two human and nonhuman societies, to demonstrate almost any similarity that one cares to choose between human beings and the other primates, and thereby to propose almost any trait of behavior as ancestral. Second, if one performs an extensive comparison of the social behavior of many human and nonhuman primate societies, it turns out that rather few features are common to all of them. There is an unfortunate tendency among those who seek to make generalizations about the social behavior of all primates, including human beings, to gloss over both the enormous diversity of such societies and the great gulf between nonhuman and human societies. In particular, there is a tendency to play down the importance of language, both written and spoken, and of learned, cultural factors in contributing to the structure and diversity of human societies. This has meant that considerable effort has been put into the search for features of social life common to all primates, human and nonhuman, in the hope that this will reveal features of human society that are inherited from nonhuman ancestors, while at the same time playing down the very differences that comparative studies show up so clearly.

Even when features of social life are found that are common to all primates, their evolutionary interpretation is not necessarily straightforward. For example, nearly all primate mothers, including human mothers, look after their infants for a long period of time and in a very intimate way. Nearly all primates, including human beings, indulge in play when they are young. In cases like these, it may be reasonable to assume the behavior in question was performed by the common ancestors of all today's primates and that it is from the early, primitive behavior of these ancestors that the present-day behaviors have been evolved. That is, it may be reasonable to assume that the behaviors are homologous. However, it could well be that many features of human maternal care developed completely afresh, as a result of cultural or other factors, rather than from preexisting maternal behavior.

Third, even if social behaviors that human beings share with other primates are assumed to be homologous, it is not necessarily the case that the factors that control their performance are the same. There is quite strong evidence, for example, that human smiling and laughing are homologous with certain monkey and ape facial gestures. It is clear, however, that the factors controlling laughing and smiling vary widely from one society to another. In some societies, as Ekman and Friesen (1969) have reported, laughter is apparently customary at funerals.

The importance of this argument is that it is quite unjustifiable to argue that a behavior that man shares with other primates is necessarily caused by the same factors that control its expression in those primates. Still less is it justifiable to assume that human beings have no voluntary control of those behaviors. Thus, if it were to be discovered that human beings shared with other primates a tendency to perform, say, aggressive behavior, and if it seemed reasonable that this behavior was homologous in human and nonhuman primates, it would still be quite invalid to argue that human beings are therefore unable to control their aggressive behavior voluntarily.

This preamble may suggest that nonhuman primate studies have no insights to offer into human behavior. This, however, is too pessimistic a view. It is worth comparing nonhuman and human primate societies not only to reveal any similarities between them, but also differences, trends, and patterns. It is useful, for example, to discover whether any features of nonhuman primate social behavior come to resemble features of human social behavior, the more closely related are the nonhuman primates to human beings. Where such features are found, it is especially fruitful to examine them in species that are most closely related to human beings, such as the chimpanzee. It is also valid and useful to discover what degree of social complexity can be achieved in nonhuman social primates with the simple behavior (in comparison with human beings) that they are capable of performing. One can then discover how far the complexities of human societies necessarily depend upon uniquely human attributes of social behavior.

Abilities Necessary for the Use of Symbols

It is clear that certain fundamental behavioral abilities are necessary if human beings are to be able to make use of symbols. There is space here to mention only three of these. The first is an ability to distinguish objects from one another, and to classify them. The second is an ability to infer from a sign or a stimulus information that is not directly contained in that stimulus. The third is the ability to pretend or to act "as if" something were the case. It is interesting to try to discover to what extent these abilities are present in monkeys and apes. If it turns out that they are present, then one is faced with the problem of deciding what, if anything, this shows about human beings' use of symbols.

The first of these abilities can be dealt with briefly. There is abundant evidence from the psychological literature that primates and many other kinds of animals can classify objects. A substantial proportion of the literature on instrumental conditioning reports on animals' abilities to respond to classes of stimuli that vary from each other to greater or lesser extents. If two objects that differ from each other slightly evoke the same response, the observer is forced to conclude that the animal does not distinguish between them. If two objects, no matter now closely similar they might be, reliably evoke different responses, the observer is forced to conclude that the animal does distinguish between them.

Perhaps more interesting for the purposes of the present discussion is the work that has been carried out on the signing ability of chimpanzees, by Gardner and Gardner (1971), Premack (1971), and Rumbaugh et al. (1976). Whatever interpretation is made of the results of these studies with respect to the animal's linguistic abilities, and this is a matter over which there has been some controversy, there is no doubt that the animals used in these studies can be trained to respond differently to different classes of visual stimuli. The precise nature of the stimuli varies from one group of workers to another. The Gardners use the manual-gestures of the American Sign Language (ASL); Premack uses colored plastic chips; Rumbaugh et al. use pictograms projected onto screens, and presented also on keyboards.

Inferring Information from a Stimulus Not Directly Present in the Stimulus

Written or spoken words, or symbols such as the Christian cross, are all stimuli that impinge upon the human senses and that people value at far more than their face value. They are not responded to simply as patterns of lines or bursts of sound. Human beings attach a meaning to those symbols far greater than is present in their simple visual or auditory content. It is interesting, therefore, to see whether other primates do the same. Since much, if not all, of human symbolism is bound up with communication between people, the obvious area of behavior to investigate in monkeys and apes is that of communication. More precisely, one needs to investigate how these animals communicate with members of their own species.

Monkeys and apes communicate by means of facial gestures, bodily postures, calls, and smells. Depending upon their species, they bark, grunt, twitter, squeak, yawn, grind their teeth, smack their lips, stare, raise their eyebrows, and so on. The question of prime interest here is "What are they communicating?" Briefly, research has shown that at least three different kinds of information are communicated. The first kind is simply the presence of the signaling animal. Some monkeys and also many bushbabies, lemurs, and their relatives deposit a pungent and long-lasting scent that appears to signal that the owner of the scent was at some time present, and may therefore indicate ownership of land. If the signaling animal is a mature female, the scent may also indicate her reproductive state. Many monkeys and also gibbons give loud, penetrating calls, which have been shown, particularly in a series of experiments by Waser (1977), to keep neighboring groups apart.

This kind of communication would seem to have very little to offer to the subject of symbolism, since the information communicated is so directly a property of the communicating mechanism. More relevant is a second function of communication. Many monkey and ape calls and gestures communicate the motivation state of the animal. As was explained earlier, an animal's motivation is not open to direct observation, and one can only infer the nature of its motivation during the performance of a gesture from the overt behaviors that accompany that gesture. An example from my own work on an arboreal monkey found in the forests of tropical Africa, the white-cheeked mangabey, *Cercocebus albigena,* illustrates this point (Chalmers, 1968).

Like many other species of Old World monkeys, these animals give three especially distinctive facial gestures. First, they stare fixedly at their opponents, raise their eyebrows, and tense themselves in a preparatory movement of springing forward. Second, they yawn, exposing the teeth. This is especially noticeable in adult males, because they possess long, dagger-like canine teeth. Third, they *lip-smack*; that is, they rapidly open and close the mouth rhythmically, several times, smacking the lips together in the process. Table 1 shows the behaviors that the displaying animals performed immediately after giving the displays. Staring and yawning are quite likely to be followed by attack, whereas lip-smacking is not.

TABLE 1
Number of Times Different Types of Behavior followed Three Kinds of Gestures [Adapted from Chalmers, 1968].

Gesture	Behavior of displaying monkey after giving gesture		
	Attacks	Remains with	Flees
Stare	6	12	0
Yawn	9	16	19
Lip-smack	0	21	9

TABLE 2
Reactions of Monkeys to Different Gestures

Gesture	Reaction		
	Attacks	Approaches and/or remains with	Flees
Stare	0	2	12
Yawn	1	7	6
Lip-smack	0	14	0

Table 2, which is most relevant to the purposes of the present discussion, shows the reaction of the animals at whom the displays were directed.

Table 2 shows that animals sometimes fled from monkeys who stared or yawned, but never from monkeys who lip-smacked. I, as a human observer, can say that the recipients of the gestures are reacting to the stares and yawns as threats.

Since the monkeys sometimes flee from yawning or staring animals, even when the latter do not follow up their gestures with active attack, one can infer that the recipients of the gestures are responding to the gestures per se, rather than anything else. These animals can be said to infer from the gestures information about the performer's probable future behavior.

This ability does not seem to be very remarkable, however, for two reasons. The first is that a monkey grows up among its fellows, and sees gestures being given and observes their effects throughout its life. It must sooner or later, therefore, learn the situations in which these gestures are typically given and the behavior that typically follows their performance. This means that quite ordinary processes of learning and memory will account for a monkey's responding to a gesture, even though that gesture may not be backed up, on a specific occasion, by outright attack.

The second reason is that most primate gestures, if not all, are not arbitrary signs, in the way that, say, letters of the alphabet might be. As mentioned in the preceding, a staring animal crouches in just the way that it would if it were in fact about to spring upon its partner. A yawning male displays its impressive teeth. The relationship between the nature of the gesture and its function is in fact a close one. Similarly, lip-smacking, which seems to promote affiliative behavior is derived, as Chevalier-Skolnikoff (1974) has shown, from the smacking movements that the infant makes when sucking its mother's nipple. Indeed, early ethological work on animal communication showed that many animal gestures and postures seem to emphasize the main features of attack or appeasement behavior. The parts of the bodies involved in the emphasis are often vividly colored, or move rhythmically or in exaggerated fashion, or are inflated. The evolution of such conspicuous communicatory devices is termed ritualization. Furthermore, when different displays have completely opposite functions, such as threat and appeasement, the displays are often directly antithetical to one another. For example, Tinbergen *et al.* (1959) showed that all of the threat postures of the black-headed gull involved the bird pointing its dark face mask directly at its opponent, whereas appeasement postures involved turning the head away so that the dark face mask was completely concealed.

Given that animal displays need to be clear and unambiguous if they are to function successfully, and given that the same is true of human symbols, it is possibly not surprising to find that both tend to be conspicuous and to make use, on occasions, of antithesis. The fact that the same ends are often achieved in human symbolism and animal communication, in no way means, of course, that the mechanisms by which those ends are achieved are the same. Convergence towards the same end by totally different means is a very common feature of biological evolution.

A third kind of information that can be communicated concerns items in the animal's environment. This has been demonstrated in an intriguing set of experiments by Menzel (1971) on young chimpanzees. Menzel was able to show that a young chimpanzee kept in a large outdoor enclosure could indicate to its fellow chimpanzees the location and quality of certain items that had been placed by experimenters in the enclosure, and of which only the one chimpanzee had any knowledge. If the objects placed in the enclosure were food, the *leader* chimpanzee's behavior would induce the other chimpanzees to move towards the food; if the object were something apparently noxious, like a plastic snake, the leader's behavior would direct the chimpanzees away from it.

The title *leader* is perhaps inappropriate here, for the chimp concerned did not necessarily lead the others to the spot, in the sense of moving on ahead of them. Nor did it give any special and obvious facial gestures to the other animals. Its fellows seemed able to interpret from very subtle postures and movements of the leader that, in Menzel's words, "something was out there in front."

Here, what is being communicated does not seem to be directly displayed in the sign used in communication. Nonetheless, it is not difficult to see how such communication could have developed through quite orthodox associative learning. Chimpanzees living in the compound would, over the weeks and months, have observed the behavior of their fellows, and would have noticed the detailed features of their postures and movements when moving towards food or away from noxious objects. In the light of this past experience, they would therefore have no difficulty in interpreting the leader chimpanzee's behavior during Menzel's experiments.

Associative learning abilities of monkeys and apes have, of course, been investigated very thoroughly by psychologists in the laboratory, and the many experiments showing that chimpanzees will perform an instrumental task for a token reward (which in turn can be used to obtain a "real" reward such as food) also show that a chimpanzee's ability to associate reinforcements with quite arbitrary and apparently nonemotive stimuli is highly developed.

The ability to associate *meanings* with quite arbitrary signs is, of course, demonstrated in the signing work mentioned earlier. The experimental animal needs to be able to associate a particular manual gesture, or plastic chip, or pictogram, with an object or action, or something more abstract such as "Yes" or "No." Using techniques such as these, it has been possible to show that chimpanzees have certain abilities that appear to be similar to those that are basic to human language. For example, Lana, a chimpanzee used by Rumbaugh and his colleagues, developed the ability to ask the name of an unknown object, and then to incorporate the name immediately into a request to be given that object (Rumbaugh, 1976).

It is probably worth distinguishing quite carefully between two different sets of abilities that chimpanzees display while performing such feats. The first is the ability to associate *meanings* with signs. As argued above, this would appear to involve no more than a normal ability to perform associative learning. The second is the ability to master certain linguistic skills.

To summarize this discussion of communication, research into primate communication shows that monkeys and apes have the ability to respond to displays performed by their conspecifics, that these displays usually represent fairly vividly the information that is to be conveyed, but that monkeys and apes can also respond to signs and stimuli whose resemblance to the information being communicated is not at all close. Insofar as human symbolic communication depends upon associative learning abilities, there is little problem in showing that other primates also have this ability in a well-developed state.

The strictures outlined at the beginning of this chapter need to be repeated at this point, however. The fact that monkeys and apes have well-developed associative learning abilities does not mean that human associative learning abilities are necessarily homologous with them. The fact that chimpanzees under certain conditions can display certain linguistic abilities similar to those that need to be used when humans speak in no way guarantees that the two sets of abilities are homologous. The neural processes underlying human linguistic ability might well be quite different from those underlying the signing abilities of chimpanzees. The chief point of interest that emerges from the chimpanzee work on signing, is that it shows what advanced and interesting things can be achieved by an animal with a chimpanzee's level of brain, rather than directing one to the possibility that the early ancestors of modern man and chimpanzees had a rudimentary linguistic ability, from which human speech and chimpanzee signing have evolved.

The Ability to Pretend

Human symbolic behavior often seems to involve a degree of pretence, or a suspension of belief about the superficially obvious nature of things. The bread and wine taken at the communion service, for example, either represent, or become, depending upon which branch of the Christian church is consulted, the body and blood of Jesus. It is interesting, therefore, to investigate whether nonhuman primates show any ability to pretend or act "as if" something were the case.

Of course, framed in these terms, the question is unanswerable for the reasons outlined earlier. Whether an animal is aware of its own behavior, whether it consciously plans that behavior, and whether it adopts strategies such as pretense are aspects of its behavior that are inaccessible to scientific analysis. One is forced, therefore, to take an altogether more indirect approach to the problem. One can do no more than ask whether any aspect of an animal's observable behavior or of its underlying physiological processes (which are themselves observable, given suitable instrumentation) suggest that the animal is performing its behavior outside the usual context in which it occurs. The area of behavior that seems most relevant here is play, and the remainder of this chapter deals with this topic. The aim of the discussion that follows is to analyze briefly what play consists of and what abilities it involves. Having obtained at least preliminary answers to these two questions, it is then possible to see how far an understanding of play in nonhuman primates illuminates human behavior.

The Nature of Play

Play is a poorly defined concept. Different authors use the term to include a wide assortment of seemingly different behaviors. These include, for example, the exploration of objects with the hands and mouth, as well as with other sense organs; gamboling and other "babyish" locomotor patterns, whether they are performed by a young animal on its own or by young animals during sequences of chasing and wrestling; and immature attempts to perform certain behaviors typical of and important to the adult. An example of this last usage comes from a field study of vervet monkeys, *Cercopithecus aethiops*, by Lancaster (1972), who describes the behavior in which adolescent females carry and hold infants in a mother-like way as "play-mothering." Another class of behaviors usually considered to be playful are *games*. Bertrand (1969), for example, describes in several different primate species a number of games, including "king of the castle," "hide-and-seek," and "tag." The definitive features of each game are not so much the particular motor patterns that the participants use, as the effects of these behaviors on the participants' position relative to each other and, often, relative to some distinctive feature of the environment such as a branch, termite mound, or creeper.

Games feature prominently, of course, in the play of children, as well as in the play of other primates. Not only do children play games defined in physical terms, such as "king of the castle" and "tag," they also play games in which they adopt certain roles: They play being mother, father, shopkeeper, and so on. Speech plays an important part in such games, and it is clear that man's verbal abilities make his play altogether more complicated and intricate than the play of other animals. This is particularly clear, of course, in formal games and sports, performed not only by children but by adults as well.

It would be very surprising if all of the types of behavior mentioned in the preceding, which at different times have been called play, had the same set of fundamental characteristics, were given in the same situations, and had the same functions. For this reason it is only likely to cause confusion if one indiscriminately lumps them all together, and analyzes play as a single category of behavior, either in human beings or in any nonhuman primate. If one is to discover what, if anything, the various behaviors listed in the preceding have in common, it is first necessary to analyze the causation, function, and ontogeny of each separately. It was in an attempt to do this that I carried out a 6-month field study on the olive baboon, *Papio anubis*, in Kenya (Chalmers, 1980). The group of baboons that I studied contained 66 animals at the beginning of the study and 71 at the end. Through the previous work of Dr. R. Harding and S. Strum at the site, all the individual animals in the group were distinguishable, and the ages of all animals that were less than 13 months old at the beginning of the study were exactly known. The ages of older animals were only approximately known. Since several infants were born into the group during the 6 months that I studied the group, it was possible to observe the behavior of individuals of ages ranging from newborn infants through to adults. By observing animals on a regular schedule at specific ages and by recording how often they performed various behaviors at each age, it was possible to obtain a detailed picture of how these behaviors developed with age.

While a subject was being watched, two different situations were distinguished. These were termed, respectively, *encounters* and *nonencounters*. Encounters involved the subject's interactions with group members other than the mother, and were defined by a consistent set of criteria. A subject did not spend all of its time engaged in encounters. In the intervening periods, it would either cling to its mother, or be close by her, and might either interact with her directly, or engage in solitary activities such as handling or mouthing the surrounding vegetation, making brief expeditions away from her, and so on.

Two results from this study are especially relevant to the present discussion. The first is that the various behaviors that are commonly lumped together as playful show quite substantial differences from one another in their development. In particular, two groups of behaviors could be distinguished. One contained a number of vigorous and acrobatic activities, such as running, jumping, climbing, and hanging. These first appeared during both encounters and nonencounters when the infant was 4 weeks old and rose to a peak frequency at about 16–20 weeks. A contrast was provided by a second group of behaviors, the most obvious characteristic of which was that each behavior in the group involved the use of the mouth, usually in association with the hands. They are referred to below as *hands and mouth* behaviors. One of these behaviors is commonly called the *play face* in the literature, but since this prejudges the issue being investigated, namely the issue of what constitutes play, it was given a different name in the present study, namely, *open mouth* (*distant*). Another behavior in this group was called *mouth and wrestle*, and consisted of a rough-and-tumble wrestling bout, in which the participants would frequently mouth each other. The other two behaviors differed in detail from the preceding two, but involved rather similar use of the mouth.

The four *hands and mouth* behaviors mentioned in the preceding almost certainly have a lot in common, and can be grouped together. It is possible to see, for example, how the more elaborate of the behaviors in this group develop during ontogeny out of the simpler behaviors. These four behaviors show a very different pattern of development from the vigorous and acrobatic behaviors mentioned earlier. They do not rise to a peak frequency at 16–20 weeks. *Open mouth* (*distant*), for example, was observed in 1-week-olds and reached its peak frequency from 2 to 8 weeks. The successively more elaborate behaviors each appeared in turn rather later, rose to a low peak, and then declined slowly. The last behavior to appear was *mouth and wrestle*, which appeared at 16 weeks, rose gradually in frequency to a peak in 2- and 3-year-olds, and then declined rapidly.

The fact that these *hands and mouth* behaviors show a different time course of development from the *vigorous and acrobatic* behaviors, together with other evidence that is not presented here, suggests strongly that these two groups of behaviors are different from each other. By "different" I mean that they differ in their ontogeny and in the causal factors that control their expression. It is interesting that both groups of behavior are widely regarded as components of play. Young animals run, jump, and climb a lot and thereby give the impression of playfulness. Similarly, the *hands and mouth* behaviors, which include the *open mouth* (*distant*) gesture (i.e., the *play face*) and *mouthing and wrestling,* are generally agreed by those who study primates to be playful.

There is evidence, therefore, that playful behavior in nonhuman primates involves at least two separate sets of behaviors, and probably more, if one takes into account the behaviors involved during the performance of games, or such activities as play-mothering. If this is the case in a nonhuman primate such as the olive baboon, it would seem that the situation is likely to be at least as complex, and probably a lot more complex, in human play. In short, if one is to investigate the abilities that are involved in playing, in behaving "as if" something were the case, or indeed the abilities that are involved in other uses of symbols, one must be prepared to face the fact that these abilities are likely to be highly diverse, controlled by a diverse set of neural systems, and elicited in response to an equally diverse set of external stimuli. It is unlikely, therefore, that any explanation of the neural substrate of human playful or related behaviors that is simplistic, or implies a unity in the behaviors under investigation, is likely to be successful.

A second point relevant to the present discussion emerges after examining the context and the order in which the *hands and mouth* behaviors appear during ontogeny. The earliest of these behaviors to appear during development is the *open mouth* (*distant*) face (the *play face*). This was frequently observed during formal observation sessions of 1-week-old animals, and was also seen during casual observation periods in animals younger than this. The gesture was rarely given during nonencounters, and rarely given towards mothers by their infants. It was almost entirely confined to encounters with other troop members, excluding the mothers. As the infant develops, so it becomes more mobile and spends more of its time off its mother. As it moves about, it tends to hold on to and mouth any objects that are not too large. This behavior is quite characteristic in appearance, and I gave it the name *grasp plus open mouth* (*contact*). The behavior appeared to be given indiscriminately towards any object of the right size, whether it was a fellow baboon, a leaf, a stone, or a twig. It first appeared in 4-week-old animals, and rose to a peak in 8-week-olds, and the time course up to 8 weeks was very similar both in encounters and nonencounters. After 8 weeks, the behavior rapidly disappears from nonencounters, but continues to be performed in encounters at or close to its peak frequency up to 36 weeks. The decline in nonencounter performance of this behavior is explained by the fact that over the 8–12 week period, the infant rapidly develops the ability, not just to contact objects with its mouth, but to put them into its mouth, to chew them, and to swallow them. Once the developing animal can eat solid objects, *grasp plus open mouth* (*contact*), which is an early and imperfect version of eating, is dropped from the nonencounter repertoire.

It is interesting to note, however, that this behavior is not dropped from the developing animal's social repertoire. It continues to be used in encounters with other group members, and it is one of the behaviors that most observers would regard as characterizing play. One can therefore see that components of playful behavior may originate in ontogeny from behaviors that are not limited specifically to playful situations, and that the situations that evoke these components can change during ontogeny. Again, this information may be relevant to studies of children's play. If one wishes to discover how children's play develops, it is essential not only to analyze objectively identifiable components of play, and to compare the time course of their development, as argued earlier, but also to look for the ontogenetic precursors of these behaviors, and to examine which situations, if any, specifically evoke both the components of play and their ontogenetic precursors. By doing this it should be possible to obtain a much clearer picture both of the components of play and of their ontogenetic origin. Once this is done, it may be possible to see whether the abilities that children use while playing have anything in common with each other and with the abilities that they use during other forms of behavior involving symbols.

Conclusions

Two final issues need to be mentioned in the light of the material discussed in the preceding. The first is the question of how symbolic behavior originates ontogenetically, the second is how it originated phylogenetically.

The data presented on the ontogeny of play in baboons show that a behavior that appears to have something in common with symbolic behavior has a complex ontogenetic origin, and is in fact a cluster of behaviors, some of which have more in common with one another than others. Some, indeed, appear to have more in common with behaviors not normally regarded as playful than they do with other components of playful behavior. It is likely, therefore, that the ontogenetic origin of human behaviors that involve symbolism is at least as complicated and diverse. This also suggests that one should beware of elevating *symbolism* to the status of a class of behavior, distinct and separate from other classes of behavior. Rather, its components should be investigated separately, and their relationships with one another analyzed.

The question of how symbolic abilities might have originated phylogenetically is, of course, more speculative. It used to be fashionable in biology to argue that the ontogenetic sequence of development of an organism recapitulated its phylogenetic history; that is, that by investigating the sequence in which features developed during ontogeny, it would be possible to discover the sequence in which the same features developed in adults during evolutionary history. As De Beer (1958), and, more recently, Gould (1977) have shown, such a simple view is nowadays untenable. Certainly the relationship between ontogeny and phylogeny is a crucial one. As both of the preceding authors have shown, changes in the rate of development of certain morphological features during development can have profound evolutionary consequences. However, one cannot obtain a potted version of a species' evolutionary history simply by looking at its ontogeny.

There is, however, another way of gaining information about a species' phylogeny that is potentially available. This is the method similar to that used by comparative anatomists, and mentioned at the beginning of this chapter. This is to survey a group of related animals and to look for features that are common to all of them. If such features are found, and if they are sufficiently similar to be thought to be homologous, then it follows than the ancestors of these animals would have possessed them too.

Looking back over the abilities described earlier in this chapter, it seems that two of the abilities described there, the ability to classify objects and the ability to infer from a stimulus information that is not directly contained in that stimulus, are present in monkeys and apes as well as humans. It also seems that these abilities, at least in their simpler manifestations, can be explained in terms of orthodox associative learning abilities. One can therefore argue that if these abilities are homologous, then the ancestors of present-day human beings possessed them too. With the abilities that are involved in language, it is very difficult to be certain whether the signing abilities of chimpanzees and the linguistic abilities of humans are homologous, and it becomes correspondingly difficult to decide at what stage in human evolutionary history these abilities first appeared.

References

Bertrand, Mireille
   1969   *The behavioural repertoire of the stumptail macaque.* (*Bibliotheca Primatologica* No. 11). Basel: Karger.
Chalmers, Neil R.
   1968   The visual and vocal communication of free-living mangabeys in Uganda. *Folia primatologica* **9**, 258–280.
   1979   *Social behavior in primates* London: Edw. Arnold.
   1980   The ontogeny of play in feral olive baboons (*Papio anubis*). *Animal Behaviour* **28**. (In press)
Chevalier-Skolnikoff, Suzanne
   1974   The ontogeny of communication in the stumptail macaque (*Macaca arctoides*). *Contributions to Primatology* (No. 2.) Basel: Karger.
Dawkins, Richard
   1976   Hierarchical organization: A candidate principle for ethology. In *Growing points in ethology*, edited by P. P. G. Bateson and R. A. Hinde. London and New York: Cambridge Univ. Press. Pp. 7–54.
de Beer, Gavin
   1958   *Embryos and ancestors,* 3rd ed. London and New York: Oxford Univ. Press (Clarendon).
Ekman, Paul and Wallace V. Friesen
   1969   The repertoire of nonverbal behaviour: Categories, origins, usage and coding. *Semiotica* **1**, 49–98.
Gardner, Beatrice, and R. Allen Gardner
   1971   Two-way communication with an infant chimpanzee. In *Behavior of nonhuman primates*. Vol. 4, edited by A. H. Schrier and F. Stollnitz. London: Academic Press. Pp. 117–184.
Gould, Stephen J.
   1977   *Ontogeny and phylogeny*. Cambridge, Massachusetts: Harvard Univ. Press (Belknap).

146 | NEIL CHALMERS

Lancaster, Jane B.
  1972 Play-mothering: The relations between juvenile females and young infants among free-ranging vervet monkeys. In *Primate socialization,* edited by F. E. Poirier. New York: Random House. Pp. 83–104.
Menzel, Emil W.
  1971 Communication about the environment in a group of young chimpanzees. *Folia primatologica* **15,** 220–232.
Premack, David
  1971 On the assessment of language competence in the chimpanzee. In *Behavior of non-human primates.* Vol. 4, edited by A. M. Schrier and F. Stollnitz. New York: Academic Press. Pp. 185–228.
Rumbaugh, Duane M.
  1976 *Language learning by a chimpanzee: The Lana project.* New York: Academic Press.
Tinbergen, Niko
  1959 Comparative studies on the behaviour of gulls (*Laridae*): A Progress report. *Behaviour* **15,** 1–70.
Waser, Peter M.
  1977 Individual recognition, intra-group cohesion and intergroup spacing: Evidence from sound playback to forest monkeys. *Behaviour* **60,** 28–74.

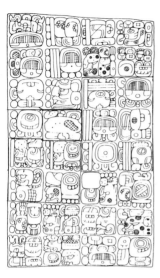

11

Neurofunctional Foundations of Symbolic Communication

JOHN T. LAMENDELLA

Introduction

The nature of cultural, including linguistic, interaction depends on the uniquely human capacity for employing complex symbolic representations in the expression of meaning. Research in the neurosciences has been making steady advances in understanding the physiological mechanisms determining the biological and psychological response of members of our species to the environment in which development takes place. At the same time, studies of symbolic behavior in the social sciences have enhanced our understanding of the cultural and psychological factors underlying particular patterns of social behavior. In the belief that both types of research endeavors can be significantly advanced if the phenomena described from each perspective are correlated, I have attempted in this chapter to present a neurofunctional model that I hope has the potential to support such correlations. The approach is based on certain well-established neurophysiological and psychological facts combined with some conjectural leaps, derived from empirical evidence that is highly suggestive, but not as yet thoroughly substantiated.

This chapter provides a provisional synthesis of an interlocking body of empirical results and theoretical conclusions spanning many years and several disciplines. In order to relate macrobehavior to microbehavior within a unified framework, I will abstract relevant characteristics of neurofunctional organization and present them as general principles. Some of these principles have been taken intact from the *organismic–holistic* approach to development (see, for example, Werner and Kaplan, 1963), Piagetian *genetic epistomology* (Piaget, 1971), and the *functional* approach to neural organization (Milner, 1967). Certain theoretical applications of these principles to the area of second-language acquisition may be found in Lamendella (1977a, 1978) and Selinker and Lamendella (1978).

Any adequate theory of symbolic behavior necessarily encompasses developmental considerations, since at birth, the human infant is clearly not yet physiologically or psychologically equipped to make complex symbolic responses to the environment. As functional systems in the brain become progressively activated during the process of ontogenetic maturation, there gradually arises the capacity for engaging in symbolic interactions that characterizes the normal human adult. The neurofunctional systems responsible for this capacity are integrated with all other brain systems in a complex hierarchical fashion. Their character in particular individuals derives from some specific combination of genetic and environmental factors operating over the span of development. The activity of neurofunctional systems, based in neurophysiological microbehavior, becomes manifested overtly in publicly observable macrobehavior, and leads to the successive implementation of behavioral responses and strategies described in the chapters by Bowerman and Shotwell *et al.* in this volume.

The fuctional capacities for semiotic behavior that characterize the modern human species are clearly the product of the long evolutionary history of vertebrates. Thus, the comparative study of mammalian behavior and physiology, especially that of our closest primate relatives (see Chalmers, this volume), coupled with a thorough study of the archaeological record (see Kitahara-Frisch, Conkey, this volume), provides two additional bases for a temporally extended understanding of the nature of human symbolic activity, an understanding that can be usefully correlated with insights into ontogenetic development and normal adult behavior to provide a more comprehensive grasp of symbolic behavior.

The investigation of symbolic information processing can also be furthered by a study of neurological disorders, especially aphasic disorders of speech (see, for example, Lamendella, 1979). Pathological manifestations of human symbolizing behavior arising from disruption of neural information processing systems can provide useful information concerning the normal human condition that is otherwise difficult to obtain, information that (in principle) cannot be obtained from the study of other species.

It should be noted, however, that most of the work in neurolinguistics and neuropsychology has been carried out from a microbehavioral perspective that stresses the anatomical structure and physiological activity of neurons and neuron aggregates. In both experimental neuropsychology and theoretical neurolinguistics, one is more likely to find discussions of overt changes in behavior resulting from damage to specific anatomical brain structures, than comprehensive models of the functional organization of neural information processing systems (Pribram, 1971, being one exception to this rule). Anthropologists and linguists who feel that the study of the brain must have contributions to make to an understanding of culture and language may therefore be led to believe that the neurosciences have not yet progressed sufficiently to be useful to them precisely because most empirical results have been formulated in microbehavioral terms that are difficult to relate to a sociocultural perspective. Until these results are translated into functional models of neural systems (see Laughlin, this volume), they will likely be of little use to social scientists untrained in the intricacies of neuroanatomy and neurophysiology. Even though functional models such as that attempted here are provisional, and sometimes amount to little more than "best guesses" derived from a synthesis of suggestive (rather than definitive) studies, these models can nevertheless serve as theoretical bridges between microbehavioral approaches in neurophysiology and macrobehavioral approaches in the social sciences.

Whereas social scientists interested in symbolic behavior are obviously not obliged themselves to operate from a neural perspective, they would do well at least to become aware of developments in this area since any complete theory of symbolic behavior must be consistent with known properties of the neural systems producing that behavior. Correlating a neurofunctional theory with sociofunctional hypotheses concerning the nature of symbolic behavior can be of relevance both to normal and pathological functioning in social interaction. Such a theory is simultaneously relevant to understanding both the ontogenetic development of symbols and the nature of the evolutionary processes that have given rise to the capacity for symbolic interaction that is characteristic of modern *Homo sapiens*.

From whichever perspective the problem is approached, it is clear that many of the controversies surrounding the investigation of symbols have been terminological rather than substantive. Some investigators argue categorically that the relation between a *symbol* and what is symbolized is *arbitrary*, while other argue with equal conviction that the sole basis for the relationship is *similarity*, or *continuity*, or *part-for-whole relationships*. In fact, an examination of the full range of human semiotic functioning shows that each of these types of relationships plays a part. Rather than use the term *symbol* generically for the entire range of human semiotic activity, here the term will be applied by definition to only one main category of semiotic information processing, without any implication that this category somehow inherently deserves the label *symbol* in favor of other semiotic categories. Thus, the focus of this chapter is a series of six, hierarchically integrated semiotic functions: *sign, index, signal, icon, metaphor,* and *symbol* (see Table 1).

Here, a symbol will be viewed as a specialized type of internal cognitive representation rather than the publicly observable product of symbolic information processing activity (here called the *symbolic vehicle* in accord

TABLE 1
Outline of Semiotic Functions from a Neurofunctional Perspective

Signifier	Basis for establishing the relationship	Semiotic perspective	Communication perspective	Information processing basis
Sign	Spatial or temporal continuity	Primary sign coding	One-way communication	Action coding
Index	Spatial or temporal continuity	Index coding	One-way communication	Correlative coding
			Interactive communication	⊛
Signal	Part-for-whole relationship	Signal coding	Intentional communication	Part-for-whole coding
Icon	Perceptual similarity	Iconic representation	Icon communication	Equivalence mapping
			Somatic depiction communication	
Metaphor	Conceptual similarity	Metaphoric association	Metaphoric communication	Similarity mapping
Symbol	Arbitrary relationship, established by convention	Autonomous symbolic representation	Gestural communication	Realization maps
			Lexical communication	Semantic maps
		Propositional symbolic representation	Language communication	Actualization rules

with Werner and Kaplan, 1963). It is further assumed that the nature of human symbol systems is constrained by the general patterns of neurofunctional organization and that, over the course of human neural evolution, the "blueprints" for these systems became encoded into the genotype of the species in varying degrees and manners. As a result of this evolutionary process, patterns of symbolic behavior emerge in particular ontogenetic sequences, permitting adaptive types of behavior to arise in the normal infant and child, provided that the appropriate environmental conditions are present during development.

Functional Organization of the Brain

The nervous system as a whole coordinates the adaptive behavior of the individual, thereby promoting both self and species survival. From a functional perspective, the nervous system may be viewed as being composed of a set of *neurofunctional systems,* emergent gestalts in terms of which culture, cognition, and communication may be investigated and understood. Neurofunctional systems have both anatomical and physiological correlates which, at present, can be localized within the nervous system only to a limited degree. Each of these systems governs information processing activity in specialized functional domains. The *function* of any given system may be identified in terms of its specialized input–output relations, and its *functional role(s)* by the net result of the system's activity for the organism as a whole.

The vertebrate nervous system is arranged into an ordered series of interpenetrating anatomical strata, each stratum being characterized by unique patterns of physiological activity. Information processing functions arise from the activity of neurofunctional systems correlated with given levels of anatomical structure and physiological activity (see Figure 1). The levels and types of cognitive information processing possible for any given mammalian species is independent on the nature of neural organization present in that species, and exists in direct proportion to the degree and nature of anatomical, physiological, and functional specializations. The six-layered neocortex of the *cerebral hemisphers* (Figure 1) is the highest level of anatomical organization present in the human brain, and neocortical systems are responsible for the cognitive capabilities characteristic of our species.

The degree of functional complexity that marks human neural systems is the end result of a long evolutionary process during which new anatomical structures and functions developed in succession, in relatively discrete stages, from existing structures. These changes often involved an increase in the anatomical size and configuration of particular structures, qualitative changes in physiological and functional organization, and increases in overall information processing potential as existing structures took on new functions. New structures arose and carried out old functions in new ways. Functionally, the hierarchical nature of brain organization is manifested by the manner in which systems at a lower level become incorporated (in either phylogenetic evolution or ontogenetic development) into higher level gestalts, *metasystems,* which may be viewed as systems made up of systems. The information processing capabilities of a metasystem cannot be predicted a priori by the properties of its component systems, but arise from the novel pattern of activity characteristic of the metasystem as a whole (Novikoff, 1945; Schneirla, 1957).

Phylogeny of Neurofunctional Systems

Comparative studies of existing species show that the overall trend in the evolution of the nervous system has been toward a progressive structural differentiation, with increased functional specialization and interdependence of components. As the vertebrate brain evolved, it developed a hierarchial functional organization in which more recently developed anatomical and physiological correlates of functional systems tend to sit at higher levels than

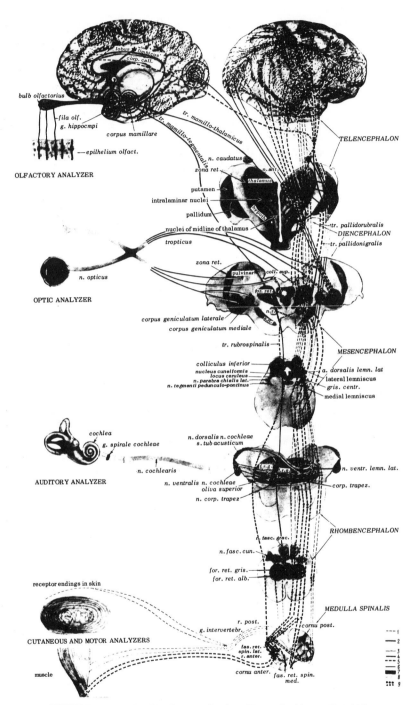

OLFACTORY ANALYZER

OPTIC ANALYZER

AUDITORY ANALYZER

CUTANEOUS AND MOTOR ANALYZERS

TELENCEPHALON

DIENCEPHALON

MESENCEPHALON

RHOMBENCEPHALON

MEDULLA SPINALIS

FIGURE 1. Levels of brain organization. (From Sarkisov, 1966:232).

those that had evolved earlier. The anatomical organization of the structural correlates of a higher-level neurofunctional system initially tends to preserve the segmental or topological organizational pattern of the lower structures out of which they evolved (Milner, 1967). As new functional systems arose, their genetic substrata became incorporated into the gene pool of the species. The successive stages of phylogenetic evolution gave rise to a general pattern of more-or-less parallel maturational stages in the ontogenetic development of the individual (Waddington, 1966). For this reason, ontogenesis can (when appropriate cautions are employed; see Lamendella, 1976, for discussion) serve as a guide for the reconstruction of hypothetical phylogenetic stages in neural and functional evolution. This is fortunate, since comparative anatomy and physiology can carry us only so far in view of the sizable behavioral and functional gap existing between us and our closest existing primate relatives.

The evolutionary development of the vertebrate nervous system took place in such a way that new structures came to be added to existing structures located at the head end of the organism, with older structures remaining present in a modified form (see Milner, 1967). This process has resulted in a more-or-less steady increase in absolute and relative brain size along the ascending phylogenetic scale (see Jerison, 1973). The *telencephalon* division of the forebrain (see Figure 1) has shown the most dramatic increase in size and complexity over the course of mammalian evolution. Less dramatic, but significant changes have, however, occurred in the midbrain and hindbrain, and also in the lower divisions of the forebrain. The *limbic system,* the primary source of affective arousal and social communication in mammals (see Lamendella, 1977b), while often neglected in considerations of neural advances in human evolution, has in fact also been marked by increases in size and complexity (Crosby and Humphrey, 1941; Stephan and Andy, 1970).

Basic aspects of the evolution of the human brain can be deduced by comparative investigations of existing species since the neuroanatomy and neurophysiology of our species is, up to some point, *homologous* with (i.e., has the same evolutionary origin and function) structures and activities in other species (see Dingwall, 1979). Such comparisons suggest a series of progressive stages in the development of the hominoid and hominid brain leading to the functional specializations characteristic of modern *Homo sapiens.*

As each new anatomical structure arose during evolution, there has been a general tendency for that structure to be involved with already existing functions, with new functional capacities for that system arising only at some later point as the new anatomy and physiology become more specialized (Mayr, 1963). The full range of human symbolic activity is possible only because of the high degree of functional specialization in the highest-level neocortical systems of the telencephalon, even while these high-level systems remain tightly integrated with lower-level systems in a complex, hierarchical fashion. It seems clear, then, that the functional basis for symbolic communication in *Homo sapiens* did not emerge from a mere "reorganization" of brain parts already existing in ancestral vertebrates. Our cultural, cognitive, and communicative potentials rest on anatomical, physiological, and functional adaptations that no other existing species possesses (see Dingwall, 1979; Geschwind, 1964).

The manner in which human symbolic information processing capabilities arose evolutionarily is obviously far from being completely understood, but our understanding of the phylogenetic development of capacities for symbolic and linguistic behavior has been steadily advancing (see Dingwall, 1979; Harnad *et al.*, 1976). There can be little doubt that the reflex of phylogenetic stages in symbolic development has become encoded into the human genotype. The degree to which even our closest primate relative, the chimpanzee, shares this genetic potential is not yet clear. The precise extent to which, under laboratory training conditions, other primates can muster symbolic and linguistic capabilities has been a matter of some dispute (see Hill, 1978). Even though chimpanzees have been found capable of behavioral learning that is to some extent comparable to human symbolizing, the significance of these behaviors cannot be understood until more is known about the functional process systems homolgous to those that trained chimpanzees are actually employing, then the capacity of chimpanzees to learn rudimentary symbolic and verbal behavior can have only limited value in illuminating human symbolic evolution. If it should turn out that neural homologues do, in fact, exist in humans, then, exercising due caution, we could eventually draw far-reaching inferences about major aspects of the evolution of symbolic behavior in ancestral hominids that led to the more complex communicational capabilities of modern humans.

Another avenue for making probabilistic inferences about the neurofunctional evolution of the genus *Homo* is the investigation of progressive changes of behavioral patterns manifested in the archaeological record. Since we know a good deal concerning the types of behavioral potential that accompanies specific neurofunctional changes during the human maturational process, we can perhaps support hypotheses concerning the point at which these same behaviors existed in prehistory, and assume that the appropriate neurofunctional systems were also already operational. This comparative analysis has scarcely begun, but archaeological studies focused on stages of behavioral development, such as those of Kitahara-Frisch and Conkey (this volume) provide an initial framework to which the type of functional model proposed here can be compared. Even at this stage, one can see the developmental levels posited in the two approaches are rather similar. Future research should take such similarities into account as further hypotheses are tested against the ontological and behavioral phylogenetic evidence.

The Ontogeny of Neurofunctional Systems

Each new human infant is the benefactor of our long evolutionary history. The progressive manner in which species-wide neurofunctional systems become operational in human ontogeny is the result of genetically regulated responses to the environment in which development takes place. However, at successive ontogenetic maturational stages, the child possesses radically different functional capacities arising from different neural substrata. Little would be gained, for example, in positing the existence of any sort of symbolic behavior (in the sense defined here) for the neonate or young infant, since the neural systems responsible for symbolic behavior are not yet operational at this point. Identifying the manner in which particular semiotic systems become operational and contribute to the emergence of new functional gestalts is an essential part of any comprehensive theory of symbolic information processing.

Observationally and experimentally, one may identify the gradual unfolding of the full range of human communicative capacities in regular species-wide developmental stages. Nonverbal and verbal communication skills proceed along a regular developmental schedule that is correlated with other genetically based maturational developments (see Lenneberg, 1967). Even for high-level language systems, certain cross-cultural regularities may be observed during the process of ontogenetic development (see Slobin, 1973). Precisely which aspects of communication development may be attributed primarily to "nature" and which to "nurture" is an empirical question of enduring concern. For our purposes, it will be sufficient to note that symbolic behavior, just like the macrobehavioral product of any other functional domain, is some blend of the two.

The neurofunctional systems responsible for symbolic information processing reside at the highest levels of neural organization and may be correlated with the activity of secondary association cortex. These systems do not become operational until approximately 1 year after the time of birth and continue to be subject to genetically regulated maturational development up to approximately the time of puberty. The fact that our species has the longest period of neural development of any existing species correlates with our attainment of high degrees of functional complexity (see Nissen, 1951). The maturation of operational, but immature systems in the presence of appropriate environmental experience relieves the genetic code of a great burden of detailed specicifity and promotes greater adaptability to highly variable environments whose character may not be predictable in advance. In general, the lower a system is in the levels of the nervous system, the more completely its mature form is genetically determined. The higher the system, the greater the degree of environmental intraction that is necessary for its normal development (Jacobson, 1970). Additionally, it tends to be the case that the lower a system is within the nervous system, the earlier it becomes operational. Overall, the infant is constrained by the need to have systems operational that are adapted to the environment of that stage (Arey, 1965).

In the development of the human infant and child, symbolic information structures may be viewed as operating in two main functional spheres: (a) They facilitate the exchange of conceptual messages and the transmission of conceptual and affective associational evocations in acts of *interpersonal communication;* and (b) they serve as the formative elements in a variety of cognitive information processing activities in *intrapersonal representation.* In this latter domain, symbols contribute to an elaboration of the internal functional models of *mind, self, body, world,* and *other persons,* potential contributors to the phenomenological awareness of the individual. Any comprehensive theory of symbolization should take cognizance of the fact that the *reality* that individuals experience and communicate to other persons is an internal functional construct related in some undetermined fashion to anatomical and physiological correlates in the brain. Although these constructs may vary widely from culture to culture and individual to individual (for one example of individual variation, see Shotwell *et al.,* this volume), they also operate under species-wide constraints imposed by the nature of the neurofunctional systems that produce them. As the individual matures, progressively higher and higher levels of neurofunctional systems become operational and take prime control over behavior, thus leading to the progressive development of radically different sorts of potential phenomenological experience.

When the highest-level operational systems are within the midbrain and lower-level forebrain (see Figure 1), the external world impinges on the individual and affects behavior by means of physical stimuli that directly evoke or block stereotyped responses. After the limbic system becomes operational, the intake potential of the individual changes (thereby defining a new *umwelt,* or *vital field,* in the sense of Uexküll, 1921), and the nature of the transactions between individual and environment are transformed by the operation of these higher systems. Now the child begins to "will," to act upon the entities in the environment as part of goal-directed action patterns related to self and species survival. After the higher-level neocortical systems are superimposed on limbic systems, and take over prime control for behavior, the retransformed external world is not only reacted to and acted upon, but is "cognized" and "known" (Werner and Kaplan, 1963).

At lower levels of neurofunctional organization, there seems to be no discrimination among elements in the diffuse field making up the infant's global awareness. Both phylogenetically and ontogenetically, as higher-level systems become operational, an increasing degree of distancing and discrimination occurs between awareness of the self, the body, the world, the mind, and other persons. Each of these co-emergent components of the child's phenomenological awareness comes to be experienced as a stable configuration against the field of its transactions.

At some level of neurofunctional organization there emerges as a distinct component of experience a functional construct we may call the *model of the body* or *body-model*. This internal construct has two aspects: a *body frame* resulting in part from the individual's introspective establishment of the limits of proprioception, sensation, and feeling; and a *body schema* resulting partly from the identification of those segments of perceptual experience that can be controlled by intentional and/or volitional acts. The integration of these two facets of the body-model results in the "total" body experience of the adult and the differentiation of the body-model as a distinct, bounded component of phenomenological awareness.

The model of the body is differentiated from yet another functional construct in terms of which the child's developing awareness is organized. This structure, which we may call a *model of the world* (or world-model), is experienced not as percepts within the brain, (where it actually resides) but is projected outside the individual. Thus, at this point, the child inhabits a reality that includes an "external" world that is distinct from the body. The projection of a world-model outside the individual comes to be manifested behaviorally in a variety of ways during ontogenetic development, including reaching-to-touch, turning-to-look, and pointing to the elements of the world-model. At some point, as part of a social sharing of experience, the individual begins to make intentional *acts of denotational reference* to objects and events in the real world. The world-state entities denoted, i.e., the *denotative referents,* may be viewed as the *extensional meaning* of denotational acts (see Werner and Kaplan, 1963).

At some point in ontogenetic development, there emerges a personal experience of *self* as the child becomes an experiential object–configuration in his or her own transactional field. The self-awareness that emerges comes to involve two distinct aspects: an *outer self* oriented extrinsically and serving as the focus of goal-directed actions; and an *inner self* oriented intrinsically and serving as the focus of apperception and reactive awarness. These two facets of self come to be integrated and balanced at later stages of neurofunctional maturation.

After the highest level of the limbic system becomes operational in human ontogeny (from about the third postnatal month), and in conjunction with the maturation of pyramidal motor systems, increasing degrees of *intentionality* and *volitional control* over both internal processes and external behavior arise (see Lamendella, 1977b). As an expression of the emerging self, the child begins to *will,* to act upon the environment, to initiate choices, make decisions, etc. In the adult human, lower-level functional domains remain under strictly automatic control. Some higher-level functions are under dual automatic–volitional direction. Perhaps the earliest type of phenomenologically experienced *consciousness* arises with *sensations* based on appetitive-level limbic activity, followed shortly by *emotions* at the affective limbic level. After neocortical systems become operational, the child develops new levels and modes of conscious awareness, some of which are focused on representational constructs such as *image frames, movement schemata, conceptual representations,* and, at the highest levels, *symbolic representations.*

Certain elements of awareness emerge as an internal construct we may call a *model-of-the-mind or mind-model.* The child's phenomenological experience now includes *mind states* distinct from both world states and body states, with the self in its active role as experiencer and initiator serving as the common denominator between these other components of the individual's awareness. One of the ways in which the construction of a mind-model becomes overtly manifested is in attempts by the child to share mind states with other persons in a social context by making voluntary *acts of connotative reference* to the elements of mind states. The mind states connotated may be considered the *intensional meaning* of connotational acts. This social orientation continues as, at some point, there emerges out of the child's experimental field distinct internal representations of *other persons.* The individual becomes able to empathize, and tends to attribute to other persons a self, mind, body, and model of the world more or less equivalent to his or her own. The child gradually advances in the capacity to adopt the perspective of other persons in the perception of world states as a reflection of the progressive attainment of the abstract attitude and the diminution of an egocentric orientation (see Piaget, 1954).

Development of Low-Level Semiotic Functions in Ontogeny

Up to some order of complexity, *semiotic information processing activities* are the functional product of neurofunctional *coding circuits* that reflect the fundamental specialization of neural tissue, that is, the intercoordination of two separate spheres of functional activity. Thus, for example, in the invertebrates, the perception of some particular kinds of objects may result in the triggering of an approach or avoidance response as the output of a "hard-wired" neural circuit. At lower levels of neural organization, such coding circuits develop during ontogenetic maturation without the need for any environmental experience or learning, and are based on relatively straightforward anatomic and physiologic connections. At higher levels within the nervous system, the anatomic and physiologic bases for relating two separate spheres of functional activity are less clear, and the nature of the neural circuits involved can only be hypothesized. Additionally, at these higher levels the establishment of specific new neural circuits increasingly requires that the individual engage in trial-and-error learning in order to establish the code that reliably triggers a given response upon perceiving a given input. Even with already established anatomical connections between the structures of underlying two neurofunctional domains, it may still be necessary for the individual to learn the junctional coding pattern that co-ordinates the directed relations between the two functional domains (for example, the *perception model* of Rosenblatt, 1958). For example, in order to develop hand–eye coordination, the human infant must discover the code identifying which intentional motor impulse will send the hand where in the visual field. In a sense, the infant is in the position of a typist given a type-writer with a blank keyboard.

In this chapter, neural circuits interconnecting two functional spheres will be viewed as *relational mappings* between a source Domain and a goal Range. Some of these mappings are *cross-modal* (e.g., from visual to au-ditory modalities within sensory systems), and others are *cross-channel* (e.g., from auditory input channels to vocal output channels). Such mappings may be of different orders of complexity and can serve radically different functional roles. For our purposes, it is of particular relevance that neuro-functional coding circuits are the principal basis for the fundamental types of semiotic and communicative behavior observable in vertebrates in general and our species in particular. At the same time, relational mappings are the foundation upon which higher-level *representational, conceptual*, and *sym-bolic functions* are constructed.

In general, *semiotic coding systems* map between a Domain of *experienced world states* to a Range of *anticipated world states*. Based on this relational mapping, the individual may make a response appropriate to the anticipated state. With this type of coding, the individual, acting as *interpreter*, treats perceptual input in two ways: as experienced world states and as *indicators* of anticipated world states. It is this act that is the essence of semiotic behavior. At different levels of neural organization, semiotic coding systems are organized in different ways and involve different types of relational mappings.

The lowest levels of semiotic coding take place by means of *action coding* (see Bateson, 1975) of cross-channel stimulus–response associations that are learned by classical conditioning. Such *Primary Sign Coding* may also take place based on *analogic coding* (Bateson, 1975) in appetitive-level sub-systems of the limbic system (see Lamendella, 1977b). In primary sign be-havior, perception of one world state becomes the sufficient trigger for a response appropriate to another world state.

Based most likely on *correlative mappings* (see Bateson, 1975) at the af-fective level of limbic activity, the individual acquires the ability to identify one element in the perceptual field as being in a fixed spatial and/or temporal relation to another element in the perceptual field (e.g., smoke has both a spatial and a temporal relation to fire). An element in the Domain of cor-relative coding maps may be viewed as an *index* when it triggers a shift in the individual's attention to the signified element in the Range of the map. This signified element may be called the *indicatum*. Access to stored index coding patterns is an active process during which the interpreter perceives the index, polls sensory input in anticipation of perceiving the indicatum, and/or initiates a response appropriate to the indicatum.

A communicative transaction between two organisms may be viewed as *one-way* when the overt sign or index initiating a semiotic mapping in an interpreter is not within the (communicative) functional outlay of an individual acting as *producer*. A classic example of one-way communication occurs with the *global crying* of the human neonate. The acoustic waveform accompanying the total somatic mobilization of the infant is merely the by-product of the forceful expulsion of air from the lungs through a constricted vocal tract. It is not the outlay of specialized neurofunctional systems with the functional role of controlling acoustic behavior via the vocal tract articulators. The adaptive value of global crying arises from the ability (and willingness) of other persons in the environment to interpret this purely automatic behavior of the infant as indicating a state of extreme discomfort (see Lamendella, in preparation, for discussion).

Unlike one-way communication, *interactive communication* involves an individual (acting as producer) whose specialized outlay for some neurofunctional system includes behavior patterns serving communication functions. An interpreter perceives the behavior, and, based on the activity of the equivalent neurofunctional system in the communication domain, identifies the semiotic significance of the communicative behavior. Examples of such interactive communication in mammalian (including human) behavior may be found in the automatic, nonvolitional production of multimodal limbic behavior complexes (involving, for example, vocal production, facial expression, posture, patterned movement) as an outlay of the affective level of the limbic system. These behavior complexes are received and interpreted as indices by the affective limbic system of other mammalian individuals of either the same or a different species. In an important sense, it is the limbic system of one individual that is interacting with the limbic system of another individual. It is this interaction that is missing in one-way communication.

After the *volitional level* of limbic activity becomes operational from approximately 9–12 months after birth, the human child acquires the conscious capacity to produce and direct toward other individuals overt behavior patterns that directly, or indirectly through the construction of some material product, serve as the means for effecting a desired change in the state of the world, or in the mind states of that other individual. Either the overt behavior pattern itself or the material product constructed by the producer can serve as an intentional index, a *signal* in the sense that Morris (1946) used the term, from which an interpreter can identify the indicatum denoted. Interactive communication in which a producer intentionally produces a behavior pattern as a signal to an interpreter may be called *intentional com-*

munication. Initially, intentional communication arises in human ontogeny as a means of expressing motivational states, as a means of regulating social interactions, and later, in acts of denotational reference. From about 9 months postnatally, the human infant employs *part-for-whole coding* (Bateson, 1975) in order intentionally to produce a component of a previously automatic limbic behavior complex as a signal to some interpreter (Lamendella, in preparation).

In summary, then, we have thus far discussed the ontogenetic development and information processing basis for three different types of semiotic functions: *signs, indices,* and *signals.* These three semiotic functions differ in the levels at which they are carried out, the sorts of communicative interactions they are capable of supporting, and the types of relational mappings that are their basis. These are outlined in Table 1.

In order to discuss higher levels of semiotic functioning, it is necessary to introduce yet another aspect of human information processing, that of *representational information structures.* It is in these terms that the three remaining types of semiotic functions to be presented here—*icons, metaphors,* and *symbols*—will be discussed.

Neurofunctional Representation Systems

Based on the evolutionary development of high-level functional systems, information processing activities develop that go beyond relational mappings and neural coding circuits. While their precise functional organization is far from clear, these *representational systems* involve the construction by the individual of distinct *models* (see Laughlin, this volume) of such internal constructs as mind states and world states. Once constructed, these representational information structures make up the contents of long-term memory storage components of neocortical systems. Domain-specific long-term memory stores lend themselves to a cumulative build-up of repositories of encyclopedic and episodic knowledge about the objects of phenomenological experience, as well as repertoires of complex behavioral skills. Representational systems allow the individual to *know* the objects of experience, and it is perhaps this knowing that is the first type of neurofunctional processing that truly deserves to be termed *cognitive.* It is out of these systems that there later arise conceptual information processing activities and a recasting of phenomenological experience in conceptual terms. Symbolic information processing enters at higher levels as a specialized type of representational, conceptual activity.

Image frames are basic types of representational knowledge structures that may be correlated with the activity of lateralized neocortical systems in the back (posterior) portion of the brain. Image frames are learned representations of past perceived events, or sequences of events, based on the selective transformation and reorganization of percepts and percept arrays according to their spatial, temporal, and/or qualitative attributes (see, for example, the *iconic representation* of Bruner, 1964; the *exemplary representation* of Werner and Kaplan, 1963). Image frames are largely autonomous from action, and their retrieval to working memory by processes of recognition or recall need not lead to any direct motor output. Basic aspects of the image frame representations of particular individuals may be productively investigated by considering a class of neurological disorders called *agnosia*. Patients suffering from agnosia, often in association with bilateral tissue damage in secondary sensory regions of the cerebral hemispheres, can no longer recognize certain classes of familiar objects or action sequences through one or more sensory channels, due most probably to a functional loss of access to, or disruption of, image frame representational processes (see Geschwind, 1965).

A *movement schema* is a basic type of representational structure involving the construction of skill schemata by secondary neocrotical systems localized in the front (anterior) portion of the left (dominant) cerebral hemisphere. Movement schemata are stored in memory as procedural representations of past learned actions and coordinated action sequences. They may be retrieved independently from immediate perceptual input, and thus lend themselves to the production of complex goal-oriented behavior without needing any specific perceptual trigger. The *apraxias* are a class of neurological disorders (frequently associated with unilateral tissue damage in secondary motor neocortex of the dominant hemisphere) in which the individual "forgets" how to carry out certain classes of learned skilled movements or movement sequences, due most probably to a functional loss of access to, or disruption of, movement schema representational processes (see Geschwind, 1975).

Representational information structures of all types are organized in neural systems in such a way that the recognition or recall of a given representation to working memory can trigger the concomitant retrieval to working memory of other information structures stored in memory. Here, we shall identify two such fields of associative elements, the *associative field* and the *evocative field,* whose specific character is dependent on the actual organization of information in the memory systems of particular individuals.

The representational structures comprising an associative field at any given time may operate in either a cross-modal or cross-channel fashion and involve various types of mappings that serve to pick out particular elements in the associative field. Thus, for example, the perception of some other person combing his or her hair leads to the recognition of a stored image frame that is, in effect, our memory of what it looks like to comb hair. With this recognition, a cross-channel *equivalence mapping* may act to recall to working memory the learned movement schema that allows the perceiver to actually comb his or her own hair. Certain patients suffering agnosia can not recognize hair combing, while certain patients suffering apraxia can not comb their hair. Patients suffering from *ideomotor apraxia* can do both, but might not be able to imitate the act of hair combing, indicating a disruption of the equivalence mapping process.

Based on a perceptual similarity between an overt signal and a covert signified element, an individual acting as producer can engage in *icon communication* by intentionally producing a behavior pattern or constructing a material product, the *icon*, which when recognized by an interpreter triggers an equivalence mapping retrieval to working memory of an image frame. Icons share *significant* perceptible properties (spatial, temporal, qualitative, and/or configurational) with the image frames they represent, and therefore share common attributes between their extensional and intensional meaning. Unlike communication based on the index, no necessary spatial or temporal association with their referent is involved in icon communication, which, for this reason, lends itself to communication about absent objects.

Based in part on equivalence mappings between a recognized image frame and some movement schema, the child begins at some point during the first year of life to engage in *imitative depiction*. This type of "true" imitation behavior must be distinguished from earlier, lower-level *co-active movements* in which there is no differentiation between internal representations of both the external model and the motor-reaction pattern (Werner and Kaplan, 1963). Thus, the imitation of tongue protrusion that may be observed in neonates (Meltzoff, 1977), as a *co-active movement*, must be functionally distinguished from the imitative depiction found in onomatopoetic imitations of such sounds as a dog's bark on representational processing in the vocal–auditory channels.

A second type of icon communication, *gestural communication*, arises when the child implements movement schemata in order to output an overt somatic behavior sequence that will give rise to a particular image frame or sequence of image frames in the mind of an interpreter. This type of communicative interaction is based on shared formal properties between depictive behavior patterns and their referents. Upon perceiving such a behavior pattern, the attention of an interpreter is associatively shifted by equivalence mappings to an internal representation of an image frame (i.e., the intensional meaning of the somatic icon), and the corresponding image frame is retrieved to working memory from the associative field. From about 7–9 months postnatally, the human child begins to produce multimodal *gesture complexes* to represent holistically image frames of actions, action sequences, or objects.

A second field of elements that may be related to a given representational information structure is what will be called here the *evocative field* of a representation. The recognition or recall of a given representation to working memory may lead to the *evocation* of particular appetitive limbic sensations (as when a photograph of food makes one hungry), affective level limbic emotions (as when the depiction of a social injustice makes one angry), or limbic behavioral reactions (as when the recognition of a dangerous situation leads to a flight response). The evocative field of representational information structures may also include specifically right (nondominant) hemisphere associative reactions, since it is the right hemisphere that plays a special role in the elaboration of affective processing in the limbic system (see Lamendella, 1977b). The set of relational mappings that serve to evoke elements in the evocative field of a representational information structure is what will be here termed *emotive maps*.

Conceptual Representations

The manner in which the world-model is experienced changes radically when representational information structures called *concepts* arise. Conceptual representations emerge out of movement schemata and image frame processing after higher levels of neocortical systems become operational and extract and store in memory *criterial properties* of objects as a means of defining abstract generic conceptual categories. Conceptual memory contains structured arrays of conceptual categories organized into inclusion hierarchies with each category being distinguished from its superordinates and coordinates by its local defining properties. World states are now experienced in terms of image frames and movement schemata that are *tokens* (or instances) of generic categories in conceptual memory (see Lamendella, in preparation).

From approximately 7–8 months postnatally, the first type of concept to develop, *object concepts,* becomes manifested behaviorally as the infant stops dealing only with *movement* and *location* and begins to deal with *objects* that move from place to place (Bower, 1977). The world-model is now populated with objects that are tokens of generic object concepts, and the infant begins to search for hidden objects and give over manifestations of the attainment of the stage of *object permanence* (Piaget, 1954).

Between about 9–12 months after birth, the human infant develops two higher-level types of concept: (*a*) *activity concepts,* 'abstract conceptual representations of the actions initiated by or undergone by objects'; and (*b*) *relation concepts,* 'an abstract conceptual representation of the relationship between objects.' Activity and relation concepts are important steps in cognitive development since they become the first two types of predication employed in representational systems. At some point during this period, the infant begins organizing complexes of conceptual representations that we may call *propositions.* Propositional representations are initially of two types: (*a*) *states,* defined according to relations predicated between objects; and (*b*) *events,* defined according to activities predicated of objects. During later stages of conceptual development, more complex types of propositional representations arise as propositions themselves become embedded into higher-order propositions. At some point in development, the individual begins experiencing both the world and his or her own mind states in propositional terms.

Within the associative field for each concept, there may be identified a subset of concepts that share properties with that concept. *Similarity maps* pick out that subset of the associative field of a concept whose criterial property descriptions overlap. As a type of volitional, conceptually based communication, a producer may produce behavior that, after recognition of a concept by an interpreter, triggers in the interpreter the operation of similarity maps leading to the retrieval to working memory of some similar concept(s) within the associative field of the recognized concept. The original concept may be viewed as a *metaphor* for the recalled concept and, in a sense, involves a type of nonarbitrary pseudo-symbolization. There is also a sense in which the metaphor, as defined here, is a type of conceptual icon.

Symbolic Conceptual Systems

In the preceding sections, a neurofunctional perspective was presented on the following categories of semiotic functioning: *signs, indices, signals, icons,* and *metaphors.* The first three of these were discussed in relation to neural coding circuits, and the last two in terms of representational processing. Each of the five derives its semiotic significance from a different sort of motivation between the signified and the signifier (see Table 1). In the view presented here, a metaphor is based on conceptual processing in which similarity maps account for the motivated relationship between the metaphor and the conceptual element it represents. Here, a symbol will be defined as yet another type of conceptual structure, one for which the relationship between the symbol and its symbolic meaning is: (*a*) *arbitrary,* and therefore in general cannot reliably be inferred by an interpreter apart from inductive learning; and (*b*) *conventional,* in that, for sociocultural symbols, the relationship between symbol and symbolic meaning rests on interpersonal convention and consensus, and for private symbols on intrapersonal conventions.

As representational information structures, symbol concepts automatically have an associative field and an evocative field independently of either the symbolic meaning or the evocations and associations of that symbolic meaning. For some types of symbolic interactions, it is precisely the associations and/or evocations of the symbol concept itself that are significant, with the symbolic meaning being neither here nor there. Thus, for example, the propositional content of insults is often irrelevant, and the motivation for the insult lies in the elicitation of particular evocations and associations in the interpreter.

As a type of conceptual representation, symbols are defined by the individual in terms of generic property descriptions. Based on the nature of these properties, a symbol may be metaphorically related to other concepts independently of its symbolic meaning. Symbol systems allow the construction of complex, abstract associative fields and a new level of representational information storage and manipulation. These characteristics of symbolic information processing are to a large extent responsible for the specific quality of human cognitive processing (see in Bruner, 1964, the discussion of the advantages of *symbolic representation* over either *enactive* or *iconic representation*). These symbolic capabilities are simultaneously the source and the product of the evolution of human culture and human language. It is the acquisition of symbolic information processing capabilities that provides the human infant with the means to assimilate into the culture of the environment.

Symbolic behavior is highly adaptive both for complex social communication and acculturation as well as for the personal attainment of complex cognitive information processing capacities. Overt acts of symbolic behavior are based on the covert activity of neurofunctional systems and involve:

1. A structured set of *symbol concepts* in long-term memory
2. An overt *symbolic vehicle*, and its corresponding internal representation as an image frame or movement schema representation
3. A connoted *symbolic meaning*
4. An *associative field*
5. An *evocative field*

Certain relationships between these elements of symbolic information processing are diagramed in Figure 2.

Thus, from a neurofunctional perspective, a *symbol* may be viewed as a neocortical conceptual structure stored in a particular subdomain of conceptual memory and retrieved to working memory under appropriate conditions during symbolic information processing activities. Symbol concepts arise at some point in development as functional constructs separate from both their symbolic meaning and the image frames or movement schemata associated with symbolic vehicles. Symbolic vehicles are external entities that may either be some patterned behavior or a material product that is the result of a producer's behavior (Werner and Kaplan, 1963). The symbolic vehicle need bear no spatiotemporal contiguity relationship to the symbolic meaning it indirectly stands for (as does an index to its indicatum), nor is it based on either part-for-whole coding (as are some signals) or a sharing of perceptual or conceptual properties with a referent (as happens with icons and metaphors, respectively). The relationship between a symbolic vehicle and a symbolic concept and between a symbol concept and a symbolic meaning must be explicitly acquired by each individual after the creation of the symbol. If a symbol is to be regularly shared between individuals in social

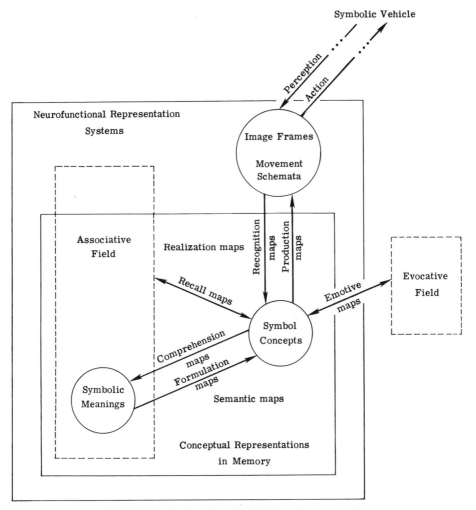

FIGURE 2. Outline of symbolic information processing.

acts of *symbolic communication,* particular sorts of relational mappings must be conventionally established within the social group and thereafter acquired through inductive learning by other individuals.

Depending on the specific input–output channels employed, symbol concepts require for their behavioral implementation a channel-specific set of *realization maps,* specialized recall maps that relate abstract symbol concepts in memory and conventionally associated image frames and/or movement schemata. Two basic types of realization maps may be distinguished according to the direction of information flow: (*a*) *production maps* employed by a producer in symbolic encoding; and (*b*) *recognition maps* employed by an interpreter in symbolic decoding.

The functional significance of the symbolic vehicle lies neither in its extensional meaning nor in the image frame or movement schema associated to it. The symbolic vehicle is the outward manifestation of a symbol concept that stands for, or substitutes for, some connotative conceptual meaning. We will call the set of conceptual representations that serve as the intensional meaning of a symbolic vehicle the *symbolic meaning* of a symbol concept, noting that the symbolic meaning lies within the associative field of the symbol concept. For symbolic communication to take place, both the producer and the interpreter of acts of symbolic behavior (perhaps the same individual) must have access to specialized types of recall mappings called *semantic maps*. Semantic maps relate a symbol concept and the symbolic meaning(s) it stands for. Two basic types of semantic mappings may be distinguished, based on the direction of information flow: (*a*) a set of *comprehension maps*, employed by an interpreter and having the set of symbol concepts as its Domain and the entire set of conceptual representations as its Range; and (*b*) a set of *formulation maps*, employed by a producer and having the entire set of conceptual representations as its Domain and the set of symbol concepts as its Range.

From about 9–12 months, the human infant begins to acquire and store in memory a set of *gestural symbols* whose overt expression in somatic behavior is integrated with multimodal limbic index and signal complexes, as well as somatic icons. From about 12 months, the child begins to produce external *symbolic gestural complexes* whose component elements manifest all of these types of semiotic functions at the same time. During this period, gestural complexes with symbolic components are the child's basic means of intentional communication with other persons (see Carter, 1974; Lamendella, in preparation; Reed, 1971).

A significant development takes place from about 9–12 months after birth, when the child develops a set of *verbal* representations based on phonologically structured auditory image frames. This verbal processing contributes to the acquisition and storage in memory of a set of *lexical symbol concepts*. Lexical forms (roughly equivalent to *words*) are also related to phonologically structured vocal articulatory movement schemata of secondary motor systems of the neocortex in the dominant hemisphere. The initial symbolic meanings of lexical symbols are probably at the level of object concepts, but lexical symbols soon begin to be used to express propositional meanings, first in a holistic, and later in an analytic fashion (see Table 2).

From about 1 year after birth, the child overtly manifests the development of lexical memory systems by producing verbal forms that make denotative reference to entities in the external world (i.e., in the projected world-model). During this period, the child produces *naming utterances* that do not typically constitute an attempt to communicate either conceptual messages or affective states to other persons, even though they may serve as

TABLE 2
Outline of the Maturational Stages in the Development of Communication Systems by the Child[a]

---

1. *Preconceptual limbic stages*

    From about two weeks postnatally, the infant exhibits a fixed set of multimodal *sign complexes* that allow a receiver to infer a closed set of graded messages. The perception of specified internal or external conditions results in the automatic implementation of a set of differentiated responses produced by action schemata of subcortical components of the limbic system. From about 6 mo., higher level paleocortical limbic components integrate with the neocortical motor systems that control voluntary motor activity to allow the intentional production of existing limbic responses as a conscious means of communicating motivational states to those in the environment. The infant becomes more responsive to the affective and conative content of adult behavior and, from about 9 mo., prosodic features such as intonation contours become part of limbic *signal complexes*. Certain universal limbic 'words' (e.g., *mam* "food"), while retaining roughly the same phonetic form, make the transition from involuntary sign to intentional signal.

2. *Prelanguage communication systems*

    (*a*) *Gestural stages*: Multimodal *gesture complexes* output by secondary neocortical movement schemata are systematically and willfully used in particular contexts to communicate the substantive and relational content of an open set of propositional conceptualizations. As various components of gesture complexes become non-representational and conventionalized, the transition is made from signal to *symbol*. Vocalizations have no special high status as against the other components of a given schema such as facial expression, visual orientation, body orientation, body configuration, rhythmic and patterned movements.

    (*b*) *Phonological labeling stages* (Naming stage): Phonologically structured names act as labels on object-level and propositional concepts in such a way that hearing a given phonological form can lead to the retrieval of a concept from long-term memory. Perceptions that lead to the conceptual recognition or recall of a given generic or token concept may result in the overt vocal production of the child's label for that concept. Such articulatory output is organized by lateralized neocortical movement schemata based in Broca's convolution. Though apparently not used to communicate propositional messages, labeling vocalizations are used in social interactions to identify objects and as vocatives.

    (*c*) *Propositional focus stages* (Holophrastic stage): Neocortically based communication systems insert phonologically structured labels into previously existing gesture complexes. One function of the verbal component of a gesture complex is to draw an addressee's attention to the information focus of a given propositional message. The conceptual content of one word utterances becomes increasingly differentiated over and above that of the gestural substratum. For the most part, both the messages the child encodes and those decoded from adult speech are still approached in terms of an immediate action strategy.

    (*d*) *Propositional focus-assertion stages* (Pivot-Open stage, Two-Word stage): Two-word utterances accompany gestural complexes, functioning to identify the information focus and also to make an assertion or predication regarding this focus. While relational concepts are still expressed almost exclusively by gestures, or by relying on the contextual situation, the child increasingly opts for the auditory-vocal communication channel. Vocalizations more and more begin to independently communicate substantive concepts that are part of the message.

    (*e*) *Lexical stages* (Telegraphic stage): The mean length of utterances goes up as the child outputs strings of lexical items capable of assuming a major burden in communicating the substantive content of messages including some relational notions. No syntactic structure

TABLE 2 *(Continued)*

exists, although word order may be fixed. Even though lexical strings remain subject to misinterpretation, the limbic and gestural systems are of diminished importance in the child's overall communicative repertoire.

3. *Linguistic stages*

Lateralized neocortical systems produce *sentences* that communicate both relations and substantives by means of *syntactic devices* and *grammatical morphemes* used with lexical items. In general, the conceptual grasp of a given distinction precedes its linguistic expression. The mastery of linguistic forms is subject to certain universal constraints. Sentences become increasingly independent of accompanying gestures and situational context.

a From Lamendella, 1976: 408.

the basis for a phatic sharing of experience. During the period from approximately 12–15 months, somatic gestural complexes remain the infant's most "advanced" means of communication. It is at approximately 15–18 months of age that lexical forms are integrated into existing gestural complexes to produce the *holophrastic stage* of prelanguage development. Phonologically structured names begin to serve to identify the *information focus* of propositional messages that the child intentionally communicates to other persons (see Lamendella, in preparation).

That naming behavior remains a functionally isolable domain even in the adult is demonstrated by the class of neurological disorders called *anomia* (amnesic aphasia). The main symptoms of anomia involve a disruption of the naming function and, in a general sense, a loss of the ability to directly and appropriately apply words as symbols. To varying degrees, and in diverse manners, patients suffering anomia exhibit a diminished ability to retrieve and/or produce verbal labels as part of naming behavior, especially in confrontation naming situations (e.g., "What is this?"). These symptoms are frequently associated with tissue damage in the posterior portion of the dominant hemisphere (see Brown, 1972; Goldstein, 1948).

From about 18–24 months higher-order *propositional symbolic representations* realized in terms of progressively more complex organizational patterns imposed on single symbol concepts in memory emerge. This capacity is based on the organization of symbolic representations of objects, relations, and activities into propositional *symbolic patterns*. Propositional symbolic patterns begin to allow the child to represent propositional conceptual meanings in a systematic, analytic fashion rather than holistically and globally. At this point it becomes possible to produce symbolic vehicles in structured *arrays* into which at some point there are introduced symbols whose function is to express the relationship between other symbols. It is this capacity that is the basis for human language and many aspects of cognitive information processing. The first type of symbolic vehicle arrays occur in the verbal domain with the Focus–Assertion (or Pivot–Open) stage of prelanguage development at approximately 18–21 months, when the child's two-word utterances for the first time contain an expression of both the information focus of the message and a predicate asserted of that focus (see Lamendella, in preparation).

Arising out of realization maps, *actualization rules* establish the correspondences between propositional symbolic patterns in long-term memory and the actualization of these higher-order symbol constructs as patterns of image frames or movement schemata for input and output. We may identify two main types of channel-specific actualization rules: (*a*) *production rules* responsible for output mappings during the production of propositional symbolic behavior; and (*b*) *recognition rules* responsible for input mappings during the interpretation of propositional symbolic behavior.

As part of the development of propositional symbol systems, rule structures arise that are higher-order semantic mappings relating propositional conceptual meanings with propositional symbol patterns in memory. Two types of such channel-specific *semantic rules* may be distinguished: (*a*) *formulation rules* related to the producer's encoding of propositional concepts into propositional symbolic patterns; and (*b*) *comprehension maps* employed by an interpreter in decoding patterns of propositional symbolic representations (see Figure 3).

One important means of investigating the internal organization of symbolic information processing activities is to study individuals who have suffered behavioral disorders of symbolic functions due to lesions in brain tissue. While little has been done up to this point to investigate the specific extent to which more fundamental disorders of symbolic functioning lie at the heart of the classic aphasic disorders of language, the area holds great promise for providing data applicable to the understanding of symbol systems (see Gainotti and Lemmo, 1976). Studies of *asymbolia* (Finkelnberg, 1870; Gainotti and Lemmo, 1976; Goldstein, 1948) and aphasia (see, for example, Brown, 1972) have already shed considerable light on the functional organization of those brain systems responsible for symbolic information processing.

Conclusions

The fact that neurological, neuropsychological, and comparative investigations of human information processing activities are still in their infancy should not prevent the realization that even vague hints from these areas can make significant contributions to the formulation of comprehensive functional models of symbolic information processing direct relevance to social scientists. Conversely, a willingness on the part of empirical investigators to operate from even sketchy theoretical models of functional organization in neural systems can help guide future empirical studies in the most productive direction.

In this chapter, an attempt was made to present a synthesis of available ontogenetic, phylogenetic, psychological, and neurological evidence in the form of a provisional neurofunctional model of various levels and types of semiotic information processing. It is hoped that this model can contribute to the establishment of a fundamental framework in terms of which symbolic behavior and symbolic communication in particular can be investigated and understood.

Acknowledgments

I wish to thank the members of the symposium for many insights into the topic of symbolic behavior and for substantive contributions to this chapter. I would also like to thank J. Halverson, P. Kenez, L. Selinker, S. Straight, and the editors of this volume for their comments.

References

Arey, L. B.
  1965 *Developmental anatomy,* 7th ed. Philadelphia, Pennsylvania: Saunders.
Bateson, G.
  1975 Reality and redundancy. *CoEvolution Quarterly* **6,** 132–135.
Bower, T. G. R.
  1977 *A primer of infant development.* San Francisco, California: Freeman.
Bronson, G.
  1965 Hierarchical organization of the central nervous system. *Behavioral Science* **10**(1), 7–25.
Brown, J.
  1972 *Aphasia, apraxia, and agnosia.* Springfield, Illinois: Thomas.
Bruner, J. S.
  1964 The course of cognitive growth. *American Psychologist* **19,** 1–15.
Carter, A. L.
  1974 *The development of communication in the sensorimotor period: A case study.* Ph.D. dissertation, University of California, Berkeley.
Crosby, E. C. and T. Humphrey
  1941 Studies of the vertebrate telencephalon. II. The nuclear pattern of the anterior olfactory nucleus, tuberculum olfactorum, and the amygdaloid complex in adult man. *Journal of Comparative Neurology* **74**(2), 309–352.
Dingwall, W. O.
  1979 The evolution of human communication systems. In *Studies in neurolinguistics* (Vol. 4), edited by H. Whitaker and H. A. Whitaker. New York: Academic Press. Pp. 1–95.
Eccles, J.
  1973 *The understanding of the brain.* New York: McGraw-Hill.
Finkelnburg, F. C.
  1870 Niederrheinische gesellschaft, Sitzung vom 21 März 1970. *Berlin klinik Wochenschr* **7,** 449–460.

Gainotti, G., and M. A. Lemmo
1976   Comprehension of symbolic gestures in aphasia. *Brain and Language* **3**, 451–460.
Geschwind, N.
1964   *Development of the brain and the evolution of language.* Georgetown Monograph Series on Language and Linguistics. Washington, D.C.: Georgetown Univ. Press.
1965   Disconnexion syndromes in animals and man. Part I. *Brain* **88**(2), 237–294. Part II. *Brain* **88**(3), 585–644.
1975   The apraxias: Neural mechanisms of disorders of learned movement. *American Scientist* **63**(2), 188–195.
Goldstein, K.
1948   *Language and language disturbances.* New York: Grune & Stratton.
Harnad, S. R., H. D. Steklis, and J. Lancaster (eds.)
1976   *Origins and evolution of language and speech. Annals of the New York Academy of Science 230.* New York: New York Academy of Sciences.
Hill, J.
1978   Apes and language. *Annual Review of Anthropology* (Vol. 7) Palo Alto: Annual Reviews Inc. Pp. 89–112.
Jacobson, M.
1970   *Developmental neurobiology.* New York: Holt.
Jerison, H. J.
1973   *Evolution of the brain and intelligence.* New York: Academic Press.
Johns, D. F., and L. L. LaPointe
1976   Neurogenic disorders of output processing: Apraxia of speech. In *Studies in neurolinguistics* (vol. 1), edited by H. Whitaker & H. A. Whitaker. New York: Academic Press, Pp. 161–191.
Lamendella, J. T.
1976   Relations between the ontogeny and phylogeny of language: A neurecapitulationist view. In *Origins and evolution of language and speech,* edited by S. Harnard *et al.* New York: New York Academy of Science. Pp. 396–412.
1977a   General principles of neurofunctional organization and their manifestation in primary and nonprimary language acquisition. *Language Learning* **27**:155–196.
1977b   The limbic system in human communication. In *Studies in neurolinguistics* (vol. 3), edited by H. Whitaker & H. A. Whitaker. New York: Academic Press. Pp. 157–122.
1978   Neurofunctional basis of pattern practice. Paper read before the 1978 TESOL Convention, Mexico City, April, 1978.
1979   Neurolinguistics. *Annual Review of Anthropology* **8**, 373–391. Palo Alto: Annual Reviews Inc.
In press   Genetically based neural idiosyncracies as the primary etiology of specific language disabilities in children. *Proceedings of the International Symposium on Child Language Acquisition* (México City, November, 1976).
In preparation   *Early growth of cognition and communication.*
Lenneberg, E. H.
1967   *Biological foundations of language.* New York: Wiley.
Mayr, E.
1963   *Animal species and evolution.* Cambridge, Massachusetts: Harvard Univ. Press.
Meltzoff, A. N.
1977   Imitation of facial and manual gestures by human neonates. *Science* **198**, 75–78.
Milner, E.
1967   *Human neural and behavioral development: A relational inquiry.* Springfield, Illinois: Thomas.
Milner, P. M.
1970   *Physiological psychology.* New York: Holt.

Morris, C.
1946   *Signs, language, and behavior.* Englewood Cliffs, New Jersey: Prentice-Hall.
Nissen, H. W.
1951   Phylogenetic comparison. *Handbook of experimental psychology,* edited by S. S. Stevens. New York: Wiley. Pp. 346–385.
Noback, C. R., and W. Montagna
1970   *The primate brain, Advances in primatology.* Vol. 1. New York: Appleton.
Novikoff, A. B.
1945   The concept of integrative levels and biology. *Science* **101,** 209–2
Piaget, J.
1954   *The construction of reality in the child.* Translated by M. Cook. New York: Basic Books.
1971   *Biology and Knowledge.* Chicago, Illinois: Univ. of Chicago Press.
Pribram, K. H.
1971   *Languages of the brain.* Englewood Cliffs, New Jersey: Prentice-Hall.
Reed, J. W.
1971   *A grammar of the holophrastic phrase.* Unpublished. Ph.D. dissertation, Southern Illinois University.
Rosenblatt, F.
1958   The perceptron: A probabilistic model for information storage and organization in the brain. *Psychology Review* **65,** 386–408.
Sarkisov, S. A.
1966   *The structure and functions of the brain.* Bloomington, Indiana: Indiana Univ. Press.
Schneirla, T. C.
1957   The concept of development in comparative psychology. In *The concept of development,* edited by D. B. Harris. Minneapolis: Univ. of Minnesota Press.
Selinker, L., and J. Lamendella
1978   Two perspectives on fossilization in interlanguage learning. Paper read before the 1978 TESOL Convention (México City, April, 1978).
Slobin, D. I.
1973   Cognitive prerequisites for the development of grammar. In *Studies of child language development,* edited by C. Ferguson and D. I. Slobin. New York: Holt. Pp. 175–208.
Stephen, H., and O. J. Andy
1970   The allocortex in primates. In *The primate brain: Advances in primatology* (vol. 1), edited by C. R. Noback & W. Montagna. New York: Appleton. Pp. 109–135.
Uexküll, J. von
1921   *Umwelt und innerwelt der tiere.* Berling: Springer-Verlag.
Waddington, C. H.
1966   *Principles of development and differentiation.* New York: Macmillan.
Werner, H., and B. Kaplan
1963   *Symbol formation.* New York: Wiley.
Whitaker, H., and H. A. Whitaker (eds.)
1976a   *Studies in neurolinguistics* (vol. 1). New York: Academic Press.
1976b   *Studies in neurolinguistics* (vol. 2). New York: Academic Press.
1977   *Studies in neurolinguistics* (vol. 3). New York: Academic Press.
(In press)   *Studies in neurolinguistics* (vol. 4). New York: Academic Press.

12

Styles of Achievement in Early Symbol Use[1]

JENNIFER M. SHOTWELL
DENNIE WOLF
HOWARD GARDNER

Introduction

The capacity to use symbols has often been considered the hallmark of human cognition. While infrahuman organisms have at most a limited capacity to produce and comprehend meaning-bearing vehicles, adult humans in all cultures utilize (and even devise) a wide range of symbol systems, ranging from language and gesture, to drawing, sculpture, music, and dance. Acknowledging the centrality of such symbol use, students of human development have portrayed the acquisition of proficiency in symbolization as a primary achievement of the first years of life (see Bruner, Olver, and Greenfield, 1966; Piaget, 1962; Werner and Kaplan, 1963). And, indeed, by the time children are 5, 6, or 7, they are generally quite skilled in the use of several symbol systems, exhibiting the capacities both to produce "legible" messages in these systems and to "read" those communications fashioned by other members of the culture.

Even though an insistence on the importance of symbol use is not in itself controversial, very little has been established concerning the early course of this crucial human ability. Although few scholars have assumed that the acquisition of symbolic competence is a simple process, much previous investigation has tended either to lump all symbolic systems together or to

[1] An earlier version of this chapter was presented at the Symposium on "Fundamentals of Symbolism," Burg Wartenstein, Austria, July 16–24, 1977. The research described herein has been supported by the Spencer Foundation.

study one in depth, while ignoring its relation to other symbolic systems. As a result, the universal properties of symbol use, those aspects of symbolization that may differ across media or across cultures, and the nature of possible differences among individuals in patterns of symbol use all have yet to be ascertained.

To secure preliminary answers to this set of issues, our colleagues and we have, over the past 5 years, been examining the early course of symbolization (see Gardner, 1976; Gardner, Wolf, and Smith, 1975; Wolf and Gardner, 1979). The chief source of information has been a longitudinal study of nine first-born, middle-class children. These subjects have been observed on a regular (weekly or biweekly) basis since the age of 1, as they have developed symbolic competence in seven different areas: language (particularly storytelling and metaphor), symbolic play, two-dimensional depiction (drawing), three-dimensional construction (modeling with clay and building with blocks), movement, music, and number. We have employed a variety of measures, ranging from standard tests of intelligence and cognition, to our own tests of symbolic competence, to intensive transcripts of free-play sessions. Though the study is still in progress, we are far enough along to justify a preliminary report on some salient features of the first years of symbolic activity.

In what follows, we shall describe the early course of symbolization in two of the media under study: symbolic play and three-dimensional construction. These media can serve as a useful introduction to the symbolic spectrum we have been monitoring, for whereas both are grounded in a child's everyday experience of object handling, together they encompass a wide range of ways in which this experience can be explored. In fact, it should be noted that young children's play is, initially at least, hardly differentiated by *media* concerns. As researchers, we have had, in a sense, to define boundaries somewhat artificial to children's everyday play. We have viewed symbolic play as the ability to represent actual or imagined experience through the combined use of objects, motions, and language. (These skills "grow up" to become capacities of storytelling, metaphor-making, and dramatic enactment.) The medium of three-dimensional construction has been conceived as entailing the meaningful articulation of spatial relationships, especially as exemplified in the subject's activities in block play and clay modeling. (Older children's participation in these pursuits is often incorporated into culture-wide activities, such as building or sculpting.)

Another of our chief discoveries is that there are both universal patterns of symbolic growth and considerable individual variation in how these patterns are realized. To the extent that one can generalize about so small a population there appear to be at least two discrete paths to (or styles of) early symbol mastery. One group of children (hereafter called *patterners*) shows a strong interest and skill in configurational uses of materials—an interest apparently rooted in a persistent curiosity about the object world around them, how it works, how it is constructed, how it can be named, varied, or explored. Such children are typically more interested in design and mechanical possibilities of materials than in their uses for communication or for the re-creation of personal experience. For instance, given a set of variously shaped blocks, patterners tend to be interested foremost in the physical dimensions of these objects, in exploring problems of symmetry, pattern, balance, or the dynamics of physical relationships between the blocks; such subjects might well create a design by matching a number of small blocks to a single, larger one.

In contrast, the other group of children (hereafter called *dramatists*) exhibits an interest in sequences of interpersonal events, ones having dramatic or narrational structures. Commencing with a strong interest in the world of persons and feelings, such children consistently seek to embed objects within interpersonal exchanges or to exploit representationality in the service of sharing experience in effective communication with others. For instance, given the same set of variously shaped blocks, a dramatist is likely to call a large one "the mommy," a small one "the baby," and have them reenact a shopping trip.

As we have come to know these styles more intimately, we have become convinced that they go beyond *media preferences, verbal versus visual inclinations,* or *person- versus object-centeredness*—though each of these entrenched characterizations bears some truth. Rather, they seem to represent fundamentally different, but equally valid, routes toward general symbolic competence—routes originating in children's overall personalities, their social contexts, and their underlying mental structures. (Phrased in terms of this volume, we might say that biological, social, and cognitive factors combine to guide and constrain symbolic growth along one of two contrasting paths.) The depth and complexity of these two paths, however, are best conveyed through rich example. Consequently, we now turn to the central tasks of our chapter: first, as a background to our own findings, a brief sketch at three early ages of general cognitive and media milestones; next, a summary of the principal steps entailed in the development of skills in the two relevant media; and then, a fuller discussion of how the acquisition of such media-specific accomplishments (common to all the children) may be effected quite differently by patterners and dramatists. Although our chapter concentrates on symbolic development in the opening years of life, there will be some discussion of how styles of symbolic use manifest themselves in early school-age children.

Early Cognitive Development across Media: Shared Achievements

Any investigation of styles of early symbolization should take into account two bodies of data. There is, first of all, the general trajectory of cognitive development, which has been set forth over the past few decades by Piaget and his followers (see Piaget, 1970). Second, and of equal importance, are those capacities and constraints that color the ways in which children will utilize any medium or symbol system. In Table 1, drawing both on the accumulated insights of developmental psychology and on our own sources of data, we have summarized these background factors at each of the three ages to be treated here: 12–14 months, 24 months, and 30–36 months of age. Taken together, these various indices of development suggest certain broad understandings that children have developed—understandings common to the various media: They represent universal aspects of early cognitive growth.

Just as certain broad patterns characterize the cognitive development of every normal child, stages of basic skills characterize manipulation of particular media, as shown in Tables 2 and 3. These common skills provide a preliminary answer to one of the questions guiding our inquiry: It appears that progress in the medium under consideration does indeed follow an ordinal scale, with any child who gains competence in symbolic play or in three-dimensional play passing through the same set of milestones in the same order (though we should add, at widely varying speeds). Milestones of both clay and block materials are shown in Table 2. Table 3 shows early stages of achievement in *replaying* (the capacity to reenact pieces of experience) and in *object substitution* (the capacity to treat one object as if it were another).

Patterners and Dramatists: Styles of Achieving Milestones

Although the milestones outlined in the preceding were negotiated by all the subjects in our longitudinal study, each child's history of achieving these stages was quite different. To the extent that children do achieve symbolic competence in a medium via somewhat diverse routes and varying time schemes, the identification of major steps in medium development has been instrumental in separating out critical individual differences among children—differences that may coalesce in stable constellations of traits persisting over time and across wide variations in format and materials. By conceiving of these sets of frequently associated characteristics as *styles* of symbol use, we suggest that they entail coherent manners of working, of selecting information, capturing it in forms, organizing it so that the desired effects will be accomplished. As such, differences in style between children may signal markedly different routes toward achieving the same basic steps in ordinal scale development. Moreover, these differences may well be enduring: They may continue significantly to guide the ways in which older children operate with unfamiliar materials, master cultural artifacts, and represent more abstract forms of information. Some aspects of these differences

TABLE 1
Some Early Achievements of Human Development

Approximate age in months	Cognitive milestones	Achievements across media
12–14	Stage 5 of Piaget's sensorimotor intelligence (1954) Action schemes no longer tied to immediate objects and persons; becoming independent of "here and now" Advent of single-word utterances	Formulation of units of action Emergence of basic vocabularies of schemes associated with different media (e.g., in drawing: marking arcs, dots, continuous scrawls) Media become separated from other fields of action (e.g., originally marking activity was a blend of motor, visual, and often, sound effects); fields of interaction defined between self and others
24	Stage 6 of sensorimotor intelligence Capacity for internal representations of past experience Ability to make organized searches for hidden objects, to perform deferred imitations Two-word utterances	Ability to combine units of action into meaningful sequences Representational possibilities exploited in language and symbolic play (e.g., two-word utterances allow formulation of simple semantic relations) Renaming and romancing Flexibility of signifier–signified relationship explored, as children frequently give another appropriate name to a familiar object (e.g., a shoe held by its laces is an "airplane") or donate elaborate meanings to unarticulated products (e.g., a scribble is called a "picnic")
30–36	Preoperational stage Semiotic (symbol-using) function acquired; thought remains primarily egocentric, limited in terms of inventive flexibility Simple sentences	Hierarchical organization of information sequences Units previously chained together by relatively simple relations are now integrated into a coherent structure (e.g., now can build arches, supply tuneful renditions of familiar songs) Representational possibilities realized in two- and three-dimensional media Interest in and ability to use common social dimensions, categories (e.g., number, shape, size, and color) Effort to make explicit the processes of representation For example, directing adults on how to draw a face or to be a frog

TABLE 2
Three-Dimensional Achievements

Approximate age in months	Block material	Clay material	Symbolic function
12–14	Stacking Exploration of specific locales ("here–there," "on–off," "in–out") A refinement of a "dropping" motor scheme into directed placements Stacking scheme transferred across a variety of appropriate materials (e.g., blocks, cans, etc.)	Product awareness A limited set of manipulatory techniques (e.g., squeezing, patting to flatten, attempting to roll coils, poking deep holes, tearing of huge wads) Crude attempts made to repair broken clay models (e.g., pressing a broken circular coil back together again).	Locations of blocks do not yet represent "real-world" spatial relations Occasional use of ritualistic play schemes suggestive of attempts to donate meaning to forms (e.g., pushing two blocks along the floor with "vroom" sound effects as if a car).
24	Constructions now combine vertical, horizontal axes. Significance attached to visual aspects of certain forms, arrays; e.g., repeated building of ritualistic "house" forms; interest in symmetry within one plane	First specifications of particular loci and forms in displays modeled by others; e.g., naming a line of small upright cones as "seals" Shaping techniques explored with more control Some assembly of premade forms Adding on to a model is usually a circular reaction but often appropriate in terms of general spatial location (e.g., adding a wad as "nose" onto the already present nose of a clay face)	Simple ritualistic forms or linguistic techniques still relied upon in attempts to render meaning (e.g., naming towers "houses," or simply designating unformed wads of clay as a "man") Initial emergence of spatial location as significant for meaning (e.g., poking holes in upper half of wad as "eyes")

30–36

Construction along vertical, horizontal, sagittal planes
Ability to build arches
Little production of solid structures with blocks

Elementary shaping
Simple modulation of meaning through shaping, but primarily at level of meaningful assembly of previously made forms (e.g., child can put together a person-figure with appropriately placed head, features, arms, legs, feet, when using already shaped coils and balls)

Meaning modulated by principles of three-dimensional organization (e.g., meaning contributed primarily by spatial location, not language)
Growing differentiation and specificity of spatial relations provides basis for assignment of significance to certain spatial relations (be it in terms of order, design, or depiction) (e.g., children use large enclosed space as house with smaller subspaces within set off as "rooms")
Symbolic play crucial in fleshing out referential potential: It donates meaning and provides a vehicle for replicating large-space experience on smaller scale (e.g., child builds an arch and drives a car through it; or child carefully forms a clay circle, says "donut," and pretends to eat it)

TABLE 3
Symbolic Play Achievements

Approximate age in months	
12–14	**Replaying** Exploration of relation between self and other through imitation and replaying rudimentary abbreviations of familiar events (e.g., feeding games; hello–good-bye). **Object substitution** Substitution of one generally similar object for another (e.g., a spoon for a phone receiver; a concave round block for a cup). **Replicas** Initial understanding that small toys can be used as, or made to act like, corresponding objects in the real world (e.g., can pretend to feed a doll).
24	**Replaying** Acquisition of simple signifier–signified relationship (e.g., pretending different blocks are "applesauce" and "milk" in an imaginary feeding situation); Combination of fragments of events into a sequence of familiar daily events that can be replayed (e.g., getting in car, going on shopping trip, returning home); Simple stereotypic roles (e.g., kitten, caretaker) can be played, as role-switching becomes increasingly available. **Object substitution** Ability freely to transform numerous objects into items needed for play; Use of renaming to capture perceived significant similarities between objects (e.g., the top of a salt cellar is called "phone" because of its shape and pattern of small holes).
30–36	Emergence of Inventive Fantasy Play **Replaying** Scenes cohere through a dynamic of *event* rather than pure sequential or additive recall (e.g., child pretends to go to store to buy ice cream cone, drops it, pretends to cry, goes home to get more money, and returns to store); Mood, character, less stereotyped emotions portrayed in more dramatically detailed role play. **Object substitution** Child now adept at animating numerous toy figures, regarding them as person-like; Emerging ability to imagine and act upon make-believe objects (e.g., pretends to see a fly, swat it, carry it to trash, wash hands).

as manifest across a range of ages and materials are presented in Tables 4 and 5.

Our two different styles can be discerned quite early (even before the vocabularies of specific medium use have been defined) in the type of relational play with objects favored by certain children. Dramatists' play with small objects often includes other people (e.g., dropping objects into an adult's hand), while patterners are, from the start, fascinated with relations between two objects (e.g., repeatedly putting a ball in and out of a cup). As children reach 12–14 months of age, differences in stylistic preference emerge more clearly, particularly as the areas of three-dimensional construction and symbolic play begin to take shape as media *fields* for action and reenactment. In the following discussion, using examples drawn primarily from two young girls, Julie and Anita, we will examine how mastery of these two media is modulated by the patterner–dramatist differences. These two children were chosen because, although they have contrasting styles of play, they are of the same sex and close to the same age.

12–14 Months: Emergence of Styles in Three-Dimensional Construction and Symbolic Play

Some of the earliest three-dimensional materials provided for children are blocks and clay. Children learn to make conventional stacks of blocks at approximately the same age but do not immediately acquire enough control and flexibility in the three-dimensional medium to introduce much variation into the stacking activity itself. As a consequence, a clue concerning early individual differences are those activities that prove sufficiently interesting to divert the child away from independent conventional uses of the materials (i.e., stacking). Children's extra-media responses may indicate individual directions in later three-dimensional usage.

We found that dramatists tend to exploit the occasion of block stacking as a turn-taking game (e.g., after the adult adds a block, Julie adds a block, then the adult, then Julie, etc.), or to accord special meanings to blocks for the purpose of symbolic play, without troubling to effect appropriate spatial locations or recombinations. Thus, Julie, in response to a request to build a train, pushes a single block around like a train. This strategy allows her to respond to the train task, in contrast to Anita's lack of response to the same task, which is, in fact, too *three-dimensionally* sophisticated for a 1-year-old. Later Julie will continue to animate her response as a tool of interaction, gradually adding more blocks and eventually achieving a train form several months before we see it in Anita's play.

Anita's interests lead to a different trajectory of achievement. At 12–14 months, patterners, when diverted from such conventional uses of three-dimensional materials as stacking, tend to get caught up in examining or organizing attributes of the small objects. For example, rather than build a tower as requested, Anita carefully picks out all the coin-shaped blocks from

TABLE 4
General Characteristics of Patterners and Dramatists

Dimension	Patterner	Dramatist
	Play process	
1. Emphasis given to aspects of the symbolic act (listed in order of importance):	formal (design) properties, reference, communication	communication, reference, formal (design) properties
2. Relations to others:	private, independent	interactive
3. Focus of attention:	exploration of object properties	re-creation of personal experience
4. Level of symbolic involvement:	tending to stay close to object properties: where substitutions and/or renamings of objects occur, they are based on object similarities; relatively low incidence of fantasy, but relatively high incidence of metaphoric behaviors.	tending to override object properties: substitutions and/or renamings occur frequently and are based more often on need or desire than physical similarity of objects; high incidence of fantasy, but relatively low incidence of metaphoric behaviors.
	Play products	
1. Favored materials:	blocks, puzzles, drawing materials	symbolic play props (e.g., dolls, dishes, toy animals, etc.)
2. Favored media (i.e., media in which children move along more rapidly or develop possibilities more broadly):	constructional, graphic	language, symbolic play
3. Modal qualities (properties that signal a basic manner of organizing information and appear to structure the bulk of children's activity with materials):	configurational; atemporal	narrational; temporal

the assortment and shows them to her mother. Or, at another point, she picks up each block, one at a time, examining each with great deliberateness, and then mouths and drops each, making no effort to combine them. This attention to the object's attributes of shape, size, and feel lays the groundwork for her later explorations of complex shape and mass relationships—explorations in which Julie lags several months behind.

Differences among children with respect to the amount of attention paid to the physical aspects of the materials also seem to have some early implications regarding sophistication of clay modeling. Those children whom we have classified as patterners display persistent interest in exploring a range of effective techniques with clay (e.g., pressing, pulling small pieces off, squeezing, poking, crude rolling attempts, attempting to rejoin pieces). Dramatists, on the other hand, tend to become engaged with clay at a more superficial level (e.g., primarily employing techniques immediately modeled, or simpler techniques such as pulling apart, eating, throwing, or placing it into an adult's hand).

Emergent individual differences prove even more salient in the realm of symbolic play. The visibility of these early discrepant paths reflects in part the tremendous flexibility as to the *means* that can be employed (children can utilize movement, language, or spatial orientation, in varying combinations); another factor that highlights early styles of play is the child's freedom to chose *which* aspects of personal experience to be emphasized or replayed.

Profoundly concerned with establishing structures suited to the mutual sharing of experience, dramatists' earliest communications center on imitations and simple role-exchange games like peek-a-boo and teasing. These children may mimic the actions of others, or signify action through gesture. As dramatists replay familiar experiences, they use gestural abbreviation to draw a wide range of persons and objects into exemplification of the same role in similar events. For example, Julie uses dolls and a small spoon and cup from a tea set to pretend to feed herself, to feed her mother, to give her mother a drink, and to feed one of the dolls.

By comparison, patterners seek effective means to capture and explore the salient aspects of the object world. Interested in the possible uses and transformations of objects, from the first year a patterner's earliest communications are often "sharing" and "showing" games that center on exchange or manipulation of small objects. At the stage where flexible manipulation and association give way to simple symbols, such children appear to pursue representation as a way of distinguishing between objects. Patterners rarely use objects to replay past experience, but rather exploit their configurations to explore object–attribute relations. For example, when Anita is presented with a toy tea set and dolls, she briefly groups the cup, spoon, and doll together, but then becomes deeply involved with collecting and stacking all the four small plates, all four of the large ones, and then nesting the stack of small plates inside the stack of larger ones. As she places

TABLE 5
Developments in Patterning and Dramatizing Behavior in Several Media

Medium	Initial Behaviors (12–20 months)		Peak Behaviors (20–30 months)	
	Patterners	Dramatists	Patterners	Dramatists
Three-dimensional construction	Block play is exploited as opportunity to examine or organize attributes of small objects (i.e., size, shape, feel); clay modeling is explored with range of effective techniques.	Block stacking is exploited as turn-taking or exchange game; meanings are donated to blocks through simple symbolic play behavior; clay modeling uses only very punitive techniques.	Block building involves complex experiments with problems of spatial location: balance, symmetry, shape, weight, and size; clay modeling is viewed as problem of careful shaping into pleasing configurations.	Children are less interested in experimental constructions than in transferring familiar forms suggested by interpersonal interests across a range of materials; clay tends to be simply renamed rather than reshaped.

Symbolic play	Communications are principally "showing" and "sharing" games centering on exchange or manipulation of small objects; play centers on exploring object-attribute relations rather than playing out personal events.	Communications are principally imitations of others' actions or simple role-exchange games (e.g., peek-a-boo or teasing); object-substitutions occur in context of replaying events, and use renaming to fit wide range of persons and objects into the same role in the event.	Children operate on attributes of objects for representational purposes: Renamings are often based on visual similarities (e.g., using a soup spoon as an ice cream cone); rehearsal of event-structures is primitive, rarely spontaneous; children are uncomfortable with imaginary objects and often demand that a real item be brought into the play.	Simple signifier–signified relationships are used as children replay short event-structures, though renamings occur with relative independence from visual similarities (e.g., using anything as an ice cream cone); rehearsal of event-structures is frequent, detailed, and often sophisticated. Children spontaneously introduce imaginary content (e.g., make-believe companions or a needed prop implied by the use of gestures and language).
Language	High proportion of words are names of objects, animals, locations.	High proportion of words are proper names, greetings, expressions of feelings.	Strong emphasis is placed on terms to encode color, size, number, physical relationships (i.e., "bigger").	Strong emphasis is placed on terms to encode emotions, moods, qualities in people.

three spoons on top of this display, she makes smacking noises with her lips and starts to hold a spoon toward the adults, but then turns back again as she once more becomes entranced with the problem of unstacking and rearranging the plates.

These examples illustrate that, just as in three-dimensional construction where children of both types are able to build towers at an earlier age, they have now attained a common stage of understanding how objects may be used as replicas and how personal experience may be replayed symbolically. However, the extent to which a child of each type will exploit this understanding in later development and the direction of exploitation may vary considerably.

24 Months: Consolidation of Styles

The power of individual differences becomes dramatically evident as the children increasingly use the two media (blocks and clay) for the symbolic re-creation of significant aspects of their experiential worlds. Children's growing control over these media by the age of 24 months both facilitates and is molded by the consolidation of some of the personal style concerns that were just revealing themselves at children's first birthdays. The strengthening of interests and approaches has, in turn, its own implications with regard to the development of symbolic interests.

The children's contrasting attitudes toward possible relationships entailed by objects exerts a powerful effect on the way in which they manipulate a set of materials, and, in fact, may determine which aspects of those materials are teased out as subject matter for the child's knowledge. Consider, for instance, how the patterner and dramatist behave when presented with a set of 12 blocks, evenly varied over color (red, yellow, and blue), size (large and small), and shape (round and square):

> *Observation 1.* Anita selects all the small round blocks and puts them in one hand, then selects all the large round blocks and holds them in the other. After she sets these groups down, she gathers all the small square blocks in one hand, stacks the large square ones, then stacks all the small square ones on top. Later, the Experimenter makes a long line of square blocks, with all the large blocks grouped together, followed by all the small ones. Without prompting, Anita makes a corresponding array with the round blocks.

> *Observation 2.* Julie builds a tower of the large circles, placing a small red round one on top. Then she makes pairs by placing blocks on top of one another: a large yellow square on a large yellow circle, a large red square on a large blue circle, and a large blue square on a small red circle. As she does this she repeats "applesauce, applesauce" softly. Then she hands one of the pairs to her mother and one to the Experimenter, who both pretend to eat them as Julie pretends to eat hers. The Experimenter asks for some milk, and Julie hands her another block, and one to her mother also. When she becomes distressed at not having a block as "milk" for herself, she is satisfied by her mother's offer to share the block Julie has just given her.

Although both children share stacking as one way of organizing the materials, the context in which they embed this activity is very different. The patterner thoroughly investigates the relationships between objects based on size and shape, while the dramatist quickly moves on to exploit the materials as props to explore familiar interpersonal dynamics and fantasy through symbolic play.

At age 2, because of the less flexible form of the grammar of three-dimensional construction and its inherent dependence on attention to attributes of physical objects, dramatists, who tend to overlook such aspects of experience, display a somewhat restricted articulation of their spatial environment. Although both patterners and dramatists combine blocks in constructions involving horizontal and vertical axes, dramatists seem less interested in experimenting with the construction itself and more interested in using a variety of material forms to symbolize aspects of an interesting interpersonal event. In contrast, patterners experiment in complex ways with problems of balance and symmetry. Thus Julie's block play is infused with an interpersonal flavor derived from her interest in feeding situations, mother–child relations, and family–house themes, with little exploitation of three-dimensional possibilities. Over a period of play sessions, she consistently builds "houses" with at least two vertical elements, using the simplest forms of visual symmetry (see Figure 1). She also "builds" houses by making a bridge

FIGURE 1. Simple structures built by a 22-month-old dramatist.

across her mother's knees or by lining up two chairs turned upside down. Somewhat later, as she gets a firmer hold on vertical–horizontal combination, she makes houses that, while still simple, at least include a variety of different shapes (see Figure 2).

FIGURE 2. Combinatorial structures built by a 24-month-old dramatist.

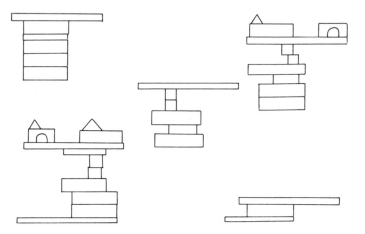

FIGURE 3. Complex combinational structures built by a 24-month-old patterner.

At 24 months, Anita's block play, although making use of the same horizontal–vertical combinational skills as Julie's structures, reflects her persistent interest in the attributes of objects and the variety of ways such objects can be combined and patterned. The simpler relations of repetitive visual symmetry that Julie is currently exploring emerged in Anita several months earlier. Anita is now expanding her earlier interest in the shape and feel of blocks into an ability to use both shape and mass in essentially nonconservative and exploratory block relations meticulously carried out. In one session she carefully makes the series of more complex constructions shown in Figure 3.

These constructions exhibit a more complex form of symmetry than that commonly seen in dramatists' block play—a symmetry based on *balanced proportions* rather than a *repetitive* symmetry (or symmetry based on an exact correspondence between parts). Patterners generally seem to acquire the skills for creating exact symmetry somewhat earlier than dramatists, and then go on to explore the more complex form. This symmetry of balance is never developed as richly by dramatists, who continue to concentrate on more repetitive forms of correspondence in block construction.

Children's differing styles also continue to inform their methods of modeling clay. Although both groups of children are equipped with a similar range of manipulatory clay techniques, dramatists tend to rush by problems of careful shaping, and would rather rename the clay, thereby transforming it into objects of current experiential interest. At this age, for example, Julie holds up a wad she has only superficially squeezed and calls it "hamburgers and French fries." Patterners, on the other hand, tend to get caught up in problems of shaping or of making pleasing configurations with the materials. Thus Anita, at the same age, forms a number of rings from the large and small coils the experimenter has rolled, and holds each finished form up for display. Experimenting for several minutes with the contours of one ring, she finally arrives at a satisfactorily (and inventively) curved circle and lays it aside as "finished."

While the behavior of dramatists appears somewhat conservative within the grammar of three-dimensional activity, it is the patterners who seem less daring in bringing to fruition the possibilities of symbolic play. As described in Observation 2, the dramatist has donated a simple event-structure to a previously ambiguous situation, thereby engaging in clear symbolic behavior: She has achieved a simple form of the signified–signifier relationship. In contrast, the patterner's play in Observation 1 seems to differ from her play a year ago only by her ability to re-create order across a more divergent set of objects. Do the two children share a fundamental acquisition, which has simply been masked by an apparent disparity in performance, or has the patterner's stylistic focus blocked development in the realm of symbolic play? It is essential to probe just how far patterners have progressed in grasping some form of the signifier–signified relationship.

During the latter part of the second year, such children begin to be able to make symbolic use of their sensitivity to object attributes: A capacity arises for discerning *similarity relations,* as patterners become avid practitioners of seeing one object as if it were another. The groundwork for this metaphoric capacity has been laid by early manipulative exploratory play in which objects have been grouped by size, arranged in rows of the same number, or matched by shape or color. What changes toward the end of the second year, yielding patterners their own characteristic forms of object substitution, is that children go from simply noticing attributes to *operating* on them for representational purposes. The effects, in the realm of symbolic play, of patterners' operations on attribute-mapping structures (their own form of signified–signifier relations) are illustrated by the following example:

> *Observation 3.* Anita is given the set of blocks and invited to tell a story with them. Anita comments, "Make house." Anita (with some help from the Experimenter) builds an arch and then places a small conical block on top of it. She changes her mind and places the conical block in the center space under the arch. She again changes her mind and builds a tower of blocks, using the cone, beside the arch. She knocks it over all at once with a laugh, but then quickly rebuilds the arch. When she again places the conical block atop it, she comments, "Hat."

30–36 Months: Complementarity of Styles

At the age of 2, the child's characteristic style of approaching media is clearly evident and serves as a point of departure for the majority of her activities. But by the age of $2\frac{1}{2}$ or so, the child's increasing elaboration of each style launches a period of complementarity, whereby children favoring one stylistic approach master the rudiments of the other style: Dramatists often elaborate narratives to a point where they can make use of attribute-mapping skills, while patterners' classifications and constructions become articulate enough to imply events. Thus, we see the patterner, Anita, sorting out a range of small items that vary in color (red, yellow, blue), size (large, small), and type (people, cars, and animals). In response to the experimenter's request to "put all the ones that are alike together," she lifts the items one by one from the heap and places each in a locale on the floor, grouped according to type. During the process she names the little girl doll "this be Anita," and the grandmother doll, "that gonna be mommy," with no other comments. It is Anita's interest in the classificatory scheme and her careful attention to each object, that provide the setting for the interpersonal relationship that she is able to map onto two of the objects. On the other hand, when Julie is posed the same task, she puts one of the dolls on top of a small block, and comments that he is "sleeping . . . cover him?" She then wants to make "other things for him . . . need a . . . need a . . . make a house for him" and goes on to construct a simple house. In the process of making a bed for another small figure, she lines up all the large blocks flat on the floor, then places two small blocks upright at each end of the line. The two small blocks match the respective colors of the end blocks. Here, it is her interest in providing for the needs of a doll-replica that leads Julie to a structure carefully ordered by shape, symmetry, and color.

At the same time, increased exposure and sensitivity to the symbolic productions of a wider circle of symbolizers (including peers) may facilitate the acquisition of complementary styles. Not only do children become acquainted with different symbol-user models, but new demands may be placed on the child. As it must behoove dramatists to become comfortably adept at handling culturally valued categories of number, size, shape, and color, so it must be advantageous for patterners to develop better tools to handle increasingly wider and more complex forms of interpersonal dynamics. At this same time children become highly sensitive to the typical uses of materials (e.g., even the most convinced dramatist eventually makes structures with blocks because that is what blocks "are for").

As the following examples illustrate, it is clear that patterners' and dramatists' play has, by now, come to share a pool of attribute-structure and interpersonal event-structure skills.

Observation 4. With a set of ambiguously shaped blocks (some of which suggest people, some of which are more conventionally blocklike) and cars, the Experimenter starts a story of a "lady"-block in a car, hunting for a parking space along a row of cars. One car has pulled out of the row so there is an empty space. The experimenter then leaves the story to Anita to resolve. Anita slides the lady's car into the empty space, "Goin' here." The Experimenter asks what else the lady will do.

Anita: "No room." (This is an imitation of an expression used by the Experimenter in the part of the story already started.)

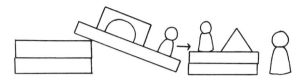

FIGURE 4. Symbolic play block scene built by a patterner.

Experimenter: "Now that she has a parking space she can go somewhere. Where shall she go?"

Anita: "Up the hill." (She makes a walking gesture with the person-block up a ramp of blocks previously designated as "hill.") She becomes more engaged with the ramp, laughing as she slides the lady-block down it. She walks the lady over to a yellow man figure and says "Hi, man." Then she builds an arrangement of blocks and figures. (See Figure 4.) She slides the lady-block down the ramp toward the man, then places the lady-block at the foot of the ramp and experiments with sliding a variety of blocks down the ramp.

Observation 5. Given a set of ambiguously shaped blocks, Julie first sets up two rectangular blocks on end, announcing "This one's a woods . . . here's the woods"; then she adds a block arching across the first two, saying "that for a hole." She pushes another one through underneath, saying "beep beep." She continues to build onto the structure, ending up with a construction as pictured in Figure 5. She then replaces the triangle and square block with two more barrel blocks, saying "that's the dinner . . . that's Froggie's dinner . . . it's a table for him." Then she says "He wants to eat with a spoon," and she feeds Froggie (a large stuffed frog), repeating twice "Here's some for you." She gives him the blocks shaped and patterned like bricks, saying "Dis a for him." Then she puts one brick block in each of the four barrels that are on top of the structure, saying "Here we go now . . . ah put this in here too." She takes up a clothespin that has a face drawn on its head, and the Experimenter names it "Fred," and greets it, "Hi, Fred." Julie also greets the clothespin, "Hi Fred"; then names the clothespin "George," and calls the Experimenter "George."

By the age of $2\frac{1}{2}$, then, patterners are able to create interpersonal events (Anita speaks for the lady, continues the action a bit further, makes the lady speak to another figure) while continuing to exhibit their enduring interest in object interrelations (block building; sliding various figures down the

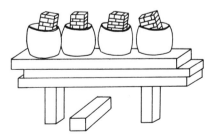

FIGURE 5. Symbolic play block scene built by a dramatist.

ramp). Dramatists can just as well exploit the attributes of objects (naming upright blocks, "woods"; making an orderly symmetrical block construction; exploring the notion of correspondences between objects by placing each brick-patterned block in a barrel) while maintaining a compelling interest in the playing out of personal events (Froggie's dinner, feeding Froggie). Both Julie's and Anita's play sequences demonstrate creditable performances in patterning and dramatizing.

While children may be led to the development of a complementary set of skills through the articulation and elaboration of their originally favored modes, much of their play, nonetheless, retains the flavor of this first-flowered style. Consider what happens when both types of children are encouraged to enter into a "pretend" game, where the experimenter "makes believe" that one of their friends has come to visit for a tea party. Both the patterner and dramatist are initially confused and only gradually enter into the symbolic play to the extent of being able to address the imagined person. It is illuminating, though, to note how each child takes grasp of an unfamiliar play demand and also how each brings such play to a conclusion. The patterner needs prompting at first to attend to the imagined guest's needs, but then connects by providing herself and the guest with *real* objects (i.e., forks and plates). She ends the play by stepping out of the imaginary realm, drawing the activity instead to concrete objects by requesting the experimenter to name a number of the props used in the play event. The dramatist, on the other hand, enters into the play by spontaneously answering the guest's needs with an *imaginary* object (i.e., offering the guest her "coat"). Likewise she ends the play within the structure of the imagined event by telling the invisible guest "bye bye" and providing the imaginary props necessary for her departure. Both children have not only coped with, but have been able to insert themselves into, a difficult and unfamiliar play situation. However, each child has made use of a different *means of access*.

Avenues to Later Symbolization

As the world of children enlarges beyond the family-and-friends circle, children must not only meet new contexts but also learn highly unfamiliar and seemingly arbitrary forms of cultural information. Although it is true that normal school-age children share performance skills in patterning and dramatizing, it may be crucial to make the most of their favored *means of access* as they are asked to become competent users of such cultural forms as texts, maps, and number.

As the children in our study have come into contact with some of these issues, we have had the opportunity to observe differences in how they handle both mapping and writing problems. Often their approaches seem to be mediated by skills that have already taken root in patterning or dramatizing. By the age of 4, the dramatist's interest in interpersonal roles and narrative sequences, contrasted with the patterner's interest in object attributes, spatial relationships, and symbolic correspondences, have culminated in strikingly different forms of emergent mapping skills. Thus, when asked to enact a pretend picnic trip and to later make a map of the trip, children vary as to which task focus is performed most strongly (though both aspects are performed with some degree of competence). Our dramatist Julie enters into the symbolic play sequence confidently and fully, often directing the play herself. Anita, on the other hand, joins in, but infrequently takes the initiative in imaginary play.

The youngsters' maps also differ. When asked to map the event, Julie's map is cursory: She draws a jaggedly curved enclosure and then points out the trip's highlights as the Experimenter requests them. Although she apparently has a very general idea of where to place points to represent their actual spatial layout, she only orders them linearly by situating them roughly (but appropriately) from right to left on the enclosure. (This ordering is also appropriate in terms of the narrative sequence of the events.) Anita's map, however, demonstrates a clear and careful concern to reproduce the spatial layout of the trip in graphic form. She can not only orient points in two-dimensional space, but can also draw the shapes of various objects at the highlight points as well (e.g., the picnic blanket, the waves, etc.).

The children also seem to approach writing issues with characteristically different attitudes, which either reflect or make use of their level of mapping skills and their stylistic concerns. Thus Julie's main interest in writing is initially to be able to sign her name at the bottom of all her pictures. This interest evolves into endless practicing of her full name, then many hours spent writing all the words she can think to ask her mother to spell out—at first copying her mother's model, and then writing it as her mother simply calls out the letters. Over a period of months she learns several words that her mother no longer has to spell out letter by letter. However, these words are learned almost as whole units—one word does not bear any relation to another—and she has little notion of how the same letters combine to make different words.

Julie does not exploit the correspondence of letters to sound—the map between spoken and written. Rather, she operates on correspondences between different unit-combinations of letters and events and people. For example, she quickly learns "Carol" for her mother, "Julie" for herself, "Merry Christmas" for the holidays, "cat" for a picture of a cat. Overall, she seems primarily to be concerned with the map between the written and the social world of object and person interaction. Thus, in one task session, when she is almost 4 (3;11), she is asked to write a grocery list; as can be seen in Figure 6, she makes a simple letter-like enclosure shape for each item,

FIGURE 6. Grocery list written by a dramatist.

commenting as she writes: "One package of butterfly, one package of butter mix, one package of batteries, and one package of hamburgers, one package of markers, one package of film, and one package of camera . . ."

Patterners' interest in mapping correspondences and shapes guides their writing concerns in a somewhat different direction. In general, there is less reliance on ritualistic practicing of whole words and less interest in the interactional dynamics of having the parent spell out words. Patterners focus first on practicing the individual letter shapes, going on eventually to learn some letter recognition skills, along with simple correspondences between letters and the sounds represented. Their interest in writing stems less from labeling than in discerning and repatterning the structure of spoken words. At just over 4 years of age (4;1) these kinds of interests lead Anita to respond to the task of making up a grocery list in an instructively different way. As can be seen in Figure 7, she announces what the writing means to her as "h, b, i, a, that's how I write down hamburgers . . . k, for kitten, that's how you make i, p, . . . ketchup, 'tato chips . . . o, o, i, . . . 'tato chips! . . . toothpaste . . ."

In this attempt to render words, Anita is clearly drawing upon her mapping skills. She not only uses several letters for each word, but also seems to capture some very global grapheme–phoneme relationships. The close ties between her writing and mapping are emphasized by her picture-writing solution for "toothpaste."

Patterners and dramatists have thus highlighted very different aspects of writing and mapping abilities in their first encounters with graphic languages.

FIGURE 7. Grocery list written by a patterner.

While we wish to stress that all normal children seem to achieve a pool of complementary stylistic approaches that provide the means of effective symbol use, we feel it is worth examining the extent to which a child's original style may persist—and may offer privileged access in the case of novel or difficult-to-master symbolic forms.

Conclusion

Against the background of those aspects of symbolic growth that characterize every individual, we have described two diverse routes of early symbolization, tracing their characteristics in the domains of symbolic play and three-dimensional depiction. One route, which we have termed *patterning,* has its origins in the young child's curiosity about the tangible and perceptible properties of objects; it manifests itself in early childhood through a persistent interest in the shapes and placement of objects, and it remains a major influence in the older child's involvement with the configurational possibilities of various symbol systems. The other route, which we have called *dramatizing,* has its first manifestations in the young child's social interactions; it reveals itself in the preschool years in a constant fascination with the world of persons and social events and can be discerned in the older child's continuing involvement with affective or narrative possibilities of symbolic expression.

We regard the findings sketched in the preceding as both partial and preliminary—partial because they represent only one part of a broader investigation of the processes of symbol use; and preliminary, because we are still gathering and analyzing data.

We have also regarded our findings as parochial to some degree. First we must consider that our findings are based on a small sample that has been studied under atypical conditions. In order to determine whether patterning and dramatizing are indeed widespread rather than "special" phenomena, we have initiated a control study that will examine a much larger group of young subjects—subjects who have not been subjected to the kind of intensive scrutiny that has characterized our involvement with the nine longitudinal subjects. Results of this study should test our claims regarding the universality of the routes we have discerned.

Second, our conclusions may be parochial to the degree that the materials and tasks we have used in our investigations may be appropriate for only Western middle-class subjects. Activities like symbolic play, so widespread in American society, may not occur in remote parts of the world; alternatively, such activities may occur in strikingly different forms and varieties. Other symbolic forms—such as ritual—that apparently play only a limited role in our society may assume greater prominence in preliterate or traditional societies. Only cross-cultural studies can reveal the range of symbolic behaviors; and only comparative work can indicate whether the portrait presented here will have to be significantly revised.

Despite these and other limitations, we feel that our intensive study of a small group of children has provided a logical point of departure for the study of symbolic development. As a result of the long-term intimacy we have acquired with our small population, we will be able eventually to posit ordinal scales for each symbolic medium, ordinal scales for each individual style, and an overall portrait describing the continuities in early symbolic development. The resulting descriptive model, along with the tools and techniques used to construct it, can then be made available to other researchers. Once our claims have been tested by other social scientists, working in a range of social and cultural settings, a much more comprehensive and accurate view of symbolization should be forthcoming.

In addition to suggesting the need for various forms of supplemental information, our study also raises a number of issues in need of further investigation. One pressing issue centers on the developmental significance of the proposed scales and styles. We have suggested that the ways in which children master some of the tasks posed by the culture—for example, mapping and writing—may utilize their first-favored cognitive style. In our view these findings suggest that, even as there exists a range of expressive media, there may also be a variety of routes that individuals can follow in mastering one or several of those media. It seems probable that most people could (and eventually do) become relatively adept in both of the dominant stylistic approaches: But what does it mean when an individual seems to have recourse to only one mode of symbolic expression? Stylistic rigidity may signal the limited world of the emotionally disturbed, learning disabled, or even the psychotic individual. Our findings also raise the question of whether the missing skills can be taught or a single style sufficiently exploited to "make up for" the missing skills—and the role of education in this process. And the possibility also arises that certain persons, such as great artists or scientists, may be similarly wedded to a single style, finding in that commitment the highly personal tools essential to forging a truly original viewpoint.

Finally, there is room for speculation about the possible sources of the styles of symbolization—are they carried genetically; are they modeled after parents, siblings, or other members of the society; do they result from a subtle interaction between predispositions on the part of the child and adjustments on the part of the parents; do they correspond to specific neural substrates or cortical zones? At this point our data allow us only to raise these issues. And, given the great difficulty in unraveling these factors from one another, it may be impossible to fix the precise contribution of each potential source. But, whatever the ultimate reasons for these contrasting styles, it is intriguing to reflect that in the case of a capacity as fundamental as symbolization, the human may have evolved at least two alternative routes to attaining competence.

Acknowledgments

We thank Shelley Rubin, Ann Smith, and Pat Mckernon for their help with all phases of the study; Jen Silverman for making the illustrations; and Judith Fram for the careful preparation of several drafts of this chapter.

References

Bruner, Jerome S., Rose R. Oliver, and Patricia M. Greenfield
  1966   *Studies in cognition and growth.* New York: Wiley.
Gardner, Howard
  1976   Promising paths to knowledge. *Journal of Aesthetic Education* **10**, 201–207.
Gardner, Howard, Dennie Wolf, and Ann Smith
  1975   Artistic symbols in early childhood. *New York University Education Quarterly* **6**, 13–21.
Piaget, Jean
  1954   *The construction of reality in the child.* New York: Basic Books.
  1961   *Play, dreams, and imitation.* New York: Norton.
  1970   Piaget's theory. In *Carmichael's Manual of Child Psychology,* edited by Paul Mussen. New York: Wiley.
Werner, Heinz, and Bernard Kaplan
  1963   *Symbol formation.* New York: Wiley.
Wolf, Dennie, and Howard Gardner
  1979   Style and sequence in symbolic play. In *Early Symbolization,* edited by Margery Franklin and Nancy Smith. Hillsdale, New Jersey: Lawrence Erlbaum.

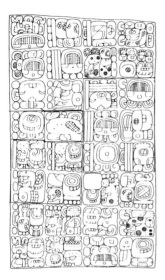

IV
TECHNOLOGY AS TRANSFORMER

13

Introduction

MARY LeCRON
STANLEY H. BRANDES

There has been a surprising neglect by anthropologists of the effect of technology on the symbolic process. Of individual authors, Lévi-Strauss considers it only on the most elementary transformational level, using the raw–cooked dichotomy as a metaphor for man's relation to nature and his cultural innovations (Lévi-Strauss, 1969). Symbolic conceptualization through *bricolage* presumably allows for an introduction of technologies and their products as one source of the elements from which symbols are created (Lévi-Strauss, 1969). Symbol systems are also technologically reflected, as in the organization of dwellings and villages (Lévi-Strauss, 1963).

Transmuted objects are similarly given *bricolage* status as elements used in various kinds of ritual by such authors as Douglas (1966), Turner (1967), and Firth (1973). Readers on symbolism (for example, Rossi, 1974; Geertz, 1971) give technology equally short shrift. That of Dolgin *et al.* (1977) introduces it only indirectly by means of a Marxist orientation in which *unreal* mediational ideologies grow in response to a technologically induced distance between labor and control of its products (see Lefebvre, 1977).

The approaches cited in the preceding, with limited exception of those of Marx and Lévi-Strauss, recognize the use of technology in implementing symbolic structures but not its role in symbolic transformation. Since both Lévi-Strauss and Marx approach it at only the most generalized level—the first as the impact of the invention of fire on man's perception of himself as a cultural being, and the second as the impact of the introduction of

SYMBOL AS SENSE

industrial technologies on social relationships—neither throws a great deal of light on the role of technology per se in creating and transforming symbols.

Although focus on *material culture* went out of style for ethnologists during the 1930s and 1940s, archaeologists have of necessity continued to make it their central concern, thus widening the intellectual gulf between themselves and those studying contemporary peoples. To reintroduce it as central to the concerns of symbolic anthropology we must turn to the work of a physical anthropologist (Kitahara-Frisch), an archaeologist (Conkey), and a nonanthropologist interested in technology as communication (Cherry).

It is appropriate to introduce technology at this stage in our discussion because Shotwell *et al.* have shown us the central importance of object manipulation and material constructions during ontogeny. It is clear both from their analysis and from Lamendella's survey that linguistic and technological proficiency have similar ontogenetic time schedules. Like those of Conkey and Kitahara-Frisch, phylogenetic studies should take this developmental feature into consideration. Cherry, working at a smaller time scale, also views language and technology as interlocked in a single, more comprehensive, symbolic process.

If we define symbolism as a process of representation of socially organized relationships, we find that the development of technological skills: (*a*) is fundamental to the production of representations; (*b*) generates in itself the need for new or revised symbolic structures; and (*c*) serves as the primary vehicle by which symbolic systems are maintained through time. Although language is not a technology in the narrowest sense of the term, if fulfills all of the other definitional criteria. Kitahara-Frisch and Cherry build this perspective into their arguments in this section, and both Kitahara-Frisch and Conkey view language as the central technology without which others, except the very simple and direct primitive tool use of lower animals (for a review of this topic, see Alcock, 1977), could not have existed.

Before technologies came into being, man and his environment were one; his environment included only nature, of which he and his fellows formed a part. Culture, in all of its present-day complexity, arose and has flourished because of the human discovery of the adaptive advantage of the transformation of nature. Through human (but in its inception hominoid rather than hominid) intervention, an element or elements from the natural environment were transformed into something both *unnatural* and efficacious. While efficacy was direct or minimally indirect in the period described by Kitahara-Frisch, its indirection steadily expanded over time.

As *unnatural* elements proliferated, the environment itself became *unnatural*. Proliferation at first progressed slowly, but as technology built upon technology (in Kitahara-Frisch's words, "tools to make tools") the rate accelerated until, at the present time, there is little of nature that has not been altered to a greater or lesser, overt or covert, extent by the manipulations of man.

Technological manifestations are cultural symbols, standing in systemic relationships to other symbols just as surely as the symbols underlying religious rituals or myth. Like words, tools are defined by the uses to which they are put, but, also like language, technologies have nonreferential uses, as Marx so clearly recognized (Lefebvre, 1977). They generate ideologies and mystiques of their own that interdigitate with social relationships of all kinds.

The three chapters included here attack the problem of technology as symbolic transformation from the standpoint of three distinct slices of time. That treated by Kitahara-Frisch explores the earliest known beginnings of technology in the Pleistocene (the Lower Paleolithic, from about 2 million to 100,000 years ago), a temporally extended slice of many millennia during which change was extremely slow. That considered by Conkey is of shorter relative duration; a perioid of perhaps 25,000 years (the Upper Paleolithic, from about 35,000 to 10,000 years ago) during which the groundwork for symbolism as we know it was well laid. Cherry examines a much shorter period, at the most 2 millennia, but with major focus on this century, during which the transformational potential of technology has almost literally exploded.

Conkey speaks of technological transformations as *rubicons,* in the sense that they are not an either/or matter. From the time they occur, they are irrevocably in existence, and affect just as inevitably the structure of society from that moment onward.

Kitahara-Frisch dicusses the rubicon of making simple stone tools through use of tools to make tools, as necessitating planning, with all of the cognitive distance that this implies. In examining this problem we move from an observational consideration of the symbolic potential of man's closest primate ancestors, in the last chapter, to deductions as to the nature of the transition that can be made from inferences about the structure of the act as revealed in the archaeological record: a complex intellectual endeavor, far removed from ethological processing of data. To make deductions of this sort, every aspect of the situation most be carefully examined. Kitahara-Frisch points out that it is not *just* tool-making that distinguishes the presymbolic phase that he is discussing, but the making of *stone* tools that, because of the nature of the material, require not just on-the-spot use of hands or teeth but the search for, and finally manufacture of, another tool that is able to fracture stone.

Today, tools to make tools are so fundamental as to be quite taken for granted. All present technologies are dependent on the process, from the knife used to peel vegetables for the stew, or the needle used to sew a seam, to the elaborate layering of tool manufacture involved in the production of automobiles or spaceships, tools for transportation.

Between the earliest stone tool manufacture and the period discussed by Conkey, tool types had gradually increased in a steady progression of specialization and elaboration. Efficacy was given a quite new dimension with the invention of the means of depicting objects and activities: in other words, art. Not until very much later, and in very few cultures, did it become art for art's sake. There can be little doubt that at its inception, art was itself a tool in that representation was used to bring about a desired result. There is also little doubt that the result had to do with man's own survival, either through continuance of his own species or continuance of other species that he needed for sustenance.

Following Leroi-Gourhan (1965), Clark (1977) argues that cave art focuses on human and animal sexuality and the commonality between the human and animal kingdoms that this sexuality provides. He points out the numerous male and female signs and conjunctions of these found on both walls and portable objects. Details can often be equally well interpreted as sexual or concerned with the hunt. For example,

> both the "tectiforms," formerly interpreted as huts or traps, and the "clavi-forms" once classed as clubs or throwing-sticks are convincingly accepted by Leroi-Gourhan as female symbols. Again, the "wounds" of the famous bison of Niaux can as well be interpreted as vulva and the "arrows" as male organs; indeed a bison on the central panel at Bernifal actually carries oval vulva signs instead of wounds and male baton signs in place of darts or arrows . . . . In the representation of masked figures with animal heads, antlers and skins strapped over human forms, we need not recognize hunting magic but rather a deeply felt community between man and the animals he hunted for food [Clark, 1977:412–413].

Metaphoric linkages by means of symbols in which two conceptually different items are made one are crucial to the symbolic process. Shotwell *et al.* have shown us that this type of classification is ontogenetically early. It can be seen to be well-developed by the Upper Paleolithic, where womb-like cave enclosures or phallic bones or tools were the primary surfaces on which sexual and animal depictions were made. We can speculate that the identification of sexual activity with killing goes back at least to the Acheulean and Mousterian periods during which weapons became increasingly pointed and symmetrical (i.e., phallic) in shape. We can also hypothesize that the major purpose of this symbolism stems from the desire to counter something bad (death) with something good (propagation and birth). The motive behind burial (first appearing around 70,000 years B.P.) seems to be much the same. Birth and death are, even today, unconsciously equated through the act of enclosure, which, because it is good in the first instance is to be seen as good in the second, or, because it leads to life in the first instance, must lead metaphorically to a renewal of life in the second.

Figurative symbolism was apparently an efficacious tool in the Upper Paleolithic, and we have little reason to suppose that it is any less efficacious today. Even if we are not always able to say what it is good for, it cannot be doubted that it is believed to be efficacious in some sense, or it would hardly be continued. One reason that its efficacy is difficult to assess is that it is so multivalent.

Conkey discusses the emergence of style in the designs superimposed on bone or manufactured artifact and the relationship of style to boundary maintenance. Cherry also stresses the importance of style as a communicative barrier. The potential for style and stylistic variation also provides a dynamic flexibility for all symbolic manifestations including technology and language (see also Shotwell *et al.,* in the preceding). Representational rules are never so rigid that they do not allow for manipulation.

The various types and functions of boundaries cry out for further exploration. Kitahara-Frisch discusses species differentiation as a function of boundaries and suggests that the lack of such differentiation in the genus *Homo* is provided by the communicational potential of culture. Conkey discusses the introduction of stylistic boundaries as a fairly late evolutionary innovation. Although these two positions are, in some sense, contradictory, it may be that stylistic boundaries impede but do not prevent encroachment. Human beings are both imitative and innovative, and the human ability to act "as if" may provide a boundary-leaping potential that both eliminates species differentiation and provides for group identification with its necessary security of belonging.

Stylistic innovations must always be individually intentional, but they are so inevitably copied as to seem a group effort. What concerns us here is the impact of the individual upon his own culture. There is historical documentation for this impact in the period that Cherry is considering. We know the roles of Alexander Graham Bell and Henry Ford or Thomas Edison, for example, and the degree to which their innovative technologies have transformed our world. Cherry shows us how innovations in communication have completely altered the nature of communication itself, and in so doing have created symbolic problems that require new solutions.

Although Cherry is speaking primarily of language-related communication, all symbolic systems, including other technologies, that seem to have less to do with communication actually turn out to be communicative in his unilateral sense. In unilateral systems, requiring no immediate, or only a very indirect, response, the sender of the message is often unspecified, that is, generalized rather than specific. Responses are often delayed and lie rather in whether subsequent behavior of the recipient reflects in any way agreement or disagreement with the message. This behavior is extremely diffuse, hence difficult to assess. In the United States, public opinion polls attempt such assessment.

Both Conkey and Cherry speak of communication explosions. As Cherry points out, new technologies and new communicational avenues significantly change the structure and content of messages. And although we cannot "know" the structure of linguistic communication in the Upper Paleolithic (but see Foster, this volume), for further clues to its nature, we can be reasonably sure that by that period it was as symbolically sophisticated as the technology, art, and ritual practices that we can "know" more directly from their material remains.

Both Conkey and Cherry also stress the interpretive advantages of a structural approach that recognizes that no contextual detail is devoid of symbolic information. Thus, even what seems to be nonrepresentational may well have communicative value (Conkey, p. 234). Certain symbolically significant details may be abstracted to represent the whole, while others are omitted or deliberately tabooed or replaced with an acceptable alternative. Introduction of both extreme realism and extreme abstraction in the earliest known art forms suggests either that the two arose simultaneously or that abstraction preceded realism. This is reinforced by the ontogenetic parallel of children's drawings in which symbolic abstraction occurs before the production of realistic detail. (See Shotwell *et al.*, this volume, for examples.)

Conkey also discusses artistic *projection* (the mental ascription of a potential image to an actual shape), which Shotwell *et al.* have described as a characteristic of childhood fantasy and which we might with justification suggest as the cognitive catalyst to the whole symbolic process.

References

Alcock, John
  1977 The evolution of the use of tools by feeding animals. In *Anthropology full circle*, edited by I. Rossi, J. Buettner-Janusch, and D. Coppenhaver. New York: Praeger. Pp. 76–86.
Clark, Grahame
  1977 The cave artists. In *Anthropology full circle*, edited by I. Rossi, J. Buettner-Janusch, and D. Coppenhaver. New York: Praeger. Pp. 411–413.
Dolgin, Janet L., David S. Kemnitzer, and David M. Schneider (eds.)
  1977 *Symbolic anthropology: A reader in the study of symbols and meanings.* New York: Columbia Univ. Press.
Douglas, Mary
  1966 *Purity and danger: An analysis of concepts of polution and taboo.* Middlesex, England: Pelican.
Firth, Raymond
  1973 *Symbols: Public and private.* Ithaca, New York: Cornell Univ. Press.
Geertz, Clifford (ed.)
  1971 *Myth, symbol and culture.* New York: Norton.
Lefebvre, Henri
  1977 Ideology and the sociology of knowledge. In *Symbolic anthropology: A reader in the study of symbols and meanings,* edited by J. Dolgin, D. S. Kemnitzer, and D. M. Schneider. New York: Columbia Univ. Press. Pp. 254–269.
Leroi-Gourhan, André
  1965 *Treasures of prehistoric art.* New York: Abrams.
Lévi-Strauss, Claude
  1962 *The savage mind.* Chicago: Univ. of Chicago Press.
  1963 *Structural anthropology.* New York: Basic Books.
  1969 *The raw and the cooked: Introduction to a science of mythology* Vol. 1. New York: Harper.

Rossi, Ino (ed.)
    1974   *The unconscious in culture: The structuralism of Claude Lévi-Strauss in perspective.*
        New York: Dutton.
Turner, Victor
    1967   *The forest of symbols: Aspects of Ndembu ritual.* Ithaca, New York: Cornell Univ.
        Press.

14

Symbolizing Technology as a Key to Human Evolution

JEAN KITAHARA-FRISCH

Introduction

As a physical anthropologist interested in the study of human origins, I have long been fascinated by the way the hominid pattern of evolution came to differ from that characteristic of animal evolution as a whole, including that of nonhuman primates (Frisch, 1965). In this chapter I wish to explore one such difference: the development in hominids of a full-blown symbolizing capacity, manifested in language and tool use, both of which radically influenced hominid evolution.

As is well known, the evolution of a newly arisen animal phylum occurs usually by way of a progressive differentiation into distinct branches, each exploiting a particular section or aspect of the environment (Simpson, 1953). This phenomenon, termed *adaptive radiation,* or, in Teilhard de Chardin's terms, *diverging evolution* (1956:99), accounts for the multiplication of genera and species within each phylum, as well as for the peculiar specializations proper to each animal form. Adaptive radiation characterizes the history of most animal phyla and is particularly noticeable at landmarks in the history of life, e.g., at the origin of land vertebrates, of mammals, etc.

The origins of the hominid family constitute no exception. When a number of australopithecine fossils came to light in South Africa, some 30 years ago, it soon became apparent that the large morphological differences seen between specimens probably called for the recognition of at least two different types of early hominids, a gracile and a robust one. To be sure, there was

Copyright © 1980 by Academic Press, Inc.
All rights of reproduction in any form reserved.
ISBN 0-12-262680-x

divergence of opinion, but this was largely confined to whether the observed differences were to be accorded specific or generic significance. That the process of diverging adaptation was at work in the newly arisen hominid family was not disputed. Subsequent finds of early hominids in Olduvai, Lake Turkana, Omo, and, lately, Hadar have confirmed the widespread coexistence of these two hominid types (Howell, 1978; Leakey, 1976). Whatever the taxonomic level ascribed to these types, we would expect, by analogy with similar radiations studied in other animal phyla, that the differences between the types would have increased over time. To the contrary, however, the next stage of hominid evolution, starting apparently with the appearance of the genus *Homo*, reveals an entirely unexpected pattern.

Although the finds belonging to the age of *Homo erectus* are still too scarce and too limited in distribution to allow a firm judgment, all the available African evidence (from Ternifine, Olduvai, and, more recently the 1.5 million-year-old skull from Lake Turkana [Leakey and Walker, 1976]) points to similarities with the earlier known Far Eastern specimens, from Java and China. Nowhere, over this wide area, is there to be seen the sort of differentiation observed in South and East Africa between early hominids coexisting within a much narrower region.

Even more significant is the pattern evidenced by the subsequent and latest stage of hominid evolution, in Upper Pleistocene times. There then appears, for the first time, a tendency *opposite* to the pattern of diverging adaptation. Populations contemporary with Western Europe's Neanderthal man (as known from Africa, the Near East, and Eastern Europe) show that early *Homo sapiens* varied considerably more in morphology than later varieties of man, which suggests that the diversity of physical types in *Homo sapiens* was much greater 100,000 years ago than it is now. The fossil evidence thus indicates that recent hominid evolution has followed a converging pattern instead of the usual diverging one.

In this Chapter, I wish to ask whether the uniqueness evidenced by the hominid evolutionary pattern from the appearance of *Homo* onwards can be related to characteristics of human behavior that cultural anthropologists have long regarded as species-specific, i.e., as restricted to *Homo sapiens* as we know him. In other words, can the behavior characteristic of *Homo* yield the key to this unique evolutionary pattern? If so, in what ways were these behavioral capacities responsible for deviation from the usual pattern in animal evolution? Among the capacities regarded by cultural anthropologists as specific to living mankind, three deserve special consideration: (*a*) *human technology,* in that man is the only primate known systematically to transform his environment, in the widest sense of the term, and to depend on this transformation for his survival; (*b*) *language,* in that man is the only primate found to make use of verbal concepts to communicate with others of his species; and (*c*) *symbolizing,* in that man is the only primate capable of organizing sensory experience into a set of meaningful representations

of perceived reality. Further, there is evidence that both language and technology depend upon the capacity to symbolize.

The task of this chapter, then, is to explain how these three capacities
and, ultimately, the capacity to symbolize may have brought about the
unique evolutionary shift that occurred during the development of the hominid phylum.

Technology

In order to identify the properties of human technology that had an impact
on hominid evolution, we must first examine how human tool-use differs
from similar behavior in nonhuman primates, particularly our closest relatives, the chimpanzees. Our knowledge of the way wild chimpanzees use
tools has considerably increased during the last 10 years. Several scientific
syntheses (Goodall, 1968; Lancaster, 1968), as well as a number of more
popular presentations (Goodall, 1971), make it unnecessary to describe these
data here. Instead, to appreciate recent advances in our understanding of
tool-use, both human and nonhuman, we should compare what is known
now about chimpanzee behavior with assumptions made in the oft-quoted
review article by Oakley, published in 1954.

Oakley mentioned as specific to human tool-making: (a) the amount of
foresight involved; (b) the making of tools to a set pattern; and (c) the use
of tools to make tools. It now appears, however, that the amount of foresight
exhibited by chimpanzee tool-use considerably surpasses what had been first
suspected. Also, some pattern can be perceived in the sequence of chimpanzee movements required for the making and using of termite fishing tools,
and this patterning, it is important to note, must be learned by trial and error
(Teleki, 1974). (The elementary nature of the patterns is somewhat reminiscent of the very small amount of patterning evidenced by the earliest
known stone tools [Merrick et al., 1973]). Thus, of the three characteristics
of human tool-making listed by Oakley, the one that emerges clearly as
unique to humans is the use of secondary tools, i.e., tools to make tools.
In fact, laboratory experiments (Khroustov, 1964) have further corroborated
this point.

Another clarification has to do with the role played by tool-use and tool-
making in the human and chimpanzee subsistence patterns. Technology is
absolutely necessary for human survival, as was originally pointed out by
Bartholomew and Birdsell (1953). Chimpanzees, on the other hand, are far
from dependent on the tools they are occasionally seen to handle. This limited dependency is manifested in many ways: the small number of animals
within the group that practice intensive tool-use (Nishida, 1973:358); the
existence of groups where no tool-use has yet been observed (which suggests
at least a very modest reliance on tools, even if further observations reveal

their presence); and the short annual time span when productive tool-use is well in evidence, at least in some places (Suzuki, 1966).

It is tempting to suppose that the unique features of human tool-use contributed to the evolutionary pattern characteristic of hominids. What makes this assumption particularly attractive is that it is at the stage where these features become better marked (in Middle Pleistocene times, with *Homo erectus*) that evolution becomes unambiguously monophyletic. Indeed, only with the appearance of *Homo erectus* have archaeologists found it necessary to use a large number of categories for characterizing stone industries and describing tool assemblages (Isaac, 1972). This great diversity of tool types can reasonably be thought to reflect a closer integration between technology and subsistence. And it is precisely at this time that the monophyletic nature of human evolution becomes evident, so evident, in fact, that it was correctly recognized by Dobzhansky (1944) more than 30 years ago.

To understand the simultaneous appearance of extended tool-use and monophyletic evolution, we should recall the mechanism responsible for the adaptive radiation characteristic of most animal phyla. As a particular phylum spreads into a number of different biotopes, local populations become subject to diverse forms of selective pressures causing the genetic composition of each to become progressively distinct from that of other populations adapting to different environments. A similar process was no doubt responsible for the formation of a number of reproductively isolated hominid species in late Pliocene and early Pleistocene times. With the development of technology, however, a new adaptive mechanism came into action: Local populations could now adjust to their respective environments not by undergoing a genetic change but by building a technological buffer between the environment and the human organism. To build such a buffer, a number of cognitive capacities were needed, among them the ability to foresee environmental changes well in advance and to prepare oneself accordingly, as well as the capability to devise complex and efficient implements, through reliance on secondary tools.

Thus technology prepared the shift to a monophyletic pattern of evolution in two ways. Most directly, it obviated the need for human populations to develop genetic adaptations to their living environments, thereby releasing these populations from the selective pressures leading to the formation of reproductively isolated groups. Perhaps more important in the long run, technology set a premium on the development of cognitive capacities. Man's immediate ancestors were able to keep in mind ever wider sections of space and time, on the one hand, and to grasp increasingly complex connections between elements of technical processes, on the other. Through technological adaptations to the environment, the human phylum was spared the need for further organic specialization.

If this view of the influence of technology is accepted, we can attempt to identify a point in time when human tool-use and the capacities it presupposes became developed enough to bring about convergent evolution. Some light on that problem can be shed by the requirements of stone tool manufacture. Stoneworking is based on mental capacities unique to human technology. Specifically, stone tool manufacture requires the use of stone on stone. To this end, an object (a pebble, for instance) must be perceived as a potential implement to make a tool out of another object, without any benefit resulting immediately and evidently from the first stage in the tool-making process.

Such a reduplication in the manufacturing process is not necessary for modifying the shape of less resistant material. Hands or teeth suffice to transform vegetal material into fishing sticks, to strip vegetal stalks for probing, or to wad leaves to make them absorbent, as is well exemplified by the chimpanzee behavior observed by Goodall (1970) and others (McGrew, 1974; Nishida, 1973; Teleki, 1974).

The mere presence of stone tools, unlike tools made of other material, automatically indicates the existence of secondary tools. Stone tools bear witness to an activity reflecting on itself.

In addition, the number of manufacturing operations that necessarily intervene between the perception and selection of the appropriate unaltered stone and its use as a tool (chopper, scraper, etc.) implies a highly protracted period of activity aimed towards a distant end. Nothing on this scale has ever been observed in cases of chimpanzee tool preparation. Moreover, early hominids found raw material for their tools in sites several miles distant from their places of manufacture and use (Merrick et al., 1973). This compares with a maximum distance of 75 meters reported for most chimpanzee tool preparation (McGrew, 1974; Nishida, 1973). Obviously, making tools out of stone calls for a much wider range of foresight than has been so far demonstrated in nonhuman primates' tool-use.

Finally, judging from contemporary ethnological evidence, it is clear that a number of activites that are an essential part of human subsistence (such as killing large animals, skinning and dismembering carcasses, cutting down trees, etc.) can be performed successfully only with the help of implements as or more resistant than stone. This indicates that, prior to the use of metals, stone tools formed an essential component of the human subsistence pattern. In this, their role was very unlike that played by chimpanzee tools made of vegetal matter. The presence of stone tools, no matter how rudimentary, may be taken to indicate the close integration between human technology and subsistence. Both by their greater efficiency in helping man to exploit the environment and by the mental abilities that they presuppose, stone tools thus appear as the best marker for determining the time period when human technology began to modify the pattern of hominid evolution.

Summing up the above, the evidence from naturalistic studies of chimpanzee tool behavior as well as that from paleoanthropology strongly suggest that human technology was one of the main factors responsible for causing the hominid phylum to assume a monophyletic pattern of evolution. Moreover, the crucial time for this major event appears to be marked in the archaeological record by the appearance of stone tools.

Language

We began our inquiry with a consideration of the differences between early human technology and that of nonhuman primates. A similar inquiry must now be attempted with regard to human language. I shall try to show that both the properties of human language and the function it may have performed in the subsistence pattern of *Homo* contributed to a convergent evolutionary pattern.

We must first remember that modern evolutionary theory considers new species to arise only if a particular population or group of populations is somehow prevented from interbreeding freely with other populations of the same species. "The essential component of speciation, that of the genetic repatterning of populations," writes Mayr (1963), "can take place only if these populations are temporarily protected from the disturbing inflow of alien genes" /(p. 480). Obstacles to interbreeding can be physical (sea, rivers, mountains), ecological (vegetation zones), or behavioral (maintenance of territories, different communication signals) to name just a few of the numerous possible sources of isolation. But any circumstance preventing communication between neighboring populations is likely to favor the formation of distinct species under the influence of selective pressures causing each population to adapt to its respective habitat.

By contrast, any agent tending to prevent isolation and promote communication between populations renders the formation of distinct species less likely and even impossible. In the case of hominids, the development of technology, because it eventually created possibilities for migrating across the surface of the earth and facilitated seasonal displacements from one habitat to another, doubtless constituted a major factor in preventing isolation and in fostering communication among temporarily separated populations. But it is evident that language herein played the more important role.

The ability to communicate through language with neighboring populations, eventually resulting in mutual understanding and intermarriage, not only mitigates against genetic isolation but also operates positively to obliterate already extant subspecific genetic differences. When Spaniards landed in the New World at the end of the fifteenth century, populations of *Homo sapiens* that had been reproductively isolated for at least 30,000 years met and were able to communicate adequately through language in a matter of months. The exchange of genes promptly followed. Technology may have sufficed to put an end to the diverging process of evolution, but language appears to have reversed its very direction.

In this context, it is interesting that the rudimentary linguistic abilities reported for nonhuman primates, particularly chimpanzees, appear not to bring together unrelated individuals. The several instances of communication by gesture described by Goodall (1968) in the Gombe Stream colony of wild chimpanzees always occur between animals already familiar with each other, not between animals belonging to different groups. Likewise, it is unclear in reports of language experiments (Gardner and Gardner, 1971; Premack, 1976; Rumbaugh, 1977) whether chimpanzees' capacity for abstraction, displacement, and conceptualization, important as indicators of linguistic abilities, are ever used for communication within the natural chimpanzee group (or, *a fortiori*, between groups). Nor have experiments meant to encourage sign communication between young chimpanzees (Fouts, 1973) produced clear evidence regarding the effectiveness of this newly learned mode of communication. It would thus seem that the communicative function of language, which was decisive in modifying the hominid pattern of evolution, is unique to human beings.

While it is not hard to describe *how* the emergence of language would have resulted in breaking down population barriers, *when* this momentous change took place still remains a matter for speculation. As is well known, anthropologists have so far failed to identify a sure sign of the emergence of linguistic behavior in the paleoanthropological record. Attempts at determining anatomical correlates of linguistic abilities, either in the cranial skeleton or in the morphology of the brain as revealed by endocasts, have met with notoriously little success (von Bonin, 1963). Paleontological finds, accordingly, are not likely to reveal the origin of language.

It is more promising to observe that the cognitive abilities commonly regarded by linguists as prerequisite to the emergence of language are similar to those that are required for the development of stone technology. This similarity is evident, for instance, if one reviews the list of design features considered by Hockett (1959) to characterize all human languages. Among these, *displacement* occupies an important place. Displacement is the property of language by which the speaker refers to objects, persons, events, and so on, remote in space and/or time. As Bronowski and Bellugi (1970) remind us, displacement presupposes at least the capacity to insert a delay between the perception of a stimulus and the utterance of the message it provokes. Human language thus requires the ability for the speaker to detach himself from the ongoing flux of experience, from the present time and place, just as the tool-maker must temporarily divert his attention from the ultimate purpose of his tool-making activity, while nevertheless keeping the purpose in mind as his guiding principle. In other words, both tool-making and language call for a capacity conceptually to relate discrete times and places.

Hockett, in a later elaboration of design features (Hockett and Altmann, 1968), adds *reflexiveness* to the key elements of his language description. With this term, he denotes the property of language by which the speaker can talk about his speech. This feature originates in what Bronowski and Bellugi (1970) consider to be a further step in the capacity for displacement, namely, the internalization of language, making it an instrument fit for reflection and exploration. Linguistic reflexiveness, perhaps even more than displacement, shows a parallel with the capacity to make stone tools. Because both language and stone technology require the capacity for an activity to reflect on itself, they are, in Holloway's (1969) terms, *concordant*. They provide two different illustrations of the same psychological ability. Out of this common root, the human pattern of tool-making and the human type of communication have both arisen.

The similarities, briefly outlined in the preceding, allow us to infer that the first appearance of stone tools, no matter how simple their manufacture, presupposed that their makers had at least rudimentary linguistic abilities. The question that remains to be asked is whether these rudiments would have sufficed to bring about the type of intergroup communication required for preventing the formation of genetic isolates.

Significantly, it is only when technology reaches a level of sophistication corresponding to the second threshold of complexity figured by Isaac (1972: Figure 5) that hominids clearly evidence a monophyletic pattern of evolution. This correlation suggests that further progress in cognitive abilities was indeed required before language had developed enough to promote intergroup communication.

The Symbolic Faculty

As mentioned above, the cognitive similarities underlying language and stone tool-making suggest that thest two phenomena did not appear separately, but that they are rather different expressions of a single more basic ability. Hewes (1973), who is among the few to have proposed a plausible model explicating the relationship between the rise of tool-making and the emergence of language, sees this basic ability as the acquisition and utilization of complex patterned sequences of action. "It could be," he writes, "that, in the long course of hominization, it is the evolutionary growth of this kind of syntactic capacity that has been so important, and not its separate manifestations in technology and language" (Hewes, 1973:109).

I suggest that the common root out of which sprang a number of distinctively human characteristics, and which was also ultimately responsible for determining convergent evolution, is best searched for at an even more general level than that proposed by Hewes. This root can be identified as what Sapir (1937) termed "the tendency to see reality symbolically." We should note that both language and stone technology manifest attempts by man to impose arbitrary forms on his activity. Man imposes arbitrary forms either in order to alter and control his environment, as in technology, or in order to reflect upon his communicatory activity and to master it, as happens in language. The imposition of arbitrary forms, in as much as it organizes the data of sensory experience into a set of representations of the perceived reality, constitutes a process that many anthropologists would call symbolic. Holloway (1969), for instance, defines *symbolization* as "the capacity to structure the environment arbitrarily," and points out that a number of capacities often considered uniquely human are, in actuality, fully human only when they manifest attributes of *symbolization*, defined as "the arbitrary imposition of forms."

As discussed in the preceding, recent research on nonhuman primate behavior has indeed shown that incipient tool-making, rudimentary conceptualization, and limited displacement are not beyond the capacities of the chimpanzee. However, as Holloway (1969) points out, it is when these abilities are integrated with symbolization, understood as the imposition of arbitrary forms, that man *qua* cultural being appears.

This is not to deny, of course, that there is evidence for the capacity to impose arbitrary forms in the behavior of nonhuman primates. The naming of new objects by Washoe (Linden, 1976:111) through sign combinations apparently not learned from her human companions could represent an example of such an incipient capacity—provided, that is, that this combination of signs constitutes more than a passing chance occurrence. What needs emphasizing here is the fact that, in man, the exercise of the capacity to impose arbitrary forms has become essential to human subsistence. Only under this condition, it appears, does the capacity give rise to a complex of activities, like stone technology and language use, which account for the reversal of direction in the pattern of hominid evolution.

Technology and language emphasize two different functions of the symbolic process. In the one instance, man uses symbols as tools for changing the world, in the other as conceptual representations for understanding the world and himself. But, while technology and language stress different aspects of the symbolic process, it is important to note that both aspects are coexistent and interrelated. No human technology is possible without the making and using of secondary tools. Thus technology always implies reflection: The tool-maker must plan his activity to bring about a desired goal. Similarly, language always implies a transformation, a specification and control of the speaker's innate but undifferentiated ability to name objects and actions; first into language as a *particular* language, then into speech for individual ends. If technology and language are responsible for bringing about the monophyletic and convergent pattern of human evolution, it now appears that, at a deeper level, it is the capacity to symbolize, to see reality symbolically, that lies at the root of the transformation that caused evolution to assume human shape.

Confirmation of this view is found in both the work and the practice of prehistorians and psychologists. For example, wherever undoubted evidence of symbolic behavior is found, as in the funerary practices associated with the burials of Upper Pleistocene hominids, no prehistorian hesitates to recognize in these remains a fully developed humanity. Likewise, commenting on aggressive behavior, the psychologist Bertalanffy (1958) points out that what differentiates human aggression from that of other animals is the role played by symbols. Even where individual or social survival is not at stake, man will fight if motivated by symbolically expressed ideals.

The common rooting of human technology and human language in the symbolic faculty made it possible for these two phenomena, once they started developing, to promote each other's growth. On the one hand, the progressive adaptation of man to a way of life where stone tool-making had become increasingly necessary must have considerably exercised the capacity to reflect upon one's actions, which in itself constituted a preadaptation for linguistic reflection and communication. Selection for stone-tool-making abilities would have placed a premium on the capacity to distance oneself from the task to be performed with the tool, thereby providing the early tool-maker with another of the conditions necessary for the emergence of human language. In the words of Bastian and Bermant (1973), "the evolution of instrumental adaptations set the evolutionary stage in a way that made possible the subsequent specializations and linguistic capacities" (p. 250).

On the other hand, it is not hard to see how the syntactic, abstractive, and reflective capacities exercised daily in linguistic communication would contribute powerfully to the development of a more complex and more efficient stone tool technology. It is probably no accident that Isaac's (1972) third threshold in the evolution of stone tool-making coincides broadly with the appearance in the archaeological record of funeral practices providing evidence of symbolizing and linguistic capacities. Moreover if, as claimed by Isaac, in the Upper Pleistocene the degree of standardization and maximum complexity of rule systems governing design changed drastically, this change can also be interpreted to reflect the emergence of standardized and rule-patterned behavior in linguistic communication and in human behavior generally. Once more, the emerging characteristics are those highly typical of the symbolization process.

Remarkably, it is precisely when the archaeological record provides increasing evidence of characteristics proper to the symbolic process that the biological differentiation between contemporary populations of *Homo sapiens,* as known from the fossil evidence, tends to decrease in importance. For it is in the Upper Paleolithic, with the appearance of modern man, that the already monophyletic pattern of human evolution now takes a decisive converging aspect.

Though one should beware, as Isaac warns us, of reading too much into the still imperfect archaeological record, and though a similar prudence is made mandatory by the fragmentary nature of the distribution of fossil finds, even in the Upper Pleistocene, the striking coincidence between the advance in technological skill and the progressive uniformization of fossil man's morphology can hardly be regarded as an artifact of the discoverers' research techniques.

Conclusion

Though the precise nature of the process responsible for the coincidence between technological differentiation, standardization, and rule patterning on the one hand, and biological convergence on the other, still escapes us, there can be little doubt that the progressively sophisticated systems of tool-making of which Isaac speaks reflect a progressive and multifaceted reinforcement of the symbolizing faculty, and led *Homo sapiens* towards culture as we know it.

Holloway (1969) in defining the specificity of human culture argues that the critical factor must be searched for in the way man organizes his experience. The fossil record documents that successive thresholds in such organization led to the singularity of the human evolutionary pattern. Progress in linguistic communication must have paralleled technological evolution, and the combination must have been a decisive factor in the distinctive convergence that is characteristic of hominid evolution. The common process, based as it is on symbolization, is more important than the media themselves. Both tools and words reflect man's basic symbolizing faculty. In technology, symbols are used as tools for action and for transforming the world, in language they are used as representations of man's understanding of the world and of himself. Thus, both *Homo faber* and *Homo sapiens* were responsible for making man's phylogenetic history unlike that of any other primate.

References

Bartholomew, G. A., and J. B. Birdsell
    1953   Ecology and the protohominids. *American Anthropologist* **55**, 481–498.
Bastian, J., and G. Bermant
    1973   Animal communication: An overview and conceptual analysis. In *Perspectives on animal behavior*, edited by G. Bermant. Glenview, Illinois: Scott, Foresman & Co. Pp. 307–358.
Bertalanffy, L. von
    1958   Comments on aggression. *Bulletin of the Menninger Clinic* **22**, 50–57.
Bonin, G. von
    1963   *The evolution of the human brain.* Illinois: Univ. of Chicago Press.
Bronowski, J. and U. Bellugi
    1970   Language, name and concept. *Science* **168**, 669–673.

Dobzhansky, Th.
1944   On species and races of living and fossil man. *American Journal of Physical Anthropology*, n.s. **2**, 251–265.

Fouts, R. S.
1973   Acquisition and testing of gestural signs in four young chimpanzees. *Science* **180**, 978–980.

Frisch, J.
1965   On a paleontological definition of the genus *Homo*. *Annals of the Japan Association for Philosophy of Science* **2**, 11–15.

Gardner, B. T., and R. A. Gardner
1971   Two-way communication with an infant chimpanzee. In *Behavior in nonhuman primates*, edited by A. Schrier and Stollintz. New York: Academic Press. Pp. 117–184.

Goodall, J. van Lawick
1968   The behavior of free-living chimpanzees in the Gombe Stream area. *Animal Behavior Monographs* **1** (3), 161–311.
1970   Tool-using in primates and other vertebrates. In *Advances in the study of behavior.* Vol. 3, edited by D. S. Lehrman, R. A. Hinde, and E. Shaw. New York: Academic Press. Pp. 195–249.
1971   *In the shadow of man.* London: Collins.

Hewes, Gordon W.
1973   An explicit formulation of the relationship between tool-using, tool-making, and the emergence of language. *Visible Language* **7**, 101–127.

Hockett, C. F.
1959   Animal "languages" and human language. In *The evolution of man's capacity for culture,* edited by J. N. Spuhler. Detroit, Michigan: Wayne State Univ. Press. Pp. 32–39.

Hockett, C. F., and S. A. Altmann
1968   A note on design features. In *Animal communication,* edited by T. A. Sebeok. Bloomington, Indiana: Univ. of Indiana Press, Pp. 61–72.

Holloway, R. L.
1969   Culture: A human domain. *Current Anthropology* **10**, 395–407.

Howell, F. C.
1978   Hominidae. In *Evolution of African mammals,* edited by V. J. Maglio and H. B. S. Cooke. Cambridge, Massachusetts: Harvard Univ. Press. Pp. 154–248.

Isaac, Glynn Ll.
1972   Chronology and the tempo of cultural change during the Pleistocene. In *The calibration of human evolution,* edited by W. W. Bishop and J. A. Miller. Edinburgh: Scottish Academic Press. Pp. 381–430.

Khroustov, G. F.
1968   Formation and highest frontier of the implemental activity of anthropoids. VII International Congress of Anthropology, Ethnology, and Science, Moscow. Vol 3. August 1964, 503–509.

Lancaster, J.
1968   On the evolution of tool-using behavior. *American Anthropologist* **70**, 58–66.

Leakey, R. E.
1976   Hominids in Africa. *American Scientist* **64**, 174–178.

Leakey, R., and A. C. Walker
1976   *Australopithecus, Homo erectus* and the single species hypothesis. *Nature* **261**, 572–574.

Linden, E.
1976   *Apes, men and language* . New York: Penguin Books.

Mayr, Ernst
1963   *Animal species and evolution.* Cambridge, Massachusetts: Harvard Univ. Press.

McGrew, W. C.
1974 Tool use by wild chimpanzees in feeding upon driver ants. *Journal of Human Evolution* **3**, 501–508.
Merrick, H. V. *et al.*
1973 Archeological occurrences of early Pleistocene age from the Shungura formation, Lower Omo valley, Ethiopia. *Science* **242**, 572–575.
Nishida, T.
1973 The ant-gathering behavior by the use of tools among wild chimpanzees of the Mahali Mountains. *Journal of Human Evolution* **2**, 357–370.
Oakley, K. P.
1954 Skill as a human possession. In *A history of technology*. Vol. 1, edited by C. Singer *et al.* London and New York: Oxford Univ. Press (Clarendon). Pp. 1–37.
Premack, D.
1976 *Intelligence in ape and man.* New York: Wiley.
Rumbaugh, D. M.
1977 *Language learning by a chimpanzee: The Lana project.* New York: Academic Press.
Sapir, E.
1937 Language. In *Encyclopedia of the Social Sciences.* New York: Macmillan.
Simpson, G. G.
1953 *The major features of evolution.* New Haven, Connecticut: Yale Univ. Press.
Suzuki, A.
1966 On the insect-eating habits among wild chimps living in the savannah woodland of W. Tanzania. *Primates* **7**, 481–487.
Teilhard de Chardin, P.
1956 *Le groupe zoologique humain.* Paris: Albin Michel.
Teleki, G.
1974 Chimpanzee subsistence technology: Materials and skills. *Journal of Human Evolution* **3**, 575–594.

15

Context, Structure, and Efficacy in Paleolithic Art and Design

MARGARET W. CONKEY

Introduction

The archaeological record shows that over a period of approximately 3 million years hominid populations developed toward culture through refinements and changes in adaptive techniques. While the accretion took many millennia, transitions are apparent that must have been fairly abrupt. Discernible rubicons in hominid cultural evolution can now be discussed.

One such major rubicon was crossed around 40,000 years ago, during the Upper Paleolithic. By that point it is said that the genus *Homo* had become truly *sapiens,* and the cultural mode of adaptation is but another variant of those known to us from the ethnographic record. Artifacts and art forms survive to indicate a cultural system based on fully symbolic conceptual organization. A careful analysis of artifactual structure should reveal certain major features of this organization. Structural analysis should shed light both on these early systems of conceptualization and on stylistic variability within such systems, as well as on their significance for the social interrelationships of these human groups. These topics will be considered here.

Much of this volume is devoted to understanding why and how humans engage in symbolic behaviors, and to the ontogenetic and phylogenetic acquisition of this behavioral mode. In formulating an evolutionary perspective on symbolic behavior, archaeologists must ask which of the many components of symbolism (components that have been elucidated by the studies in this volume) are knowable for past human groups. Like all observers of

SYMBOL AS SENSE

human behavior and its by-products, archaeologists must deal with limited evidence. Intentionality, for example, is no more "seen" by ethnographers than by the archaeologist. However, with richer sources of contextual information, an ethnographic interpretation is expectably richer in detail and more refined in scale. The archaeological visibility of past human behaviors is often lacking, complete, or uneven. For example, we have been able to infer more about prehistoric subsistence systems than about other behavioral systems, partly because the archaeological visibility of certain subsistence activities is much more obvious. But regardless of the behavior being investigated, the nature of the observations that archaeologists can make demands that we make our inferences from structure: the relationships between elements in cultural constructs. Further, the scale of analysis and interpretation is, by definition, different for the archaeologist than for the ethnographer. Details of daily life are not to be expected in prehistoric reconstructions. Our temporal framework is more likely either to be a single event, such as an elephant kill, or to encompass processes occurring over a generation or even a millenium.

Diachronic questions, and those that can be answered by the analysis of material culture, are, at present, the questions that archaeologists can deal with best. This chapter is an attempt to base inferences about prehistoric human behaviors—behaviors occurring over several thousand years—on observations of the structure of material culture. The difference in scale from other analyses in this volume (e.g., Bloch's) will be apparent, yet the interpretive results should add depth to our understanding of the evolutionary perspective on human symbolic behavior. My intent is to develop perspectives on the context, the structure, and the notion of efficacy in Paleolithic art and Upper Paleolithic design systems, particularly as derived from recent studies of Magdalenian engraved bones and antlers from Cantabrian Spain (Conkey, 1978a). These perspectives are provocative because they support the hypothesis that it is in the Upper Paleolithic that we find for the first time manifestations of fully human symbolism, not only in form but in structure.

There have been few attempts to make inferences about the evolution of symbolic behavior from structural features of the archaeological record of the Pleistocene. The works of Isaac (1976) and Marshack (e.g., 1972) stand out as exceptions. Archaeologists may be justified in feeling uncomfortable in the study of the evolution of symbolic behavior for we cannot assume the same or even a similar organization of adaptive behavior for the evolving hominids of the Plio–Pleistocene as we do for those existing in the ethnographic present (see L. R. Binford, 1972). For some time now (see Fritz, 1973), I have been working on the description and explanation of what I view as an explosion of symbolic behavior during the Late Pleistocene. This seems particularly impressive after 40,000 years B.P., but I would not go so far as to say that symbolic behaviors, as manifest in material culture, did not exist earlier. It is well known that Neanderthals prepared graves, and made collections of shells, pretty stones, and ochre (as coloring material?), and that perhaps even earlier hominids executed a few deliberate incisings on pieces of bone (see Bordes, 1969; Marshack, 1978). But these evidences of symbolism are sporadic and relatively unsystematic.

Evolutionary Rubicons

The kind of qualitative and quantitative transformation generally assumed by a rubicon or critical point theory of cultural evolution may well have taken place during the Late Pleistocene, particularly as manifested by Upper Paleolithic material culture systems after 40,000 years ago. Anthropologists have successfully laid away the *cerebral rubicon* theory that held that culture was an all-or-nothing phenomenon; that is, that evolving hominids crossed a critical boundary in cerebral development that not only allowed for but resulted in culture. Lamendella (this volume) gives ontogenetic evidence for progressive development of the symbolic faculty requisite to culture. Yet phylogenetically:

> the greater part of human cortical expansion has followed, not preceded, the "beginning" of culture, a rather inexplicable circumstance if the capacity for culture is considered to have been the unitary outcome of a quantitatively slight but qualitatively metastatic change of the freezing-of water sort [Geertz, 1962:721].

This denial does *not* mean that the *organization* of cultural and adaptive behavior typical of the ethnographic present has also existed since the Australopithecines, whose archaeological remains have supported the denunciation of the critical point theory. There seem to be at least two significant components of human cultural behavior that appeared suddenly and must be all-or-nothing phenomena. In analyzing the process of the creation of material culture, there is increasing reason to believe that neither stone toolmaking nor stylistically decorated cave walls and portable objects evolved gradually in terms of slow and accumulative transformations. Although by no means a Late Pleistocene development, the first—tool manufacture—is a most significant component of all anthropologists' visions of hominid evolution and of the "making" of humanity. Isaac has argued plausibly (1977; 1975:29–30) that "the initial discovery of conchoidal fracture was a quantum jump" that may be thought of "in part as a threshold phenomenon":

> The discovery by hominids that stone fractures in a predictable way when struck may well have given rise immediately to a wide range of forms. The two fundamental series are both unavoidable consequences of the discovery; there have

to be cores, and there have to be flakes . . . . Higher levels of technical organization are achieved when additional steps in manufacture are added [Isaac, 1975:29].

The Emergence of Style

Isaac (1975) and others (see, for example, Clark and Haynes, 1969; Gould, Koster, and Sontz, 1972; White, 1969) note that opportunistically produced tool forms, particularly those that are not (or are only minimally) further prepared, such as a small untrimmed flake, are *not* "appreciably less effective than the more elaborately shaped rule-bound forms that occur in other cultures" [Isaac, 1975:29]. (See also Isaac, 1976.) That is, a sharp unmodified flake struck from a core could do a butchering job as effectively as a more rule-bound flake tool that was further modified according to the restraints of a technological design system. But without either, the butchering would probably not take place. Clearly, the appearance of stone tools must have contributed to an expansion of the hominid potential for energy extraction. Kitahara-Frisch (this volume) discussed this first so-called quantum jump in some detail. However, we must also address the questions of why, when, and how hominid material culture—lithic or otherwise—became rule-bound in form and most probably in function.

Ontogenetically (see Gardner, and Bowerman, this volume) and phylogenetically (see Kitahara-Frisch, this volume) humans become classifiers and develop styles of pattern-recognition at many levels, from that of the individual to wider and more inclusive social groupings. But humans are also pattern-generators; the on-going feedback between these two processes is a baseline for thinking about the growth and diversification of meaning. Even if we were to limit our analysis of the feedback process between pattern-generation and pattern-recognition to material culture systems, the potential for variability at all points in the process should be apparent—variability in interpretation, representation, transformation, form, or use, to cite but a few. However, variability among certain classes of prehistoric material culture has become not only constrained, or rule-bound, but constrained *differentially* in ways peculiar to different groups.

Just as it is difficult to imagine a piece of flint that has been only *incipiently* fractured, an item of material culture can hardly be incipiently modified stylistically, or incipiently rule-bound; either it is or it isn't. Style is the second component of the human cultural behavioral repertoire that I see as an all-or-nothing phenomenon. Although style has been at the methodological core of much archaeological research, particularly as it is manifest among hominid material culture systems, Paleolithic archaeologists are hampered by the lack of coherent analyses and concepts of style, particularly perhaps for lithics (Kleindienst and Keller, 1976). We are only just beginning to make explicit the fact that stylistic behavior, particularly as we know it in the ethnographic present, was not operative during much of the Pleistocene, nor is it manifest in those components of the archaeological record that we most often have to analyze. For analysts of prehistoric material culture, this means that:

1. We have yet to formulate an explicit concept of style, particularly one that will facilitate our identification of its operation in prehistoric cultural systems;
2. We must recognize that we cannot necessarily except to demonstrate stylistic variability among all classes of prehistoric material culture; or, in some contexts, we cannot expect style at all; and
3. We need to build models to explain the appearance of stylistic behavior among hominid populations.

I have discussed points 1 and 2 elsewhere (Conkey, 1978b), and wish here only to elaborate on the third point. To this end it is necessary to formulate a working concept of style that will not necessarily be all-inclusive.

The term *style* implies a conceptually based process that produces variability in the formal attributes of material culture. Wobst (1977) has offered a straightforward definition along these lines. He equates style with "that part of the formal variability in material culture which can be related to the participation of artifacts in the processes of information exchange" (p. 321). Style implies not only participation in a similar encoding–decoding strategy but also the *transformation* of that code into material culture. This transformation, itself a form of communication, is based on a mutually intelligible communication system, and produces material culture exhibiting some degree of standardization. Foster (1975, and this volume) is concerned with transformation as a new means of representation from old materials—transformation as another mode for providing meaning. Participation in a common cultural encoding strategy, transmission of this code via stylistic treatment of artifacts, and standardization of the informational content borne by material culture may operate as processes of cultural integration. Participation in a style enhances the predictability of a message by restraining it. But, just as participation in a style may contribute to integration, it may also serve as an isolating mechanism. In the ethnographic present, we observe the existence of cultural entities that are often internally integrated and externally differentiated from other cultural entities, at least partially, on the basis of style. This is why many archaeologists employ style as an indicator of social boundaries.

A more dynamic approach, however, focuses on style not as an indicator of social boundaries but as a component in the process of boundary-maintenance. Stylistically imbued material culture is not just a reflection of boundaries, but is an active part of the social process (see Bloch, this volume, for a similar perspective on the role of ritual). Barth (1969:15) has argued that analysis should focus on boundaries rather than the "cultural stuff" they contain. Of greater concern to me is the set of conditions under which boundaries are created and the processes by which they are not merely maintained but also mediated. If, in the Upper Paleolithic, these processes involve stylistic modification of material culture, not only can we assume that those humans were organizing their behaviors in such a way as to encode and employ information related to boundary-maintenance in an "artifactual mode" (see Wobst, 1977), but also—and more basically—there must have been recognition of and needs for dealing with boundaries per se. In the evolutionary perspective, the question is one of elucidating the appearance of the noncontinuous component in the human social world.

From Species to Pattern Diversity

The interpretations that have been made of available data from the Middle Pleistocene and earlier (see Bindord, 1972; Isaac, 1969, 1972a,b,c) do not indicate the cultural entities that ethnographers distinguish. Continuing discoveries of hominid remains, both biological and cultural, have pushed back into earlier time ranges the evidence of Australopithecines, stone tool manufacture, earliest *sapiens* populations, and so on. The impressive array of earlier and earlier dates has only elongated the developmental biocultural phases prior to the appearance of *Homo sapiens sapiens* and the associated cultural remains of the Upper Paleolithic. It is not until 70,000 years ago, *at the earliest,* that we can begin to discern critical changes in tempo and mode of cultural evolution (see Conkey, 1978b; Isaac, 1972a:382). We may hypothesize that the selective pressures favoring the processes of internal cohesion and external differentiation among human social groups, as well as the transformation of material culture to effect such cohesion and differentiation, did not exist until the Late Pleistocene. Between 70,000–100,000 years ago, there were important hominid groups that were coping with the fluctuating climate of a periglacial and low latitude tundra habitat associated with the onset of a major glaciation. These groups became located within the ecological circumscription of southwestern Europe; an area bounded by the Atlantic, the Mediterranean, a glacial front, and high mountain regions, which often experienced local high altitude glaciations. Under such conditions, it may have become increasingly difficult for a total population to interact and mix without undergoing some kind of differentiation. This may have been particularly the case in terms of the reception and processing of information.

New modes of dealing with conspecifics under these circumstances may have been characteristic responses by both hominids and other gregarious mammalian groups. Geist's study (1971) of mountain sheep adaptations, for example, elucidates the development of genetically differentiated characteristics possessing social significance, such as horns. Acquisition of these attributes enhanced intragroup dynamics while retaining the unity and viability of the species in a precarious periglacial environment. It seems probable that, for hominids, stylistic differentiation was similarly adaptive, and that certain classes of material culture were provided with group-specific attributes that contributed to the definition and maintenance of group boundaries.

Since that time, human evolution has been characterized not by species diversity but by pattern diversity; that is, cultural differentiation within a singly polytypic species (see Kitahara-Frisch, this volume). That hominids would affect ways for managing both intragroup and intergroup dynamics primarily in terms of symbolic behavior instead of genetically based (especially secondary sex) characteristics as did the mountain sheep is predictable (see Margalef, 1968:97–190). Most views on the evolution of human symbolic behavior suggest that a shift in the organization of adaptive behavior led toward behavior dependent on symbolization (see Geertz, 1964). When such organizational shifts occur, diversity within the new organizational level is predictable. Paleolithic art is clearly one manifestation of the diversification of symbolic behavior systems (see Conkey, 1978a).

One can see that for Upper Paleolithic groups, as for modern ones, a common art style, different from that of their neighbors, could have promoted intragroup solidarity. Replication of a restricted repertoire of designs and the ability of group members to predict the stylistic features of the art forms would have contributed to the standardization of responses among the group. However, just as we can no longer assume that all hominid groups engaged in stylistic behavior, we cannot assume that all material culture of Upper Paleolithic (and later) hominids carried stylistic information.

Although it has been argued that the archaeological visibility of those classes of material culture most likely to bear stylistic information is minimal (see Wobst, 1977), it would seem that among the material remains of the Late Pleistocene populations, even within the domain of Paleolithic art, some media are more predictably and effectively encoded with messages that serve to maintain boundaries. I have argued elsewhere that. *art mobilier,* or 'portable art,' is probably more informed with messages of this sort than either stone tools or cave–wall art (Conkey, 1978a).

Some bones and antlers found in Upper Paleolithic sites are engraved and some are not. In assessing the significance of the observed variability among the engraved pieces, it is not yet clear that we can demonstrate distinct regional or local design codes or systems (see Conkey, 1978a). Nonetheless, once a bone or antler is treated stylistically and becomes a bearer of a stylistic message, it has lost, as Wobst has pointed out (1977), its *signaling innocence* or 'neutrality.' That only *some* bone–antler implements are engraved (that is, the fact that some are and some are not) is, in itself, significant, particularly if these are used, and/or made, in a culturally stipulated mode or as part of a culturally defined context. The loss of signaling neutrality in

Wobst's theory of style predicts precisely the kind of behavioral phenomenon suggested here: "A state of no-stylistic messaging should *suddenly* be replaced by a state in which stylistic form has pervaded at least one (or more) categories of material culture" (Wobst, 1977; 326; italics added). The socioecological context in which human boundary-maintenance modes appeared seems not to have existed before the Late Pleistocene, and style—the behaviors that encode information to be employed in this process—also did not appear before this time. Style could not have evolved cumulatively, so the transition from no-stylistic message to stylistic message must have been abrupt. Stylistic evolution and diversification followed.

One way to view culture is as a mode of organizing diversity to restrain potential chaos (Rappaport, 1971). This organization must be implicitly known by the participants in the cultural system. It is argued that hominids have not always organized diversity into bounded sets, and not always recognized and mediated the boundaries among such sets by symbolic behaviors and the creation of material culture. The hypothesis that hominids have not always organized diversity in this manner is supported in part by the lack of systematic differentiation among artifact assemblages during the many early millenia of tool-use. Boundedness implies a basic social dichotomy of "us *versus* them" (Foster, 1975). Social distinctions create systematic differentiation in behavioral products, and vice-versa. Wherever or whenever bounded sets occur, the cultural continuum is necessarily interrupted. Entities that might otherwise become confounded are made discrete.

The Structure of Upper Paleolithic Art

The art of the Upper Paleolithic appears at a time when the existence of some cultural boundaries is assumed. Style, although we do not understand all of its characteristics, had come into existence. Two important principles of Upper Paleolithic conceptual orientation have been inferred from a structural analysis of Paleolithic art. These I have called (*a*) merging or nondifferentiation of levels; and (*b*) extension of class (after Gombrich, 1961). Both principles involve modes of symbolic association that also imply disassociation or opposition (see Foster, this volume).

I originally derived the identification of these two characteristics of Paleolithic art from an analysis of more than 1200 engraved bones and antlers from Magdalenian (c. 15,000–12,000 years ago) sites in northcoastal (Cantabrian) Spain, but they are, to greater or lesser extent, applicable to a wide range of depictions and forms of both wall and mobile Paleolithic art. In referring to engravings and paintings, I want to stress that not all depictions conform to the characteristics being discussed. Just as we can expect a multiplicity of contexts, of uses, and, therefore, interpretations of and for Paleolithic art (see Ucko and Roseneld, 1967:280–281), we can expect that some engraved pieces, for example, may be more plausibly referable to notational systems (see, for example, Marshack, 1970), some to gaming pieces (see Dewez, 1974), some rather to idiosyncratic incising and/or "noise" than to participation in (a) decorative or incising tradition(s) that generated patterns and structures discussed in the following.

Merging or Nondifferentiation of Levels

The process of artifact manufacture, a transformation of nature into culture (which then is most often used to mediate between nature and culture), creates a form from raw materials. These forms—pots, stone tools, harpoons, cloth—may then be imbued with further information: painted or woven designs, retouch patterns, incised elements. Operationally, the creation of the form and the additional treatment constitute separate levels in the design process. For example, the two levels are clearly involved in Greek vase painting. The vase form is made by the potter; the painted decoration is applied by the painter. In this case, the differentiation of levels is made explicit in that different specialists attend to each level. Most Paleolithic wall art and some of the portable art appears on unprepared surfaces rather than on preexistent forms, such as canvas or artifact. There is not the same kind of differentiation of levels as in Greek vase painting.

Furthermore, many researchers have noted and documented the lack of explicit borders in Paleolithic depictions (deLaguna, 1933:100). In terms of categories that present-day analysts use in the study of visual systems, the lack of explicit design field is striking (see Conkey, 1978a; Fritz, 1975). The lack of consistent, explicit orientation features, such as a ground line, and the need for rotation of engraved pieces in order to observe all of the design seem not to effect the recognizability or interpretability of the art. An indifference to rotation and an indifference to orientation, as we define these features, seem to have existed.

In analyzing decorated material forms, archaeologists are concerned with pattern-generation (Friedrich, 1970; Washburn, 1974a, 1974b). At the same time, we must be concerned with pattern-recognition. We need to know what features make Paleolithic art forms recognizable to us, as well as those features that made the patterns recognizable to Paleolithic observers. But can we know the latter? This may be a critical question, particularly if we argue that at least some patterns or structures have been employed in the process of group boundary-maintenance, whereby structure and content, as well as context, may affect the recognition, and hence efficacy, of a given form.

The lack of certain forms of orientational discrimination in Paleolithic art (see Neisser, 1967:56) reveals something about the pattern-generation process and, in particular, the nondifferentiation of levels. We may also gain insight into pattern-generation processes by investigating the work of ethnographically known artists. Studies of Eskimo carvers suggest that the artists do not conceive that they are applying or adding a pattern or form to the raw material. Rather, the form or pattern exists *in* the raw material, and they view their work as being about releasing those forms from the material (Carpenter, 1973). There is no conceptual or operational differentiation of the level of artifact from the level of decoration. Nondifferentiation of levels, then, is a characteristic of both Eskimo and some Paleolithic art, particularly on art forms that are made by a substractive process, such as carving.

It is easier for us to recognize the *release* from the material of a substractive sculptured Paleolithic form, such as an animal, anthropomorph, or human figure than the *release* of a form that seems to us nonrepresentational. But, as Leach argues (1954), designs that appear as nonrepresentational to us may not necessarily be so to the manufacturer. Although naturalistic forms are common in Paleolithic art, most of the engravings are geometric or apparent nonrealistic depictions.

There have been analyses of Paleolithic art that have attempted to identify characteristic themes or organizational principles. Although both Chollot (1963a, 1963b) and deLaguna (1932, 1933) argue more for idiosyncratic engraving than for any standardization of code among engraved portable art from French sites, both that material and the Spanish engraved material that I have studied show that not only is there a close connection between the engraving and the form of the material being engraved but also there is a restricted set of elements incised on these pieces. Among the Spanish materials, the arrangement of these elements is often carried out according to one of 15 different structural principles (Conkey 1978a; see also deLaguna, 1933:102).

For some engraved materials, it is possible that what may be significant is simply that a particular item is engraved, and has thus lost its *signaling innocence* in Wobst's terms (1977). In addition, there may be a selection of certain elements, which in turn may be ordered according to a certain principle, perhaps one that is consistent with the morphology of the piece that is incised. The incising system is rule-bound in a way that seems less arbitrary.

Figure 1 shows an example of Paleolithic design structure where the morphology of the incised object seems to have dictated the form of the en-

(schematic)

FIGURE 1. Laugerie-Basse: Nondifferentiation of artifact level from depiction level.

graving. This piece of reindeer antler from the French site of Laugerie-Basse depicts a reindeer whose incised rack is positioned to correspond to the point at which the original rack (on which the engraving was executed) was attached to the head of the living animal. This congruence provides a continuity between nature and design, and exemplifies perfectly nondifferentiation of levels.

Here and elsewhere in Paleolithic art, the iconic component is striking. A strong case can be made for an element of iconicity among these engravings. We can identify attributes such as elongation, longitudinality, or zigzags that characterize both the morphological form and the incisings on that form. The replication of these features in the incisions makes them characteristic of the whole artifact, not only of the incisions. Figure 2a shows recognizable incised animal shapes that replicate the shapes of the engraved surface. Those of Figure 2b (c and f) clearly correspond to the elongations, indentations, and protrusions of the engraved surface. The three-dimensional morphology of the incised piece provides a directionality for the two-dimensional incising; this relationship is thus not differentiation of level but continuation of level through decorative emphasis.

It would seem that both engraved pieces from Upper Paleolithic deposits and certain cave paintings are part of a conceptual system that "sees" the whole thing at once, and is not disassociative in the sense of viewing "the-pot-to-be-painted," "the-bone-out-there-onto which . . . ." Rather, the cave walls and the bone–antler items are wholes from which an element, a pattern, is derived, rather than a field onto which a pattern is applied. Given this, it is not surprising to note the lack of an explicit design field.

Congruence of levels is an *associative* pattern-generating process. The earliest portable art includes the famous figurines that, as products of a *subtractive* process of transformation, are not an *applied art* in the sense that Greek vase painting is. In fact, one of the characteristics of these forms is the cutting-out process below the brows and around the nose that yields facial features, *if* they are shown (deLaguna, 1932:496–497). It is not until relatively late in the Upper Paleolithic that decorative treatment becomes widespread on already existing artifact forms, such as harpoons, points, or beveled pieces (see Barandiaran, 1973; Leroi-Gourhan, 1965).

It may be worth an empirical investigation of these datable pieces of Paleolithic art to test the hypothesis that earlier decorated, sculptured, and/or incised art work tended to be executed on nonartifact forms, such as ribs, antler racks, scapulae, slabs, plaques, or were sculpted per se, as in the case of the figurines, whereas later examples of art tended toward increasing application of decoration to forms that were already culturally modified. These latter have at least two potential levels of transformation; first, the manufacture of the artifact, for example, a harpoon, and second, the incising of the patterns into the artifact. It might be argued that subtractive processes of transformation are evolutionarily fundamental. Early tool-making is pre-

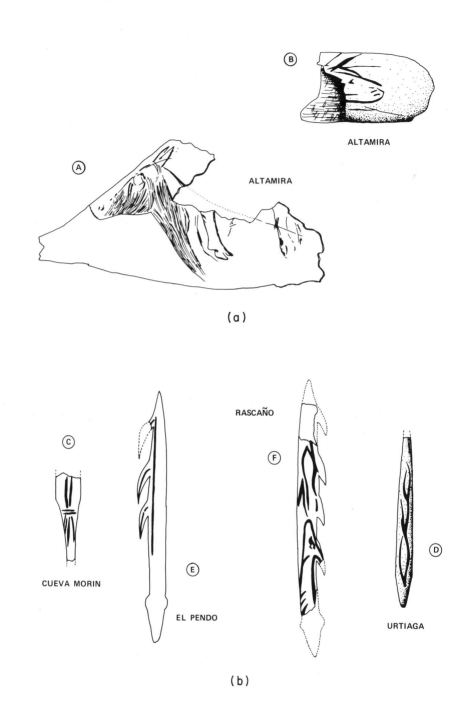

(a)

RASCAÑO

CUEVA MORIN

EL PENDO

URTIAGA

(b)

FIGURE 2. (a and b). Incised patterns as replications or transformations of basic morphological attributes: merging or nondifferentiation of levels.

dominantly subtractive, right through the use of the Levallois technique. It is only in the Upper Paleolithic, with the development of composite tools, that there is significant evidence for tool-making as an additive process as well.

Although I am arguing for a congruence of levels, this can be viewed more hierarchically. The "decision" that a harpoon is to be incised, for example, can then restrain the potential set of incisions to those in congruence with the morphology of that artifact. In a hierarchic approach that assumes at least some degree of differentiation of levels (at least from the analytical, if not also the operational, point of view), a key feature is to what extent are the degrees of freedom of the *parts* restricted by the existence of the whole? (Whyte, 1968:xv–xvi). This freedom seems to be considerably restricted in Paleolithic design. Not only in the engravings on the portable art do we find this kind of replication of attributes of the whole, particularly the morphological whole, but also in wall art, compositions or prearranged elements are unusual.

In the Altamira ceiling the different painted forms may well form such a composition (Freeman: personal communication). Although frequent utilization of natural *bosses* of the wall morphology is a highlight of these paintings, the arrangement of the animals (a central group of dynamic bison—females giving birth?—surrounded by single representatives of other animal species, e.g., a hind, a boar) indicates that more planning was involved than merely seizing upon suggestive wall shapes. But overall it is not composition,

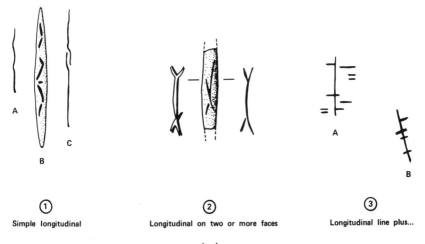

① Simple longitudinal   ② Longitudinal on two or more faces   ③ Longitudinal line plus...

(a)

FIGURE 3. Structural principles of Cantabrian engraved bone–antlers. (a–c) Class I: Longitudinal principle, nine variants. (d) Class II: Closing structures, three variants. (e) Class III: Continuous structures, three variants. (*See pages 238–239.*)

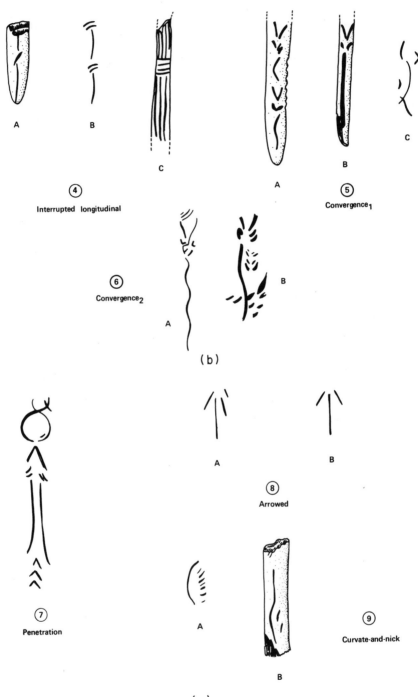

FIGURE 3. (b and c).

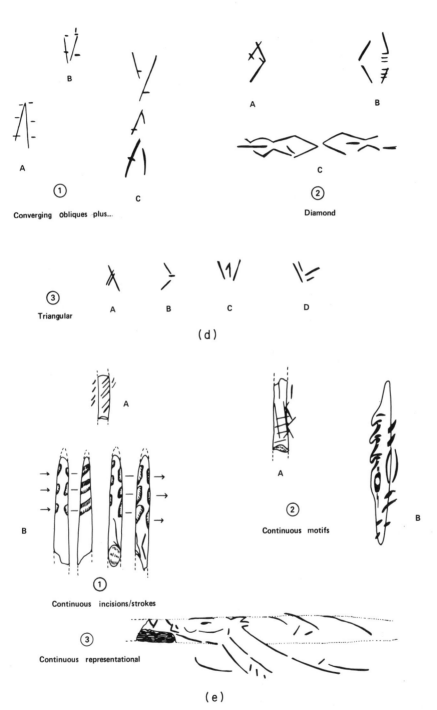

B

A

① Converging obliques plus...

C

A

B

C

② Diamond

③ Triangular   A   B   C   D

(d)

A

B

A

② Continuous motifs

B

① Continuous incisions/strokes

③ Continuous representational

(e)

FIGURE 3. (d and e).

in the sense of predetermined design forms to be applied to the surface, that restrains the selection and use of decorative elements in wall and mobile art. Rather, the characteristics of the morphological whole more often restrain the selection of the parts. Some implications that can be drawn from this as to the efficacy of Paleolithic art will be considered later.

To understand the power of the whole over its parts we need to examine the structuring or arrangement of the design elements. Some analyses of engraved designs have, at one level, contributed much to our understanding of the features that presumably made Paleolithic engravings recognizable (see especially Barandianan, 1973; Chollot, 1963a,b; deLaguna, 1932, 1933; Leroi-Gourhan, 1965). Although these researchers have contributed to our definitions of the elements or themes that are incised, they have not identified specific ordering principles underlying the designs. In searching for differentiation of stylistic schemata among Paleolithic portable art, I expected that variability in structural principles would distinguish styles. Both my work and that of Chollot (1963 a and b, in which she argues for idiosyncratic use of 27 design elements) are consistent with Washburn's (1974a: 3) observations on prehistoric ceramic design systems of the U.S. Southwest: "most design elements are widespread phenomena well-known and used by many . . . who work within a broad temporal and spatial area." Unlike Chollot, who suggests that it is the presence–absence or frequency of different elements that is sufficient to recognize Paleolithic *art mobilier,* I believe that there is more systematic usage of these elements according to certain parameters of meaning, efficacy, and appropriateness.

The symmetry classes that Washburn used to differentiate among Southwestern ceramic design systems or styles (Washburn, 1974a, 1977) proved *not* applicable as discriminators of intraregional (i.e., Cantabrian) design systems (Fritz, 1975). I found that the symmetry that *does* exist, the structural principles that *do* characterize the use of many design elements on many pieces, and the selection of many elements were closely tied to piece morphology. Figure 3 illustrates these structural principles, which are easily classed into three broad categories, each relating in a different way to use of space: (*a*) longitudinal principle (nine variants); (*b*) closing structures (three variants); and (*c*) continuous principle (three variants). Figure 4 shows shapes of frequently engraved artifacts.

The design elements arranged according to any of the longitudinal principles serve to emphasize the elongation or attenuation of the item being engraved. Most of these (if not all) are found on types of artifacts or implements such as points or rods, illustrated in Figure 4—preexisting forms very similar in shape and size to our pens or pencils. The structure of some designs is continuous in that the design field is the whole object, with no bounding, banding, or definition of the space to be engraved on any one surface of the supporting raw material. Boundaries suggested by the lateral edge of the morphological face are ignored as the design continues and encircles the

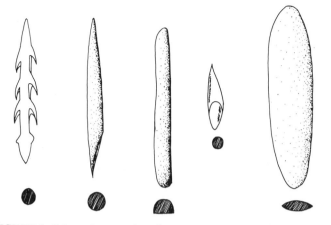

FIGURE 4. Schematic examples of types of artifacts frequently engraved.

entire piece (see Figure 3, Class II). Yet, as deLaguna has also suggested (1933:102), the surface to be engraved usually does not seem to be approached conceptually as three-dimensional. The incisings often constitute patterns and arrangements around the piece, but they are most easily comprehended by us when "unrolled" onto two-dimensional space, and some are best viewed as one would a cylinder seal's impressions rolled out onto soft clay (see Figure 3, Class III). There are exceptions such as some sculpted pieces (e.g., the leaping horse from Bruniquel), but these are rare to absent among the Cantabrian materials.

Extension of Class

We do not really understand the relationship between the wall art and portable art, but this use of three-dimensional space as if it were flat suggests a conceptual linkage with the wall depictions. Wall art is not unidimensional but is characterized by the kind of associative aspect that Gombrich (1961) termed "extension of class." Most casual observers of cave art note the frequency with which the Paleolithic artists exploited presumably natural curves, protuberances, and shapes. By touching them up with paint, a two-dimensional design assumed a partial third dimension. The conceptual process that resulted in such visual manipulation must be part of the feedback between pattern-recognition and pattern-generation. On the one hand, some cave art interpretations suggested that these artists, influenced by their hunting world (see, for example, Breuil, 1952; Torbrugge, 1968), literally "saw" a bison or a deer in the cave wall, and released or made it articulate by a few strokes of color and line.

This implies projection: mental ascription of a potential image to an actual shape. Rorschach (1942) stressed the fact that projection is a kind of mental classification system, and Gombrich's discussion of the cross-cultural variation in interpretations of celestial constellations (1961:106–107) supports the idea that forms and shapes, whether natural or artifactual, serve in part to codify experience (see Munn, 1966:936). For those championing the hunting-image interpretation of Paleolithic art, the Paleolithic projection involved capturing and/or controlling the subject; or at the very least, the artists domesticated the subject, in the sense of making it cultural rather than natural. As noted in reference to the Altamira ceiling, this process is not one of merely seizing appropriate shapes and bosses, of projecting images onto, or "seeing" images in, any cave formation or piece of antler. Rather, an extension of class through analogy takes place. The class of bison rumps, for example, is extended to include certain cave wall shapes that, with a certain amount of treatment (e.g., painting) and in a certain context of action, can stand for a bison rump. The use of the cave wall painting as a new metaphor elicits a similar response because it is an extension of the class of bison rumps: "The test of an image is not its life-likeness but its efficacy within a context of action" (Gombrich, 1961:110). In this sense, the artistic process depends on additives; one must add not only aspects of form (e.g., paint) but also a context in order to *release* the image, to effect the extension of class. It may be that, as an associative process, extension of class is more characteristic of additive art, whereas merging or nondifferentiation of levels is more characteristic of subtractive art. However, both the projection and the extension of class, two sides of the same conceptual coin, testify to the human ability to generalize and, on the basis of partial similarity, to group physically different objects into a common class (Blesser *et al.*, 1973:210).

In some cases of Paleolithic art, nondifferentiation of levels and extensions of class seem to be two variants of the same process. Figure 5 provides two

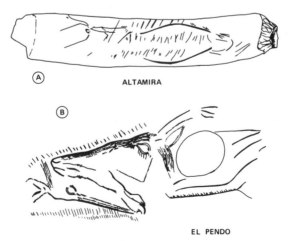

ALTAMIRA

EL PENDO

FIGURE 5. (a and b) Use of common lines: merging motifs.

examples of the way in which motifs may be merged by means of a single, common line. One figure thus becomes the analogical inspiration for another. Just as the emergence point of the antler rack and the shape of that rack suggested the shape of the animal's head in Figure 1, so protrusions on portable objects or a cave wall suggest animal shapes.

Conclusions

The transformation of a piece of raw material, whether bone, antler, or cave wall, into an artifact or cultural product is a form of communication. In Paleolithic art not just any bone, antler, or cave wall locale was selected. The superpositioning and reuse that characterize both wall (Ucko and Rosenfeld, 1967:181) and portable art (Marshack, 1976) support this observation. Given the associative characteristics of Paleolithic design, and given a greater restrictive influence of the morphological whole over the freedom of the parts (see Whyte, 1968:xv–xvi), the selection of raw material and morphology plays a great role in the design process. It is this that constrains decorative choice and generates structural principles.

Relevant properties such as durability obviously play a role in the selection of raw material, but the cultural coding or efficacy of the medium is also involved. Although experiments are being done (see, for example, Berke in Camps-Fabrer, 1978; and Newcomer in Camps-Fabrer, 1978), we do not really know how much more or less incisable antler is than bone, or exactly what processes of preparation (such as soaking) may be necessary to engrave bone and antler of different kinds and ages, or how these processes may affect the use of an engraved harpoon as a harpoon. However, we do know that a clear majority of the engraved items from Cantabrian sites are antler rather than bone, despite the fact that bones would be more available, and that the primary source of antler (in Cantabria) would have been red deer (*Cervus elaphus*), a species that was possibly less prevalent during certain phases of the Magdalenian because of the retreat of its habitat (see Gonzalez-Echegaray, 1972–1973).

Foster (1975) has suggested that the selection of antler for engraving and the use of certain cave locales for painting is governed by sexual associations. Leroi-Gourhan's (1965) hypothesis that Paleolithic art is based on a conceptual division of the world into masculine and feminine components is consistent with Foster's theory. However, a strict reading of Leroi-Gourhan fails to convey the notion of a *general meaning range* that is a most plausible characteristic of a prehistoric or primitive iconographic system (see Munn, 1966, 1973). The depictions that Leroi-Gourhan would interpret as masculine, that Breuil would interpret as weapons, and that Freud would interpret as phallic may refer to a generalized class of design elements that has a range of meanings and uses, including all of these (and more), but that derives more specific meaning from the *context* of action or use. Any separation or distinction between form (e.g., a spear or point) and meaning (e.g., masculinity) that is encoded by the design is not very obvious when the congruence between form and meaning is great. The distinction between the sign (i.e., the design) and the signified (masculinity) is also not sharp when the iconics of the sign are strong.

Thus, the engraved piece as a whole may embody a general meaning range of spear–masculinity–phallus plus other potentially associated meanings such as movement, penetration, and so on. Differentiation of these meanings into a more specific range would be dictated by the context, while choice of raw material for decoration becomes a significant element in that total context. Perhaps it could be argued that engravers or painters were often not so much applying culture to nature, or merely encoding information in an artifactual mode, as extracting culture *from* nature, for the image and part of its meaning is in the raw material that is selected for modification. The paradox of the artistic process is that, at least at one level, the artist is trying to leave culture behind and move toward nature, to create natural forms and depictions, and, in some conscious conceptual systems, such as that of some Eskimos, to release a natural form from the raw material. However, the created object is inevitably cultural, and the natural component is transformed from an object to a sign. A successful transformation

> must bring out certain fundamental properties which are common to both the sign and the object, i.e., a structure which is evident in the sign, and which is normally latent in the object, but which suddenly emerges thanks to its plastic . . . representation, and which furthermore allows a transition to be made to all sorts of different objects [Lévi-Strauss in Charbonnier, 1969:125].

Many current interpretations of prehistoric bone–antler work emphasize the constraints that the raw materials impose on the size and shape of artifacts and on the content of the depictions, but less from the perspective of a structural system than from a perspective that the limits of the raw material were not overcome by the artists (see Camps-Fabrer, 1978; also Leroi-Gourhan, 1965). The nonrandom selection of raw materials or surfaces to be decorated, the merging of form and decoration, the kinds of analogies involved in the extension of class, and the principles for incising that link the engraved design iconically to the incised object provide structural clues to the meaning of Paleolithic art that need further exploration. The variability of style that is referable to group boundaries and maintenance of such boundaries over time will not be available to us until we have mastered the more general dimensions of structure. There can be no doubt that a structural understanding of Paleolithic decorative systems, especially that of bone–antler engravings, has the potential to indicate dimensions of group variability that are still obscure.

References

d'Aquili, Eugene
1972 *The biopsychological determinants of culture*. Reading, Massachusetts: Addison-Wesley.

Barandiaran, Ignacio Maestu
1973 *Arte mueble del Paleolithico Cantabrico*. Saragossa, Spain: Monografias Arqueologicas 14. Departmento de Prehistoria y Arqueologia. Universidad de Zaragoza

Barth, Fredrik
1969 *Ethnic groups and boundaries*. Boston: Little, Brown.

Binford, Lewis R.
1972 Paradigms, model-building, and the state of Paleolithic research. In *An archeological perspective*, edited by L. R. Binford. New York: Academic Press.

Blesser, B.,R. Shillman, C. Cox, T. Kuklinski, J. Ventura, and M. Eden
1973 Character recognition based on phenomenological attributes. *Visible Language* 7(3), 209–223.

Bordes, Francois
1969 Os percé mousterien et os gravé acheuléen du Pech de l'Azé II. *Quaternaria* 2, 1–6.

Breuil, Henri
1952 *Four hundred centuries of cave art*. Paris: Sapho Press.

Camps-Fabrer, Henriette, (ed.)
1978 *Methodologie appliquée a l'industrie de l'os préhistorique*. Procedes du Colloque International. Paris: Centre National de Recherche Scenifique.

Carpenter, Edmund
1973 *Eskimo realities*. New York: Holt.

Charbonnier, Georges
1969 *Conversations with Claude Lévi-Straus*. London: Jonathan Cape (Originally published in 1961.)

Chollot-Legoux, Marthe
1963a L'art geometrique magdalenien et les origines du symbolisme d'après les collections du Musée des Antiquités Nationales. Unpublished thesis: Ecoles pratiques des Hautes Etudes, Paris.
1963b Art geometrique et symbolisme en préhistoire. *Antiquités Nationales et Internationales* **14–16** (IVe année), 32–37.

Clark, J. Desmond, and V. Haynes
1969 An elephant butchery site at Mwanganda's village, Karonga, Malawi, and its relevance for Paleolithic archeology. *World Archaeology* **1**, 390–411.

Conkey, Margaret W.
1978a An analysis of design structure: Variability among Magdalenian engraved bones from northcoastal Spain. Ph.D. dissertation, Department of Anthropology, University of Chicago.
1978b Style and information in cultural evolution: Toward a predictive model for the Paleolithic. In *Social archaeology: Beyond subsistence and dating*, edited by C. Redman *et al.* New York: Academic Press. Pp. 61–85.

deLaguna, Frederica de
1932 A comparison of Eskimo and Paleolithic art, Part I. *American Journal of Archaeology* **36**, 477–511.
1933 A comparison of Eskimo and Paleolithic art, Part II. Non-representative art. *American Journal of Archaeology* **37**, 77–107.

Dewez, Michel C.
1974 New hypotheses concerning two engraved bones from La Grotte de Remouchamps, Belgium. World Archaeology 5 (4), 338–345.

Foster, Mary LeCron
1975 Symbolic sets. Paper presented at the Annual Meeting of the Society for American Archeology, Dallas, Texas.

Friedrich, Margaret Hardin
1970 Design structure and social interaction: Archeological implications of an ethnographic analysis. *American Antiquity* **35,** 332–343.

Fritz, Margaret Conkey
1973 Style and the evolution of symbolic behavior. Paper presented to Anthropology Colloquium, University of California, Santa Cruz.
1975 The structure of Paleolithic design. Paper presented at Annual Meeting of the American Anthropological Association, San Francisco, California.

Geertz, Clifford
1962 The growth of culture and the evolution of mind. In *Theories of the mind,* edited by J. Sher. New York: Free Press of Glencoe. Pp. 713–740.
1964 The transition to humanity. In *Horizons of anthropology,* edited by S. Tax. Chicago: Univ. of Chicago Press. Pp. 37–48.

Geist, Valerius
1971 *Mountain sheep: A study in behavior and evolution.* Chicago: Univ. of Chicago Press.

Gombrich, Ernst
1961 *Art and illusion: A study in the psychology of visual representation,* 2nd ed. Bollingen Series 35, no. 5. New York: Pantheon.

Gonzalez-Echegaray, Joaquin
1972–1973 Consideraciones climaticas y ecologicas sobre el Magdeleniense III en el norte de Espana. *Zephyrus* **23–24,** 167–187.

Gould, Richard, Dorothy A. Koster, and A. H. Sontz
1971 The lithic assemblages of the western desert aborigines of Australia. *American Antiquity* **36,** 149–169.

Hallowell, A. Irving
1959 Behavioral evolution and the emergence of self. In *Evolution and anthropology, A centennial appraisal,* edited by B. Meggers. Washington, D.C.: Anthropological Society of Washington, D.C., pp. 36–40.
1961 The protocultural foundations of human adaptation. In *The social life of early man,* edited by S. L. Washburn. Chicago: Aldine. Pp. 236–255.

Isaac, Glynn, Ll.
1969 Studies of early culture in East Africa. *World Archaeology* **1** (1), 1–28.
1972a Chronology and the tempo of cultural change during the Pleistocene. In *Calibration of hominoid evolution,* edited by W. W. Bishop and J. A. Miller. New York: Scottish Academic Press, pp. 381–430.
1972b Some experiments in quantitative methods for characterizing assemblages of Acheulian artifacts. In *Congrès Panafricain de préhistoire, Dakar 1967,* edited by H. Hugot. Paris: Imprimeries Chambery. Pp. 547–555.
1972c Identification of cultural entities in the middle Pleistocene. In *Congrès Panafricain de préhistoire,* edited by H. Hugot. Paris: Impremeries Chambrey. Pp. 556–562.
1975 Early hominids in action: A commentary on the contribution of archeology to understanding the fossil record in East Africa. *Yearbook of Physical Anthropology* **19,** 19–35.
1976 Stages of cultural elaboration in the Pleistocene: Possible archaeological indicators of the development of language capabilities. In *Origins and evolution of language and speech,* edited by S. R. Harnad, H. D. Steklis, and J. Lancaster. Annals of the New York Academy of Sciences, Vol. 280, 275–288.

1977   Early stone tools—an adaptive threshold? In *Problems in economic and social archaeology*, edited by G. de G. Sieveking, I. H. Longworth, and K. E. Wilson. London: Duckworth.

Kleindienst, Maxine, and Charles Keller
1976   The elusive concept of style and stone artifacts. Paper presented at IXᵉ Congres, Union International des Sciences Préhistoriques et Protohistoriques, Nice, France.

Leach, Edmund R.
1954   A Trobriand medusa? *Man* **54** (158), 103–105.

Leroi-Gourhan, André
1965   *Treasures of prehistoric art*. New York: Abrams.

Margalef, Ramon
1968   *Perspectives in ecological theory*. Chicago: Univ. of Chicago Press.

Marshack, Alexander
1970   *Notation dans les gravures de Paleolithique superieur*. Publications de l'Institut de Préhistoire de l'Université de Bordeaux. Memoire no. 8. Bordeaux: Delmas.
1972   Cognitive aspects of Upper Paleolithic engraving. *Current Anthropology* **13**, 445–477.
1976   Use versus style in the analysis and interpretation of upper Paleolithic image and symbol. Paper presented at IXᵉ Congres International des Sciences Préhistoriques et Protohistoriques, Nice, France.
1978   The meander as a system. The analysis and recognition of iconographic units in Upper Paleolithic compositions. In *Form in indigenous art*, edited by P. Ucko. Canberra: Australian Institute of Aboriginal Studies pp. 286–317.

Munn, Nancy D.
1966   Visual categories: An approach to the study of representational systems. *American Anthropologist* **68** (4), 939–950.
1973   *Walbiri iconography. Graphic representation and cultural symbolism in a central Australian society*. Ithaca, New York: Cornell Univ. Press.

Neisser, Ulric
1967   *Cognitive psychology*. New York: Appleton.

Rappaport, Roy
1971   The sacred in human evolution. *Annual Review of Ecology and Systematics* **2**, 23–42. Palo Alto: Annual Reviews, Inc.

Rorschach, Herman
1942   Psychodiagnostics: A diagnostic test based on perception. (Translation). New York: Grune & Stratton.

Torbrugge, Walter
1968   *Prehistoric european art*. New York: Abrams.

Ucko, Peter, and A. Rosenfeld
1967   *Paleolithic cave art*. New York: McGraw-Hill.

Washburn, Dorothy K.
1974a   A symmetry classification of Pueblo ceramic design. Unpublished manuscript.
1974b   Symmetry universals in primitive design. Paper presented at 73rd annual meeting, American Anthropological Association, Mexico City.
1977   *A symmetry analysis of upper Gila area ceramic design*. Memoirs of the Peabody Museum. Cambridge, Massachusetts: Harvard Univ.

Whallon, Robert
1968   Investigations of late prehistoric social organization in New York State. In *New perspectives in archeology*, edited by L. R. Binford and S. R. Binford. Chicago: Aldine. Pp. 223–244.

White, J. P.
  1969 Typologies for some prehistoric flaked stone artifacts in the Australian New Guinea Highlands. Archeology and Physical Anthropology. *Oceania* **4**, 18–46.
Whyte, L. L. (ed.)
  1968 *Aspects of form: Introduction; A symposium on form in nature and art.* New York: Amer. Elsevier.
Wobst, H. Martin
  1977 Stylistic behavior and information exchange. In *Papers for the Director: Research essays in honor of James B. Griffin;* edited by Charles E. Cleland. Anthro-Papers. Museum of Anthropology, University of Michigan, No. 61: 317–342.

16

The Communication Explosion

COLIN CHERRY

Introduction

Differing technologies of communication can distinguish one society from another in certain major respects and serve to channel ways of thinking and feeling. These technologies also serve to constrain a society's powers of organization; and it is organization rather than merely the possession of machines that is one hallmark of the "advanced," industrialized societies. If the so-called Industrial Revolution is regarded as a triumph, it is a triumph of organization, based upon sustained progress in communication technologies, from early accountancy and record-keeping to today's computers and telecommunication services, both national and international.

The Industrial Revolution developed early and rapidly in England, in the eighteenth century, not only because of the invention of machines, nor only because of science, but also because the existing organization of the great estates gave the necessary social foundations, including their traditions of accountancy. This major change brought in its wake a drastic shift in communicational relationships that must be taken into account if we are to understand communicational symbolism in the modern world.

Many years ago I heard a popular ballad that opened with the lines:

> I shot an arrow into the air,
> It fell on earth, I know not where . . . ,

which seemed to me, in my childish innocence, to be an act of criminal irresponsibility. You should be more careful with bows and arrows. The ballad continued:

> I breathed a song into the air,
> It fell on ears, I know not where . . . ,

which seemed to be a purposeless activity.

Some 50 years later I read in my newspaper that some space scientists had simultaneously achieved both of these feats. They had shot a space vehicle into the air, towards space. A message was inscribed on the side, consisting of: (*a*) outline drawings of a man and a woman in stylized Western artform, the man's hand raised in a gesture of goodwill; and (*b*) circles representing the solar system (or wheels?) and other cryptic symbols.[1]

I will tell this tale here, because it seems to me to epitomize the problem of cross-cultural communication. If you really wish to communicate with the Martians, or with any other culture, in an attempt to reach understanding you should not bombard them with ironmongery nor challenge them with the more cryptic and erudite symbols of your own culture.

There is much wild talk today about "communicating with intelligent beings in outer space," and I must confess that I find both the ethics and the political wisdom of this highly questionable. We have enough problems of communication on this earth already, without inviting more. Communicate with the Martians? We can't communicate well enough with the Chinese yet.

Toward this goal, we will need to consider what the word *communication* really means, for it is an overworked word. However, I should like to make clear, at the outset, the sense in which I shall be using the word *technology*. I employ it in a very general, philosophical sense that I feel to be akin to the view of Kitahara-Frisch (this volume).

I write as one who cannot regard technology as applied science, nor merely as the study of useful artifacts. It is nonsense to speak of *pure technology*, in the way that someone will speak of *pure science*. Technology is essentially a social and political matter; its values are always judged in a social context; its significance changes if it is transplanted from, say, an industrial to a developing country. All human beings use technologies, of some form or other, for they are tool-makers and tool-users (Oakley, 1951), and the particular technology that a people possesses will be a major decider of how they think and feel about themselves and others and about the world around them. Their particular technology defines those people's powers of action upon each other and upon their environment, and so decides their conceivable *choices* of behavior, their liberties of action, expectations, and *rights*. Human rights are not absolutes, but relative to the conceivable liberties of

---

[1] The Pioneer 10 mission.

action open to a people and to other liberties of action revealed to them but not yet open to them (frustrations).

Technology mediates between man and his world.[2] Our particular technology gives us our own peculiar view of the world since it constrains our conceivable course of action and, therefore, of thinking. If this technology changes (as it does so quickly in industrial countries), it will compel moral change too; we must adapt to it;[3] any new technology that falls within our sphere of awareness cannot be ignored, but must be reckoned with. Thinking and action are Siamese twins.

When speaking of technology in this broad way, we need not confine the concept to tools and artifacts "in the metal," but may include social artifacts as well; organized bureaucracies in all their forms are also technological artifacts or, in Kitahari-Frisch's sense, "tools to make tools." We speak of "handling people," just as we speak of "handling tools." The purpose is to increase productivity.

Toward a Philosophy of Communication

Discussion of the values of the technology of communication, to be fruitful, must rest upon some consistent philosophy underlying the general question: What *is* communication? People speak of "communication" with animals, with computers, with people long dead, and in other ways. The philosphy that this writer has found most helpful, for rationalizing questions of communication, is derived from the work of Charles Sanders Peirce (Buchler, 1950; Cherry, 1957, 1966; Gallie, 1952; Morris, 1938, 1946; Peirce, 1931–1935).

The word *communication* means 'sharing' (from the Latin, *communico*). It does not mean sending messages, as is so often said. It is a social and mutual act of sharing; it is a sharing of concepts, mediated by the use of *signs*. For example, as you read these words you may feel that I am "sending you a message"; but I am not, because I have still got it. We may send each other goods or commodities (because we cannot both have them), but we *share* messages. Messages are not commodities (Cherry, 1957, 1966, 1978).

Peirce distinguished some 66 different types of signs, which, broadly speaking, fall into three classes: (*a*) *indexes* (that give physical indication, such as compass needles, weather vanes, etc., or denote, such as automobile numbers, etc.); (*b*) *icons* (that purport to represent, by likeness or repre-

---

[2] See, for example Tiryakian (1962:112).

[3] I would agree with Kitahara-Frisch (this volume) that the procedures of tool-making closely resemble the grammar and syntax found in all human languages and, indeed, would myself argue that language *is* a tool—the most flexible one that we have, having, as it does, an unlimited variety of purposes.

sentation, such as pictures, diagrams, etc.); and (c) *symbols* (that operate by convention, such as names, badges, flags, etc., together with language).

Not all signs are communicative signs. For example, black clouds are a sign of rain, but we do not communicate with Mother Nature—we may raise our umbrella in response, but the clouds do not, in turn, respond to us; we share nothing with them. Again, a slamming door is a sign of a draught, but it is a *causal* sign, not a communicative one. On the other hand, if we saw some person slam the door, we might interpret it communicatively, as a sign of expression of anger—and might demand an apology. All communicative signs are artifacts, uttered by persons, and they require a response sign (*reply*) to interpret them.

What makes an artifact into a sign? Any artifact may possibly be a sign (a scratch on a stone, a printed mark, a sound—anything), but its sign-hood arises solely from the observer's assumption that it *is* a sign. Peirce argued that to know some event *as* a sign is to know it as evidence of another mind. Mind reaches mind by sign usage. By this concept of *signs,* Peirce overstepped the old problem of mind–body dichotomy, arguing that all thought is in signs. He claimed that all knowledge of other people's minds arises from inference based upon *outward happenings* and behaviour called signs— and, furthermore, all knowledge of our own minds, too, for thought is sign activity. Thought, internal musing, has the nature of dialogue, between "you" and "yourself." He further argued that, on this basis, our power to *criticize* our own minds is no more than our power to criticize other people's.

Signs are outward happenings and thus are observable, which calls for interpretation, or meaning. Such interpretation is of course mental (not observable) so it is revealed by a *response sign* or reply. All signs require another sign "to interpret them"; no event can exist *as* a sign, in isolation. Signs can operate only within a working system of signs.

Such a view of the social act that is termed *communication* may be of value when considering the very difficult problem of communication between humans and animals. Neil Chalmers (this volume) addresses himself to the question: What can we infer, from observation of the behavior of nonhuman primates, about the mental processes controlling that behavior? From the Peircean viewpoint, however, there is a clear distinction between *observation* and *communication*. If we observe some behavioral act on the part of the animal, and regard this as *evidence of another mind,* we can test this hypothesis only by responding to that behavior (i.e., by replying) and then by observation of the animal's response to that reply—and so on, successively. That is to say, we can only infer what may be going on in the animal's mind by haivng *conversation* with it, and to the extent that we succeed, our inferences will be valid. *Conversation* is meant here in the general sense of interacting sign-usage between the animal and the human— not necessarily in speech, of course! As Chalmers (this volume) so rightly says, there are severe limits on the sort of inferences that can be made by mere *observation*.

The (unobservable) concept set up in a mind by a sign may be termed the *designatum* of that sign, and, in general, the designata for the utterer and for the receiver should not be assumed to be the same (for they are unobservable). The test of communication is the *relevance* of the signs. To take a simple example, consider the following exchange:

Person A: "Are you well?"
Person B: "Yes, I am well."

gives no indication of true communication, for the sign *well* is totally ambiguous; it could be his name, for example. The first sign *well* needs a response sign "to interpret it"; for example:

Person B: "Yes, I am in good health."

The test for communication rests upon the degree to which Person A's sign and Person B's response sign may be considered as relevant to the same designatum. That is to say, people can communicate only inasmuch as they can *share*.

Person B's remark requires, in turn, a further sign from Person A "to interpret it," and so on. Conversation can then, in principle, continue forever, for it is always possible to add a further relevant remark. Conversation is then possible because it can always be done better than it actually is done, not because it is a logical, conclusive, precise operation, but because it can satisfy criteria of *adequacy;* it is always possible to expand upon it.

Ritual in Communication

Fortunately conversations do terminate, but the final sign (*remark*) has no successor "to interpret it." It is therefore a sign that receives no overt interpretation with regard to the subject matter of the conversation. In fact it is usually a ritual-sign (e.g., *goodbye*) that is significant of the intended situation rather than of the subject of conversation.

Ritual-signs are of the greatest importance to the process of human communication, for they purport to denote the nature of the social situation within which signs are to be interpreted. So far we have considered communication solely in terms of semantics, but the pragmatist is concerned with how those signs operate on specific occasions, in specific situations.

Communication is not merely a matter of conveying meaning in the sense of subject matter (*designata*), but is also a matter of conveying attitudes and senses of purpose. If *conveyed*, the behavior that produced them must belong to a shared system. I. A. Richards has distinguished four different levels of meaning of an utterance (Richards, 1929).

1. *Sense,* in that it directs attention to some external item (*designatum*).
2. *Feeling,* in that it expresses feelings or attitudes toward the designatum.
3. *Tone,* in that it expresses the speaker's attitude to the person being addressed.
4. *Intention,* in that it signifies the speaker's aim or purpose in speaking (to greet, to inform, to explain, etc.).

In expressing *feeling, tone,* and *intention,* language may be said to be performing a ritual function, because it is indicating the nature of the intended social situation in which the *sense* is to be interpreted. Messages may easily be misinterpreted in cross-cultural interchanges because the ritual function is implicit only to the sender and not to the receiver of the message. Sign interpretation, as a psychological act, depends utterly upon the identification of the specific intended social situation (e.g., is it a police court, a church, an office, a situation of rebuke, or enquiry, or what?). Let me remind you, in this context, of studies that have been made of how various body-signs, e.g., stance, gestures, facial expression, intonation, and many more, are used, in a ritualistic sense, to indicate people's intended relationships (Argyle, 1969; Argyle and Kendon, 1972; Birdwhistell, 1952).

We speak with our whole bodies, not just our mouths (Birdwhistell, 1952). Also styles and arrangements of seating, interior decoration, architecture, and other environmental signs serve such ritual functions, vital to communication. They can be immediate in their impact, for they define the situation at a glance, if only to people of that particular culture. Similarly, dialect serves such a function, as do jargon, styles of clothing, and even the distance separating two people in conversation, for we carry about with us a *personal space* of a volume that depends upon our degree of intimacy or other relationships with our partners (Argyle, 1969).

Bilateral Communication Offers Freedom of Movement

For the first year or two after Alexander Graham Bell's demonstration of the telephone in 1876, it was not regarded as a means of conversation, but was used to "broadcast" songs, news, and items that today we receive by radio. There were no telephone exchanges and hence no choice of partner. Telephones were first used in ways that anticipated broadcasting by over 40 years. It was the coming of the telephone *exchange* that was the revolutionary step, because it ultimately offered the common man *choice* of whom to speak to. One consequence of this was the outdating of the social customs and rituals of personal approach, within the various social ranks, or outside persons' spheres of acquaintance, for it became possible for a person to ring up a stranger—without introduction or letters of credence.

A totally new subscriber organization arose, giving subscribers the feeling that it was within their rights to telephone other subscribers, whoever they were.

Not only did the telephone system "annihilate distance," as is so often said, but a more profound result was that people were enabled to move from one place to another without leaving home; for you can be anywhere on the network and yet establish social contacts. The telephone service thereby added feelings of security to travel. Today the traveler may speak to his home base as he moves about almost any major inhabited area of the globe. Communication from a distance had, of course, been started earlier by the postal service, reorganized in the seventeenth century into a form that eventually became available to the common man; but it was the telephone system, carrying all the psychological advantages of human conversation, that so greatly increased our feelings of security of movement, leading to the creation of innumerable institutions of business, emigration, industry, government, diplomacy, news services, and many others in which movement of people is an essential element. Today the airlines, the multinational corporations, the international organizations, banking, and many other institutions on a global scale seem to many in the industrial countries as "part of nature" by virtue of the telephone, the Telex, and other systems of bilateral communication that render their organization practical and reliable.

The telephone service is a *bilateral* system, extending the natural values of conversation between people with nonprescribed locations. Other communication systems are *unilateral*, such as radio, books, newspapers, and so on, which do not permit of an immediate reply. These have totally different social values.

Time and Unilateral Systems

When considering the social functions of various communication services, it is necessary to distinguish between bilateral and unilateral systems, for they are often confused.

Books, journals, and newspapers are early examples of unilateral systems; films, radio, and television are more recent ones. All unilateral systems require both some "professionals" (writers, speakers, performers, etc.) to act as sources, as well as some organizing body (publishers, broadcasting authorities, etc.), whereas the bilateral systems, such as the telephone service, need only the latter (e.g., the post offices). One major consequence is that the unilateral systems may greatly increase the dominance of *authorities* of many kinds—for example, sources of news, writers, performers, *experts* of various kinds. One particular modern example is the "cult of stars," so rapidly developed by the early film industry. Unilateral systems then create a social hierarchy. Messages come from "them" to "us," who cannot reply; from the "great" to the "humble." Their great power lies in their possibility for extending the influence of *authority;* the ways by which they do this and the values of so doing depend upon political wisdom, as well as upon the level of social development of the particular society and upon its degree of literacy (Lerner, 1958a,b). One of our safeguards is responsible journalism. The responsibilities thrust upon certain of our journalists today is very great, for *interpretation* of news items,[4] that is to say, for relating the necessarily isolated and incomplete news items to historical and current social contexts.

One other consequence of the spread of unilateral systems, especially of those systems that do not require literacy (e.g., films, radio, television), during this century is creation of the belief that "the world has shrunk." In the sense that items of news are now received far more quickly, though only from selected places on selected occasions, this belief is true; however, by virtue of the immense body of news items and factual information that is now presented to us every day, the opposite is the case—the world we are expected to comprehend has vastly expanded. We are now expected to know what is happening in all corners of the earth and, furthermore, to hold opinions on it. We feel it a *duty* to read our newspapers and feel guilty when we have not "heard the news." But in reality we cannot understand it, for we have inadequate knowledge of the historical, cultural, and political backgrounds from which the specific items of news have been extracted.

How many people can one be said to know, as persons? A few hundred? Perhaps as many as an average village would hold. But on no account can we be said to "know" millions. We are compelled to ritualize the situation which modern news services force upon us; we *personify* whole peoples and speak of "the Americans," "the Indians," "the Chinese," and so on. We see them as stereotyped images, as caricatures, just as we may see the "early Romans" or "ancient Greeks," but with the added force of daily reportings of their sayings and doings and with knowledge that they may profoundly affect ourselves today (Cherry, 1971). We cannot be *in* communication over long historical time. But the illusion that we can may be the more deceptive. I am, of course, not referring to anthropologists, nor to historians, when offering this opinion, but to the ordinary people who receive this news daily about people whom they have never met, let alone conversed with, and whose backgrounds and customs are unknown to them.

Unilateral Communication in Industrial and Traditional Communities

It is sometimes said that "radio continues the verbal tradition," in the sense that broadcasters are talkers, propagators of spoken news, and sto-

[4] See other UNESCO Reports and Papers on Mass Communication.

rytellers. For example, Lerner (1958a) refers to changes taking place in traditional societies of the Middle East, such as Egypt, Iran, Jordan, Lebanon, Syria, and Turkey, that are due not only to the spread of literacy but also to the unilateral systems of radio and film.

Within such countries, radio and film *may* indeed have eventual political value, by extending traditions of storytelling by the direct spoken and visual presence. Lerner quoted the late President Nasser of Egypt: "Literacy counts far less, politically, than it did 20 years ago: Radio has changed everything . . . . Today people in the most remote villages hear of what is happening everywhere and form their opinions." But Lerner rightly questions whether the word *opinions* is valid. Radio may well interest and even stimulate illiterates into awareness of certain kinds, but it is doubtful whether they could form opinions upon matters beyond their direct experience (Lerner, 1958b). Even we literates gain only a minute part of our knowledge by direct experience of this world; the bulk is obtained secondhand, and the drive to gain it and to form opinions about it has its source in our literacy. The anthropologist Doob has referred to unilateral communication as a force for bringing about the downfall of traditional societies (Doob, 1961).

In other countries, notably modern China, these unilateral techniques are used politically as instruments of social change, as loudspeakers on street corners continually blare out news and slogans from which no one can escape.

In contrast to bilateral systems, unilateral systems offer no means of answering back, of criticizing, expanding, or questioning. The receiver is frustrated in certain ways that render all such systems "against nature" and that may inspire feelings of threat. Various attempts have been made to add elements of bilateralness to them, but no amount of listener's "phone-ins," "letters to the editor," or "audience participation" can succed in this. This does not render them antisocial however, but it does thrust enormous responsibilities upon broadcasters and journalists, for these are the new propagandists, in the correct sense of that term (from the title of the committee of cardinals in the Roman curia—*congregatio de propaganda fide*). The values of responsible broadcasting for public morale were clearly seen during World War II, and it can have similar values for nation-building in "developing areas" of the world today, as has been stressed by many (Cherry, 1966; Pyre, 1963; Schramm, 1964 and n.d.; UNESCO, 1960 and 1962).

The impact upon traditional societies of radio, television, and film by continuing their verbal tradition may be greater than it has been, or will be, upon ourselves in the highly literate countries. The consequences may prove not wholly to our advantage, for it may introduce them to ourselves, or change their images of us, in ways not yet predicted and not wholly favorable, as it changes their self-images and political consciousness.

On the other hand, the effect of radio and television upon ourselves in highly literate communities may be beneficial in that it may restore to us some of the advantages of the verbal tradition that the concentration upon high literacy in education, needed in the past for development of industrialization, may have helped to reduce. Reading is a very withdrawn, private, intellectual operation, whereas we sit around the radio or televison set as those in preliterate societies sit around the feet of the storyteller. These domestic raconteurs and entertainers may do much to preserve present-day happenings and beliefs as tomorrow's myths and legends, giving an added sense of cultural continuity and sense of community. Concentration upon literacy and numeracy as prime educational goals is, in my view, not wholly beneficial; indeed there are some recent signs of a revolt against such values (e.g., the recent change in the science–arts ratio of applicants for university places in England).

I am not suggesting for one moment that literacy is outdated in industrial countries, merely that we may run the risk of overvaluing it and that radio, television, and films, like the theater, may be valuable balancers. It is unfortunately common for intellectuals in industrial countries to decry them by contemptuously terming them *mass-communication*. (Mass is derived from Greek *maza,* meaning 'porridge,' or, more strictly, 'barley meal.') What evidence do we have, for example, that television reduces the individual to "the will of the herd" (to use an expression of Nietzsche)? Serious studies of the matter do not suggest this (Himmelweit *et al.,* 1958; Schramm *et al.,* 1961).

Finally, it should not be forgotten that the unilateral nature of broadcasting reflects back upon the *sender* also; for he is talking, but does not know who he is talking to. No reactions are observed, no responses interpret his remarks. Talking is essentially a social activity, but here it is deprived of its real social nature. A writer is in a slightly different situation, for his audience is not present at the time; writing is a premeditated activity, not directed at individuals (except in letters), and the results are reflected in the more formal language style.

Problems of Timing

If we agree with Peirce that human speech is always a social process—always *between* people (even you with yourself, in thought, in the Peircean view [Gallie, 1952]), it would seem that remarks and the interpreting replies most naturally follow one another closely in time, so that the situation to which they refer is unchanged. Human languages evolve so as to operate within certain time-scales.

The technological extensions of human communication frequently disturb these time-relationships. The telephone does not; and consequently, it is as easy and "natural" as face-to-face conversation. Letter writing is a technology that does, however; and it represents one form of *delayed dialogue;* between the sending of a letter and the receiving of a reply the situation referred to may have changed. For example, the Roman Empire under Augustus organized many of its operations by a form of postal service, as had the Persian before. It operated an elaborate system of couriers, on horseback or in caravans, and used relay postal stations at regular intervals along all main roads. Each postal station kept some 40 horses and grooms, and the speed would have been about 50 miles per day. It took about 1 month for a message to pass between Londinium and Rome (Pflaum, 1950).[5] With such a long time delay between sending advice and receiving instructions, events might have taken place that rendered those instructions useless, or even dangerous (Cherry, 1971).

A postal service is essentially a bilateral system and, as such, it has many organizational functions. Today, business and industry are organized around the assumption of *reliable* communication services of many kinds. The early empires made similar assumptions (Herodotus, 1954). Xenophon and Polybius also emphasized the need for communication services for the control of scattered empires and for military operations.

A formal mathematical theory, called the *theory of control*, shows that if a response to some stimulus "feeds back" so as to affect that stimulus, and if there is an excessive time delay in so doing, instability may occur. Perhaps we should not try to apply the mathematics too literally to complex social systems (Deutsch, 1963; Cherry, 1957, 1966, and 1978). Nevertheless, Wiener's *Cybernetics* (1948)[6] powerfully argued for applying some of its lessons to many kinds of systems, including biological systems and economic systems. One of these lessons is that excessive time-delay is a recipe for instability, for example, ataxia in the nervous system, or booms and slumps in economics (Tinbergen, 1950). Similarly, excessive time-delay in bilateral communication *may* lead to instability; and within industrialized society today, rapid communication is essential. Fast communication is, of course, not a guarantee of stability, but it is a prerequisite. Undoubtedly, it is both the *speed* and *reliability* of our modern telecommunication services that enable today's global-scale systems to operate—the international organizations, the airlines, banking, diplomacy, news services, meteorological forecasting—an endless list. But they are no guarantee of success (Cherry, 1971).

These remarks apply only to the bilateral systems of communication, which involve *feedback*. The argument is different for unilateral systems such as broadcasting, the press, film, etc., for these operate from a single source to a multitudinous audience, whose individual responses have no significant effect upon the source. In a strict (Peircean) sense, these are not *communication* systems at all, for no *mutual* sharing takes place. It is better to call them *broadcast* systems.

[5] The earliest organized system may have been that of Semitic Babylonia, about 3800 B.C. Another system, used by Kublai Khan, is described by Marco Polo (1908).
[6] From the Greek Κυβερνητησ 'steersman,' a term first used by André Ampère in 1834.

Very broadly speaking, these unilateral systems are emotional in values, whereas the bilateral ones are organizational. They concern emotional satisfactions, morale, education, and group feelings—rather than planning and prediction or rational matters. It is not then surprising that they lay themselves open to much criticism and public concern, for the public cannot individually respond with any effect ("to interpret them"). As remarked previously, one great consequence is that they can enhance the status of authorities of various kinds. I have referred to the press as a unilateral system, inasmuch as individuals cannot meaningfully reply to it in the natural, conversational mode. However, the public can respond, as a whole population, statistically; in this sense there is feedback, and the consequences of time-delay can again be serious. By this I merely mean that delay in news reporting can lead to its becoming outdated by events, so that public attitudes (with possible political consequences) can be unfortunate. In the case of newspapers, I do not feel this to be serious, at least in industrial countries, for we have several alternative sources of news; furthermore, as mentioned earlier, far more serious consequences may arise from our failure to comprehend the news. However, the case of *books* may be another matter, for at least three reasons.

First, books have about them a certain charisma; they are more "serious" things then newspapers,[7] the authors may have international reputations; books are perhaps believed in more firmly. Second, books that attract widest interest will persist in circulation far longer in time, and the images they convey can become very outdated or old-fashioned. Third, whereas the common man reads only the newspapers of his own country, books are translated and may enjoy wide circulation among foreign populations. Those that are regarded locally as the most important literature of the source country are often used for educational purposes. One wonders whether the reading of Dickens in the USSR or of Dostoevsky in Western countries have serious effects upon national attitudes and feelings.

I personally doubt, too, whether tourism does much to correct our international attitudes, for we are likely to go and see what we have been taught to see. Our attentions are directed by our education, reading, and folk tales, for we still identify with home. The case of immigration and settlement is rather different, for transfer of identity is accepted and the person is subject to a continuing stream of new experiences in his new country, above all, that of earning his living there (Deutsch, 1963).

Communication: Human, Animal, and Machine

The question is sometimes asked: Do we communicate with animals, birds, insects—or even with machines (computers)? It is very much a matter of

---

[7] The contemptuous term *mass-communication* is rarely applied to books.

definition, but what is more important is that the various classes of communication should not be confused and that it should not be assumed that all are linguistic in form. Certainly, when I pat a dog, it responds by tail-wagging, which in turn I respond to by further patting—and so on. We share, in that sense, and so *communicate*. But the dog does not appear to have a wide range of alternative signs to choose from, in order "to interpret" my pats. The field of discourse open to us is rather limited!

The whole question has been raised again by the interesting case of Washoe, the chimpanzee, who has been taught to communicate with its trainer by gesture, based upon the standard American Sign Language of the deaf (Gardner and Gardner, 1969).[8] Not only did Washoe use single signs relevantly, but she used them in combination. Such combinations suggest a rudimentary syntax, but it is not syntax in the full *generative* sense that Chomsky refers to (Chomsky, 1975). Sebeok (1976) has noted that Washoe's sign-usage shows that she has learned to use gestures directly at the pragmatic level without syntax; that is to say, as opposed to human language, Washoe has not necessarily learned grammatical rules per se, with which to construct meaningful "sentences."[9] Such comment clarifies but does not detract from the value of such painstaking work.

In the early stages of learning a first language, a child will employ nouns and verbs, because he or she can touch or point to objects, or carry out actions. Words like *although, whether,* and so on are functors, which are abstract and learned much later. At first the child learns reduced subject–verb or verb–subject sentences (e.g., "Daddy go," "Hit ball"). But the child does not continue merely to learn a list of standard sentences; rather it learns grammatical structures of various types into which its increasing vocabulary may be fitted. Furthermore, a child will suddenly come out with a sentence that it has never heard before—with correct grammatical structure. To learn grammatical rules a child tests for relevance of particular signs in particular contexts in exactly the Peircean sense touched upon in the preceding (see Bowerman, this volume). A child demonstrates its ability to objectify grammar quite early, by inventing its own nonsense words, but using them in a syntactically correct way.

Grammar is a system of *rules*, habits that determine *both* syntactic and semantic properties of sentences (e.g., change of word order can convert a statement into a question in English), and for this to be used generatively, by humans, cognition is necessary. Chomsky's argument is in line with the philosophy of Peirce; the meaning of an utterance is revealed by the *relevance* of the reply or, in other words, we first attribute a meaning to someone's utterance by cognition, as an intermediate step, and then *re*-signify that concept into our own, different response (Chomsky, 1975).

---

[8] Other such work with primates and dolphins has also been published.

[9] See Kitahara-Frisch's chapter concerning symbolic behavior of nonhuman primates.

For example, the following question is ambiguous: "Is George a good painter?" It cannot be responded to relevantly until it is first decided whether *painter* refers to an artist or to a house painter. The choice is a semantic, operational, conceptual one, not syntactic (see Foster, this volume).

Systems of signing show increasing specificity of purposes as we proceed down the evolutionary scale, and we humans use innumerable signs, other than language, that serve analogous functions: fashions of dress, badges, flags, and other *indicators* of group membership; various *tokens* that signify claims; involuntary *reflexes* like blushing and trembling, and so on. But the extreme is reached when it comes to "communicating" with inanimate machines, such as computers.

It is conventional to speak of computer *languages* in reference to the instructions fed into the machine; but, strictly speaking, these are not languages but rather *codes*. The various functional operations carried out by a computer (multiplying, adding, etc.) are certainly operational and therefore semantic; nevertheless, they are *definable*, and remain at the syntactic level. It is the human programmer who carries out the cognitive, semantic processes and converts them into syntactic instructions.

There was a fashion some 25 years ago, but now fortunately passing, to compare computers with brains.[10] It was a revival of a concern in the seventeenth and eighteenth centuries with robots, perhaps stemming from the work of Leibnitz and Descartes upon "logic machines." However, logical reasoning operates, not with ordinary language, but with *language-systems* that use a fixed range of signs and rules of usage defined in a metalanguage.

A human being, when interactively operating a computer, is not in conversation with it. Cognitive effort is required on his part, which involves considerable training and skill, but the machine has no such powers. The computer responds to its instructions by direct syntactic operations; its apparent powers of interpreting instructions semantically derive from its programed mechanism for converting these into syntactic operations—a mechanism constructed by the human programmer.

It is interesting to speculate upon the future of computers. It is my personal opinion that these machines will not develop so as to appear increasingly "clever" or as challengers to human thought, nor will they come to "dominate" us as some science fiction writers imagine. On the contrary, it is more likely that progress will be steadily made in the so-called machine languages by which an operator instructs the machine. Early machine languages required operators to have specialized training, and this is still true; it is likely that, as time passes, ability to operate computers will increasingly require less skill until, perhaps, they can be operated by ordinary, untrained people. In that case the machine "fades away," and the person is left with his own

---

[10] In his book *Cybernetics*, Wiener (1948) made only modest claims in this respect.

thoughts—communicating with himself. An ideal machine is one that is not noticed as such, so that it does not divert the user's attention away from his main purpose.

There is no particular cultural merit in numeration, as such, nor (unless you are a designer or repairman) in understanding the internal operations of any machine. Years ago children were taught to recite the arithmetic tables; later they were allowed to use slide rules; today they take pocket calculators into the examination room. Their attention is on their work, not on the workings of the machine. In the future they may have access to computers for innumerable purposes and will give no thought to them.

If such a trend comes about, it will require not only operating language systems needing little skill to use, but also much further development in the symbolism with which the computer presents its output to the user. Such a study is called *computer graphics,* and it has already made great strides, especially for computers used as aids to solving design problems. Numerous forms of symbolism are needed, in particular, *iconic* signs by which a concept is immediately impressed upon the user with little cognitive effort required (Murrell, 1976). Such computer usage would not only benefit the industrial countries, but the "developing" countries too, though this will require much study of symbolism of scientific and technical concepts to be interpretable within the context of their cultures, especially if such machines are to be an aid towards their industrialization.

So what of the future of computer learning? My own view is not that of pupils sitting alone, seeing the computer as their teacher. On the contrary, as the machine becomes more facile in usage and more obliging in its symbolism, it will gradually "fade away," and the pupil will be in more human contact with human teachers. If not, technology will have failed.

Human Communication Studies: The Inadequacies of Physical Science

It is sometimes argued that mathematics and even science are international languages and can easily be put to the service of intercultural understanding. This perhaps motivated the sending of iconic symbols into outer space, as mentioned in the Introduction. The belief seems implicit that, if "intelligent life" exists there, it will "naturally" be very concerned with science and so be able to interpret the cryptic symbols as signifying scientific concepts. But, as we have seen, no icon without a context can be a sign of specific meaning, for in isolation it could have an infinite number of interpretations.

The problem is one of epistemology as well as semantics. The particular framework of scientific concepts that have evolved on earth has derived out of our own historical experience. It rests upon certain "fundamental," primary concepts accepted by faith, or pure assumption. Further, these elementary foundations were laid largely by people who could express themselves in Latin. There is no reason to believe that a science could not have evolved upon a totally different epistemological system, based upon different primary, fundamental concepts, had language and history been different.

Physical science, as it has evolved within Europe, may be regarded as an epistemology that aims to describe the world without any reference to symbolic values. It distinguishes objective and subjective aspects of observations. For instance, we could describe the printed words on this page objectively in terms of the chemistry of ink and of the geometry of letters, and soon, but we could not similarly say anything about what the words *mean*. But, as the philosopher Collingwood (1938) has pointed out, feeling something and feeling *about* it are one and the same experience. So too with other sensory experiences; they are two sides of the same coin (Collingwood, 1938:160). Their separation was an idea born of the Renaissance, which became thinkably and morally possible only then. As a result of this thinking, of separating the objective from the subjective, man was no longer a creature *of* the world; henceforth he was *in* the world, a thing among other things.

Through all forms of symbolic activity (sign-usage, language), the unity is phenomenologically restored. Signs, words, phrases, and icons are, on the one hand, physical entities, but they also have meanings *to* a particular person, in a particular situation. This fact may be forgotten by those who speak about "communicating with beings in outer space," and so on. It is certainly meaningful and often useful to speak objectively of objects, events, artifacts—in their own right, but the moment we perceive anything *as* a sign, it has significance—the nexus between the objective and the subjective becomes clear as they become related in a single experience. The experience is phenomenological but it is also cultural. Because of this, science as taught and understood in the West is not necessarily a good tool for cross-cultural communication.

Yet there may be ways of overcoming this problem, for science is above all else a means of understanding the material world. If it is expressed in symbolism that relates to the culture, it can be used as technology for problem-solving. Some current studies are exploring such an approach. One such study has been carried out by Keith Warren with the support of UNICEF (Warren, n.d.).

Briefly, Warren argues that the "developing" countries (e.g., of the Indian subcontinent and elsewhere) are handicapped with regard to the spread of scientific understanding for two basic reasons: (a) Science and scientific concepts have been channeled, through the use of Western technological laboratory equipment (itself the product of Western industrial society), into its forms as we know them; and (b) their language may not necessarily form a good epistemological base for the building of scientific theory in the form that it is known within Western cultures.

Warren is particularly concerned with the former, and has shown over a period of years means to arouse the spirit of scientific enquiry at elementary school level, by designing experiments that require no Western apparatus, but only local materials (e.g, pieces of bamboo, stones, cooking pots, coconut shells), domestic materials that are *familiar* to the young people in villages and towns. He gets them to make such instruments as rain-gauges, pin-hole cameras, string-bow fire raisers, magnifying glasses, and so on, arguing that imported Western equipment cannot fail to carry certain Western values with it, that this is learning science, and that an introduction to a sense of controlled change over the natural world can be given to peoples long imbued with unchanging attitudes to nature, without necessarily imposing Western values.

In such an experiment, the scientific method is divorced from the cultural implications of its Western origins and used as a technology for communication about natural laws and the uses to which they can be put in increasing human productivity. *What* is produced and *how* the product is to be utilized need not be communicated. It is hoped that on the phenomonological level the sign–meaning nexus remains culturally untainted while the human benefits of the scientific method are perceived through its local application.

References

Argyle, M.
  1969 *Social interaction.* London: Methuen.
Argyle, M., and A. Kendon
  1972 *The experimental analysis of social performance: Communication in face-to-face interaction.* London: Penguin Books.
Birdwhistell, R. L.
  1952 *Introduction to kinesics.* Louisville: Univ. of Kentucky Press.
Buchler, J. (ed.)
  1950 *The philosophy of Peirce: Selected writings.* London: Routledge & Kegan Paul.
Cherry, E. C.
  1957 *On human communication.* Cambridge, Massachusetts: MIT Press.
  1966 *On human communication* (second edition). Cambridge, Massachusetts, MIT Press.
  1978 *On human communication* (enlarged edition). Cambridge, Massachusetts: MIT Press.
  1971 *World communication: Threat or promise?* London: Wiley.
Chomsky, N.
  1975 *Reflections on language.* London: Temple Smith.
Collingwood, R. G.
  1938 *The principles of art.* London: Oxford Univ. Press.
Deutsch, K. W.
  1953 *Nationalism and social communication.* Cambridge, Massachusetts: MIT Press.
  1956 *Nationalism and social communication.* Cambridge, Massachusetts: MIT Press.
  1963 *The nerves of government: Models of political communication and control.* Glencoe, Illinois: Free Press.
Doob, L. W.
  1961 *Communication in Africa: A search for boundaries.* New Haven: Yale Univ. Press.

Encyclopedia Britannica
1910   *Encyclopedia Britannica*. Cambridge, England: Cambridge Univ. Press.
Gallie, W. B.
1952   *Peirce and pragmatism*. London: Pelican Books.
Gardner, R. A., and B. T. Gardner
1969   Teaching sign language to a chimpanzee. *Science* **165**, 664.
Herodotus
1954   *The histories*. Translated by Aubrey de Selincourt. London: Penguin Books.
Himmelweit, H., A. N. Oppenheim, and P. Vince
1958   *Television and the child: An empirical study of the effects of television on the young*.
        London: Oxford Univ. Press.
Hjelmslev, L.
1961   *A prolegomena to a theory of language*. Translated by J. Whitfield. Madison: Univ.
        of Wisconsin Press. (Originally in Danish, 1943.)
Lerner, D.
1958a   *The passing of traditional society*. Glencoe, Illinois: Free Press.
1958b   Editor's introduction. *The Public Opinion Quarterly* **22** (3), 217.
Morris, C. W.
1938   *Foundations of the theory of signs*. Vol. 1, no. 2. Chicago: Univ. of Chicago Press.
1946   *Signs, language and behavior*. New York: Prentice-Hall.
Murrell, H.
1976   *Men and machines*, edited by P. Herriot. London: Essential Psychology.
Oakley, K.
1951   *A definition of man*. Penguin Service News, no. 20. London: Penguin.
Peirce, C. S.
1931–1935   *The collected papers of Charles Sanders Peirce*. Vols. 1–4. Cambridge, Mas-
            sachusetts: Harvard Univ. Press.
Pflaum, H. G.
1950   *Essai sur la "Cursus Publicus" sous le Haut-Empire Romain*. Paris: Imprimerie Na-
        tionale.
Polo, Marco
1908   *Travels*. London: Dent (Everyman's Library).
Pye, L.
1963   *Communication and political development*. Princeton, New Jersey: Princeton Univ.
        Press.
Richards, I. A.
1929   *Practical Criticism*. London: Kegan Paul. (1964 reprinted by Routledge Paperbacks,
        London).
Schramm, W.
1964   *Mass media and national development*. Palo Alto, California: Stanford Univ. Press.
n.d.   *The role of information in national development*. UNESCO.
Schramm, W., J. Lyle, and E. B. Parker
1961   *Television in the lives of our children*. Palo Alto, California: Stanford Univ. Press.
Sebeok, T. A.
1976   *Contribution to the doctrine of signs*. Lisse, Netherlands: Indiana Univ. and the Peter
        de Ridder Press.
Tinbergen, J.
1950   *The dynamics of business cycles*. Translated by J. J. Polak. London: Routledge &
        Kegan Paul.
1951   *Business Cycles in the United Kingdom, 1870–1914*. Amsterdam: North Holland Publ.
Tiryakian, A.
1962   *Sociologism and existentialism*. London: Prentice-Hall.

Warren, Keith
  n.d. *Elementary and secondary school texts in native languages.* Kathmandu, Nepal: UN-
       ICEF.
  1960 *Developing mass media in Asia.* Report no. 30 on Mass Communication. Paris:
       UNESCO.
  1962 *Developing information media in Africa.* Report no. 37 on Mass Communication.
       Paris: UNESCO.
Wiener, N.
  1948 *Cybernetics.* New York: Wiley.

V

FORM THROUGH TIME

17
Introduction

MARY LeCRON FOSTER
STANLEY H. BRANDES

The structures of culture, whether primarily referential, like language, or primarily figurative, like ritual, are highly formalized (as we saw in Part II) in order that they may be learned and reproduced with a high degree of conformity to norms despite the passage of time and the entry and exit of individuals from the culturally constructed scene. We say "in order that" because the continuity that formalization provides must have adaptive value, yet maintenance of the cultural structure requires not just continuity but also sufficient flexibility to adapt to change. The chapters in this part of the book suggest cultural means by which cohesion may be maintained, changes be bridged, and creativity to allow for novel solutions be fostered. All the chapters are concerned with the interaction of act, actors, and internalized structure in promulgating this tripartite adaptive process. The symposium on which this volume is based tended to stress symbolic being and becoming rather than to describe structure as such. Our two language chapters fit the more dynamic model. We have already seen in Bolinger's chapter (this volume) how the individual (albeit, also in formalized ways) may intrude his intentionality upon the referential forms of language. That of Bowerman, in this section, gives us the input of the young individual as she (in this case) actively internalized the language with which her culture has provided her. Like Lamendella, Laughlin and Stephens build from a linguistic base within a neurofunctional framework, interrelating the denotative and connotative aspects of culture. Language as referential structure is thus implicit in conference and book rather than spelled out.

Copyright © 1980 by Academic Press, Inc.
All rights of reproduction in any form reserved.
ISBN 0-12-262680-x

Ardener's discussion brings us back to the problem introduced by Sperber: the difficulty in making valid application of linguistic models to analysis of data from nonreferential systems. In this connection Ardener introduces another complication: that of the relationship between the synchronic and the diachronic aspects of culture. He confronts us with the extreme difficulties that behavioral scientists face in forging analytic tools adequate to the task of describing human culture in all of its complexity. Building from Ardener's position, Laughlin and Stephens indicate how steps in such an undertaking might begin to be taken.

Laughlin and Stephens's chapter has the virtue, in the present context, of assimilating not only Ardener's model for the unconscious dynamics of social action but also the ontogenetic flexibility of Bowerman's model for language learning, which, of course, Laughlin was also exposed to before writing the chapter reproduced here. The formality of the processing of spontaneous events of the type discussed by Ardener is usually less noticed by the anthropologist as observer than is the processing of calendrically cyclic rituals such as religious rites of various kinds, greeting formulae, mealtime etiquette, and the like. This is because the processing occurs at irregular intervals, and is triggered by abnormalcy, such as crises requiring solution, rather than the normalcy of expectable social relationships, or the yearly round.

The processing of linguistic events by children, as described by Bowerman, has also, until recently, gone largely unnoticed by scholars of any stripe, not because it was infrequent but probably because as the product of an untrained minority it seemed relatively unimportant. (For another view of minority production, see Part II.) In both the Ardener and the Bowerman processing of events, participants formulate models that depend both on previous input and the uniqueness of the situation at the time that the processing takes place. It is this combination of memory storage and the need for immediate response to triggering circumstances that provides the creativity of culture—coupled, it goes without saying, with individual intentionality.

In emphasizing symbolic relationships through time as an ongoing and dynamic process, we part company from traditional structuralist analysis that, as Laughlin says, has tended to avoid problems of social action in favor of the symbolic devices of cyclical normalcy. According to Lane (1970), in structuralism, "the synchronic structure is seen as being constituted or determined not by any historical process, but by the network of existing structural relations" (p. 17).

Ardener speaks of the theoretical realignment of the *poststructuralist* period, in which "the capturing of the life of events as they articulate with structures will certainly be one outstanding problem requiring a new phase of specially collected data." Traditional ethnographies contain a minimum of the kind of data that such an approach requires. Ardener says that such data would involve *simultaneities*. To capture these, anthropologists would do well to emulate the meticulously detailed data-gathering of ethologists such as Chalmers or psycholinguists such as Bowerman, in which every simultaneity of the event under consideration is meticulously recorded. This would perhaps be not so much a "new anthropology" as a "new ethnography" to be used as the basis for poststructuralist theorizing.

According to Lamendella, both a rudimentary capacity for categorization of causality and a rudimentary capacity for analogic categorization are present almost immediately after birth. Depictive representation begins imitatively through gesture. At about the same time that language learning begins, the infant is also organizing propositions and events based on the relationships of objects in space. Use of these concepts involves metaphoric association and intercommunicational sharing. The language-learning picture painted by Bowerman is very much in keeping with this neurofunctional model. First, as she points out, the language-learning child does not distinguish between reference and metaphoric extension. This presumably develops when the child becomes capable of "as if" playing. By that time she is in possession of a fairly sizable vocabulary built up through imitative modeling and analogic extension from a prototype: either associated with original adult modeling or with the most repeated adult modeling. The sliding scale between reference and figuration that she posits for the learning of a referential system in ontogenesis is, then, very similar to that which we proposed in the symbolic model outlined in our preface to the book.

Intercommunicational sharing means that the child's verbal representation must gradually be brought into phase with adult modeling. This is probably always incompletely realized. Prototypes undoubtedly persist at some level into adulthood. One can often detect this in one's own usages. This is similar to the persistence of repressed latent content in mature individuals, and probably depends upon the degree to which incomplete models (prototypes) were modeled with high affectivity by interacting adults.

That spatial relationships involved in events are early prototypical meanings is not surprising considering the conceptual organization described by Lamendella and the gestural nature of early imitative activities. Since children must strive to discover the boundaries of the meanings that adults attach to signs, if those meanings are not bundles of distinctive features but prototypically closer to or more distant from a central content core, the *bricolage* involved in the restructuring of prototypes must depend upon the structure of the events in which a given sign is successively produced.

The prototype theory of word meaning seems a productive advance over the hitherto current concept of the word as a distinctive feature bundle. From the standpoint of language change, it would mean that the prototypical focus would undergo imperceptible shifts because of differential usage, probably both during ontogeny and adulthood. Bowerman's analysis provides a plausible point of departure for such a theory.

In addition to Laughlin and Stephens's chapter, we are aware of two developments that build upon Ardener's approach. The first is a series of papers published in S. Ardener (1975). Here E. Ardener's *p-structures* loom large as the idealized product of a dominant male *norm*, against which less culturally salient female ideologies are projected and, with which, at least to some extent, they are brought into phase. The second is a paper by Hastrup (1978), in which she explores the possible dimensions of *poststructuralism* as foreshadowed by Ardener and two other writers.

Hastrup emphasizes (following Ardener) that language is an inadequate model for portraying relationships that do not follow a communicational line of lineal causality and unidimensional sequence, and that to portray these, new methods will need to be devised. In our opinion, Laughlin and Stephens's diagram (p. 339) is a step in this direction because it is three- rather than two-dimensional.

Ardener's p-structures have a variety of precursors: e.g., Marx's "ideology," Kroeber's *superoganic*, Chomsky's *deep structure*, Lévi-Strauss's *elementary structure* (or simply *structure*), Kuhn's *paradigm*, Foucault's *episteme*, or simply the notion of *culture* itself in anthropology. Foucault's episteme is similar to, but more comprehensive than, Ardener's *p*-structure. Foucault postulates an unconscious order underlying encoded order that determines the direction that encoding will take. This underlying order can be detected by discovering relationships reflected in various systems of encoding in a given culture during a given time period:

> This middle region, then, in so far as it makes manifest the modes of being of order, can be posited as the most fundamental of all: anterior to words, perceptions, and gestures, which are then taken to be more or less exact, more or less happy, expressions of it (which is why this experience of order in its primary state always plays a critical role); more solid, more archaic, less dubious, always more 'true' than the theories that attempt to give those expressions explicit form, exhaustive application, or philosphical foundation. Thus, in every culture, between the use of what one might call the ordering codes and reflections upon order itself, there is the pure experience of order and of its modes of being [Foucault, 1973: xxi].

Ardener's *world structures*, while more comprehensive than *p*-structures, are not comparable to epistemes either, because they seem to be overarching institutions that rely, at the same time, for their direction on both *p*-structures and individuals acting in accordance with *p*-structures. Foucault's epistemes are more like *p*-structures at their most comprehensive level, composed of the multitude of lesser *p*-structures that guide events into more specific channels.

Laughlin and Stephens's chapter is an attempt to reduce the "black box" aspect of unconscious models in culture. They show that *p*-structures are both represented through action and canalized through replication in successive events. By means of this replication (each an *s*-structure), *p*-structures enter the cognitive systems of individuals (cognized environments) where they lie dormant until conditions are such in the operational environment that they are neurofunctionally reactivated as a new s-structure. The variables of *p*-structures constrain potential action through the intentionality of the individuals who participate in that action.

Intentionality, for Laughlin and Stephens, is somewhat different from intentionality as we have presented it, since for them it comprises the meanings of all kinds that underlie symbols while we have restricted it to the individual interplay between affect and meaning (both figurative and denotative) that motivates action. It is here that we believe, with Foucault, that psychoanalysis has much to say to us, for, as he says (1973) it "advances and leaps over representation, overflows it on the side of finitude, and thus reveals, where one had expected functions bearing their norms, conflicts burdened with rules, and significations forming a system, the simple fact that it is possible for there to be system (therefore signification), rule (therefore conflict), norm (therefore function)" (p. 374). In this, Foucault finds a kinship between psychoanalysis and ethnology: Both see as emerging behind the fact of human representations the norms and rules through which events are experienced and activated and consciousness molded and defined. The ideal ethnology, for Foucault (1973), would be one that would

> deliberately . . . seek its object in the area of the unconscious processes that characterize the system of a given culture . . . it would define as a system of cultural unconsciouses the totality of formal structures which render mythical discourse significant, give their coherence and necessity to the rules that regulate needs, and provide the norms of life with a foundation other than that to be found in nature, or in pure biological functions [pp. 379–380].

Counter to Foucault and with Laughlin and Stephens, we believe that for man there is no "pure biological function" that is divorced from the symbolic process; that is, biological function and ethnological and individual function are part and parcel of the same human process. Therefore, the kind of models proposed by Ardener and strengthened by Laughlin and Stephens's neurofunctional equations seem to us to hold significant promise for a structuralism that will shed light, not just on human systems, but on human actions.

References

Ardener, Shirley (ed.)
1975 *Perceiving women.* New York: Wiley.

Foucault, Michel
  1973   *The order of things: An archaeology of the human sciences*. New York: Vintage.
Hastrup, Kirsten
  1978   The post-structuralist position of social anthropology. In *The yearbook of symbolic anthropology*, edited by E. Schwimmer. London: Hurst. Pp. 123–147.
Lane, Michael (ed.)
  1970   *Introduction to structuralism*. New York: Basic Books.

18

The Structure and Origin of Semantic Categories in the Language-Learning Child

MELISSA BOWERMAN

Introduction

Scholars have often sought clues to the ultimate nature of the human symbolic capacity in the process by which children acquire man's foremost symbolic tool, language. Most studies of language as an emerging symbol system have focused on how the child becomes capable of using one item to stand for or represent another (see, for example, Bates *et al.*, 1977; Piaget, 1962). But symbolism draws heavily on a second cognitive capacity into which language development also offers intriguing glimpses: the ability to regard discriminably different stimuli as equivalent, or to categorize.

In the present chapter, two basic aspects of the development of categorization as it relates to symbolism are explored through a study of how children acquire and use words in the second year of life. First, what categorizational processes are available to very young children as they attempt to identify novel referents for a word? The structural principles children use in categorizing for purposes of word use are found to be far more similar to those used by adults than is often supposed. Prototype-based models of category structure that have been proposed for adult categories are particularly applicable. Second, where do the categories symbolized by children's early words come from? In a former era, the tutorial role of linguistic input was emphasized. More recent theorizing, in contrast, has granted almost no role at all to input, but instead stresses the contribution of the child's language-independent cognitive growth. Data presented here indicate that both these positions are too one-sided: There appears to be a complex interaction in word acquisition between children's own predispositions to categorize things in certain ways and their attention to the words of adult language as guides to concept formation.

The primary data used in investigating these issues were collected from my two daughters, Christy and Eva. Christy is the older by 2½ years. Their semantic and syntactic development has been followed closely by tape recording and daily diary notes from the time of their first words. Detailed records cover the developmental history of almost all their early words from the time they began speaking to about 24 months, with more selective records continuing beyond that point.

The Structure of Categories in Childhood and Adulthood

The ability to categorize plays at least two important roles in symbolic activity. First, it permits symbols such as words to stand not only for unique objects and events but also for whole arrays of discriminably different stimuli. Consider, for example, the diversity among the objects, actions, spatial relationships, events, etc. that we regard as essentially the same kind of thing and classify together as *chair, open, in, justice,* and so on. A second critical role that categorization plays in symbolism is to enable us to leap established category boundaries to equate items that are normally thought of as belonging to *different* categories. This is at the heart of man's ability to create and understand nonarbitrary symbols, including metaphors.

When children are in the early stages of language development, it is often impossible to determine whether in applying a word to a certain referent they intend it literally or metaphorically. For example, when a child calls a cat *doggie,* should we assume, along with Clark (1973) and many others, that he is identifying the cat as a member of the category symbolized by his word *doggie*? Or is it more likely, as Bloom (1973) and Nelson *et al.* (1978) have argued, that he means to express the idea that the cat is *like* a doggie (although it is not really a doggie)?

No principled grounds have yet been advanced for selecting between these alternatives in individual instances of word use. The metaphor argument is not implausible, but it has two important drawbacks. First, it does not provide any account of how children draw category boundaries in the first place—for example, how they decide what is and is not a member of the "doggie" category. Second, inferences about which word uses are literal and which are metaphorical are hopelessly subjective, usually being based on our knowledge of where *adult* category boundaries fall.[1] The hypothesis that word use in young children involves routine acts of categorization rather than metaphorical extension at least does not by-pass the problem of initial boundary formation, and it also has consistency to recommend it, since all word uses are interpreted in the same way.

Still a third possibility should be considered: that early in development it makes little sense to ask whether a child intends a word literally or metaphorically because he has not yet drawn any sort of boundary between the two. Rather, he simply sees some sort of similarity between an "old" object or event (one for which he already knows a word) and a new object or event, and extends the word accordingly. Only later does he gradually come to sense that there is such a thing as a distinction between literal and metaphorical usage and begin to get an idea of where the former leaves off and the latter begins. This hypothesis is favored by the fact that the exact placement of the lines between category membership, membership by metaphorical extension, and nonmembership is often culture-specific, as will be discussed at the end of this chapter. Since children do not come predisposed to learn one language rather than another, it seems unlikely that they prejudge the position of these boundaries. It is more plausible that they learn them gradually on the basis of experience with the language to which they are exposed.

Regardless of whether we interpret young children's word usage as strictly literal, sometimes metaphorical, or not clearly either one or the other, it provides an excellent guide to the structural principles available to young children when they categorize.

Noncomplexive versus Complexive Categories

Children's categorizational abilities are commonly considered both qualitatively different from and inferior to those of adults. When faced with a concept formation or concept identification task, they generally do not, as adults do, attempt to sort or group objects or rationalize their choices on the basis of one or more attributes shared by all exemplars. Rather, they form *complexes* in which items are grouped by principles other than possession of a common attribute (Bruner *et al.,* 1966; Piaget and Inhelder, 1959; Vygotsky, 1962). For example, in the familiar chain complex, which Vygotsky considered the purest form of complexive thinking, the child links new exemplars to older ones by a process of end-to-end matching. In a block sorting task, for instance, he might put a red triangle with a blue triangle,

---

[1] Oddly, the application of this knowledge of adult category boundaries is usually limited to "miscategorized" *objects*. Thus, *doggie* for a cat is often considered a metaphorical extension, but no one has suggested that when a child says *open* while turning on a TV or *off* while unfolding a newspaper (as in examples to be discussed in the following) she "really" means 'this action is *like* opening something' or '. . . *like* taking something off.'

then add a red circle, then a yellow circle, then a yellow square, and so on. Vygotsky and others have argued that children's complexive groupings stem from their inability to abstract out an attribute from a concrete object or event and endow it with special, concept-defining status.

Many investigators (see, for example, Vygotsky, 1962; Werner, 1948) have supported their assumption that children initially think in complexes with examples of early complexive word use. An often cited example is that of the child who applied *quah* first to a duck swimming in a pond, then to liquids in general, including milk in his bottle, then to a coin with an eagle on it, and then to round, coinlike objects in general (Vygotsky, 1962: 70). Vygotsky argued (1962) that "complex formations make up the entire first chapter of the developmental history of children's words [p. 70]."

The view that young children's early use of words is necessarily complexive contrasts interestingly with more recent theories of the acquisition of word meaning proposed by Clark (1973) and Nelson (1974). Although these investigators differ from each other in many respects, both have assumed that children identify words from the start with one or more stable elements of meaning that determine how the word will be applied in new situations. For example, *doggie* might be identified with the meaning 'four-legged,' and thereby be extended to all four-legged creatures; similarly, *ball* might be identified with the meaning 'something that bounces and rolls' and extended to all objects that show this behavior.

Bloom (1973) has attempted to integrate evidence for both complexive word use (e.g., *quah*) and noncomplexive word use (e.g., *doggie* only for four-legged animals) by proposing that the two styles of word use predominate at different periods of development. Like Vygotsky, she argues that complexive usage is more primitive, and suggests that it is associated with lack of the concept of object permanence. According to her hypothesis, only when the child achieves the concept that objects have a stable, enduring existence (about 18–24 months in Piagetian theory) can he begin to identify words (at least for objects) with consistent features.

How accurate is this view of the young child's categorizational abilities as revealed through his use of words? The supporting data provided by most investigators—for example, isolated examples like *quah* or *doggie* collected from different children—are insufficient proof. In order to make a careful test of the hypothesis that complexive word use reflects an earlier and more primitive stage of concept development, one must inspect in detail the history of word use in *individual* children. Such an analysis of the data collected from Christy and Eva offers little support for the hypothesis (Bowerman, 1976, 1978).

Early Noncomplexive Categories

According to the "stage" theory, complexive usage reflects a primitive stage of mental development and tends to fade out, being gradually replaced by the putatively more advanced noncomplexive use of words in which all referents for a word share one or more attributes. However, both Christy and Eva used some words noncomplexively virtually from the start of the one-word period. That is, they stuck to consistent classificational criteria in extending certain words to novel situations; their attention was not diverted by salient but irrelevant attributes of the new referents or by possibilities for thematic groupings.

Three examples are presented in Table 1. Example 1 shows that from 13 months Eva used *ball* exclusively in connection with rounded objects of a size suitable for handling and throwing (Christy's early use of *ball* was similarly consistent). From 15 months, Christy used [a:] *off/on* (Example 2) (these were among her first words; lack of final consonants in her speech at this time made it difficult to tell if one word or two were involved) in connection with the separation and joining of objects or parts of objects. It was broader than any everyday adult category, being applied not only to

TABLE 1
Some Words used Noncomplexively[a]

---

1. Eva, *ball.* From 13;5 for rounded objects of a size suitable for handling and throwing.

   Fourteenth month: (first use) as spies a large round ball in adjoining room, then goes to pick it up; as picks up rounded cork pincushion, then throws it; as looks at a red balloon; later, also as handles it. Fifteenth mo.: whenever sees or plays with balls or balloons; as holds an Easter egg, then throws it; after picking up a small round stone, then throws it; as sees plastic egg-shaped toy; as holds a round cannister lid, then throws it; etc.

2. Christy, [a:] *off/on* (not clear if two words or one). From 15;12 in connection with situations involving separation or rejoining of parts.

   Sixteenth to seventeenth months: in connection with getting socks on or off; getting on or off spring-horse; pulling pop-beads apart and putting them together; separating stacked paper cups; unfolding a newspaper; pushing hair out of M's face; opening boxes (with separate or hinged lids as well as sliding drawers); putting lids on jars, cap on chapstick, phone on hook, doll into highchair, pieces back into puzzle; while M takes her diaper off; trying to join foil-wrapped torn-apart towelettes, etc.

3. Eva, *off.* From 14;18 in connection with separation of things *from the body* only (as request or comment).

   Fifteenth to seventeenth months: for sleepshades, shoes, car safety harness, glasses, pinned-on pacifier, diaper, bib. Starting in sixteenth mo.: *open* begins to be used in other 'separation' situations; e.g., for opening doors, boxes, cans, toothpaste tubes; pulling pop beads apart; taking books out of case, tip off door stop, wrapper off soap; cracking peanuts; peeling paper off book cover, etc. *Off* still used for taking things off the body.

---

[a] Ages given in months and days, or examples listed chronologically within the month. All examples in all tables are spontaneous; there was no prior modeling of the word in the immediate context. All utterances were single words unless otherwise marked. M = Mother

situations in which adults would say *take off* or *put on* but also to those they would encode with *unfold* or *fold, take apart* or *put together, take out* or *put in,* and *open* or *close.* Eva's use of *off* (Example 3) was just as consistent as Christy's, but the category underlying it was much less abstract: The word referred only to the removal of objects from the body and did not generalize beyond this domain, even to other situations an adult would refer to by *take off,* for many months. During this time Eva simply did not refer to other kinds of separation, although she engaged in activities involving the separation and joining of objects and their parts as much as Christy had.

The complexive use of words also began during the one-word period for both children, but it flowered somewhat later than these early noncomplex- ive uses and continued into the third year and even beyond for certain words (examples will be introduced in the following). This pattern (early onset of noncomplexive word use; later contemporaneous occurrence of words used complexively and words used noncomplexively) indicates that the com- plexive use of words does not necessarily stem, as Vygotsky (1962), Bloom (1973), and others have postulated, from an inability to abstract out attributes and hold them constant over a wide range of referents. To the contrary, early consistent uses like Eva's *ball* and *off* in the fourteenth and fifteenth months suggest that the capacity of very young children to form categories on the basis of stable, consistent attributes has been underestimated.[2] How- ever, if complexive word use does not reflect an incapacity to form non- complexive categories, why does it occur? Recent evidence on the nature of adult semantic categories, coupled with close analyses of children's com- plexes, helps to answer this question.

The Role of Prototypes in Adult and Child Categories

Conceptions of the nature of adult categories have been undergoing radical change in the last few years. No longer do investigators assume that most categories entertained by mature, sane, conscious, and civilized represen- tatives of the human species are definable in terms of a conjunction of *cri- terial attributes,* with category membership being an all-or-nothing matter. According to an alternative conception, category membership is more typ- ically a matter of degree. At the core of a category there may be one or more prototypical, or "best," exemplars; these are "surrounded by" other less

---

[2] Rosch *et al.* (1976) have recently shown that children at least as young as 3 (the youngest age tested) can sort objects noncomplexively as long as the objects provided permit sorting according to *basic level* categories (e.g., dogs, cars) rather than superordinate categories (e.g., animals, vehicles). Like the present data, this indicates that children are capable of using adult- like categorization principles when they are free to group at their preferred level of abstraction. (However, the extremely abstract category underlying Christy's use of *off* at 15 months indicates that children's preferred level is by no means always relatively concrete, as is often assumed).

prototypical members at increasing distances from the center. Noncentral instances shade off at some point from being poor or peripheral members of the category to being nonmembers, but the borderline between membership and nonmembership, or membership only by metaphorical extension, is often fuzzy and ill-defined (Fillmore, 1975; Rosch, 1975; Smith *et al.,* 1974). The prototype model of category structure accounts well for certain phenomena that embarrass the "categories-as-conjunctions-of-criterial-attributes" model—for example, the fact that criterial attributes are impossible to identify for many categories (e.g., "furniture"; see Rosch and Mervis, 1975) and the fact that some category members seem to speakers to be more central to or representative of their category than others (Rosch, 1973).

Several researchers have suggested the applicability of the prototype model of category structure to children (see, for example, Anglin, 1977; Fillmore, 1975; Rosch and Mervis, 1975), but the matter has been relatively little explored, especially with children under two years of age. A close examination of Christy's and Eva's early language records indicates that the model is indeed useful: It provides an excellent account of their early complexive word uses, almost all of which are describable as a set of variations around prototypical exemplars.

Prototypicality could not be determined, of course, by directly probing the child's view on the representativeness of various category exemplars. It was judged instead on the basis of how the attributes of category exemplars were distributed within the category. Among the referents to which each complexively used word was extended, a small set of attributes repeatedly figured. Although many referents shared no discernible attributes with each other (which is, of course, why the category had to be considered complexive), there was at least one referent (or group of highly similar referents) with which they *all* shared one or more attributes. In this prototypical referent, all the attributes associated with the category (to judge from the way in which the word was extended to novel referents) were maximally clustered. This structure conforms closely to Rosch and Mervis's (1975) "family resemblances" model of the internal structure of prototype-based categories. According to Rosch and Mervis's studies, the degree to which adults perceive category members as prototypical is, for many semantic categories (e.g., "furniture," "chair"), a function of the internal distribution of attributes. Category members that are seen as most prototypical share many attributes with other category members (and particularly with each other), while category members perceived as less prototypical or as poor exemplars share fewer attributes with other category members.

In addition to being central in terms of the way the attributes associated with a given category were distributed within the category, the children's prototypes had other claims to special status. In almost all cases, the prototype was the child's *first* referent for a word. Additionally, it was invariably the referent to which the word had been applied most frequently or exclusively in parental speech. It appears, then, that the children learned and first used certain words in connection with frequently modeled category exemplars. After periods ranging from a few days to a few months they began to extend the words to never-modeled referents sharing one or some combination of the attributes of the original. The interval between first use and extension beyond prototypical exemplars may reflect the length of time it took the child to analyze the prototype into some of its attributes and to begin to recognize these attributes when they occurred independently of each other, recombined with other attributes in new configurations.

Some examples of word use revolving around prototypical exemplars are presented in Table 2. Consider Example 1, Eva's use of *kick*. She produced

TABLE 2
Some Complexively Used Words with Prototypical Referents

---

1. Eva, *kick*.

Prototype: kicking a ball with the foot so that it is propelled forward.

Features: (*a*) *waving limb;* (*b*) *sudden sharp contact* (especially between body part and other object); (*c*) an *object propelled.*

Selected samples. Eighteenth month: (first use) as kicks a floor fan with her foot (Features *a, b*); looking at picture of kitten with ball near its paw (all features, in anticipated event?); watching moth fluttering on a table (*a*), watching row of cartoon turtles on television doing can-can (*a*). Nineteenth mo.: just before throwing something (*a, c*); "kick bottle," after pushing bottle with her feet, making it roll (all features). Twenty-first mo.: as makes ball roll by bumping it with front wheel of kiddicar (*b, c*) pushing teddy bear's stomach against Christy's chest (*b*), pushing her stomach against a mirror (*b*); pushing her chest against a sink (*b*), etc.

2. Christy, *night night*.

Prototype: person (or doll) lying down on bed or crib.

Features: (*a*) crib, bed; (*b*) blanket; (*c*) nonnormative horizontal position of object (animate or inanimate).

Selected examples. Sixteenth month: (first use) pushing a doll over in her crib; from this time on, frequent for putting dolls to bed, covering, and kissing them (Features *a, b, c*). Seventeenth mo.: laying her bottle on its side (*c*). Eighteenth mo.: watching Christmas tree being pulled away on its side (*c*); after puts piano stool legs in box, one lying horizontally (*c*); after putting a piece of cucumber flat in her dish and pushing it into a corner (*c*). Nineteenth mo.: as M flattens out cartons, laying them in pile on floor (*c*); often while looking at pictures of empty beds or cribs or wanting a toy bed given to her (*a*, sometimes *b*); laying kiddicar on its side (*c*). Twentieth mo.: "awant night night," (request for M to hand her blanket); she then drapes it over shoulders as rides on toy horse (*b*), etc.

3. Eva, *close*.

Prototype: closing drawers, doors, boxes, etc.

Features: (*a*) *bringing together* two objects or parts of the same object until they are in close contact; (*b*) causing something to become *concealed* or inaccessible.

Selected examples. From Sixteenth month: for closing gates, doors, drawers (Features *a, b*). Nineteenth mo.: "open, close," taking peg people out of their holes in bus built for them and putting them back in (*a*). Twenty-first mo.: Frequent from now on while pushing handles of scissors, tongs, tweezers together and for getting people to put arms or legs together, e.g., "close knees" (*a*); "close

---

(*continued*)

TABLE 2 (*Continued*)

it,'' as tries to push pieces of cut peach slice together (*a*); trying to fold up a towelette (*a*, (*b*?)); ''open, close,'' as unfolds and folds a dollar bill (*a*, (*b*?)). Twenty-second mo.: ''open, close,'' after M has spread doll's arms out, then folded them back over chest (*a*). Twenty-fourth mo.: ''that one close,'' trying to fit piece into jigsaw puzzle (*a*, [*b*?]); ''I close it,'' as turns knob on television set until picture completely darkens (*b*); ''Mommy close me,'' (twenty-sixth mo:) ''I will close you, o.k.?'' both in connection with pushing chair into table (*a*), etc.

4. Christy, *open.*

Prototype: opening drawers, doors, boxes, etc.

Features: (*a*) *separation* of parts which were in contact; (*b*) causing something to be *revealed* or become accessible.

From middle of seventeenth month: *open* starts to take over the function of *off* (see Example 2, Table 1) for 'separation' situations, both with and without 'revealing.' (First use) for cupboard door opening (*a*, *b*); pointing to spout in salt container that M had just opened (*a*, *b*); trying to separate two frisbees (*a*). Eighteenth mo: for opening boxes, doors, tube of ointment, jars (*a*, *b*); trying to push legs of hand-operated can opener wider apart than they can go; spreading legs of nail scissors apart (both *a*). Nineteenth mo.: several times in connection with pictures in magazine; wants M to somehow get at the pictured objects for her (*b*); request for M to unscrew plastic stake from a block (*a*); request for M to take out metal brad that holds 3 flat pieces of plastic together (*a*). Twentieth mo.: request for M to take stem off apple (*a*); ''awant mommy . . . open,'' request for M to pry pen out of piece of styrofoam (*a*); request for M to take pegs out of pounding bench (*a*); ''awant open hand,'' request for M to take leg off plastic doll (*a*); request for M to turn on electric typewriter (*b*); trying to pull pop beads apart (*a*). Twenty-first month: request for M to turn on water faucet (*b*); request for M to take pieces out of jigsaw puzzle (*a*, (*b*?)); trying to get grandma's shoe off her foot (*a*); ''open light,'' after M has turned light off, request to have it turned on again (*b*). Twenty-second mo.: ''awant that open,'' trying to pull handle off of riding toy (*a*), etc.

5. Eva, *open.* (See Table 1, Example 3 for initial uses.)

Selected examples. Eighteenth month: request for M to take apart a broken toothbrush (*a*), and for M to pull apart two pop beads (*a*), and for M to take pieces out of jigsaw puzzle (*a*, (*b*?)). Nineteenth mo.: pulling bathrobe off M's knee to inspect knee (*a*, *b*); request for M to turn television on (*b*); ''open tape,'' request for M to pull strip off masking tape (*a*). Twentieth mo.: ''open tangle,'' bringing M pile of tangled yarns to separate (*a*); taking stubby candle out of shallow glass cup (*a*). Twenty-first mo.: ''open mommy,'' trying to unbend a small flexible ''mommy'' doll (*a*); unfolding a towelette (*a*, *b*); request for M to put legs apart (*a*). Twenty-second mo.: ''open slide,'' request for M to set slide in yard upright (*a*, (*b*?)); ''I'm open it,'' after rips apart two tiny shoes that were stuck together (*a*). Twenty-third mo. and beyond: ''my knee open,'' as unbends her knee (*a*); ''I will open it for you,'' before taking napkin out of its ring for M, does not unfold it, then says ''I open it'' as report on completed action (*a*); ''I'm gonna leave this chair open like this, I'm not gonna shut it,'' as leaves table with chair pulled out (*a*), etc.

6. Eva, [gi]. (from ''giddiup'')

Prototype: bouncing on a spring-horse

Features: (*a*) *horse* (later, other large animals and riding toys which one sits astraddle); (*b*) *bouncing motion;* (*c*) *sitting* on toy (especially astraddle).

Selected examples. Fifteenth month: (first use) bouncing on spring-horse or as request to be lifted onto it (*a*, *b*, *c*); as picks up tiny plastic horse, then tries to

(continued)

TABLE 2 *(Continued)*

straddle it (*a, c*); getting on toy tractor (*c*); looking at horses on television (*a*); getting on trike (*c*); seeing picture of horse (*a*); bouncing on heels while crouching in tub (*b*); climbing into tiny plastic blow-up chair (*c*); looking at hobby horse (*a*); bouncing astraddle M's legs (*b, c*). Later, continues to be used for pointing out horses, generalizes to other large animals like cows, and while pointing out or riding on trikes, tractors, kiddicars.

7. Eva, *moon.*

Prototype: the real moon

Features: (*a*) shape: circular, crescent, half-moon (these shapes were distinct—i.e., a stretch of curved surface not enough to elicit "moon"; (*b*) *yellow* color; (*c*) *shiny* surface; (*d*) *viewing position:* seen at an angle from below: (*e*) *flatness;* (*f*) *broad expanse* as background.

Selected examples. Sixteenth mo.: (first use) looking at the moon (all features). Seventeenth mo.: looking at peel-side of half-grapefruit obliquely from below (*a, b, d*); playing with half-moon-shaped lemon slice (*a, b, e*); touching circular chrome dial on dishwasher (*a, c, d, e, f*); playing with shiny rounded green leaf she'd just picked (*a, c, e*); touching ball of spinach M offers her (*a.* Spheres were usually called "ball." There was perhaps a limited chaining effect here to the leaf, a referent earlier the same day, through shared greenness). Eighteenth mo.: holding crescent-shaped bit of paper she'd torn off yellow pad (*a, b, e*). Nineteenth mo.: looking up at inside of shade of lit floor lamp (*a, b, d*); looking up at pictures of yellow and green vegetables (squash, peas) on wall in grocery store (*a, b, d, e, f*); looking up at wall-hanging with pink and purple circles (*a, d, e, f*). Twentieth mo.: pointing at orange crescent-shaped blinker light on a car (*a, (b?), c, e*). Twenty-first mo.: looking up at curved steer horns mounted on wall (*a, d, f*); putting green magnetic capital letter D on refrigerator (*a, d, e, f*); picking up half a Cheerio, then eats it (*a, (b?)*); looking at black, irregular kidney-shaped piece of paper on a wall (*a, d, e, f*). Twenty-fourth mo.: "my moon is off" after pulling a hangnail (a routine usage) (*a, e*).

this word starting at seventeen and one-half months both in situations in which an adult would also be able to use *kick,* as when she kicked a fan, and in strangely diverse and (to adult eyes) inappropriate situations such as while she watched a fluttering moth, when she bumped a ball with the front wheel of her kiddicar, making it roll, and when she pushed her stomach up against a mirror. What does the bumping of a ball with a kiddicar wheel or the pushing of a stomach against a mirror have in common with a fluttering moth? Probably nothing. But all three referents share one or more attributes with a very common referent for *kick* (exceptionally, not Eva's first referent but implicit in her second referent), the situation in which someone kicks a ball with a foot, propelling it forward. The moth referent shares with it an attribute we may refer to (very schematically) as 'a waving limb.' The kiddicar referent shares with it 'sudden sharp contact' and 'an object (ball) propelled.' And the stomach-against-mirror referent shares with it—and with the kiddicar referent but not with the moth referent—'sudden sharp contact.'

Example 2 illustrates that for Christy, *night night* was associated with at least three features that are all present simultaneously in the typical situations in which children learn this word: beds or cribs, blankets, and the horizontal position of an object that is usually vertical. These features were present one-, two-, or three-at-a-time in the various situations to which Christy extended *night night*. For example, her attention to 'nonnormative horizontal position' in the absence of beds or blankets is found in her production of *night night* while watching cardboard cartons being flattened, while witnessing a Christmas tree being hauled away, and after laying her kiddicar on its side.

Examples 3, 4, and 5 show that, for both Christy and Eva, *open* was associated with the 'separation of parts' and the 'revealing of something,' while *close* was associated with the reverse features of 'joining' and 'concealment.' Both features of each pair co-occur in typical *open* and *close* situations involving doors, jars, boxes, and the like (these were the children's first referents for *open* and *close*), and they occur one-at-a-time in referents like turning on or off water faucets, lights, television, or radio (revealing or concealing without separation or joining) and taking a stem off an apple, buckling a wrist strap, and pulling a chair out from a table or pushing it in (separation and joining without revealing or concealing).

Eva first used *giddiup* in connection with bouncing on her spring-horse, the only referent situation in which it had ever been modeled to her. Example 6 shows that she subsequently extended it to horses and other large animals, riding toys, sitting on or (particularly) astraddle, and a bouncing motion, all of which were present simultaneously in the original spring-horse situation.

Example 7 shows Eva's use of *moon*. This was first applied to the real moon, then extended to a variety of objects that shared shape (circular, half-moon, or crescent) with the moon and that were also characterized by one or more of the following attributes of the moon or of the situation in which it is viewed: flatness, yellowness, shininess, having a broad expanse as a background, and being seen obliquely from below. This example is particularly interesting because it reveals that the child may assign different weights or values to the attributes she associates with a category. *Shape* was obviously criterial for Eva's use of *moon,* since no matter how flat, shiny, yellow, etc. an object might have been she never called it *moon* unless it was also shaped like the real moon in one of its phases. Unlike shape, attributes like flatness, shininess, and so on were only probabilistically associated with the category labeled *moon*. The differential weighting of attributes according to their relative degree of criteriality for a category is a central part of a model of prototype structure (for adult categories) outlined by Smith *et al.* (1974).

To summarize, the preceding discussion of the structure of semantic categories in the early period of word acquisition reveals little discontinuity between childhood and adulthood in the structural processes used in categorizing. While data from only two children have been presented here, there is no reason to suppose they are unrepresentative. To the contrary, there is at least preliminary evidence to suggest that the phenomenon of extending a word on the basis of similarities that new referents bear to prototypical referents is quite general in the early period of word acquisition. For example, Labov and Labov (1974) describe such a usage for *cat,* one of their daughter's first two words, and Clark (1975) reanalyzes examples of word use from the early diary literature in a way that is quite compatible with the present model.

The argument that children are capable of using essentially the same principles in categorizing objects and events as adults do supports Rosch *et al.*'s (1976) contention that the structural principles of category formation are universal. In addition, it is in keeping with the more inclusive hypothesis that is currently enjoying much popularity, that man's biologically given propensities for organizing experiences in certain ways will, because they are so basic, manifest themselves early in childhood (as well as in other domains such as universals of linguistic structure and constraints on the way languages change over time; see Rosch, 1975; Slobin, 1975, for general discussions). This approach to the child's abilities regards maturation as a process consisting largely of acquiring an overlay of detail, much of it culture-specific, on an underlying universal cognitive base that is common to both children and adults. In this emphasis, it differs from accounts of child development (including those of Vygotsky and other theorists who have written about complexe thought processes) that stress ways in which children are both different from and deficient with respect to adults.

On the Origins of Children's Categories

Old and New Hypotheses

The current theoretical emphasis on the extent of man's inherent cognitive capacities stands in striking contrast not only to the different-and-deficient view of children referred to above but also to the view, widely accepted earlier in this century, that cognitive development is heavily dependent on language acquisition. According to this latter position, embodied most strongly in the Sapir–Whorf hypothesis, the categorization schemes adopted by different cultures are essentially arbitrary, there being nothing in either man's make-up or in the real world that calls for experiences to be divided up one way rather than another. The growing child, in this view, is socialized into the locally prevailing system of categorizing largely through his acquisition of language. Thus, language acquisition precedes and guides cognitive development.

This hypothesis has been turned upside down in the last few years, with many researchers now arguing for the opposite view, that cognitive development precedes, paces, and guides language development. An important early determinant of this shift was the recognition in the early 1970s that children's early sentences everywhere are largely limited to the expression of a small set of putatively universal operations and semantic relationships,[3] coupled with the realization that Piaget's theory of cognitive development in the sensory–motor period (birth to 24 months) provides a compelling account of how children arrive at these concepts independently of language input (Brown, 1973). The cognition-precedes-language hypothesis has gained additional strength from studies showing that children employ many non-linguistic strategies in trying to process and interpret linguistic structures (see, for example, Slobin, 1973; Clark, 1975), from the generally negative outcomes of attempts to test the hypothesis that language structure influences cognitive structure or processing (Lenneberg, 1967), and from the recently adduced evidence that certain categorization schemes are far less arbitrary and variable from language to language than has been supposed (Berlin and Kay, 1969; Rosch, 1975; Rosch et al., 1976).

According to the currently prevalent view of the relationship between linguistic and cognitive development, the prelinguistic child is engaged in building up a repertoire of basic concepts and ways of organizing his experiences on the basis of his own dealings with the world and in accordance with biologically given constraints on the possible form that human concepts can take. The task of acquiring language, in this view, is to learn the linguistic devices with which the local language *encodes* concepts that the child has already formulated independently of language. In other words, learning to talk involves learning a system for mapping or translating from one representational system (cognition) into another (language) (see, for example, Clark, 1973; Nelson, 1974; Slobin, 1973). No one would deny that language at some point becomes instrumental in introducing the child to new concepts or in refining his existing concepts so they conform to adult norms, but this is typically seen as a phenomenon of later language acquisition—say, beyond the period of early sentences at about 18 to 30 months. During the early period of acquisition, the child is thought not to acquire linguistic forms—perhaps not even to notice them—until he has already arrived, on his own, at an understanding of the meanings they express. Then he will actively start searching for the needed expressive devices.

In the following discussion, I will argue that this account is far too extreme. In our enthusiasm to acknowledge the many ways in which language acquisition depends on prior cognitive growth, we should not be so easily

---

[3] These include the predication of existence, nonexistence or disappearance, and recurrence of objects and events by words such as *that, there, no more, allgone,* and *more,* and the expression of relations among agents, actions, and objects acted upon, between locations and objects located, between possessors and possessions, and between objects and their attributes (see Bloom, 1970; Bowerman, 1973; and Brown, 1973).

persuaded that linguistic forms are always mapped onto preformulated concepts, and never concepts built to account for received linguistic forms.

Some Relevant Data

Speculation on the role of language in early cognitive development has generally been hampered by a lack of specific and detailed information on the contexts in which children learn particular words and the ways in which they use them. The following analyses of data from my two subjects are brief, but I think they are sufficient to suggest that the relationship between language and cognition in early development is more complex than either the current cognition-precedes-language theory or the earlier language-precedes-cognition theory can account for. There seem to be complex interactions in word learning among such factors as the child's own prelinguistic conceptual activity in a particular semantic domain, the nature of the input provided, and the child's attempts to make sense of this input.

The relative contribution of linguistic input and autonomous cognitive development in the child's acquisition of the concept underlying her use of a particular word can be roughly inferred from several types of evidence. A first consideration is whether the word is one the child has been exposed to, or instead is idiosyncratic. Children sometimes appear to make up words; Nelson (1974) suggests that this occurs when they have formulated concepts independently of language and cannot find suitable words in the speech they hear with which to express them. A second consideration is whether the range of situations across which a child applies a recognizable word of the adult language is similar to the semantic range across which it has been applied in the input to her, or whether she uses it in a consistent but deviant way—for example, either for only a subset of the situations in which the adult uses it (underextension) or for those situations plus many more besides (overextension). Gross deviations from the input in terms of the size and make-up of the child's semantic category suggest a relatively strong role for the child's independent conceptual activity. A third consideration is whether the concept underlying a child's word, as inferred from the situations in which she uses it, is at all likely to have originated completely autonomously, or whether, instead, there has been a specific kind of verbal input to which the concept can more plausibly be traced.

When these admittedly somewhat rough criteria are applied in analyzing Christy's and Eva's early words, at least two general patterns emerge (probably these are merely opposite ends of a continuum representing the relative contribution of language-independent cognition and linguistic input in the genesis of the child's semantic categories). In one pattern, the underlying concept seems to have originated with minimal or no assistance from adult linguistic input; this, of course, is exactly and *only* what one should expect to find according to the current hypothesis that early language learning consists of mapping linguistic forms onto preformulated concepts. In the second pattern, in contrast, considerable influence of adult linguistic input is apparent.

Some examples of the first pattern include Christy's *off/on*, Eva's *off* (Examples 2 and 3, respectively, in Table 1) and Eva's [bidi] (Example 1 in Table 3). As noted earlier, Christy's *off/on* was applied over a much broader semantic domain than in adult speech. It apparently referred to almost any kind of separation or joining of two objects or parts of the same object. Eva's use of *off* contrasts strikingly in that its range of application was very restricted by adult standards (to objects being removed from the body). These patterns of word usage suggest that Christy regarded taking clothes and other objects off the body as similar, at some level of abstraction, to opening boxes, unfolding papers, and pulling pop beads apart—all could be referred to by the same word. Like Christy, Eva regarded manipulations

TABLE 3
Words Illustrating Differences in the Relative Contribution of Language-Independent Cognition and Linguistic Input to Concept Formation

1. Eva, [bidi]. Concept: *pinching* or *touching* someone, especially on *leg*, or unexpectedly *bare skin*.

   Selected examples. Seventeenth month: as pinches M's leg; as pinches her own leg; coming up to pinch leg of visitor; soon after, as pinches M's leg. Eighteenth mo.: looking at picture of boy on a swing, his shirt is pulled up so bare skin shows in back; approaching strange child in theater and touching his bare back; after father appears in unfamiliar shorts, E going up to touch bottom edge of the shorts.

2. Christy, *hi*. Concept: *things on or covering hands or feet*. (As a greeting, *hi* had already been known for several months.)

   Selected examples. Nineteenth month: sticking hand inside snowsuit hood and holding it up; as washrag drifts across her foot in tub; as shows M tiny object balanced on end of her finger; as hold up finger with drop of milk from her bottle on the end of it; as looks at M's finger which is stuck in toy tube of straw; as slides her hands under her blanket and holds them up; as puts a mitten-shaped potholder over her hand; as sticks her hand down into silverware holder of dishdrainer; as holds up finger with wing-nut balanced on it; when shirt falls off side of crib and lands over her foot.

3. Eva, [gidi]. Concept: *physical displacement* of object, or anticipated potential displacement.

   Selected examples. Nineteenth month: "gidi towel," as climbs on chair, brushing against towel hanging on stove; as climbs over father's legs on couch; as tries to squeeze past Christy in narrow hall; "gidi book," as clambers over magazine on couch. Twentieth mo.: "gidi Mommy," as tries to squeeze behind and past M in hallway; "gidi miau," as pushes aside a rabbit riding toy (which she calls "miau") so she can push doll carriage through; "gidi Mommy," pushing M's arm, which is over her head, away; "gidi Christy," trying to shove a chair in at kitchen counter beside chair C is standing on; "gidi beads," pushing toy car through pile of beads, shoving them aside. Twenty-first mo.: "Christy gidi!" distressed after C has encroached on her space in tub, trying to shove her back.

with pop beads, folded paper, boxes, and so on as similar enough to be referred to by the same word, although the word she used was *open* rather than *off*. But taking things off the body did not appear to share in this concept for Eva, since she always referred to this action by a different word, *off*.

It is difficult to account for these differences on the basis of the linguistic or other input to the children, since their linguistic and physical environments were quite similar at this age (same parent, babysitter, house, toys, etc., although of course Eva had an older sibling while Christy did not). An alternative and more persuasive hypothesis is that the children had, on the basis of their own dealings with the physical world, arrived at different ways of categorizing and organizing their experiences involving separations of various types. Different children may make the cuts in their experiences in different places. The things that one child sees as going together might not exactly coincide with what another child regards as similar, and—as in the case of the two *offs*—neither child may make the cuts in the places they might be expected to if they were relying primarily on linguistic input to instruct them on how to categorize things.

Eva's word [bidi] (Example 1, Table 3) reflects a concept that seems even more independent of adult input than Christy's *off/on* and Eva's *off*. Eva used this word extensively in her seventeenth and eighteenth months in connection with her act of pinching someone's leg or, later, touching someone wherever bare skin was somewhat surprisingly on view. As far as I can determine, both [bidi] and the concept it encoded originated with Eva; no plausible adult model suggests itself. We did not pinch or talk about pinching; we did tickle, but Eva had a separate word for this, *ticky,* which was associated with toes. The salience and interest value for Eva of "surprising" bare skin also seems to have been independent of any adult linguistic input. In short, [bidi] seems to have been a purely spontaneous invention on Eva's part, in both word and governing concept.

Now consider Christy's *hi* and Eva's [gidi] (Examples 2 and 3 in Table 3). Unlike *off/on, off,* and [bidi], these words were acquired and used in such a way as to suggest considerable influence of linguistic input on concept formation. That is, there is strong reason to infer that the children did *not* formulate the concepts independently of language and then look around for convenient labels with which to encode them. Rather, the concepts seem to have originated with the children's attempts to make sense of the way they heard certain words used to them. In both cases, the child's efforts to understand resulted in her construction of a concept that was not the same as the adult concept governing the use of the word. But it seems unlikely that her concept would have been formed and labeled at all unless she had been exposed to adult usage of the word and had attended to it without yet having a notion of what the word meant in those contexts. Notice that this kind of behavior is precisely what is *not* predicted by the hypothesis that children initially learn language only to encode those concepts that they already have acquired on a nonlinguistic basis.

The first example shows that Christy at 18 months began to develop a peculiar use for *hi* (she had used it normally as a greeting for some time). The governing concept appears to have been 'situations in which something rests on or covers the hand or foot' (see examples in Table 3 from which this inference is made). What would cause a child to develop a concept like this? I think it is implausible to suppose that the concept was formulated independently of language, not only because it is such a peculiar one, but, more importantly, because there is an easily located linguistic source for it. When playing with Christy, I would sometimes put a finger puppet or object like the cap of a pen on my finger and pretend it was a little person, coming to say *hi*. Thus, she heard *hi* modeled in connection with seeing something stuck on the end of a finger. Rather than interpreting *hi* in its intended and known (to her) sense as a greeting, she apparently concentrated on making sense of the co-currence of *hi* with something on the finger, and from there constructed a rather ingenious and consistent hypothesis—albeit the wrong one—to account for the usage.

The concept governing Eva's use of [gidi] (Example 3, Table 3) seems to have involved the actual or anticipated physical displacement of objects. For example, starting in the nineteenth month, she produced the word as she brushed against a hanging towel, as she set a hairbrush to one side, as she shoved a toy car through a pile of beads, and as she pushed past people or objects in narrow hallways. It is not inconceivable that a child would formulate a category involving the physical displacement of objects and people on her own, and, not finding a suitable adult word to encode it, make up her own. But consider how much sense this concept makes if we identify Eva's [gidi] with adult *'scuse me*. [gidi] was a plausible rendition for *'scuse me* in Eva's phonology, and she had certainly been exposed to the phrase on many occasions in which someone was squeezing past her in the hall or moving her to one side. I would hypothesize that Eva's attention was drawn to 'physical displacement' because she had heard the same phrase used repeatedly across a variety of superficially diverse situations, most of which shared this abstract element. In other words, repeated exposure to the word served as a "lure to cognition" (Brown, 1958:206) and started her working on a concept she probably would not have formulated at that time in the absence of this specific kind of linguistic input.

The examples presented so far all involve categories for which there appear to be criterial attributes. Determining the source of such categories in the child's development involves making inferences about what brings a certain cross-situational invariance to a child's attention and/or sets a certain categorizational principle in motion at a particular time. What about categories revolving around prototypical exemplars? Determining the origin of these involves making an additional type of inference: Why do certain objects or events, complete with all their attributes, take on central or core significance while others are relegated to more peripheral status?

Rosch (1973, 1975) suggests a number of principles by which prototypes might arise. In some of these, certain category exemplars take on prototype status as a result of the learner's experience with a variety of category instances. For example, the learner may become implicitly aware, through principles of information processing, that certain exemplars represent the central tendency of the category taken as a whole. The data presented in the preceding section indicate that early in children's development prototypes do not arise by this type of processing, but rather are salient from the beginning, constituting the growing points around which the categories are subsequently formed. Rosch postulates that there may be several ways in which certain stimuli take on special salience before the formation of their categories. For example, some items (e.g., certain colors, "good gestalt" shapes) appear to have prototype status universally due to the characteristics of man's perceptual apparatus. Other items might acquire special salience because they are the exemplars of their category that the learner hears identified first or most frequently.

The hypothesis that early word acquisition consists of mapping words onto preformulated concepts would predict that the child would be little influenced in his selection of prototypes by which items he hears labeled by a particular word first or most frequently. Rather, certain stimuli should assume special salience for the child on grounds quite independent of language. This is no doubt true in many cases. For example, consider Eva's *moon* (Example 7, Table 2). Because the real moon is unique and perceptually highly salient, its preeminence over hangnails, scraps of paper, and other more peripheral members of the category labeled by Eva's *moon* is easy to understand. It would seem implausible, in fact, for a child to form a category (such as, perhaps, *paper*) including scraps of paper as the prototype and the real moon as a peripheral member. In short, it is not necessary to suppose that linguistic input played a critical role in singling the moon out from other "similar" objects and giving it special status in Eva's eyes. It is quite plausible, to the contrary, that she conceptualized it for herself and only then adopted the word offered for it in parental speech.

However, now consider Eva's use of *kick*. Should we assume that there is also something highly salient about kicking a ball that would lead a child to elevate this event to prototype status on nonlinguistic grounds? It is not clear that kicking a ball has the necessary perceptual or functional salience over other similar events, such as kicking one's sister or throwing a ball, to make it the core of a concept that includes these other events as more peripheral members. An equally or more plausible explanation for the prototypical status of kicking a ball in the category labeled by Eva's *kick* is that the word *kick* was modeled to her in connection with this referent far more frequently than with any other referent. This alone could have highlighted it and caused it to assume focal importance over all "similar" competing referents for *kick*.

Frequency probably also correlates with firstness. That is, the referents in connection with which parents model words most frequently would also tend to be the first or certainly among the first referents with which they introduce the word. Brown (1977) suggests that parents' choice of first referent when introducing a word is not random, but rather is dictated by their own (adult) knowledge of the internal structure of the category labeled by that word: "Given any choice at all . . . a parent will surely prefer to introduce a word with a highly prototypical instance. Indeed, I suspect there is a little law to the effect that words will be ostensively introduced to children with the most prototypical or representative example available. For *vegetable,* peas or carrots, not mushrooms. For *furniture,* a chair or sofa, not a clock. And for *bird,* something like [a jay], rather than a penguin [pp. 6–7]."

If it is indeed true that when parents talk to children they select highly prototypical category members as first (and probably most frequent) referents for a given word, and if children use parental speech as a guide in selecting referents to serve as prototypes for their own incipient semantic categories, as the data discussed in the preceding suggest, then the core examples of children's semantic categories would tend to be the same as those of adult categories virtually from the start. In the case of categories whose prototypes are favored on grounds of universal cognitive–perceptual salience, the adult input would simply tend to affirm and reinforce children's inherent language-independent categorizational predispositions. But in the case of categories lacking biologically given prototypes, which no doubt constitute the majority of those to be learned, the road to adultlike knowledge would be considerably shortened if the child were attentive to adult linguistic input and willing to accept as his own prototypes the category members that adults label first and most frequently for him, rather than simply matching adult words to self-generated and presumably often rather idiosyncratic concepts.

The Role of Nonlinguistic Categorizational Biases in Human Symbolic Activity

According to the hypothesis that the initial stage of language acquisition involves a mapping of language forms onto concepts generated independently of language, the role of children's categorizational predispositions would be to provide the concepts—or prototypes for the concepts—that the child subsequently learns to encode linguistically. However, if early language acquisition involves an interaction rather than a one-way mapping between cognition and language, as I have argued, then we can expect categorizational predilections to manifest themselves in additional ways: as characteristic biases in the way children learning the same and different languages try to make sense of words whose meanings they don't yet know (see also Clark, 1975) and in the way they assimilate novel referents to the prototypical category instances presented to them through language. Children's tendencies to attend to certain sorts of resemblances and not others among objects and events might be expected, on grounds that they are exceedingly basic, to show up in areas of human symbolic activity other than language acquisition. There is preliminary evidence that this is so.

Most work on nonlinguistic categorizational biases among children has been limited to the domain of object classification. A number of studies indicate that young children regardless of language tend to extend words for objects to novel referents most frequently on the basis of shared *perceptual characteristics,* especially of shape (Anglin, 1977; Bowerman, 1976, 1978; Clark, 1973). Clark (1977) suggests that children's reliance on visual perceptual similarities in extending words arises from universal nonlinguistic categorization processes that manifest themselves not only in children but also in the classifier systems of many natural languages. In both classifiers and children, "objects are categorized primarily on the basis of shape, and the same properties of shape appear to be relevant in acquisition and in classifier systems. Roundness and length . . . appear to be very salient [1977; p. 263 in 1979 reprint]." Similarity of overall contour is also an important basis upon which metaphors and other symbols are selected by both adults and children.

Little evidence is yet available on children's ways of recognizing similarities between actions or spatial relationships, as opposed to objects. But data from my two subjects suggest that universal cognitive predispositions may also operate in these domains to guide children's hypotheses about what words mean. It is intriguing to note that many of the ways in which Christy and Eva overextended nonobject words reflect classifications that, although "incorrect" in the English modeled to them, are found in other languages, in dialects or special uses of English, or in possible metaphorical extensions of English words. For example, one does not normally *open* or *close* the television, radio, or water faucet in standard English, but one can *shut* them off; and one routinely *opens* and *closes* the water in Spanish and the television or radio in Finnish. Similarly, although a foot is normally required for the application of English *kick* to be appropriate, one speaks metaphorically of the *kick* of a gun against a shoulder—a usage only trivially different from Eva's application of *kick* to situations in which she bumped her stomach or chest up against an object.

Even when word usage superficially seems whimsical or wildly unreasonable, a closer look often reveals a hidden logic. For example, Christy's extension of *hi* from situations involving things on the hand (as had been modeled to her) to those involving things on the feet reflects an underlying equation of hands and feet. The same equation was demonstrated about a month later when she requested help in getting a tiny plastic doll's leg off with "awant open hand." A parallel equation of arms and legs was also shown in her frequent reference to pant legs as *sleeves,* in Eva's extension of *kick* to the throwing of a ball, and in Eva's one-time reference to her wrists as *ankles.* While these equations are not directly encoded in the English lexicon with which the children were familiar, they are routine in other languages (e.g., many languages use the same term for both fingers and toes; see Anderson, 1978:353–4).

A related example is Christy's extension of *night night* to normally vertical objects now horizontal. This reflects a sensitivity to spatial orientation that plays a relatively minor role in English (e.g, *stand* versus *lie* [*down*]), but that is of central importance in certain American Indian languages, in which the *position* (standing, sitting, or lying) of both animate and inanimate objects is obligatorily encoded in almost every sentence (Watkins, 1976).

These examples suggest that children's hypotheses about what might be relevant to the meanings of the words they are learning are not randomly generated, but are guided by universally shared categorizational propensities. The role of linguistic input in the very early stages of language development may thus not be primarily to instruct the child that she should become aware of certain similarities among stimuli, as in traditional language-precedes-cognition accounts (although this may become important later in development). Rather, the input may at first serve the more limited function of activating a search for the relevant classificational principle(s) from among a somewhat constrained set of candidates. When the child hits upon a certain principle to guide her extension of a word to novel referents, the correctness of her hypothesis will be to a large extent dependent on the language she is learning. A usage that is acceptable literally in one language may be either acceptable only by metaphorical extension in another or simply incorrect. Even when it is incorrect, however, the usage may reflect a classifying principle that is important in some other area of the lexicon or morphology of the child's language or other languages, or in a symbolic domain other than language. Ultimately, an important role of linguistic input must be to inform the child of how the classificational principles she favors are formally recognized in the culture in which she finds herself.

References

Anderson, Elaine S.
1978 Lexical universals and body-part terminology. In *Universals of human language* (vol. 3): *Word Structure*, edited by J. H. Greenberg. California: Stanford Univ. Press. Pp. 335–368.

Anglin, Jeremy
   1977   *Word, object, and conceptual development.* New York: Norton.
Bates, Elizabeth, Laura Benigni, Inge Bretherton, Luigia Camaioni, and Virginia Volterra
   1977   From gesture to the first word: On cognitive and social prerequisites. In *Interaction, conversation, and the development of language,* edited by M. Lewis & L. Rosenblum. New York: Wiley, Pp. 247–307.
Berlin, Brent, and Paul Kay
   1969   *Basic color terms.* Berkeley: Univ. of California Press.
Bloom, Lois
   1970   *Language development: Form and function in emerging grammars.* Cambridge, Massachusetts: MIT Press.
   1973   *One word at a time: The use of single-word utterances before syntax.* The Hague: Mouton.
Bowerman, Melissa
   1973   *Early syntactic development: A cross-linguistic study with special reference to Finnish.* London and New York: Cambridge Univ. Press.
   1976   Semantic factors in the acquisition of rules for word use and sentence construction. In *Normal and deficient child language,* edited by D. Morehead & A. Morehead. Baltimore, Maryland: University Park Press. Pp. 99–179.
   1978   The acquisition of word meaning: An investigation into some current conflicts. In *Development of communication,* edited by N. Waterson and C. Snow. New York: Wiley. Pp. 263–287.
Brown, Roger
   1958   *Words and things.* New York: The Free Press.
   1973   *A first language: The early stages.* Cambridge, Massachusetts: Harvard Univ. Press.
   1977   Word from the language acquisition front. Paper presented before the Eastern Psychological Association Meetings.
Bruner, Jerome, Patricia Greenfield, and Rose Olver
   1966   *Studies in cognitive growth.* New York: Wiley.
Clark, Eve V.
   1973   What's in a word? On the child's acquisition of semantics in his first language. In *Cognitive development and the acquisition of language,* edited by T. E. Moore. New York: Academic Press. Pp. 65–110.
   1975   Knowledge, context, and strategy in the acquisition of meaning. In *Georgetown University Round Table on Languages and Linguistics,* edited by D. P. Dato. Washington, D.C.: Georgetown Univ. Press. Pp. 77–98.
   1977   Universal categories: On the semantics of classifiers and children's early word meanings. In *Linguistic studies offered to Joseph Greenberg: On the occasion of his sixtieth birthday,* edited by A. Juilland. Saratoga, California: Anma Libri. Pp. 449–462. Reprinted in Eve V. Clark, *The ontogenesis of meaning.* Wiesbaden: Athenaion, 1979. Pp. 253–267.
Fillmore, Charles
   1975   An alternative to checklist theories of meaning. In *Proceedings of the First Annual Meeting of the Berkeley Linguistics Society,* edited by C. Cogen *et al.* Pp. 123–131.
Labov, William, and Teresa Labov
   1974   The grammar of *cat* and *mama.* Paper presented at the 49th Annual Meeting of the Linguistic Society of America, New York.
Lenneberg, Eric
   1967   *The biological foundations of language.* New York: Wiley.
Nelson, Katherine
   1974   Concept, word, and sentence: Interrelations in acquisition and development. *Psychological Review* **81,** 267–285.

Nelson, Katherine, Leslie Rescorla, and Janice Gruendel
  1978   Early lexicons: What do they mean? *Child Development* **49**, 960–968.
Piaget, Jean
  1962   *Play, dreams, and imitation in childhood.* New York: Norton.
Piaget, Jean, and Bärbel Inhelder
  1959   *La genèse des structures logiques élémentaires: classifications and sériations.* Neuchâtel: Delchaux et Neistlé.
Rosch, Eleanor
  1973   On the internal structure of perceptual and semantic categories. In *Cognitive development and the acquisition of language,* edited by T. E. Moore. New York: Academic Press. Pp. 111–144.
  1975   Universals and cultural specifics in human categorization. In *Cross-cultural perspectives on learning,* edited by R. Brislin, S. Bochner, and W. Lonner. New York: Halsted Press. Pp. 177–206.
Rosch, Eleanor, and Carolyn B. Mervis
  1975   Family resemblances: Studies in the internal structure of categories. *Cognitive Psychology* **7**, 573–605.
Rosch, Eleanor, Carolyn B. Mervis, Wayne D. Gray, David M. Johnson, and Penny Boyes-Braem
  1976   Basic objects in natural categories. *Cognitive Psychology,* **8**, 382–439.
Slobin, Dan I.
  1973   Cognitive prerequisites for the development of grammar. In *Studies of child language development,* edited by C. Ferguson and D. Slobin. New York: Holt. Pp. 175–208.
  1975   The more it changes . . . : On understanding language by watching it move through time. *Papers and Reports on Child Language Development.* (Stanford University), **10**, 1–30.
Smith, Edward E., Edward J. Shoben, and Lance J. Rips
  1974   Structure and process in semantic memory: A featural model for semantic decisions. *Psychological Review* **81**, 214–241.
Vygotsky, Lev
  1962   *Thought and language* (originally published in 1934). Cambridge, Massachusetts: MIT Press.
Watkins, Laurel
  1976   Shape versus position: Classificatory verbs in North America. Paper presented at the Linguistic Society of America Annual Meeting, Philadelphia.
Werner, Heinz
  1948   *Comparative psychology of mental development.* New York: Science Editions, Inc.

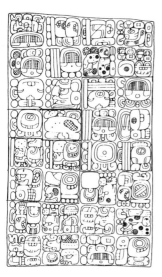

19

Some Outstanding Problems in the Analysis of Events[1]

EDWIN ARDENER

Recent theoretical developments in social anthropology have moved so fast that it will perhaps at least be helpful to clarify or develop some of my own usages, scattered in various places. I regard most of them as mere stepping stones to understanding. I shall inevitably be touching on the place of the linguistic in the social, but the time has come when social anthropology must reject some criticisms couched merely in terms of the data of other subject matters. I have exercised almost total self-restraint in citing parallels from other disciplines or from other anthropological writers whose views I have considered to have had priority, or to have matched mine in some respects. Nowadays, so many authorities recant or revise their views (with an admirable provisionality), that instead of referring to them, I shall present my argument from anthropological scratch, and relatively unadorned. I have cited numerous references elsewhere. On this occasion, I shall begin from the point reached in the "The New Anthropology and Its Critics" (Ardener, 1971c), and take some of the implications of poststructural theory for our view of the social as a manifold of both *thought* and *behavior*. In this chapter I try to lighten the heavy load that specific terms lay across analysis.

Events as Output

The image of a stream of events that the social anthropologist's initial task was to meter was never far from the minds of early fieldworkers. The jour-

[1] This material was first published in E. Schwimner (Ed.), *Yearbook of Symbolic Anthropology I*. London: Hurst (McGill–Queen's University Press: Montreal), 1978.

ISBN 0-12-262680-x

nalist's idea of a "newspaper of record," the old historian's conception of a "chronicle" or "annals," and the whole modern development of methods of *documentation* suffice to show that the image of the notionally complete registration of events has a respectable genealogy—respectable enough for its implications to have the invisibility of either the self-evident or the unexamined. Everybody now knows and acknowledges that the "events" that are registered are inseparably related to the mode of registration. Yet, as commonsense beings, we are used to identifying an event determined by one mode with an event determined by another, as by sight and by sound; or (at another level) by radio, press, and television, or by document and by an oral communication; or (at another level still) by a theory of economics and a theory of psychology. Still, we come at once to an intractability about events; they have to be recognized, detected, or picked up by modes of registration. We must know as much as possible about these modes.

Let us suppose that the stream of events is there, "as advertised." A simple output model would suffice. The "events" pass the social anthropologist as on a conveyor belt. He describes them according to selected criteria. He defines the events as if they were carburetors. From records of stretches of output he sets out relations, redefinitions, and the like. On a real conveyor belt a sequence from "carburetors" to "dynamos" is a more significant one than that from one carburetor to another. In our output of events, however, we pass figuratively from carburetor to dynamo without guidance. The first dynamos are described as aberrant carburetors, or a new term is invented to subsume both types. Given enough "output," classifications may fit more and more closely to the new units. But it will be seen at once that the view of our subject matter as an output of events leaves us gravely handicapped because of the retrospective nature of our interpretations and our inability to return to check our original specifications, save through our record of them. Nevertheless, even this simple picture enables us to grasp the nature of one use of *significant* as applied to events.

If the output model is now strengthened by the addition of a programmatic component, we see that a discontinuity as between carburetors and dynamos would be discoverable in the program (see Ardener, 1971c:452). On a conveyor belt it is a laborious waste of time to observe the output in order to determine the nature of the units in it, for the program is available—not only laying down the significant units: carburetors or dynamos, but specifying, perhaps, that 10 carburetors will be followed by 50 dynamos. Even the superior combination, "output and program" is only of a crude and elementary assistance to us—a temporary crutch—for two reasons:

First, our definition of units in the output—the "events"—depends upon the modes of registration available to us. And second, the program for the stream of events does not "exist" in a separate box or office from the output—at least not as far as we are concerned.

This must be the end of that image, therefore. Nevertheless, it throws light on some dilemmas. If you wish to continue to separate the anthropologist observer from the object of his study as heretofore, you must visualize that the program is located in the output, and generated simultaneously with it. Or if you like, each event is differently "marked" for programmatic content—some are nearly all "output"; others are nearly all "program"; others in between. Even the anthropologist as observer is thus required to see himself as a being with a mode of registration somewhat more sophisticated than that of a camera. As the *programmatic* content is not crudely observable, we shall need a definition of *event* that includes the supposedly unobservable. Since the so-called observer can himself only register his apprehensions of those events through his own mesh of social and psychological categories, we see that a satisfactory number of current anthropological concerns are before us. Before we leave the conveyor belt, therefore, it is worth noting that social anthropologists even in their most empiricist garb have rarely assumed they were only checking off output. Even when counting stocks of yams they were also charting myths. Thus the "observed" events always included (for example) linguistic events, even when these events were inadequately delineated.

Structures

The structures that social anthropologists have hypothesized out of the foregoing are: (*a*) structures homologous with those of the program; (*b*) structures homologous with those of the output; and (for the observer) (*c*) the modes of registration he has: systems of interpretation and technical and cultural categories of his own, aware and unaware.

Only (*a*) and (*b*) will occupy us for the moment. These I have termed elsewhere *paradigmatic* and *syntagmatic*. It is however unfortunate that the term *paradigm* has achieved common conversational currency as often little more than a vogue synonym of *pattern*, sometimes only of *tabulation*. It is already far gone on the road taken already by *model* and *syndrome*. In addition, those of us who have used the *paradigmatic–syntagmatic* terminology have had to cope with the different levels at which this relation can be applied. The relation is an abstract one of great power and importance. Yet it has become data-laden in different ways through its applications, quite legitimate in themselves, to the material of varied disciplines. For that reason, new terms will be used later.

I want here to demonstrate that social anthropologists do not need to turn to any material but their own to express this abstract relation. We shall consider anthropological usages. In so doing we shall discover that we are dealing with matters that are not parasitical on the terminology of other disciplines. We are concerned with certain structural universals that cannot help appearing in all fields concerned with human beings. It is with reluctance then, that I here cut the painter linking our terms with those of other disciplines for the moment. Let no one turn to a dictionary, or to Saussure or Jakobson or Roland Barthes or Kuhn or Lévi-Strauss to elucidate or to "correct" the following remarks. Erase all images of *paradigms* from the mind.

Ethnography

The necessity for a distinction between "levels" in structural analysis has been a commonplace. In considering the case of the Bakweri *nyongo* phenomenon, a distinction emerged in this way. Certain kinds of zombie manifestations were correlated with low economic performance of the mass of the population. Yet that which correlated on each occasion was not the symbolic content of the behavior. This was separately "assembled" at the different periods of manifestation, or so I hypothesized, through new symbols, or newly arranged old symbols. Thus, at one period, zombie manifestations were caused by persons who had built corrugated iron houses. They were thought to kill their younger relatives and to use them as zombie labor. At another period, the zombie phenomena were thought to be caused by "Frenchmen." The content was not continuous over time, but something else was: a repetitive, distinctive, structuring tendency that I called then the *template* (Ardener, 1970:155).

On another occasion, the Bakweri (who lived on a long-quiescent volcano) blamed a serious eruption upon Posts and Telegraphs engineers who had scraped the mountain's back to build a rough, rock-strewn road to a VHF station. A new rite of exorcism and appeasement was devised by elders for performance on the road, which upon Bakweri representation was barred to vehicles for the time being (Ardener, 1959). The content of the new rite was congruent (we see by hindsight) with other rites, but the new one did not derive from any other. It could not simply be generated from all previously extant rites. Merely to verbalize this distinction requires us to propose at least two structuring processes: one that shapes, and a second that builds. In this case, a "well-formed rite" for a Bakweri is recognized in terms quite different from one devised by Sicilians for an eruption on Mt. Etna. The Bakweri would be able to produce a rite, even in the absence of traditional props, and with the use of foreign or modern symbolic elements, that was still "well-formed." The building process may be likened to the *bricolage* of Lévi-Strauss.

To take a further example: The Bakweri mermaid (mammy-water) or *liengu* rites for women are built up from elements common to the peoples of the whole Bight of Biafra. The template in this case was peculiar to the Bakweri, with elements derived from the ambiguity in self-classification between men and women as expressed through a characteristic contradiction in the Bakweri view of the "wild" (Ardener, 1975).

Again, certain peoples like the Ibo show a remarkable lability in their symbolic forms. "New customs," "modifications," and "modernizations" follow each other rapidly. It seemed here that the *bricolage* facility was exaggerated, "overdetermined." The new shapes were "Ibo" despite their frequent transformations of content. The "novelties" were not relevant to a definition of what was Ibo. This feature seems to be characteristic of highly adaptive, "strong" but "modernizing" cultures, of which the Japanese may br a supreme example.

In all of these cases the need for a distinction between two kinds of structures is strengthened by a practical difference in the methods available for their analysis. The former are in one terminology *template structures* and the latter *structures of realizations*. The latter present no problems. All observational and recording devices provide data. In addition, linguistic and textual analyses of many kinds are possible and in order. That point must be stressed, since some "structuralists" are concerned with these structures in their own data quite as often as most "functionalists," although with characteristic differences. The s-structures then, as we may now call the structures of realization, appear in the normal flux of experience. They are studiable in the "stream of events" itself.

The p-structures, as we may now call the template structures, are a different class, set up as unknowns, posited before identified. As far as social anthropology is concerned, they are its quarks or hadrons. But we can say something about them. We apprehend (or construct) them out of the same world as the s-structure, but we can document them only by their reflections, or their *reflexes*.

S-Structures

In studying witchcraft (for example), it is a commonplace to examine the "personnel" involved. There may perhaps be an analysis of the sex, age, and socioeconomic status of the accused. It is no surprise that a category labeled *marginality* or *deviance* may frequently seem appropriate to cover the human constellations revealed. I. M. Lewis (1971) has expressed essentially the synchronic form of such an approach, K. V. Thomas (1971) the diachronic. Explanations of phenomena in terms of the observable characteristics of the participants, their demography, their relative positions in "social systems," and the like are all explanations based upon s-structures. In the Bakweri case of the zombie witchcraft, it would be possible to plot s-structures of these kinds.

The problem presented by s-structures lies in their contingent quality.

That may appear strange since such structures (or more precisely terms, whose only embodiment lies in such structures) form the common basis for conventional sociological analysis, and the "social structure" itself is simply its most inclusive example. The problem becomes acute where s-structures are considered over time. If the phenomenon that an s-structure is to explain "disappears," as for example, witchcraft in late eighteenth-century England, we may be forced to propose that the s-structure itself has no longer any validity: The formerly marginal categories no longer exist, let us say, or at least, that this kind of marginality is no longer "significant." It is obvious that we are soon in difficulties. Few students of witchcraft can nowadays bring themselves to argue that the s-structures *are* witchcraft, in some way. They nowadays admit that they are handed the term *witchcraft* "in advance" as part of a system of ideas—even as a word among words. The question of *whose* system of ideas, a world in whose language, is quite commonly discussed, but more, perhaps, by social anthropologists than by historians.

A *P*-Structure

It must follow from the argument so far that p-structures cannot appear to the analyst by the methods that will generate s-structures. It is quite wrong to be asked to be "shown" a p-structure; p-structures are unknowns, almost by definition. On the other hand, it has been stated that such structures, if they have any existence, must be revealed in the stream of events. If so, linguistic problems loom very large in their consideration. The normal terminological and onomastic process ascribes labels to s-structures with ease, for most of our categories in social studies are of s-type. We can sense what a p-structure should have in it, but the terms available to us are either overspecific or underspecific, the result of using an educated discourse brought up on s-structures.

For example, one p-structure that we require for the specification of a witchcraft system has in it some component for relating persons to misfortune through other persons. In the Bakweri zombie–witchcraft case, we can begin to shadow the elements of the p-structure with preliminary hints like this:

Individual self-betterment ↔ public misfortune

You will recall that when boom agricultural conditions occurred, the threshold of "activation" of the p-structure rose: no zombie manifestations. In slumps, the threshold fell: zombie manifestations appeared. Bakweri talked of *inona* ('envy') as being generated by *nyanga* ('pride,' 'ambitious achievement'). Self-betterment resulted from the killing of fellow Bakweri (particularly one's own children) and using the dead bodies to work as zombies. All these elements present a complicated problem for description by the anthropologist, since what is describable is realized in *s*-structures. String these emotive words together

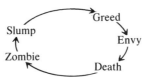

We have an impression of the *p*-structure when activated: the hollow shape of its shadow in language. Nevertheless, this one is rooted in concepts of "property," and in economic behavior, as well as in "affective," even adrenal, matters. For the moment we may just note that this structure may be difficult to express but may be easier to "locate." I fear that even this example will have overconcretized the anthropological view of such a structure. Critics should remember then that for the moment we are concerned entirely with generating such structures from purely anthropological data.

The Calibration of *P*-Structures and *S*-Structures

P-structures and *s*-structures cause difficulties because their calibrations do not directly match. To make them fit we must propose something between them—a black box, as it were, in which all calibration problems are solved. I will call it a *mode of specification*.

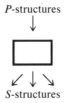

Mode of Specification

The black box specifies the particular realization of the elements of the *p*-structures. The mode of specification for the Bakweri zombie witchcraft included a very practical one: 'owners of metal-roofed houses are zombie masters.' Another was: 'all sudden deaths, especially of young persons are caused by zombie masters.' We can list a whole string. When we talk of *witchcraft* as having elements of universality, it is easy to see that we are talking of certain similarities essentially between *p*-structures. Despite the peculiarities of the observable aspects of Bakweri zombie manifestations compared with English witchcraft, the difference between the *p*-structures is much less great. We can hypothesize (the language shadow of) a *p*-

structure thus: misfortune ↔ personal cause. We require a mode of specification of the kinds of events that qualify as misfortune and where to find the personal causes. Very similar p-structures may have very different modes of specification, thus generating very different s-structures. Statements like "deprived, marginal persons" belong now in the mode of specification, through which the s-structures are generated.

When we look at this phenomenon that we have chosen to call *witchcraft,* we see at once that changes may occur in the p-structures, in the mode of specification, and in the s-structures. If the p-structure changes to: misfortune ↔ *im*personal cause, the mode of specification and the generated s-structures automatically change. Witchcraft vanishes. If the mode of specification changes, but the p-structures do not, we see different types of grounds for witchcraft emerging, or changes in the kinds of person accused. Again the s-structures inevitably change.

Why should not the s-structures change independently? This would occur (let us say) when there are no actual events that fit the specifications—no people of the sort heretofore specifiable as witches.

The introduction of the black box, the mode of specification, is merely another mechanical crutch, and we shall eventually dispense with it. It has been necessary because of the confused way in which we apprehend s-structures. The contingencies or accidents of reality set up chains of events. The observing social anthropologist may set up s-structures that are not "imperative," that is, not generated by the society concerned. As if the contingencies of reality had produced, for example, a set of temporary correlations in the Bakweri case between ownership of metal-roofed houses and blood-group O. Some such correlations might be well-founded, in the sense that they might be derived from the sorting-out effect of the mode of specification. But even such well-founded structures may be rendered inoperative by a change in the mode of specification. Consequently, certain s-structures of "observers" may seem to have "explanatory" value, for a time, and then to cease to do so. It was precisely the interest of this question that led us to hypothesize p-structures in the first place, in order to help the conceptualization of what is essential, continuous, and "imperative" in the structuring of society, and to separate it from the merely contingent and from the realization processes themselves.

The resolution of simultaneities into linear chains is a mode of exposition with many practical advantages. It is important, however, to grasp that the $p \rightarrow \square \rightarrow s$ levels are present together in our experience. Questions that leap to the lips like, "Is not the black box (the mode of specification) part of the p-structure?" should, strictly speaking, be immediately stifled. The black box does not exist: It merely shows the relationship diagrammatically.

We have already gained something in clarity by this stretching out of a simultaneity. It is helpful, for example, to see in passing that the term *paradigm* is used by various authors for quite disparate parts of the sequence.

The key to their differences lies in the placing of the black box. For some scholars, s-structures plus their modes of specification are commonly called the *paradigms* (they fail to register p-structures at all). Many structuralists, on the other hand, collapse p-structures and modes of specification together as paradigms. It is an irony that the processes in the black box, which was only a temporary hypothesis, should loom so disproportionately large in analysis. It is as if the zone of calibration between p-structures and s-structures was disproportionately magnified, was specially enlarged because of its critical importance.

A Simultaneity

It is a strain upon our language to express the nature of a simultaneity in practical anthropology, such that the p-structural, the specificatory, and the s-structural elements can be all shown to be present at a stroboscopic instant. Examine this sequence:

A crowd howl at an old man hiding under a bed. Dismantled sheets of rusty corrugated iron lie in the vicinity.

That is already part of a record masquerading as a real instant. Suppose it to represent an instant in the wave of detections of zombie-masters. Everything in that scene can be set up into s-structures by behaviorist–empiricist methods: Therein lies the power of the latter. (Count the crowd; find the age of the man and the structure of the bed; locate iron; analyze rust; measure the site; record the speech, etc.) Yet the participants "know" the significance "at a glance." Only the iron sheets can be assigned to the mode of specification, by which the old man was also specified. Thus, they are also a link with the p-structure. The "corrugated iron" then in the tiny, inadequate stretch of time is mysteriously lit up. It is a "marked" element. It is simultaneously (for that snapshot instant) part of the evidence for the p-structure, a part of the mode of specification, and an element marking the s-structure so specified—the group of builders of metal-roofed houses, the zombie-masters.

We seem to be gaining some fleeting reflected insight into *symbol, association, metaphor, metonymy,* and the rest. Once more we have only a language-shadow, this time of the articulation of p- and s-structures.

Dead Stretches

Most of our analyses are done upon dead stretches of experience, upon data as recorded. The problem that was alluded to at the beginning of this chapter, of the intervention of the recorder into the process, now emerges more clearly. We do not possess those successive instants, only our records of some of them, and from instant to instant we select aspects only. These are our "events." With the naive and unreflectingly ethnocentric observer, the General G. Custer or H. M. Stanley, events he records or registers are totally structured by specifications from the *p*-structure of his own society (Ardener, 1974). There can in such a case be no records of the other society that would yield material for the reconstruction of any *p*-structures save his own.

The step from experiencing society to analyzing a record of the experience is thus a crucial one. Unlike the historian the social anthropologist does both the living and the recording. The ethnography is a kind of slaughter of the experience and a dissecting of the corpse. That increasing modern preoccupation with attempts to understand the generative elements of a living society, which is now becoming apparent, requires some appreciation of the exact point at which the opportunity for such an understanding both exists and vanishes—the exact moment of the slaughter, as it were. That moment was exactly when we wrote: "A crowd howl at an old man hiding under a bed, etc." The opportunity existed of a record that would separate the programmatic from the accidental, read the marking on the signs, determine the signs, and note the dispositions they reveal for particular subsequent events to occur. The opportunity vanished because the language for that record has been beyond our normal powers. The language of the record quoted is merely blocked together (*bricolé*, it might said) out of the categories of English. The resulting petrification of the Bakweri experience that is given us has a different kind of weight in a normal English experience. For example, those sheets of corrugated iron strike a banal note—surely no drama could rest on them? A tinge of the ridiculous creeps in.

The good ethnographic observer must therefore use categories and labels in an ambiguous manner, or use some that have a degree of ambiguity already in his own language, and hope that by applying enough of them, he will enable the reader to create from their elements new combinations that will be closer to the "native experience" being recorded. I call this the method of language-shadows.

The Mode of Registration

The condensation of concepts to illustrate the instant at which the anthropologist apprehends his "event," has enabled us to answer questions that were raised in dispensing with the "conveyor belt" or output model. We left over from the discussion of structures the problem of the "structures of the observer": the modes of registration at which we began. We now see that the reference to the definition of events according to the mode of registration of the observer is to set up another black box. Indeed, it is not a new black box but a different aspect of our old friend the mode of specification of a $p \rightarrow s$ sequence. The registration of the simultaneity that has just been discussed is the matching of the s-structures of the observer to the s-structures of the event. If the p-structures of the observer come from the same set as the p-structures that generate the event—then the s-structures of the observer may be "imperative," "will match." If not, the s-structures will be contingent, *not* imperative. Once more that enlarged portion of the relationship, the purported "black box" area, is a curious complication. The highly self-conscious observer figure is a manipulator of some p-structures and their modes of specification into s-structures, but he may still fail to match those of the participants.

We may generalize the relationship thus:

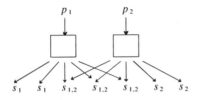

Where p_2 is a p-structure of the social anthropologist (or of his society or culture), p_1 is a p-structure of the other society; s_1 are the s-structures of events specified by p_1; s_2 are the s-structures of events specified by p_2; $s_{1,2}$ are s-structures of the observer that are "imperative"; s_2 are s-structures of p_2 that are not "imperative," are contingent, and are not generated by p_1.

I have had to put it in this lengthy way in order to show that the third element in understanding the event, the mode of registration of the event by the observer, is analyzed in the same way as the event itself. We have also been brought to consider that the p-structures of thinking individuals and those of the social continua in which they live will require some differentiation. (See the following "World Structures" section.)

So far we have progressed from the data and necessities of social anthropology itself, to the step of setting up p-structures and s-structures. We have suggested that such structures have homologies in the reality with which anthropologists work. An analytical device that the anthropologist needs to make sense of social events turns out to be a usable image of the way social events are generated. Having said that, we may like to dispense with p-structures and s-structures and tell it as it is. Dispense with the terms though we may, "telling it as it is" requires more than ordinary skills. Most anthropologists end up by still telling it in terms of such structures, disguised as technical terms, ad hoc jargon, or expressive language. That is why I must now leave these mechanical formulations, and repeat (to the regret of many) that p-structures and s-structures, embedded although they are in the particular data of social anthropology, are related as the *paradigmatic* is to the *syntagmatic,* and the properties of this relation are all available to help us from the unwieldy language of structure. The path we have followed, however, was necessary to show us that these terms, as used in linguistics, are expressed in a different reality. I want to explore some of these differences. In order to do so I must allude to some elementary linguistic matters, although many social anthropologists may wish to turn straight on to the section headed "Why Linguistics is Different."

Paradigmatic and Syntagmatic Again

We know that, in language, at each stage of a sentence the morphemes fall into place unbidden, as it were, into sequences, the structures of which are demonstrable, by examination, over the length of the sentence. Yet, simultaneously, paradigmatic relations determine the kinds of morphemes that must be selected. Where are the paradigmatic relations? No one asks that question in linguistics, any more than one asks "Where is the ten-times-table?" Yet such questions are asked in social anthropology, as if our audiences cannot hold abstractions in their heads. Still, some linguists might try the reply that they are in a paradigmatic rulebook, a kind of Liddell and Scott, just as words are conceived of as being in a lexicon, and the syntagmata are in a book of syntax. We might say, then, that in social anthropology the *p*-structures exist in the appropriate section of an ethnography.

There is no doubt that the ordinary grammarian is aided in his mental imagery by the external representations of his abstractions in real volumes, indexes, and dictionaries. To such an extent does this occur that the syntagmatic chain of utterance is commonly visualized as already in its "completed" state, as the discipline's version of "a dead stretch": that is, as a recorded sentence, or the like. The syntagmata are seen as wholes, as if taken in at a glance on the page. But in natural speech, syntagmata are generated "live," and the same questions that social anthropologists ask can in fact be asked in the live situation. We could answer then that the paradigmatic specifications are generated in the same acoustic chain as the syntagmatic. The receiving brains sort it all out almost without noticing.

But the social anthropologist asks his question because no one as far as he knows is "uttering" society, and he is not at all sure if there is anyone "receiving" it. It all gets very complicated when we note that the "utterance" of events is in three dimensions over time; and that among the behavior uttered is linguistic utterance—nesting like a small detailed replica of the whole, and yet purporting to render acoustically an image of some of the whole. It is not surprising that to some it seems easiest to see it all as an excrescence of language in the first place. Then the syntagmatic and paradigmatic axes would be coordinates inevitably based on language, giving us an artificial horizon and vertical for stabilizing our discourse at all levels.

The clear expression of this relationship outside natural language in quite simple mathematics makes it of greater interest than that (Ardener, 1971c:466).

Diachronic and Synchronic

There is an occasional anthropological misconception that the paradigmatic is diachronic, and the syntagmatic is synchronic; some think the exact opposite. Both are wrong, of course. The linguistic case will be genuinely helpful here. An utterance may be analyzed (*a*) according to the syntactical arrangements between its parts—syntagmatically; (*b*) according to the kinds of parts that are required (a choice of *I, you, we,* etc. among pronouns, for example)—paradigmatically; (*c*) diachronically—by which the utterance in all its parts is traced historically over time; and (*d*) synchronically—by which analysis is concerned only with the utterance as a system of parts at any one time.

It will be seen that the terms *diachronic* and *synchronic,* which to some seem simpler to grasp than *paradigmatic* and *syntagmatic,* are really much more confusing. It has been pointed out elsewhere that both *diachronic* and *synchronic* as terms applied to systems are *static* in nature. This is a result of looking at our data as dead stretches. Set the system moving (even in very slow motion) in natural time: Utterances are generated lineally, specified paradigmatically, unrolling well-formed syntagmata. The synchronic is a freezing of this process. The diachronic is an examination of successive freezings of the process (Ardener, 1971b). Once more the tremendous weight of the conceptualization of language in terms of kinds of records lies heavy over even Saussurean linguistics. That is why we cannot always take the usually welcome advice of linguists in examining these matters. Fictions convenient on the scale of language become cumbersome and misleading at the scale of social events.

In natural time both the paradigmatic and the syntagmatic change continuously. Consider the following sequences over three centuries (the change from an impersonal construction in the use of *like* in English illustrates all four terms: synchronic, diachronic, syntagmatic, paradigmatic).

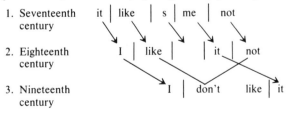

1. Seventeenth century   it | like | s | me | not

2. Eighteenth century   I | like | | it | not

3. Nineteenth century   I | don't | like | it

1,2 and 3 are each a sequence from a *synchronic* state of English (dates are only illustrative). Together they form a *diachronic* sequence. Each sentence is analyzed from left to right *syntagmatically*. Each may be divided into *paradigmatically* selected units. The arrows show the changes in paradigmatic selection over time. The sentences are staggered to the right to suggest the element of syntagmatic change over time. Once the system is visualized in continuous operation (Saussure's [1964] *panchronic* was groping towards this [Ardener, 1971a:xli]), it begins to cry out for devices like rewrite rules and transformational analysis. This is still a "dead stretch" nevertheless. In order to visualize the process in natural time we must put in all the speaking individuals, and all the versions of the utterance. Modern linguistics moves rapidly off on its own here.

Such a moving diagram for the three-dimensional grammar of even a single *ritual* over time would be a "model" worth having indeed. Some research is already in hand on this. For the living grammar of the whole set of systems that is loosely labeled a *society,* we have quite a task before us. It is because the homologies between language and society are so many and so varied that it is necessary to point out that the social expressions of the common principles involved are working through much more intractable material than the linguistic.

Why Linguistics Is Different

The social homologues of utterances churn themselves out very burdensomely compared with speech. Were language to be like that, the significant units would be occurring at generally long and always very irregular intervals, among contingent events, and on a time scale of the same order as the normal rate of deterioration of the system. As if the telephone wires had time to corrode away, or the vocal cords to mortify, before the speaker got it all out. The "system" is one of permanent emergency routing. That is why there cannot be the cosy meshing of paradigmatic with syntagmatic that occurs in speech. Circumstances so change between successive "utterances" that the actual mode of expression may have radically changed in the meantime. A kind of memory of what the system is about is stored in ad hoc ways. These are the p-structures, that are so difficult to locate. Since there is no homologue of the speaker, however, the p-structures must have a certain unconscious, blind, or automatic quality. They are not all open to awareness. They are in some direct relationship to the "infrastructure." It is no surprise, then, that we find ethologists, ecologists, biologists and psychologists converging in separate dogsledges upon this zone, where the theologian, the philosopher, and the social anthropologist already pace the ground.

The old "template" for the zombie belief of the Bakweri was a combination of infrastructural (agricultural productivity) and biopsychological elements, and theories of causality. Looked at now as a p-structure, it behaves in the appropriately immanent manner: generating an *s*-structure at one time of zombies and corrugated iron roofs, and later on of Frenchmen and deep-sea wharfs (see Ardener, 1970:155). If this were any language studied by linguists, it would require some exaggerated form of continuous restructuring, a series of repeated and unpredictable creolizations. That is why I have related it in another study to the logic of a program with continuous rewrites. We are much closer to systems as diverse as the language of infants, of the insane, or of animals. We may take a cue from this, to ask ourselves whether there is lacking a "metalinguistic" faculty in the social system, or whether if it does exist it is of only a haphazard function. The matter is a serious one because successive realizations of a *p*-structure may be so different in their *s*-forms that the supposed "actors" do not easily link the sets of events together. Once more I remind you that the successive "zombie" manifestations were apperceived as separate by those that lived through them. We are rather like high-grade aphasics of the type studied by Luria.

Storage and *Location*

These terms from warehousing have since moved into computer studies, but perhaps they are more literally appropriate when they are applied to society as a system of structures. It is beginning to appear as if what may be treated as abstractions in language have for society to be "stored" separately and "located" in the unstable series of social events. Human beings even build physical structures and rearrange the environment, and thus incorporate physical events into the system. Society is thus a "brain" trying to be a "language."

When we tried to understand *p*-structures, we found that their *location* and their evidence for existence were linked problems. The *p*-structure homologues in language (the paradigmatics) are in the last analysis "stored" no doubt somewhere in the brain—that is, outside the acoustic chain. That is one of the great steps forward we took with language. In the "social" the separation of media is rudimentary and unstable. Having asked about the "metalinguistic" faculty, which is so difficult to detect in the grunting, noise-ridden, idiot-tongue of society, we may then ask whether it is separately "stored" or "located" (I would emphasize here that the *p*-structures do not provide a "metalanguage," they are part of the "language.") A "black box" for a metalanguage of the system will require a device for monitoring the whole system, reporting on it, substituting in it, and modifying it. The only social phenomenon that is a serious candidate turns out to be real language—that is, language, properly so-called: the system of acoustic speech. If so, it shows that the social is not like real language in its detailed structure. In real language the metalinguistic faculty is expressed *in* real language, not in an independent system. We have to get used to seeing different analytical levels expressed in different media, and separations between media in ways that are momentarily surprising.

Consider the social as a surface composed of receptors operating on the slow-moving scale that I have tried to depict. Real language operates like a system of comparatively instantaneous links between receptors: Real language deteriorates more slowly than the surface. It is not surprising then that in this aspect real language is (or was) the only thing fast enough to provide a metasystem for the social. It can hardly be efficient: When we speak of the difficulty of "unpacking" nonverbal semiotics into language, we are using another terminology to express the lag in awareness that the "infrastructural" source of so much of the social "output" (leading to unconscious, automatic features) makes difficult to overcome.

The language-like continuum of society cannot be apprehended without recognizing that real language is such a great improvement on society, in some particulars, that it cannot be a perfect mirror of society. It can usefully map a lot of the social into a medium that can delineate and label structures. Thus far it stores. It is not at all bad at storing language images of s-structures. It is not good at imaging and storing p-structures. We can suggest reasons why not, but it is sufficient to note the phenomenon. To demonstrate a new p-structure through language, we have to run through metaphors, analogies, and symbols of multiple reference, until we have created a "language-shadow" of it. Those who can express the process in other than natural language—possibly mainly mathematicians—are at a great advantage, but it appears that this faculty is not widely spread in any society. Language certainly creates its own problems. Furthermore, it adds some new automaton-like processes, out of its own peculiar "wiring," even as it helps us to plot some of those due to the peculiarities of the social. The totality of action and partial awareness may be termed a *world structure* (Ardener:1974).

World Structures

A *world structure* is a manifold of the relations we have discussed; it is also a system of people. It is like a communication system in so far as it has certain properties shared by systems that have a transmitter and a receiver. It is also like a homeostatic system, in so far as the chief receiver of its communications is itself. This duality comes from the position of individuals both as elements of the system and as communicating beings themselves. There is a high degree of automatism in the world structure, and human beings, by investing their fates in it, sacrifice a great deal of their freedom of action. They cease to experience events, and instead they experience "events"—where the quotation marks express the transformation of experience through the world structure. In another place I have discussed, for example, the reduced capacity of a world structure to respond to its own demographic changes (Ardener, 1974).

In confronting the "unaware" parts of the world structure, we may recognize (with the strongest possible emphasis) that human beings as individuals are much more complicated than they are as parts of the structure. Those expensive and sophisticated intelligences may serve in their social aspect to signal relatively simple messages—many no doubt of on/off binary type (e.g., acquiescence/nonacquiescence). With certain conventions a small structural chain can be set up generating behavior in a way that is "unconsciously" constraining on each individual. Such chains are set up every day in laboratory experiments, not only with rats, but in studies of human behavior. The structure, as such, is not stored in individual nervous systems. We can, for a game, devise a bureaucracy that will work with no single individual knowing the whole structure. We can go further and say that a mature bureaucracy may work for long periods in that way. From the useful evidence of the Watergate inquiry, we note that two major "decisions"—to enter the building and to cover-up the affair–each took place in automatic sequences. Mr. Jeb Magruder said of the latter that, on the news of the Watergate arrests, the cover-up simply began. "I do not remember any discussion that there should not be a cover-up." The sleep-walking effect was very noticeable when individuals were asked to examine their consciousness of the events.

We need not jib, therefore, at accepting that human beings in a world structure will not be conscious of all of it. We may be glad just to be able to conceive that we may be in one. The Watergate case illustrates another way in which we see events as "significant" from outside. If the Nixon White House is taken as a convenient model of a world structure, the two events mentioned earlier were "significant" in the light of that world structure's subsequent collapse. To the participants, "event" followed "event," linked with syntagmatic logicality, while certain triggers set themselves unnoticed. Such "triggers" belong in the p-component. (For those who still need the "black box," they reset the mode of specification of the s-structures).

Simple predictivity in human science is revealed as a misguided goal when we consider the discontinuity of p- and s-components. A p-change may release a "trigger," leaving a disposition in the structure that does not realize itself because the precipitating conditions simply do not occur. Or, given a major social entity, over time, triggers may be released, or thresholds overridden, that are realized in the s-structures only a generation later. There seems no doubt that p-structures are labile, and may set or release triggers under the influence of infrastructural changes. We have discussed problems of "storage" and "location" and deterioration. We have hinted at the demographic problem as a modifier of the human content of the system (for details see Ardener, 1974). The major outstanding problem in the analysis of events is to spot the triggers moving—to catch the p-component in events.

The world structure occupies a space that is neither "idealist" nor "materialist." Looked at through language it is the one; looked at through "events" it is the other. I have always thought that Whorf—the fire assurance assessor who found he could not stop fires without correcting language—well understood the world structure as a sometimes dangerous generator of reality (Whorf, 1956).

What Is a World Structure Like?

At various stages in this chapter, we have set up "black boxes" to help to solve problems, and we have then dispensed with them. The whole language of structure is ultimately a process of that type, and the world structure is the biggest black box of them all. How might it work? We have suggested that it may be like a surface with particular properties. Let us compare it with a special memory surface. That surface both "registers" and "recognizes" events by fairly simple principles. The traces of different events reinforce each other only in the parts that overlap. Old traces die out if not reinforced. This creates a continuous movement across the surface. The configurations on the surface are stable or change shape, become "deeper" or "shallower," according to the degree to which they are reinforced. The newer or the rarer the event, the less readily will it be registered. Only those aspects that reinforce existing configurations will register; indeed, a deficiency of such a surface is that those configurations are thereby further strengthened.

It is unlikely on the other hand that the world structure as a surface would work with such relatively simple excitation rules as De Bono (1969) suggests for individual perception. It is both more rudimentary and more complex; for example, the surface itself has important discontinuities caused by the irregular demographic distribtuion of the human elements of the surface. On an ideal memory surface, the flow across the surface is uninterrupted save by the processes of the surface itself. Still, it is probable that any degree of mutual sensitivity between enough like organisms could set up some elements of a memory surface. Two bonding attractions would be enough: one into the physical world (say hunger) and one into like elements in the surface (say sex). A simple pair of p-structures (using our previous terms) would generate the activity of the surface. The continuity of the "social" through animal species to man may, indeed, merely exemplify this kind of proposition. Thereby, we confront once more the prospect of some automatism in our subject matter.

The rudimentary form of the surface is importantly modified by incorporating ways of scanning the surface supplementary to the operations of the surface itself. We can do this by superimposing on the surface a second surface (surface 2), which will register events on surface 1. What has been said of surface 1 applies *mutatis mutandis* to surface 2. This time it is configurations newly established on surface 1 that will not register easily. The configurations on surface 2 would tend to overdetermine the most deeply reinforced parts of the configurations on surface 1. If, furthermore, surface 1 now has the faculty of registering the configurations of surface 2 as well as physical events, we have some of the properties of a world structure. Surface 2 is like the scanning effect of language, and exemplifies some defective features in that scanning. The mutual registration of surfaces 1 and 2 creates a duality of configurations on surface 1, some registering the "environment," some the scanning process. The elaborate new surface thus registers "markers" indicating some of its own states. Some of the events that are thus registered can be said then to be "symbolic" of states of or in the surface.

To translate this back into the terms of the social anthropological subject matter, language (that is real language) provides a map of some of the main regularities of the social. I have suggested elsewhere (Ardener, 1971a:xlv) that multiple semiotic systems must have prepared the way, and must still coexist with it. Language represents a much fuller exploitation of the human capacities of the surface, but as we saw earlier, whole regions of the automatism in the surface are only inefficiently mapped through it.

We are led to the probability that even the extraordinary complexity introduced into the surface by the rapid transmission of provisional maps of its own configurations still does not utilize more than some fraction of the complexity of the individuals composing it. That may be said, even though over recent millennia the storing of language by recording devices has accelerated the process of *"linguification"* of the surface to the degree that there is now a somewhat greater resemblance between the surface and an elaborate memory surface than there can have been in the remotest past.

We have suggested that this introduces more and more complicated "automatisms." The surface registers natural events but generates a welter of "events" of its own. A state of the surface may well appear such that most events individuals contend with in that strange "real world" are mere automatisms of the surface. The failure of language to discriminate rapidly or even (as far as untechnical discourse is concerned) at all between its own processes and the processes of the surface becomes critical at this stage. In this condition, *individuals* may make the necessary discriminations, step outside the surface, as it were, but lack a common real language for their expression.

Temporary Conclusion

We have tried, in the last section, another way of visualizing how strange a world structure might look if we were not in one. Even were I to defend the attempt as a mere language-shadow, I would not claim it to be very successful. The capacious terminology of structures is more reassuring to us at the moment, and certainly more closely matches our research capacities. But we should recognize the provisional nature of even these rich theories.

The bringing of world structures to consciousness is a bigger task than social anthropology on its own can tackle. It has got the small distance that it has because of its privileged experience of a multiplicity of such structures. However, the terminology of "structure" is itself becoming exhausted. It has had a good life in social anthropology, although in the lay world its vogue is only just beginning. "Structure" does not always help us to visualize the multiple realizations that we are dealing with. We are, of course, not waiting for new terms for "structures." We are simply in a poststructuralist situation parallel to the postfunctionalist situation of the 1940s and 1950s. In the poststructuralist period the capturing of the life of events as they articulate with structures will certainly be one outstanding problem requiring a new phase of specially collected data. In this place, it is not necessary to specify the methods that could be used, but they might include the detailed study of what I have called *simultaneities*. As an alternative to the method of definition, the method of language-shadows may be used to delineate immanent structures.

We are in a *post*structuralist position, however. This means that old Durkheimian problems such as that of the *location* of structures no longer seem to require a metaphysical solution. The problem of *validation*—that is, of determining the "truth" of structural analysis, derives from the degree of "match" or "fit"—a feature I have called imperativeness. We have learned also that the human is a world on a very grand scale indeed: A world in which a consistent and relatively simple set of structuring principles are fleshed out in the most diverse ways. It still appears to me that individual human minds are much more advanced than the structures through which a kind of sleep-walking ratiocination occurs. An awareness of structure is a first stage in stepping out of it.

References

Ardener, E.
  1959   The Bakweri elephant dance. *Nigeria* **60**, 31–38.
  1970   Witchcraft, economics and the continuity of belief. In *Witchcraft confessions and accusations,* edited by M. Douglas. A. S. A. Monograph, no. 9. London: Tavistock. Pp. 141–160.
  1971a Introductory essay: Social anthropology and language. In *Social anthropology and language,* edited by E. Ardener, A. S. A. Monograph, no. 10. London: Tavistock. Pp. ix–cii.
  1971b The historicity of historical linguistics. In *Social anthropology and language,* edited by E. Ardener. A.S.A. Monograph, no. 10. London: Tavistock. Pp. 209–241.
  1971c The new anthropology and its critics (The Malinowski Lecture). *Man* n.s. **6**(3), 449–467.

1974 Social anthropology and population. In *Population and its problems,* edited by H. Parry. New York and London: Oxford Univ. Press (Clarendon). Pp. 25–50.

1975 Belief and the problem of women. And: The problem revisited. In *Perceiving women,* edited by S. Ardener. London: Malaby. Pp. 1–17; 19–27.

De Bono, E.

1969 *The mechanism of mind.* Harmondsworth, Eng.: Penguin.

Lewis, J. M.

1971 *Ecstatic religion.* Harmondsworth, Eng.: Penguin.

Saussure, F. de

1964 *Cours de linguistique générale* (translated). London: Peter Owen. (Originally published 1916)

Thomas, K. V.

1971 *Religion and the decline of magic.* London: Weidenfeld & Nicolson.

Whorf, B. L.

1964 *Language, thought and reality,* edited by J. Carroll. Cambridge, Massachusetts.: MIT Press. (Originally published 1959)

20

Symbolism, Canalization, and *P*-Structure

CHARLES D. LAUGHLIN, JR.
CHRISTOPHER D. STEPHENS

If a description is valid, then the fact that it is very complicated cannot be helped. No benign and parsimonius deity has issued us an insurance policy against complexity.

George Miller, Eugene Galanter, and Karl Pribram (1960)

Introduction

Two extreme paradigms of analysis and theory construction—structural functionalism and semiotic structuralism—predominate in present-day anthropological explanations of human nature. The first paradigm, structural functionalism, takes a generally behaviorist stance (see, for example, Watson and Skinner) on the function of social categories and institutions. Analyses of this sort are principally concerned with types of social action and how action participates in maintaining a social system (see, for example, Eggan, 1954; Parsons, 1966; Service, 1975; Radcliffe-Brown, 1940). Because of a rigid focus upon role-related action, systemic form, and contingent event structural–functional theory has experienced difficulty in modeling issues involving the psychology of human behavior. Thus, early attempts to introduce psychological variables into structural–functional models proved unsuccessful in accounting for the behaviors observed (see, for example, Gluckman, 1963, on conflict; Malinowski, 1961, on culture change; Radcliffe-Brown, 1924, on mother's brother).

The second paradigm, semiotic structuralism, takes an essentially idealist

SYMBOL AS SENSE

stance in which the purpose of analysis is to factor out the principles of logic underlying categorical and symbolic thought (see, for example, Leach, 1973; Lévi-Strauss, 1949, 1966, 1969; Maranda and Maranda, 1971; Rossi, 1974). As the result of an extreme emphasis upon the *form* of thought, semiotic structuralism has found it difficult to address issues pertaining to social action or change, and the few attempts to do so have appeared less than effective (see, for example, Castaneda, 1968, on the dynamics of shamanistic experience; Lévi-Strauss, 1972, on myth and ecology; Needham, 1962, on prescriptive cross-cousin marriage). As if in self-defense against the tainting influence of situational variables, semiotic structuralists seem to take refuge in the analysis of those aspects of cultures apparently least vulnerable to the vicissitudes of environmental strain and social action. In short, while structural functionalism generates a theory focusing upon action to the exclusion of mentation, the inverse is true of semiotic structuralism; it generates a theory focusing upon mentation to the exclusion of action.

Both paradigmatic views, if seen in this light, are inadequate. On the one hand, the structural-functionalist view yields a "black box" treatment of the nervous system and in practice tends to attribute functions to the nervous system, and brain in particular , that are simplistic and contra-empirical. On the other hand, the semiotic structuralist creed denies the systemic interconnection of mentation and action in furtherance of the dual role of the nervous system in organization *and* adaptation.

An adequate theory of human nature is one therefore that recognizes the nervous system as the organ of behavior and behavior as the external concomitant of operations internal to the nervous system. *Biogenetic structuralism* (Laughlin and d'Aquili, 1974) holds that the structure of the human nervous system constrains, predisposes, and patterns all manifestations of human behavior. It is our position that only those theories that account for how neurobiological mechanisms intervene in cognition and action— throughout evolution, ontogenesis, and on-going adaptation—will succeed in giving us a close enough view of the condition of man and the nature of his behavior. Much of our work and the work of our associates has been directed at modeling the interaction between the individual neural system and its environment.

In the present chapter we wish to discuss the process by which individual neurocognitive systems become modulated by their social and physical environments. In order to proceed we must first introduce some basic concepts that have emerged in biogenetic structural theory, and then summarize some of our work on the symbolic function and attendant phenomena (language, ritual, and myth). Once a foundation of common understanding is reached, we will handle the topic of modulation—coordination of cognitive system and environment—by reference to Edwin Ardener's concept of p-structure and by reformulation of the symbolic function material within his frame.

Cognition and Behavior

Cognition and the mental operations intervening to produce behavior are structured by the human brain. Brain constructs models of aspects of its environment by means of innumerable mechanisms. In the following, we briefly touch upon several of these mechanisms.

The principal function of the human brain is the modeling of the phenomenal world. The totality of models constructed by the nervous system and from which actions derive we call the *cognized environment* (or E_c for short). The world of actual phenomenal effects upon the cognizing organism—effects initiated both internally and externally to the organism—we call the *operational environment* (or E_o).[1] The neurobiological processes underlying cognitive modeling have been examined in detail elsewhere (see Laughlin and d'Aquili, 1974; Laughlin, McManus, and Stephens, n.d.). In the interests of space, we will simply refer to the models comprising the individual E_o as *neurognostic models* (or *neurognosis*). A word or two about the models themselves. Models constructed by the brain either function with or without a motor (behavioral) component. In other words, some models *mediate*[2] complex functions such as a complicated conceptual operation while others mediate simple functions such as a primary manual task. Either type of model may be hierarchically organized in terms of (*a*) feedback control (Powers, 1973a,b); and (*b*) *n*-order entrainment of submodels (Hebb, 1949, 1951).[3]

All cognitive operations are mediated by neurognosis and neurognostic models are the product of an *equilibration*[4] in ontogenesis between the genetic predispositions of the organism and exigencies in the E_o (Piaget, 1971). Neurognostic models become *entrained*[5] into neural subsystems that respond with systemic integrity to anomalous input from the E_o. This organization—that is, integration and order—will depend both on the predis-

---

[1] The terms *cognized* and *operational environments* are borrowed from Rappaport (1968) but have been considerably expanded elsewhere (see Laughlin and Brady, 1978).

[2] *Mediation* means causal intervention by information processing within the stimulus–response arch. Sensory stimuli must be processed by the nervous system as information before it results in behavior, if any.

[3] A neural model is a discrete pathway through a field of neural connections. A submodel may comprise a portion of the pathway. Submodels may operate at any and all levels in a hierarchically organized scheme of neurognosis. In other words, they may constitute localized or extended connections in a model. Submodels may serve therefore not only as a reference for lower-order stimulus configurations but also may link up to mediate higher-order cognitive functions (see Powers, 1973b; Hebb, 1949, 1972).

[4] *Equilibration* is the diachronic equivalent of the notion of synchronic equilibrium—the former referring to the process, the latter to the state (Waddington, 1957; Piaget, 1971).

[5] *Entrainment* refers to the process by which the nervous system links subsystems (models and submodels) in an array to form more complex arrangements.

position to system formation and on the nature of E_o exigency. In agreement with Piaget, models and systems of models will, wherever possible, operate to preserve their organization while at the same time retain a relatively open system, sufficiently flexible to permit modification of the organization in response to shifts in the E_o.

Change in E_c models occurs through a feedforward–feedback subsystem inherent in the physiology of the nervous system and which involves sensory modalities and motor subsystems in "tests" of model veridicality. More broadly, neurognostic models are constructed in ontogenesis and reformed in on-going adaptation via the *empirical modification cycle* (or EMC), which is essentially a process by which expectations derived from neurognosis are evaluated in relation to E_o responses and models modified to compensate for any perceived and salient discrepancy between the E_c and the E_o (Bruner, 1973; Laughlin and d'Aquili, 1974; Miller, Galanter, and Pribram, 1960; Piaget and Inhelder, 1969; Whitehead, 1929).

It is through this testing procedure that the nervous system maintains an *isomorphism*[6] with its operational environment that results in responses adaptive for the organism. Since no organism's cognized environment is completely isomorphic with its operational environment (in the first place, there are constraints on the neural organization of information and, in the second place, environmental stimuli are infinitely rich and varied; [see Diamond, 1976; Rosenzweig and Bennett, 1976; Rosenzweig, Bennett, and Diamond, 1972]), the EMC is the principal process by which the organism maintains a partial isomorphism comprehensive and accurate enough to permit continued survival.

Neurognostic models thus initially organize information about E_o events through attunement of intention (via the EMC) to E_o process. Hence the *intentionality*[7] of any neurognostic model is information or knowledge it contains about the entity or happening, or set of entities or happenings, in the E_o modeled by that neurognosis. The intentionality of any model will inevitably be only partially isomorphic with the E_o entity modeled. Further, the intentionality of any model will vary in its internal organization of information about an E_o process, depending upon the level of cognitive complexity at which the organism is operating.

---

[6] The term *isomorphism* refers to the correspondence between the elements and relations comprising one particular system on the one hand and the elements and relations comprising another system of a different form on the other. This term is quite precisely defined in the mathematics of the group or set theory. For a more accurate definition of isomorphism, refer to Laughlin, McManus, and d'Aquili (1978).

[7] *Intentionality* manifests several behavioral features: expectation of the outcome of an act, selection among alternative means for fullfillment of goal, sustained directionality in action sequence, an expected state to match a resultant state, and a flexible plan for instigating alternative means to compensate and correct for discrepancy, if any, between expectation and result (Bruner, 1974).

The Symbolic Function

A single formula specifies the relationship holding between the symbolic function and the general processes of cognition mediated by the human brain. It is the following: *The symbolic function of the nervous system is that by which the whole is inferred from the part.* More accurately, the total intentionality of a model is *evoked*[8] by partial sensory information pertaining to the E_o entity that has been modeled (see Laughlin, McManus, and Stephens, in press; Sperber, 1975). A model may be evoked either by a stimulus in the E_o (keeping in mind, that it may be within or without the organism), or by another model within the E_c. In either case, we customarily term the evoking stimulus or model a *symbol*.

A discussion of the neural *hardware* (i.e., the processes of topographic projection, reciprocal inhibition, pattern detection, etc.) underlying the symbolic function has been presented elsewhere (Laughlin, McManus, and Stephens, in press; see also Pribram, 1971). However, 15 issues are critical to our comprehension of symbolism and will be mentioned briefly.[9] (1) A symbol does not evoke the E_o entity that has been modeled. Rather, it evokes knowledge about the E_o; that is, information stored in models about the E_o. (2) In the context of the present discussion, the *meaning* of a symbol is the total intentionality evoked by a symbol in any particular stimulus situation. The same symbol may have different meanings depending upon a variety of factors, including the context of the stimulus situation and the intensity of evocation. (3) The *intensity* of evocation may vary depending upon a number of variables external and internal to the E_c, including mode of expression (i.e., chance occurrence or ritual event, presented through language or through the visual system, or both), and extent of penetrance of the stimulus into E_c models; the latter may be determined by the intensity of affect or attention directed at the stimulus or stimulus context (e.g., a lotus floating in a mountain pool may merely trigger a simple percept, whereas the same symbol displayed in a Buddhist ceremony may evoke an extremely complex concept) or by the level of conceptual complexity at which the individual is operating (Harvey, Hunt, and Schroder, 1961). (4) The discussion of meaning is inseparable from the discussion of *memory*, which is simply the intentionality (knowledge about an event, process, or entity in the E_o) stored in models (that is to say, a dormant model's latent function; [Liben, 1977; Piaget and Inhelder, 1973]). Hence, the intentionality of memory may comprise everything from traces of entities (i.e., aspects or features) to the structure or *scheme* of complex E_o processes (Neisser,

---

[8] *Evocation* specifically refers to the neurophysiological process by which a stimulus signal activates a neurognostic model.

[9] All of these issues have been addressed at length in Laughlin, McManus, and Stephens (in press).

1967; Piaget, 1969). Any stimulus that evokes a model or set of models is functioning as a symbol evoking intentionality, memory, or meaning.

(5) A symbol may evoke, of course, models the intentionality of which have little or no isomorphism with those entities in the E_o experienced through only a single phase of consciousness. In other words, symbols can evoke fictions (like sprites, gods, spirits, hereafters, mythical events, etc.)—this being an aspect of the symbolic function of great interest to some phenomenologists (e.g., Husserl and Schutz). (6) The symbolic function is an efficient organizer of information within the nervous system. It is an adaptive function that simultaneously provides for an economy in the organization and integrity of information. Not only may a partial stimulus evoke knowledge of a whole entity, but a single stimulus may evoke knowledge of an entire class or category of entities, some members of which may actually exist in the E_o and some of which may not (e.g., the symbol *Christmas* may, for many of us, simultaneously evoke knowledge of evergreen trees and elves). Symbols that evoke information about an entire E_o process may conceptually organize the connection between E_o events and the organism's actions and goals into a temporal sequence. We may thus speak of symbols as providing intentionality with *plans* (Miller, Galanter, and Pribram, 1960) or *strategies* (Flavell, 1970; see also Bruner, 1969a). Thus, the concept *Work of the Gods,* for Tikopia, may evoke knowledge of an annual round of ritual (Firth, 1967). The uprooting of the *rumbin* may evoke entire plans for ritual performance (Rappaport, 1968), not only triggering images of actual ritual events but also evoking strategies for performance appropriate to the sequence of events. Indeed, symbol systems may be so extensive that they pervade virtually all that is significant in a society's life (Turner, 1967).

(7) A symbol may or may not be cognized as a *symbol;* that is, the part–whole relationship between a stimulus and its intentionality may or may not be salient to an individual. For any individual or society, there are stimuli or internalized images the evocative powers of which are given cognizance and emphasized in ritually delineated bundles (i.e., embedded in ceremonial rituals, myths, monuments). We will hereafter denote a conceptualized symbol as a **symbol.** A society's **symbols** are typically those that evoke models of the most profound and ramified intentionality (e.g., flags, totems, shamanistic regalia, icons, etc.). **Symbols** are quite often hierarchically organized within systemic bundles such that one may reasonably speak of *core* **symbols** (Ortner, 1973; Schneider, 1968; Turner, 1967), the evocative fields of which contain the intentionalities of other secondary and tertiary symbols (Munn, 1973a,b; see also Marshack, 1976, with reference to the evolution of symbolism).

(8) It is biologically, evolutionarily, and ontogenetically crucial to distinguish between *symbolic integration* (the primary process by which direct experience is given coherence through symbolic organization within the E_c) and *symbolic expression* (the ancillary process by means of which experience

may be communicated between individual E_c's). (9) The process of symbolic integration follows a basic format; it is apparent both in the early organization of action and in symbolic expression itself. As for the early organization of action, an infant's intentionality is formed in-utero (Leboyer, 1975a,b; see also MacFarlane, 1977) with preliminary (both in- and post-utero) single action movements serving first to complete sensorimotor-based E_c models and then to augment *modular* performance routines (Bruner, 1970).[10] Mastering of early action sequences (two or more preliminary acts) is accomplished through play; a way of varying means-and-ends objectives to provide information on the actual pattern of combined performance required for effective regulation of a successful action sequence Bruner, 1974b), Play enables the intentionality of an E_c model (or models) to become *coded* for any part of the action sequence; sufficiently so for meaning and intention to be evoked by a stimulus about any aspect of the entire action once successive performances have provided for a smooth "run."

(10) Early action development, more accurately the operations of the organism shaping it, gives form to the communicative system of symbolic expression. Two aspects of these operations predominate: the structure of action and the structure of attention (Bruner, 1975a). Action structure underlies the case grammatical form of symbolic expression. Both action and expression order moments and sequences in relation to categories of E_o entities—agent, action itself, object of action, recipient of action, location, possession, and so on. E_o events and processes encapsulate categories and the associations between categories. The organization of action (thus, symbolic integration of information into E_c models) passes through a series of stages in which various categories of E_o entities (i.e., object and action) established separately through preliminary sensorimotor acts are grouped according to functional relationships (i.e., agent, instrument, etc.; [see Clark, 1973]); in other words, prior knowledge about particular E_o entities constructed independently of relations with other entities is further elaborated ("played with") and then combined and organized into a unified E_c model of contextualized (albeit, primitive) "frame" form (Fillmore, 1968; see also Schank, 1973; Simmons, 1973). The essential part to referencing[11] is the integrative process itself by means of which children construct a tax-

---

[10] Thus the patterned behavior (i.e., visual attention, grasping) that occurs "instinctually" in newborn infants is later converted into behavioral schemes that encompass the more varied results of post-utero play. Eye and hand, eye and mouth, and eye and sound coordinations (Bruner and Koslowski, 1972; Piaget, 1952; Leboyer, 1975b; Wertheimer, 1961) are the completion of formative intentions stemming from independent acquaintance and in-utero use.

[11] *Reference*, in a linguistic sense, is the expressive counterpart to meaning. The process by means of which entities, actions, and states in the E_0 are differentiated and discriminated is the precursor to the formation of indicative and nominal means for their expression. Referencing entails indication and naming. Referencing depends upon deixis. Indication refers to gestural, postural, and vocal means of directing attention; naming refers to the use of symbols for con-

onomy of symbols to deal with a set of extra-expressive E_o entities with which they traffic jointly with conspecifics—other children and adults (Harrison, 1972).

Attention structure underlies the subject–predicate form of the grammar for expression; a form basic to natural language (Chomsky, 1965; Greenberg, 1963). Akin to the categorical form of action structure, predication[12] is the comment upon, in our terms, the meaning evoked within the E_c about, extra-expressive E_o entities. It is information pertaining to the function of objects or persons inferent in the contexts in which children finds themselves. The development of this form entails the same operations observed as occurring for the development of action structure. The grouping together of prior separate E_o entities and unification into a single E_o event or process about which meaning can be evoked within a child's E_c is made possible through a reorganization of the separate attention and action routines; a reorganization primed by the "focus variation" pattern of play and nourished by encounters ranging from joint activity to individual management of task (Bruner, 1975b).

(11) If there is one point that deserves additional emphasis in the preceding, it is that symbols—through attention and action development—only function to organize information about the context in which social action occurs. The inference is that whatever organizing features of syntax, semantics, and pragmatics may appear in symbolic expression, they are features required, by necessity, to translate effectively the complex organization of experience achieved by the human organism about its E_o. As we have argued elsewhere (Cove and Laughlin, 1977; Laughlin and d'Aquili, 1974, n.d.; Laughlin, McManus, and Stephens, in press), the occurrence of (a) an evolutionary progression in the complexity of symbolic integration in a species opting for (b) an adaptive strategy based upon the social group is both a necessary and a sufficient condition for an evolutionary progression in the complexity of symbolic expression. The reasoning here is quite simple. The central problem for any progressively evolving social organism is the coordination of individual E_c's such that corporate action is facilitated by congruent perception and affect. The adaptive function of symbolic expression in a social context is to maintain that coordination (see d'Aquili, Laughlin, and McManus, 1978). Were the internal cognitive structuring of a species to "outstrip" its means of symbolic expression in evolutionary development,

---

veying information about entities in the E_o; and deixis refers to knowledge of spatial, temporal, and interpersonal contextual features of situations (Bruner, 1975b). To reference an entity or state therefore is first to encode the deictic features of the context in which either entity or state is apparent and then to translate deictic features via indicative and nominal elements into expression.

[12] *Predication*, in the linguistic sense, refers to the assertion of a quality, attribute, or property of the subject of a proposition (Wall, 1974). In a psychological sense, predication refers to the commentary upon a topic of a functional or argumentive nature (see Chomsky, 1965; Bruner, 1975a).

then the species would gradually lose its capacity for adaptive social action. Hence, construction of modes of expression evolutionarily or acquisition of language ontogenetically reflects a process governed by joint action and the requirements of an action dialogue. The development of early action bears testimony to this. We shall return in the following to the function of expression and language in particular.

(12) From the point of view of the present theory, a *sign*[13] is an evolutionary specialized **symbol** that participates as a constituent in a greater **symbol** system (e.g, phones, lexemes, and utterances may be seen as signs constituent, as subplans, of a larger **symbolic** unit, the *text*). Evolutionarily speaking, symbols lost their stimulus-boundness such that a system of signs, by combining the symbolic function with a structured set of *plans*, could provide its own intentional frame. But in natural sign systems, **symbolic** context is rarely lost at the highest level of intentionality. (13) The evolutionary sequence in the emergence of the symbolic function along the hominoid line was from symbol (e.g., a moving shadow evokes the model of dangerous predator), through **symbol** (e.g., meat is a special resource worthy of ritualized exchange), to sign systems (e.g., natural language, visual codes, etc.), and finally to *formal sign* systems (i.e., a sign system that may operate with total nonstimulus-boundness; e.g., an abstract mathematical or logical system). All four stages in the evolution of the symbolic function in humans have their representations in the ontogenesis of the individual cognitive system (Piaget, 1971) and may be operative in a particular individual during the course of a single event (e.g., imagine a lecture being given by a mathematics professor).

(14) Symbols order and direct the flow of experience. They determine how events are experienced; they focus attention and integrate information sufficient for meaningful re-cognition by organizing the information about events of the moment in terms of knowledge contained with the E_c of E_o events experienced in the past. Obviously then, the study of phenomenology (*consciousness*) is critical to our comprehension of symbolism.

Phenomenology is a process, not a state. It is *the* E_c function, the cognizing function of the organism. More precisely, it is a combinatory function of E_o awareness, orientation response, stimulus reception, and several moment-to-moment transformations of neural subsystems operating upon information pertaining to the E_o. One transformation, the symbolic function, determines

[13] Our definition of *sign* differs from current usage. In evolution, the loss of stimulus-boundness in **symbolic** expression created a need for context-definition. Signs make "common" the sense of a symbol by defining the sets of intrinsic relationships holding between it and its meaning. Signs thus "package" the link between symbol and meaning in a *form* that is grasped independent of recourse to a perceptual frame. In our words, signs combine the symbolic function with a structured set of *plans* such that they operate within their own intentional frame. The view is completely in consonance with pragmatic, semantic, and syntactic aspects of symbolic expression (Silverstein, 1976).

the extent of further information processing depending, for instance, on whether the encounter is novel or merely a re-cognition.

(15) *Semiosis* (the process by which a stimulus becomes a symbol in ontogenesis) and *semiotropism* (the automatic response to symbols of great phenomenological salience) are mechanisms integral to the E_c function of the organism.

Both mechanisms serve the organism with a paradox; while they operate as a control function matching pattern to input, model to stimuli, their intervention limits the organism's capacity for reorganization of the previously coded information. The logic of this argument runs as follows. On the one hand, semiosis provides for integrity and directionality in consciousness. It encodes information about an E_o event sufficient for the organism to construct a model–symbol connection. Once constructed, such models are then relegated to a lower order level outside the purview of consciousness (Sokolov, 1977). A semiotropic response to symbols circumscribed by a society's hermeneutic through semiosis maintains congruity between the meanings evoked in the E_c's of a group's members. On the other hand, by organizing information around symbols and relegating this information to lower order neural structures (i.e., those to which we "habituate"), semiosis prevents the human organism from dealing with the stricture placed upon growth by the process of cognitive development itself. Because of the change in operational complexity experienced by the organism in ontogenesis, differentially processed information gives rise to *décalages* (Inhelder, Sinclair, and Bovet, 1974); in other words, the nonsynchronous integration of information about symbols and construction of models based on dissimilar E_c operational abilities yield differentially organized arrays of information. Similarly, since semiotropism channels meaning through symbolic intercourse circumscribed by a society's hermeneutic, it limits the extent of symbolic integration of experience occurring outside the normal parameters of the E_o.

The problem for the human organism is to reorganize the *décalage* of information. A reorganization would provide for the integration of information about experience, both internal and external to the E_o, at the most advanced level of cognitive functioning. It would consequently prepare for further unfolding of the cognizing function itself.

Natural Language

As we have already implied, the primary problem facing any social species is the ongoing maintenance of corporate as opposed to individuated or simple aggregate, response to rapidly shifting operational environmental contingencies (Allee, 1951; Wynne-Edwards, 1962). These contingencies are not restricted to the physical E_o, but include the social E_o as well. Corporate response depends upon the capacity of the group to initiate coordination both within (intraorganismic) and between (interorganismic) individual E_c's.

Intraorganismic coordination involves the entrainment of the many neural subsystems (perceptual, conceptual, affective, autonomic, motor, etc.) requisite for an adaptive response. Interorganismic coordination involves some kind of cybernetic control over which alternative entrainment will be activated in the E_c's of group members. As various social deprivation studies have shown, the problem of maintaining intra- and interorganismic coordination is a complex one for animals for whom there is normally a great overlap in direct experience. The problem becomes truly profound in a species like *Homo sapiens* where there may exist a wide disparity in direct experience made possible by a cognitive system capable of penetrating into and modeling a vast expanse of the group's E_o.

The complexity of the problem becomes remarkable when the factors of attrition and birth enter the picture. Not only does this cognitively precocious animal have to constantly assure intra- and interorganismic coordination among its groups' adult members, it must replace dead and transient members via a long and arduous period of ontogenesis. To make a very long story very short, humans have not only been able to solve this complex problem, they have evolved one of the most flexible mechanisms of social adaptation known. The principal mechanism facilitating this ongoing process of equilibration is, of course, natural language. Natural language enhances the ability to transmit information pertaining to direct experiences from the experiencer to conspecifics who can, in turn, encode and store that information as vicarious experience (Cove and Laughlin, 1977; Laughlin and d'Aquili, n.d.). Thus, the experiences obtained by other group members become integral to one's own E_c, placing individuals in a better position to evaluate and respond to contingencies than had they to adapt via trial and error.

Language evolved in the context of interorganismic adaptations. The development of language was precipitated by an increasingly complex cognitive system (Miller, 1972). Language "works" because its syntax, semantics, and pragmatics are structured around the primary relationships that exist between interacting organisms. The acquisition of language in ontogenesis occurs in the context of these emergent relationships.

The one essential feature of the communicative event, then, is the relationship that prevails between experiencer and conspecific, communicator and recipient. The principles of communication formalized in natural language are predicated upon the mutual development of such relationships. *Corporate enterprise* or *joint action* governs everything from joint reference to predication (to name but two principles common to language [see Greenberg, 1963]). The more complex the interactive behavior mediated by neurognostic models (i.e., the more highly organized the *plan* [Miller, Galanter, and Pribram, 1960]) the more diverse and extensive the principles become. Even in the simplest of situations, such as the relation between infant and adult, where joint activity involves a shared knowledge of categories of use as well as spatial and temporal features within the E_o, the deictic limits governing joint reference will extend, at the least, to the modeling of a tri-partite relationship between E_o entities, conspecific, and action sequence sufficient to evoke the same meaning and consequently agreement in the performance of action (Bruner, 1975b). As we have already inferred, the nature of joint activity will also determine the need for a taxonomy of symbols with which to *code* (in neurobiological terms) and then *reference* (in linguistic terms) the E_o entity itself, the relationship between entities, or the action associated with the E_o entity, depending of course on the level of cognitive complexity at which the organism is operating. And it is the joint activity which in turn provides a context for the development of predication; in other words, it is not only through action but joint action that the pattern or relationships prevailing between a set of E_o entities or events—*inclusive* of other persons—is contextualized, encoded, and "framed" (Fillmore, 1976; Schank and Abelson, 1977).

Just as the nature of the relationships between conspecifics changes so does the nature of the relationship between communicator and recipient. The functioning communicative acts of a human organism—referencer and recipient, demander and complier, seeker and finder, task-initiator and ac-complice, and so on—give shape to discourse. Multiple contexts require both a flexible grammar to meet the ennumerable permutations in relation-ships and a semantics appropriate to each and every permutation in context. So that any growing organism is not just faced with the task of *contextual-ization,* of developing a frame for relationships, but also of *conventionali-zation* of the "frame" once formed. The problem is how to fit context to convention. The pragmatic function of signs, those specialized symbols com-bined into action or plan, in conveying information depends upon a mastery of convention—of the societally sedimented and cognitively embedded links between symbol, meaning, and plan—and it is the linkage of sign to con-vention that assures the meaningful use of any mode of expression (Jakob-son, 1960; Silverstein, 1976). It is the action dialogue between infant and adult that enables the context of an action to be matched with convention and thereafter communicated effectively through language.

Natural language, therefore, not only facilitates transmission of infor-mation between generations by means of a built-in convention of meanings, but simultaneously embraces the flexibility of tradition in relation to the changing experiences of the immature; a requirement for full use of the adaptive potential of immaturity. As Jerome Bruner puts it: "One of the major speculations about primate evolution is that it is based on the pro-gressive selection of a distinctive pattern of immaturity. It is this pattern of progressive selection that has made possible the more flexible adaptation of our species [1972:687]." It is increasingly obvious that children obtain information pertaining to vicarious experience in the context of their own direct experience; they have one eye on the adults and the other on the rest of their E_o, as it were. We shall return to this point later.

Myth

Myth plays a critical role in the integration of information about direct experience. In the first place, myth is the quintessential form of **symbol** system, operating to organize experience around a society's core symbols. A society's core symbols are invariably oriented upon the zone of uncertainty—that is, the set of events giving rise to significant effects for which there exist no readily perceivable causes for a large number of a society's members.[14] Through the mode of symbolic integration, myth thereby orders information relevant to those E_o events that remain problematic (unspecified) to individuals of a society.

In the second place, myth gains its efficacy via the organizational capacity of the symbolic function. Symbols may evoke meaning about either the contingent or operative configurations of E_o events. The meaning evoked will depend upon the degree to which information has been integrated into the E_c of the organism. The degree to which information is integrated varies in two major ways: in terms of either the level of cognitive complexity or the nature of operative knowledge within a level. Within a cognitive level, symbolic integration works in a binate fashion. The symbol may be patterned on the contingent state and descriptive features of an event (i.e., it may hold a feature in common with another event, aspects of which have already been cognized and stored in memory) or the symbol may be patterned on the event as fitted to the operation of an E_o process (Furth, 1977; Piaget, 1977). Although the latter provides for operative knowledge about the E_o, the former is a prerequisite to the construction of the operative knowledge. The former provides the data about states of the E_o, the latter the transformations and structures about the process generating those states. In either case, however, symbols evoke meanings (albeit, some more "complete" than others) about E_o events, and thus possess the capacity to organize both partially and fully integrated information at any level of cognitive complexity. Once organized within a structure of logical operators (the complexity of the system of operators depends upon the complexity, in Piaget terms, of the individual cognitive system), **symbols,** and thus their intentional fields, take on a fluid order, providing a potent system of meaning in relation to momentary experience. Thus, within the mode of symbolic integration, myth manifests its two principal cognitive functions: (*a*) as a system of *transformation* by which operations upon the myth effectively order (reorder) information both stored in memory and gleaned from immediate and direct experience; and (*b*) as a system of *transposition* permitting the reduction of complexity and richness of direct experience and the encoding of that reduced experience for storage as "meaning" within the E_c (Cove and Laughlin, 1977; Lewis, 1965).

---

[14] The *effects* may appear in many forms. They may include external contingencies (earthquakes, death, famine, etc.) and internal contingencies (dream, vertigo, etc.).

Through the mode of symbolic expression, myth may be transmitted between E_c's via natural language or ritualized drama and art. The puissance and salience of myth in expression derives, we believe, from three factors universal to all mythopoeic systems: (*a*) the fact that **symbols** comprising myth are drawn from imagery of the sort common to the (at least potential) visual experiences we all share in alternate phases of consciousness; (*b*) the fact that myths are commonly present in the ontogenesis of the child as stories that become transformed into the elements of experience in dream (Shearer, Laughlin, and McManus, 1977); and (*c*) the fact that myths address issues of uncertainty common to all members of the group (Lévi-Strauss, 1963, speaks of dilemmas to human experience; Eliade, 1964, and Burridge, 1967, speak of elements central to the human condition; Count, 1960, speaks of "the world as problem"; Tillich, 1951, mentions matters of "ultimate concern"; and Ridington, n.d., refers to the reality of the life-experience).

All three points deserve explication. Myth as mode of expression shares its imagery-based **symbols** with that class of internally generated visual experiences obtained in alternate phases of phenomenology. Dreams, visionquests, meditation, and out-of-body experiences enact the permutations generated from the matrix of meanings supplied by myth. Whether the imagery is primordially based (genetically predisposed, e.g., the mandala form) or hermeneutically derived[15] (socially cognized), myth invariably encodes and stores the meaning of the **symbol** imagery in a structure bridging polyphasic experiences (see Ridington, 1978a, for the Dunne-za; Meyerhoff, 1974, for the Huichol; Reichel-Dolmatoff, 1971, for the Tukano). The implication is simply that myth may serve to store information structured at the most complex and adaptive level of the E_c function. Hence it would furnish the most complete view, for the discursive thinker, to a cosmology the existence of which lies beyond the thinker's grasp.

Mythopoeic information organized at an advanced level of cognitive development will, by virtue of the developmental process itself, possess meaning(s) systemically coded at all levels of cognitive functioning. Myths are thus easily grasped by children and adults alike. In fact, myths constitute the preliminary dialogue between the infant and his or her social existence. They are the metastatement between knowing "that" and knowing "how." Because myths draw upon imagery that is primordially based and hermeneutically derived, a child's encoding of meaning will, of course, be phenomenologically salient. The fact that such meaning is further transformed into the elements of experience in alternate phases (i.e., dreams [see Laughlin, Shearer, and McManus, n.d.] or vision quests [see Ridington, n.d.])

---

[15] *Hermeneutic,* from our point of view, refers to the mode of specification that links a stimulus symbol with a particular evocative field in the E_c. Insofar as the stimulus of reference is a **symbol**, then the mode of specification will be determined by social convention (i.e., via the signs of symbolic expression and mythopoeia).

would only serve to access further the significance of the experience to cognition.

Mythopoeic expression facilitates the encoding and transmission of vicarious experience relative to the zone of uncertainty. As such, myth operates as a socially imposed hermeneutic for experience. The hermeneutic quality of myth is a dynamic one. Because the symbolic integration of information about E_o events and processes is patterned upon a finite number of E_o entities or stimuli, both the symbols and **symbols** of myth "invite thought" (Ricoeur, 1962) about possible meaning. That is, (*a*) they evoke wide fields of intentionality, both within the normal waking phase of consciousness, and within alternate phases; (*b*) they "channel" experience (i.e., 'provide meaning') in the sense that information is processed through the structure of myth; and (*c*) they ensure, through an expanded polysemy, that the myth remains meaningful in spite of the presence or absence of a particular contingency. Myth often provides a means of integrating experience by exploration of alternatives open to an individual or group facing uncertainty. The exploration is not restricted to specifying a charter for action (Malinowski, 1948), but rather may provide the positive and negative consequences of an entire range of alternative views or actions (Cove, 1977). In performing a series of vicarious experiments, myth may also point out the unanticipated consequences of seemingly viable solutions in social action.

Ritual

Ritual behavior, likewise a human universal, is the quintessential form of symbolic expression through (largely nonverbal) action. Common to communication among many social animals (see d'Aquili and Laughlin, 1975; Laughlin and McManus, 1978; Smith, 1977, 1978), ritual behavior for our purposes may be defined as a sequence of behavior that: (*a*) is structured or patterned with something approaching a tagmemic grammar (Kemnitzer, 1971); (*b*) is repetitive and rhythmic, tending to recur with some regularity (Laughlin, d'Aquili, and McManus, 1978; Lorenz, 1966); (*c*) has the effect of coordinating intraorganismic neural subsystems of participants (Gellhorn and Kiely, 1972; Lex, 1978); (*d*) has the additional effect of interorganismically coordinating the perceptions, affect, cognition, and response of participants (McManus, 1978a; Murphy, 1978); and (*e*) operates (in man, at least) to standardize the functional level of complexity of E_c's (McManus, 1978b).

Unlike companion modes of expression, ritual involves not only accentuation of the sequential relation between a category of E_o entity, the action with which it is linked and the event resulting, but also the development of *rules* for both sensorimotor sequence and signals. There is a crucial point here. It is that ritual has the effect of drawing attention both to communication itself (Leach, 1966) and to the structure of the *acts* in which communication is taking place (McManus, 1978a). This is simply because "mastery" or "grasp" of any number of significantly interpersonal and existentially meaningful events in the E_o is not possible without the "skeleton" of the activity, to which such events may be inextricably tied, becoming the object of focus (Hocart, 1954; Tinbergen, 1951). And ritual is the mode for dealing with activity and its *rules* of modulation and patterning (see Laughlin, McManus, and Stephens, in press) as object of attention. In the ritual mode, the segments of parts of action sequences are converted to nonutilitarian purposes—to signaling, to substitution, and to variation. Rhythm and repetition are established in the underlying structure. Both activity *and* outcome become the center of attention.

We may make the distinction between ritual behavior and **ritual** in exactly the same sense, and for exactly the same reasons, we made the distinction between symbol and **symbol.** Ritual behavior pervades our lives, as it does the lives of rhesus monkeys, but most ritual is performed outside of our awareness (Goffman, 1971; Smith, 1977). In fact, if Piaget (1976) is correct in his analysis of the role of consciousness in ontogenesis, we are aware of most rituals only momentarily, for as long as it takes to lay down the neural models requisite to their animation. Yet, in all human societies, there exist (often complex) ritual sequences that are particularly salient, cognized by actors as signal events, events to be conceptually and materially demarcated as discrete units vis-à-vis the normal flow of action. These conceptualized ritual events we label **rituals. Rituals** are, of course, **symbols,** or more properly, **symbol** systems (Turner, 1973), comprised of forms of symbolic action ranging from natural language (i.e., the longhouse orators of the Iroquois [Foster, 1974]) and music (i.e., the chants, rattles, and singing of the Yanomamo [Chagnon, 1968], or the innumerable percussive sounds of the Zinacantecos [Vogt, 1978]; [see also Dobkin de Rios and Katz, 1974]) to stylized motor activity (i.e., the *powa* sun dance of the Shoshone [Jorgensen, 1972]). **Ritual** tends to be complex, organized in a hierarchy of sequences and segments forming a congruent colloquy in form.

The distinction between ritual and myth is generally an academic one, and typically arbitrary, due to the fact that the two are inextricably bound together systemically (Eliade, 1963; Reichel-Dolmatoff, 1976; Wallace, 1976 , but compare with Lévi-Strauss, 1971). Myth is quite commonly depicted through the medium of ritual drama (e.g., Hopi *katcina* ceremonies, Balinese *kris* dance ceremony). Myth may also prescribe and legitimize the recurrence of ritual (Radin, 1957a). Quite commonly, myth and ritual may, as Count (1960) has noted, form different expressions of the same set of E_c models.

Like myth, **ritual** is never directed at the solution of trivial problems, but rather of those problems potentially productive of the greatest cognitive uncertainty and disruption (i.e., the zone of uncertainty).

Now that we have, for the moment, established a common framework for

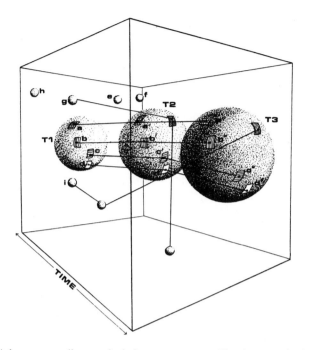

FIGURE 1. A hyperspace diagram depicting a *p*-structure. The time axes is designated. The axes running perpendicular to the time dimension represent *p*-structural (E_c and E_o) and non-*p*-structural variables. Both sets of variables are potentially involved in *s*-structures (spheres) at various times. (Modified from Waddington, 1957:28).

expressing symbolic and cognitive events, let us turn to the central issue of this chapter, the question of how individual E_c's are modulated in the course of, and in the interests of, social action.

Canalization and *P*-Structures

A potent means of addressing the question of how individual E_o's are oriented in the interests of social action is through the medium of Edwin Ardener's *p-structures*.[16] A *p*-structure is a model of all of the constraining variables (hereafter called components) operating within the E_o's of group members and the E_o of the group, which, when combined with unexpected E_o contingencies, result in momentary events (called *s-structures*). The facts

[16] Ardener has discussed the notion of *p*-structure in a number of studies, and under a variety of guises, including *template* (1970, this volume), *programme* (1971a), *paradigm* (1971b), and *p-structure* (1975, this volume).

that p-structures (a) are composed of more variables than are ever efficiently present in any particular s-structure; and (b) provide constraints to the form taken by any particular s-structure makes it fruitful to introduce the harmonious concepts of canalization and hyperspace.

Any organic system may be conceived of as existing in a multidimensional space comprised of all variables potentially operating within or upon that system. A geometrically defined portion of such a space may be called a *hyperspace* (see Figure 1).[17] The momentary position of any component of the system may be represented by a point in hyperspace (point a in Figure 1). As the system changes through time, the point representing that component will move through a trajectory (e.g., a, a', a''), and the totality of such trajectories representing the system in time forms a *canal* (Waddington, 1957:27). A component involved in the definition of a hyperspace may, or may not, participate in determining the momentary position of the system in its canal (thus, component g becomes involved in the s-structural trajectory only at time T_2). If the canal representing the course of a system in hyperspace is the result of equilibration between constraints imposed by components within the system and those imposed from without the system (but still represented within hyperspace), then the canal is termed a *creode* (Waddington, 1957:32). It is our position (congruent with that of Waddington, 1957, and Piaget, 1971, among others) that the course of all organic systems, be they at the level of organ (like the brain), at the level of organism (like a person), or at the level of population (like a society), conforms to the conditions of a creode in hyperspace.

We may view a series of observable events (a series of s-structures) as forming a creode through hyperspace (s-structural sequence of spheres in Figure 1).[18] If we were to partition the creode at any point in its trajectory, we would observe a single s-structure (a separate sphere as at discrete times T_1, T_2, or T_3). Now, we may also conceive of a p-structure as the total set of components (say a, b, c, e, f, and g) that may potentially constrain the form of an s-structure, but the subset of components within the p-structure that actually come into play (say, a, b, c at times T_1 and T_3; a, b, c, g at time T_2) will be determined by contingencies from the E_o, modeled in hyperspace, but external to the p-structure itself (say, points d, i, and h). In this way, we can see that the p-structure "generates" the s-structure, but does not "determine" it; "the (p-structure) is totally 'generative' as to kind of event, but it is not necessarily predictive as to when events will occur.

[17] The notion of hyperspace has been termed phase space, phase hyperspace, hypervolume, and has been variously applied in biology (Hutchinson, 1957, 1965; Valentine, 1969; Waddington, 1957; Piaget, 1971; Count, 1975, 1976; Welker, 1976). For a recent treatment of this concept in evolutionary biology, see Dobzhansky, Ayala, Stebbins, and Valentine (1977).

[18] The idea of using a multivariate mathematical model something on the order of hyperspace to depict p-structures is clearly implied by Ardener (1971:465).

Furthermore, the (*p*-structure) itself is finite: it may be amended or rejected. As a result it may never, even will never, generate all the kinds of events for which it is the program" [Ardener, 1971a:453].[19]

S-structures are, thus, the output of *p*-structures (Ardener, this volume), and as output, *s*-structures participate in the modification of the *p*-structures that generate them. The mechanisms providing this feedback into *p*-structures are twofold: They are (*a*) feedback through the EMC into the individual E_c's of group members; and (*b*) material effects upon the E_o of the group—both the E_c's and E_o form sets of components, all of which are modeled within our hyperspace.[20]

This leads naturally into the question of the ontological status of a *p*-structure. Is it an epiphenomenon on the order of Kroeber's *superorganic*? Is it a figment of an analyst's imagination or an "as if" model of social reality? In our view (and in Ardener's as well, as we read him), *p*-structures are characterized by none of these statements, but rather are to be seen as models of actual sets of constraining variables given momentary unity in events. It is very difficult for us to "show you a *p*-structure" (Ardener, this volume), not the least problem being that most of the *p*-structural variables are neurocognitive ones operating in a societal context. Yet *p*-structures "reveal themselves in the stream of events" (Ardener, this volume) depicted in the preceding as our creode. The components modeled by any *p*-structure "actually exist" (that is, exist within actual cognized and operational environments) as (often disparate) potentially canalizing components that gain congruence within the stream of events, and that are, in turn, affected by the stream of events as outcomes.

In more concrete terms, the kinds of components making up a *p*-structure are both contentive and structural. That is, the components constrain (*a*) the flow of information and action; (*b*) the nature of the information and action; and (*c*) the effects of information and vectored action. Within the E_c's of group members, components may take the form of categories that specifically canalize information entering the cognitive system. "The peculiar features of prescriptive categories (thou shalt do this, thou shalt not do that) are of the very essence of what I have called the (*p*-structure)" [Ardener, 1971a:455]. Categories may be as simple as a percept or as complex as a conceptual frame.

Intra-E_c components may also be structural in that the internal system of logic operating to organize relations between categories may constrain the operative "power" of cognitive subsystems intervening between the stim-

[19] Also see Ardener (1971c) for discussion of generativeness of linguistic and nonlinguistic events.

[20] In explaining certain actions of a West African people based upon beliefs centered on the existence of zombies, Ardener (1977) writes, "The old 'template' (read *p*-structure) for the zombie belief of the Bakweri was a combination of infrastructural (agricultural productivity), and biopsychological elements, and theories of causality."

ulus input and action output (Pribram and McGuinness, 1975). A cognitive system operating at minimal efficiency may be capable of only simple associations between categories (i.e., association of two or more categories on the basis of but a single common feature; a form of logic characteristic of both preoperational thought and state-specific or nonoperative knowledge, according to the Piagetian scheme, 1960, 1977), whereas a cognitive system at optimal functioning might be able to operate on the principles of logic governing the relationships between categories, which in turn would affect the lower level operations on categories (Harvey, Hunt, and Schroder, 1961). Within any level of cognitive functioning, certain associations between categories may obtain interorganismically due to: (*a*) genetic predisposition of neurognosis; or (*b*) socially derived hermeneutic embracing such associations. The former provides a principal mechanism for culturally universal *p*-structures, while the latter provides the mechanism for culture-specific *p*-structures (see further discussion of this latter point in the following).

Extra-E_c components comprising *p*-structures are, generally speaking, those E_o components that are modulated or affected by social action. *Technology*, within the present frame, may be defined as the knowledge of techniques by means of which the operational environment may be modified and the uncertainty produced by uncontrolled E_o components reduced. Increased complexity of the neurocognitive system (Sarnat and Netsky, 1974) and resultant complexity of technology are two rather remarkable features of evolutionary development along the hominid line (see Isaac, 1976, for the Lower Paleolithic; Binford, 1973 for the Middle Paleolithic; Stephens and Laughlin, n.d., for the Upper Paleolithic; and Clarke, 1977, for the Mesolithic). They rest as obvious hallmarks of a distinctly hominid *p*-structure. Technology results in modifications of the E_o, that subsequently canalize action, examples being horticulture, architecture, as well as nonmaterial constraining components such as institutions, bureaucracies, information processing and storage facilities (i.e., the West African specialists in oral history), transportation networks (i.e., the trans-Saharan trade-ways). Thus, as Ardener, himself, has noted, it is quite possible to set up a *p*-structure so vast that no single person comprehends the whole system.

A central point to emphasize is that *p*-structures are essentially anticipatory in function. Whereas the *s*-structure functions within the demands of moment-to-moment adaptation, and, hence, is (unless ritualized) highly contingent (Ardener, this volume), the *p*-structure functions as an organization of E_c and E_o constraining components generative of *s*-structures in the future. We may recognize here the two poles of equilibration, adaptation and organization, characteristic of the ontogenesis of organisms (Piaget, 1971; Waddington, 1957), and carried to the level of the group as significant unit in biological adaptation (Allee, 1951; Wynne-Edwards, 1962). This anticipatory, or feedforward, quality of *p*-structures is what gives them continuity, even in the face of disrupted (and disrupting) events. "Since both (*s*-structures) and (*p*-structures) are simultaneously delineated through events, the '(*p*-structural) primacy' probably derives from a basic and systematic, 'event-oriented,' adaptive capacity in the mentalistic structure of human society'' [Ardener, 1971a:466].

This *p-structural primacy* is, of course, mediated by the neurocognitive capacity to fit action to "*plan*" (Miller, Galanter, and Pribram, 1960); that is, the capacity of the human brain (and in particular, the frontal lobes [see Luria, 1976]) to schedule momentary actions in a sequence leading to some coherent goal. This "time-binding" ability allows humans, more than any other animal, to anticipate adaptively salient events far in the future and plan their actions accordingly (d'Aquili, 1972; Laughlin and d'Aquili, 1974). *P*-structural primacy leads to the temporal structuring of social events into repetitive patterns in response to cyclically recurring, adaptively relevant, and predictable events in the E_o. The tendency for social action to be phasically structured has been termed *diaphasis,* and the *p*-structure underlying diaphasis has been termed *diaphatic structure* (Brady, 1976a,b; Laughlin and Brady, 1978). Examples of diaphatic *p*-structures are: an alteration between sharing and long-term goal attainment at one extreme and hoarding and short-term goal attainment in response to cyclically recurring resource deprivation (Laughlin, 1974; Laughlin and Brady, 1978), an alternating broad and narrow spectrum subsistence pattern geared to periodic (long and short cycle) resource fluctuation and heterogeneous resource base (Stephens, n.d.a.), recurring migration and reliance upon exchange relations in response to cycles of deprivation (Waddell, 1975), and recurrence of epidemics of spirit possession in response to recurrent stress (Lewis, 1966). Indeed, much of the adaptive significance of technology involves the anticipatory nature of *p*-structuring. Not only have humans been able to anticipate adaptively salient events, they have increasingly been able to modify the E_o to reduce the uncertain effects of these events. This has been a bivalent advantage, as we shall see in a moment.

P-structures, because they are inextricably and causally linked to *s*-structural sequencing, are quite labile. ''The programmes for human events are self-transforming'' [Ardener, 1971a:452]. The categories and associations between categories comprising the E_c components of a *p*-structure may be changed. They may change in ontogenesis of individuals, they may change transgenerationally within a population, and they may change in response to the press of *s*-structural events. *S*-structural output has its effects upon the E_o. Thus, the E_o components to any *p*-structure are liable to (often radical) change. Change in *p*-structure is so fundamental to its adaptive significance, in fact, that we have had to use the notions of canalization and hyperspace to model it. Models of *p*-structures must look less like a homeostat and more like a field of vectors with points of transformation in time. In a very real sense, a *p*-structure is put to the test with each and every *s*-structure it generates. *P*-structures, dramatically demonstrate their adaptive significance when they must generate s-structures in response to massive *un*anticipated events in the E_o, when perhaps the easy, coherent flow of previous s-structures is suddenly nonadaptive, and a new string of s-structures must be generated for renewal of adaptive action.

A principal difficulty in maintaining adaptive p-structures in a society is the binate fact that: (a) action generated by p-structures, via s-structures, tends to modify the E_o toward simplicity; whereas (b) action generated in the E_o, and adaptively salient to a p-structure, tends to modify the p-structure toward complexity. The perennial problem of adaptation may be seen as that of balancing the drive on the part of the organism to simplify and control the E_o with the superoptimally complex nature of E_o events themselves. This is true for *intra*organismic operations upon the E_o, and is therefore constraining to the nature of *inter*organismic p-structures.

Along this line of thought, it seems apparent that most p-structures are organized at a fairly concrete level. As Ardener (this volume, p. 00) writes, "It still appears to me that individual human minds are much more advanced than the structures through which a kind of sleep-walking ratiocination occurs. An awareness of structure is a first stage in stepping out of it." The implication here is that in any society there may be, even usually are, individuals whose E_c's are more complex in operation than that requisite to participation as an actor in most of that society's p-structures (see Radin, 1957b). One might therefore wonder why p-structures become canalized at lower than optimal level. The answer, of course, is that social action depends ultimately upon unambiguous information processing, as well as some standardization of perception, cognition, and action. Information, so to speak, must be coined in the lowest and most common cognitive denomination. P-structural components and associations must be organized within the cognitive and motor capacity of all, or a majority, of participants (McManus, 1978b). We will have more to say on this in a moment.

The total set of p-structures operating within the collective E_c's and E_o of a society Ardener terms a *world structure*. "A *world structure* is a manifold of the relations we have discussed; it is also a system of people" [Ardener this volume]. More accurately, a world structure is an abstraction that models: (a) the congruency of E_c's of all actors in the society; and (b) the effects upon the E_o of all social action. Any bureaucracy may be taken as an example of a world structure. Any change in either E_c or E_o components of a world structure may precipitate morphogenesis in the world structure as a whole (e.g., a change in population [Ardener, 1972]).

By participating in a world structure, actors "sacrifice a great deal of their freedom of action . . . [they] cease to experience events, and instead they experience ''events''—where the quotation marks express the transformation of experience through the world structure''[Ardener this volume]. Through its world structure, a society *pré*pares its members for experience, provides ready-made categories and associations and actions that increase the probability of social consensus and corporate response. Yet "stepping out" of that matrix of predetermined meaning may be requisite for creativity (Koestler, 1969; Wilson, 1976) and optimal personal growth (Castaneda, 1974), perhaps even at the expense of one's comfortable social identity (Becker, 1973; Wilson, 1956).

The methodological ramifications of *p*-structures are vast and would be the stuff of another study altogether.[21] Suffice it to say here that, as Ardener (1971c) himself realizes, the only truly temporal model of human events is a *p*-structural model that controls for (*a*) all components and operations potentially efficient in generating any of a set of alternative *s*-structures; and (*b*) the set of contingencies predisposing one or another *s*-structure to be generated. Sequential observations producing a series of *s*-structures, without knowledge of the *p*-structure(s) generating them, only gives an illusion of temporality in a model; one that might look like our series of separate-spheres (*s*-structures) in Figure 1, minus the surrounding hyperspace. This may seem a tall order, but when you consider the fact that in the human sciences we are attempting to comprehend the most complex system in the known universe, the challenge seems more than appropriate.

P-Structures and Symbolism

We wish now to complete the circle and discuss briefly the way various forms of the symbolic function participate universally in the construction of *p*-structures, those elusive forms that so potently canalize human cognition and action. Remembering always that virtually all of perception operates on the symbolic function—that primordial mechanism by which a sensory stimulus providing partial information about an entity, event, or process in the E_o may evoke a total system of information about that entity, event, or process in the E_c—the potential use of the symbolic function in social canalization, and even in provision of a creode, becomes increasingly evident. All that is required, once the relationship between stimulus and model is established, is manipulation in some manner of the stimulus by other group members. In a far more complex fashion, but nonetheless using this common neurocognitive mechanism, this is precisely how social canalization through the establishment of *p*-structures occurs.

Particularly efficacious in this regard are those stimuli we have termed **symbols;** images, like Ardener's (1970) Bakweri zombies, about which a

---

[21] It is apparent from both Ardener's position and that of biogenetic structuralism that the traditional "Lone Ranger" approach to research is no longer tenable. Field research should be bolstered by congruent laboratory research in a comprehensive approach that simultaneously controls for behavioral, neurocognitive, and phenomenological variables operating in *p*-structures. If we can not yet directly observe all aspects of a *p*-structure, we can at least record data on *s*-structural manifestations from every conceivable facet.

multitude of intentionalities may be organized within the E_c. Any stimulus evoking that image (say, in the case of Ardener's zombies, a metal roof) may well call forth an enormous array of information (i.e., the entire process or "cycle" of concomitant events, or merely an associative aspect, Ardener this volume) that is brought, as it were, into the stimulating event. All of this information, of course, derives from, and is part of, the p-structure generating the event. As we have tried to emphasize in various ways, a p-structure is almost never totally mental when we are dealing with the affairs of man. The metal roof is part of the p-structure, as much so as is the image of the zombie and the cognized associations between zombies and misfortune, evil, and so on. Yet the mechanism of activation of E_c models in the presence of E_o components of a p-structure is via the symbolic function; the presence in a Catholic priest's perception of a form he cognizes as a *cross* canalizes his attention and action upon entering a *chapel*.

Each system of symbols, in its own way and through its own sensory modes, operates to canalize cognition and action. Because the mode of symbolic integration may easily result in divergence of cognition in man, social groups use the mode of symbolic expression to standardize: (*a*) the stimulus–intentionality link; (*b*) the sensory orientation and attention; (*c*) the intensity of evocation; and (*d*) the cognitive–affective association within the E_c's of group members. Three primary forms of the mode of symbolic expression, as we have seen, are natural language, myth, and ritual.

P-*Structures and Natural Language*

In most cases, the *experience* of any event by a person is a construction of that event within the person's E_c; a construction combining stimulus information about any aspect of the E_o event with information evoked by the stimulus and stored within neurognosis. Transmission of symbolic material through natural language may accompany such an event, or it may precede or succeed an event. Operating powerfully through the mechanism of the symbolic function, linguistic stimuli may be highly influential, even determinate, upon the evocation, and intensity of evocation, of models within the E_c in relation to an event. Informational components or categories and associations between categories transmitted via natural language form an integral part of the p-structure generating events.

The ontogenesis of a human organism follows a process of cognitive development, the action and attention structures of which form module "primers" to the communication system. The action dialogue between infant and adult initially works to furnish consistency and pattern in the child's E_c scheme of his operational environment. Joint activity subsequently serves to modulate and attune E_c's of the participants through the development of co*operative* rules (i.e., reference and predication) for successful completion of tasks. And language builds upon this commonality. So the capacity of language transgenerationally to structure events through transmission of vicarious experience can easily be understood. At the same time, however, we must comprehend that the language categories themselves, as well as other *p*-structural components, are never more than a significant fraction of the components involved in any *s*-structural event and its accompanying activities. Symbolic material will tend to become transformed with *s*-structures in regard to the intentionality they evoke among participants in those events. In other words, for the adult, all that is salient about an event may be transposed and transmitted via language, whereas for the child, the vicarious portion of the event derived from the adult is but a portion of his experience of the event. The model he constructs, and some of which he will store in long-term memory, will be a transformation combining elements of both direct and vicarious experience. Joint activity and, later, language may thus set the parameters for interaction but not the perimeter to independent action, experience, and alternative meaning (for a classic example, see Fynn, 1974).

We see again that the *p*-structure canalizes an event, but potentially is transformed by the event. There is a simultaneous but qualitatively different discharge of information through and from an event. On the one hand, a child, as it becomes socialized, begins increasingly to respond to "events" and "elements of events" rather than events, to use Ardener's idiom. This is the origin of what Korzybski (1958) called the *Aristotelian fallacy,* the confusion of the word with the thing signified, a phenomenon of language in social context that characterizes culture worldwide. On the other hand, a child may be constantly faced with the challenge of integrating information gleaned from direct experience, the significance or meaning of which may not be coded though vicarious experience.

Linguistic exchange of information within generations facilitates intraorganismic coordination of E_c's by adjustment interorganismically in the direction of consensus—consensus about what is salient in the E_o, about how to code events, how to feel about them, and what to do about them. In most social interactions, there is typically a gradual molding of novel aspects of any event into socially established categories (symbols and signs), associations between categories (meaning), and intentionality (plans). Thus, Bakweri zombies and tin roofs at time T_1 become Frenchmen and deep-sea wharves at time T_2 (Ardener, 1970). And each set of associations evokes a set of serviceable strategies or plans for dealing with the peculiar events (Ardener, this volume). Language participates as a major symbolic subsystem in *p*-structures by providing socially available categories and relations—in other words, signs—with which individuals may "make sense of" otherwise novel events. *P*-structures, via the provision of existential, yet socially generated, categories and relations, impose a flexible continuity of experience for actors. Again, it is clear and of phenomenological importance that individuals can "step out of" the socially generated, linguistically available categories and thus increase the novelty of events. This is the reward offered to the "outsider" who experiences such freedom from social restraint (Wilson, 1956). This is essentially Don Juan's gift to Carlos; by setting aside the *tonal*, a person may experience the *nagual* (Castaneda, 1974).

P-*Structures and Myth*

Myth, as we have said in the preceding, is a form of symbolic expression, reliant upon the media of natural language, ritual drama, and visual form for transmission, and commonly correlated with events in the zone of uncertainty. As such, a society's corpus of myth provides a prominent example of socially available information pertaining to events that would otherwise be fraught with superoptimal novelty and, hence, cognitive uncertainty for actors. And corporate, social action cannot be grounded upon unmitigated cognitive uncertainty. It is highly significant that myth narration is seldom rote repetition but is a creative and interpretive activity (Ridington, n.d.) bolstered by information drawn from polyphasic experiences and woven through several levels of reality (Ridington, 1978a). Myth as hermeneutic withstands the vagaries of time, through perpetual reorganization of constituent symbolic material in the E_c's of those who have experienced, and operated upon, the myth's meaning (see Brown, 1971). As with language, the myths themselves become transformed in relation to other components in *s*-structures. The efficacy of a myth's interpretation thus rests on the ability of the interpreter to operate on the *p*-structure while constructing links with and between generated *s*-structures. This, the ultimate test, serves to place the promulgators of myth at the most advanced level of cognitive functioning; imparting it with an all-embracing scope of, and penetration into, the E_o (see Foster, 1974, on the Iroquois longhouse speakers; and Radin, 1956, on Winnebago narration).

Although actual field research on the issue is sparse, the transgenerational transmission of vicarious experience via myth would seem to be a critical factor in maintaining continuity of adaptive action in relation to intermittent but adaptively salient events (Cove, 1978). The transgenerational transmission of vicarious experience via myth is, as we have already argued, usually reinforced with direct encounter of mythopoeic material in alternate phases of consciousness. It is through myth, then, subsequent to this foundation of experience, that the young become canalized beforehand to experience events in a given and socially adaptive way (Laughlin and Brady, 1978; Ridington, 1978b).

In the mode of symbolic integration, myth is part and parcel to *p*-structure. Only through action (i.e., expression in relation to events; expression through language, through ritual drama, through vision quests, or through other forms of action resulting from information that has been "thought through" the myth) does myth participate in *s*-structure. As *p*-structure, myth has its existence in long-term memory (i.e., information stored as intentionality in neurognosis). As *s*-structure, myth exists as canalized action in relation to uncertainty in the E_o. Thus, vicarious experience transmitted and stored in the form of myth, may provide the *p*-structural components and associations necessary to transform a catastrophic event (say a typhoon, earthquake, famine, etc.) from a socially divisive one to a socially cohesive one in its effects (Laughlin and d'Aquili, 1978; Laughlin and Brady, 1978). The event in the zone of uncertainty need not be so dramatic, of course. Issues of personal identity, inevitable or even imminent death, disease, ethnic identity, hostility, misfortune, and the like form a massive phalanx of potentially disconcerting issues. A society's mythopoeic system may address any and all of these issues, *s*-structurally organizing their actuality within a frame of *p*-structural intentionality capable (usually and for most people) of transforming negative to positive, uncertain to certain, novel to redundant, and meaningless to meaningful.

P-*Structures and Ritual*

Ritual is a transformational device. It operates to open the E_c system. It untangles (differentiates), reorganizes (discriminates), and reintegrates (incorporates) the symbols comprising the system (McManus, 1978a). Ritual functions to expose *the* structure of communication, cooperation, and action by generating the set of possible structures. It "plays" with symbols, as signals and sequences, to reinstate order and organization anew. The resultant order may be only a change in the arrangement of symbols or it may be a wholesale reorganization of the models with which the symbols are linked. In other words, either the *s*-structure or *p*-structure may change.

In Ardener's terms, ritual operates in a feedback loop from *p*-structural components, through *s*-structural events, and back to *p*-structural components. Through various neurocognitive mechanisms, ritual behavior intra- and interorganismically coordinates the E_c's of group members so that perception and action become synchronized in relation to stimulus, and corporate action, in turn, is perceived as efficacious (i.e., is seen as effectively coping with the stimulus [see d'Aquili, Laughlin, and McManus, 1978]). Ritual is at one and the same time: (*a*) action canalized by cognitive and socially available symbolic information (for example, myth) and directed at a socially salient target; and (*b*) a mechanism for canalizing information about the E_o and about effectiveness of action in the E_o reentering the information storage components of *p*-structures.

The most important actions in this respect are a society's **rituals,** those cognized and symbolically embellished strips of action that evoke and modulate such a powerful range of intentionality. Given vent through *s*-structural events, **rituals,** are capable of canalizing: (*a*) experience in normal and alternate phases of consciousness (Shearer, Laughlin, and McManus, 1977);

(b) autonomic system arousal and reactivity (including retuning the autonomic system in relation to stimulus [see Lex, 1978]); (c) the orientation response (McManus, 1978b); (d) the level of cognitive complexity at which information is being processed (McManus, 1978b), of individual participants to the action. It is easy to see that *if* an *s*-structure is generated as ritual by a *p*-structure, and *if* that *s*-structure is in confrontation with elements potentially disconcerting to a group, and *if* a vast majority of the components of the *s*-structure derive from *p*-structure, and not the disconcerting aspect of the E_o, *then* a quality of self-reinforcement through actions becomes manifest in the generative relationships between *p*-structure and *s*-structure. Put in other words, if the key elements of corporate action in the face of adversity are provided by the *p*-structure and not by the adversive field—elements like what to look for, how to code it once you see it, how to feel about it, and what to do about it—then the amount of novel information that may enter the *p*-structure and its components is limited, and more importantly, controlled (and controllable). Obviously, a *p*-structure totally closed to adversity would not last long and would look much like a society-wide psychosis. On the other hand, a *p*-structure uncontrollably open to adversive information would be incapable of sustaining social continuity. The balance must be struck—that is, a creode formed. This is yet another way of viewing the twin demands of adaptation and continuity of organization that characterize organic equilibration (McManus, 1978a; Piaget, 1971).

Conclusions

The implications of merging our understanding of the neurocognitive principles underlying the symbolic function in man with our understanding of the *p*-structural mechanisms for canalization of cognition and action are enormous and wide-ranging in scope. We have, of course, insufficient space to explore these implications. All that we can hope to do is point an inquiring finger at a few of them.

1. *Heavily technological creodes are ecologically dangerous.* Remember, man operates, not upon the E_o, but upon his knowledge of the E_o; that is, he operates out of his E_c. And his E_c is inevitably a simplification of the E_o. It is a model only. This means that when man operates from his technology to modify the E_o, he does so without controlling the totality of variables and relations between variables that comprise the E_o. This fact results in a biological bivalence to heavily technological creodes. Whereas the creode may prove of high adaptive value in the short run, it may in the long run so fundamentally alter the complex relations in the E_o that the creode produces devastating effects upon the biosphere. Again, the constraints are not mechanical, but cognitive. The human brain may have presently evolved to a

critical point of transformation where it is capable of substantially altering the biosphere in the interests of immediate adaptation, but is incapable of controlling the unintended and systemic consequences of these alterations (see Ellul, 1964). The examples of such alterations are many. International détente balances on the incredibly precarious nature of nation states' nuclear abilities; order in the world economy rests on finite energy resources which wane with increased consumption; welfare of Third World peoples depends on explosive development of third world resources.

Predominantly technological creodes are the product of science. Science thus generates far more problems in the zone of uncertainty than it resolves. While science results in alterations of our E_o, it does little to inform us of how to deal with the ramifications of these alterations (Rosenfeld, 1977). This is blatantly evident in the repercussions on cognitive development arising from medical control over human infant birth and early postnatal care (M. Stephens, 1978). The trauma wreaked by this kind of technological overdrive has yet to be reckoned. Yet the long-term consequences are staggering; the violent births of our hospital era are attended by stress, phobias, and disorders of the most varied kinds. The literature in clinical therapy attests to this (Janov, 1973, 1976), and the results of traditional nonviolent birth techniques virtually confirm it (Leboyer, 1975b).

2. *Modern anthropological theories must explain sociocultural phenomena both in terms of behavior and in terms of mentation.* The predominant focus of attention today is upon those aspects of society and culture that are most observable; that is, upon behavior as the center of focus. This myopia in the sciences must and will change. Behavior will be increasingly viewed as an output function mediated by complex neurocognitive processes that need to be understood before truly viable sociocultural theory can emerge—theory indeed capable of facilitating reasonable control of such phenomena as technological creodes.

The promise and potential of "brain and behavior" theories can be seen, to take one example, through the impact of the collaborative efforts of George Miller, Eugene Galanter, and Karl Pribram (1960) on subjects ranging from infant cognition (Bruner, 1964), to ritual (Fernandez, 1977), and the evolution of technology (Stephens and Laughlin, n.d.).

Theories of this kind are a requirement for understanding the evolution of hominid behavior. Focus on the material residue of behavior to the exclusion of the processes that intervene in the generation, formation, and patterning of that residue is singularly unenlightening (Schiffer, 1976). Equally unproductive is the predication of theories about hominid behavior on simplified notions of human behavior. It is simply not sufficient to simulate a stimulus–response link—an undeniably perverted view of the organism–environment relationship (Chomsky, 1959, 1974)—in archaeological explanations of past behavior, adaptation, or what-have-you. Most if not all paleolithic researchers are guilty of this (i.e., Binford and Binford, 1969; Higgs, 1973; Jacobi and Stephens, n.d.; Jochim, 1976), especially when it comes to accounting for observable (we hasten to add "anomalous") changes in the archaeological record (for a partial redress of this imbalance, see Binford, 1973; Clarke, n.d.; Cowgill, 1975; Stephens, n.d.a.). It is easy, but incorrect, to take a strong environmental position with respect to organismic evolution or adaptation. It is equally erroneous to overplay the role of the organism in development. The real issue, from our viewpoint and from Ardener's perspective also, is not one of either environment or organism but rather one of the character of their interaction. Modeling this interaction is not an easy feat. Nevertheless, no theory of hominid behavior will adequately account for the phenomena of man unless the multivariate interplay of cognitive system and ecosystem is comprehended. The premises upon which any archaeological perspective of the human past builds must therefore "cast" behavior in terms of the exchange between mentation and environment. We can single out in this regard the burgeoning theory of the British archaeologist David Clarke (1968, 1972). In his framework (Stephens, n.d.b.), viewing the behavioral features of man past and present, the recent and evolving hominid adaptation is not solely a function of internal system regulation but also of modification of this internal psychological system to meet conditions of the external system in which the hominid operates. In other words, for an organism to adapt both initial transformation of input from the environment to fit prior cognitive structures and subsequent modification of the encoded information to fit environmental exigencies, constraints are necessary (Clarke, 1977).

3. *A recognition of how science works is the first step to knowing what sciences does.* Science is not an alternative to mythopoeia. Science, unlike mythopoeia, does not tell us how to cope with what we know, but merely adds to our knowledge. Science systematically reduces errors in our view of the E_o while simultaneously increasing the amount of uncertainty arising from this acuity. The goals of science are set through the social prescription of open models (Laughlin and d'Aquili, 1974; Lukes, 1973). So that what is verified in scientific pursuits is that which has already been established as verifiable (Lakatas, 1970). Sciencing—the cognitive process itself—provides, however, an entré into mythopoeia via the existential prescription of open models. Truth and objectivity are no longer socially prescribed. There exists no social norm against which to check one's knowledge. The test is operability itself. Truth and objectivity are fully recognized. Thus, the existential position allows that truth is not fabricated but only our version of it. It is the correspondence between E_c and E_o that holds the interest of the existential phenomenologist. Objectivity is benign if the role of the personal ego of the scientist (the cognized model of the self within the individual's E_c) in molding the notion of objectivity is not recognized. Indeed, how can a scientist apply nonpersonal canons to the assessment of what is known,

to the evaluation of what is considered truthful, without realizing, and thus transcending, the role the personal ego plays in distorting the shape of these canons?

Knowing how science works is equivalent to knowing the formula by which *p*-structures and *s*-structures are transformed. A prerequisite to this knowledge is grasping the mode of thought by which sciencing is actually performed (Rubinstein and Laughlin, 1977).

4. *The role of the symbolic function is central to the canalization of experience in all phases of consciousness.* As we have already argued, human experience comprises a scaffolding of information within the E_c; its very growth nourishes a structural *décalage*. The eternal problem facing humans, then, is restructuring the disparately processed information gleaned from this experience. A human being attains structural unity by integrating the personal ego (in our terms, the cognized model of experience within the individual's E_c) and the true self (the individual's entire E_c, plus the rest of the internal E_o).[22] The primordial means by which a human facilitates integration of conscious and unconscious aspects of his or her organism is through the organizational principles of phenomenology and symbolism, experienced in alternate phases of consciousness. The problem becomes most apparent when it is realized that most Western social scientists are alienated from their own potential to experience through multiple phases of consciousness. It is clear, however, that many human societies and groups highly value such experiences as input into their E_c's. Thus, how societies integrate and canalize these experiences in the interests of social activity is a paramount question for social science.

5. *The full range of cultural manifestations of the symbolic function and how these operate within p-structures to canalize cognition and action need to be explored.* Up to now, anthropologists of a structuralist bent have centered their attention primarily upon myth and attendant phenomena to the exclusion of other forms of symbolism. Myth, however, is only one of the devices by which meaning is transmitted in social behavior. Recent focus on the structure of art can only, therefore, be applauded (Faris, 1973; Halpin, n.d.; Humphrey, 1971; Munn, 1973b). Nevertheless, the function of art is more often than not dropped from view (but see Bateson, 1972), so that how knowledge is translated into expression and how symbols of nonverbal expression work to generate information and guide behavior are unknown. Of particular concern to us at the moment, then, is the formation of a more sophisticated theory of art, one that controls both universal neurocognitive principles and their operation.

6. *The role of the symbolic function is central to the p-structures under-*

---

[22] This is nowhere better depicted than in the long and arduous process by which Don Juan and Don Genaro structured Carlos Castaneda's (1974) tonal (E_c plus personal ego) to confront his nagual (the more complex and novel nature of E_c minus ego, but plus internal and external environment).

lying social power. Implied in our discussion of the symbolic function and the *p*-structural canalization of cognition via that function is the importance of the process as a potential power resource in societies in which differential control of *p*-structural components is vested in actors. Indeed, the use of the symbolic function to canalize the cognitive systems of actors is probably fundamental to the functioning of polities of all kinds (see Baumgartner, Buckley, Burns, and Schuster, 1976). Furthermore, if we can come to understand how *p*-structures are initially established and how they are changed once they become established, we would possibly be in a better position to inhibit the process of bureaucratization, that insidious process by which the life-serving functions of social institutions become stultified and the institution itself becomes involuted and self-serving (Hocart, 1936).

Acknowledgments

An earlier version of this chapter was prepared for the Colloque France–Canada III Conference held at Laval University, Québec, August 20–September 8, 1977. Some of the key ideas expressed herein were derived from discussions with participants of the Fundamentals of Symbolism conference, sponsored by the Wenner-Gren Foundation at their conference center at Burg Wartenstein, Austria, July 16–July 24, 1977. Laughlin is especially grateful to Edwin Ardener for lengthy discussions at Wartenstein. However, our inclusion of his notions should in no way imply his endorsement of our conclusions. We wish also to express our debt to John McManus, John Cove, and Jon Shearer for ideas gleaned from our many projects and discussions.

References

Allee, W. C.
   1951   *Cooperation among animals,* 2nd ed. New York: Henry Schuman.
d'Aquili, Eugene G.
   1972   *The biopsychological determinants of culture.* Reading, Massachusetts: Addison-Wesley.
d'Aquili, Eugene G., and Charles D. Laughlin
   1975   The biopsychological determinants of religious ritual behaviour. *Zygon* **10**(1), 32–58.
d'Aquili, Eugene G., Charles D. Laughlin, and John McManus (eds)
   1978   *The spectrum of ritual.* New York: Columbia Univ. Press.
Ardener, Edwin
   1970   Witchcraft, economics, and the continuity of belief. In *Witchcraft: Confessions and accusations,* edited by M. Douglas. London: Tavistock. Pp. 141–160.
   1971a   The new anthropology and its critics. *Man* (n.s.) **6**(3), 449–467.
   1971b   Introductory essay: Social anthropology and language. In *Social anthropology and language,* edited by E. Ardener. London: Tavistock. Pp. ix–cii.
   1971c   The historicity of historical linguistics. In *Social anthropology and language,* edited by E. Ardener. London: Tavistock. Pp. 209–241.
   1972   Language, ethnicity and population. *Journal of the Anthropological Society of Oxford* **8**(3), 125–132.

1975 Belief and the problem of women; and The problem revisited. In *Perceiving women,* edited by S. Ardener. London: Malaby. Pp. 1–27.

1978 Some outstanding problems in the analysis of events. In *The yearbook of symbolic anthropology,* edited by E. Schwimmer. London: Hurst.

Bateson, Gregory
1972 Style, grace and information in primitive art. In *Steps to an ecology of mind,* edited by G. Bateson. New York: Balantine. Pp. 128–152.

Baumgartner, Tom, Walter Buckley, Tom R. Burns, and Peter Schuster
1976 Meta-power and the structuring of social hierarchies. In *Power and control: Social structures and their transformations,* edited by T. R. Burns and W. Buckley. Sage Studies in International Sociology. Beverly Hills, California: Sage. Pp. 215–288.

Becker, Ernest
1973 *The denial of death.* New York: The Free Press.

Binford, Lewis R.
1973 Interassemblage variability–the Mousterian and the "functional" argument. In *The explanation of culture change,* edited by C. Renfrew. London: Duckworth. Pp. 227–254.

Binford, Lewis R., and Sally R. Binford
1969 Stone tools and human behaviour. *Scientific American* **220**(4), 70–84.

Brady, Ivan A.
1976a Adaptive engineering: An overview of adoption in Oceania. In *Transactions in Kinship: Adoption and fosterage in Oceania,* edited by I. A. Brady. Honolulu: Univ. of Hawaii Press. Pp. 211–293.

1976b The sociobiology of hoarding: Some preliminary theory. Unpublished manuscript.

Brown, Joseph E. (ed.)
1971 *The sacred pipe: Black Elk's account of the seven rites of the Oglala Sioux.* Harmondsworth: Penguin.

Bruner, Jerome
1964 The course of cognitive growth. *American Psychologist* **19**(1), 1–15.

1969a Eye, hand and mind. In *Studies in cognitive development: Essays in honor of Jean Piaget,* edited by D. Elkind and J. Flavell. London: Oxford Univ. Press. Pp. 223–235.

1970 On voluntary action and its hierarchical structure. In *Beyond reductionism,* edited by A. Koestler and J. Smythies. New York: Macmillan. Pp. 161–191.

1972 Nature and uses of immaturity. *American Psychologist* **27**(8), 687–708.

1973 The growth and structure of skill. In *Beyond the information given,* edited by J. Anglin. New York: W. W. Norton. Pp. 245–269.

1974 The early organization of action. In *The integration of a child into a social world,* edited by M. P. P. Richards. Cambridge, England: Cambridge Univ. Press. Pp. 167–184.

1975a The ontogenesis of speech acts. *Journal of Child Language* **2**, 1–19.

1975b From communication to language: A psychological perspective. *Cognition* **3**(3), 255–287.

Bruner, J., and B. Koslowski
1972 Visually pre-adapted constituents of manipulatory action. *Perception* **1**, 3–14.

Burridge, Kenelm
1967 Lévi-Strauss and myth. In *The structural study of myth and totemism,* edited by E. Leach. London: Tavistock. Pp. 91–115.

Castenada, Carlos
1968 *The teachings of Don Juan.* New York: Ballantine Books.

1974 *Tales of power.* New York: Simon and Schuster.

Chagnon, Napoleon
1968 *Yanomamo: The fierce people.* New York: Holt.

Chomsky, Noam
1959 Review of *Verbal Behaviour* by B. F. Skinner. *Language* **35**(1), 26–58.
1965 *Aspects of the theory of syntax.* Cambridge, Massachusetts: MIT Press.
1972 Psychology and ideology. *Cognition* **1**(1), 11–46.

Clark, Eve
1973 What's in a word: On the child's acquisition of semantics in his first language. In *Cognitive development and the acquisition of language,* edited by T. E. Moore. New York: Academic Press. Pp. 65–110.

Clarke, David L.
1968 *Analytical archaeology.* London: Methuen.
1972 Models and paradigms in contemporary archaeology. In *Models in archaeology,* edited by D. L. Clarke. London: Methuen. Pp. 1–60.
1977 Mesolithic Europe: The economic basis. In *Problems in economic and social archaeology,* edited by G. de G. Sieveking, I. H. Longworth, and K. E. Wilson. London: Duckworth.
n.d. The interpretation of archaeological results. Unpublished manuscript.

Count, Earl W.
1960 Myth as world view. In *Culture in history,* edited by S. Diamond. New York: Columbia Univ. Press.
1975 Discussion. "Studies in Biogenetic Structuralism" symposium, annual meeting of American Anthropological Association, San Francisco.
1976 Languages of organism: Requisite fabric for an evolution of the speech function. In *Origins and evolution of language and speech,* edited by S. R. Harnad, H. D. Steklis, and J. Lancaster. *Annals of the New York Academy of Sciences* **280,** 456–466.

Cove, John J.
1978 Survival or extinction: Reflections on the problem of famine in Tsimshian and Kaguru mythology. In *Extinction and survival in human populations,* edited by C. D. Laughlin and I. A. Brady. New York: Columbia Univ. Press. Pp. 231–244.

Cove, John J., and Charles D. Laughlin
1977 Myth, cognition and adaptation. Paper presented at annual meeting, Canadian Ethnological Society, Halifax, Nova Scotia.

Cowgill, George
1975 On causes and consequences of ancient and modern population changes. *American Anthropologist* **77**(3), 505–525.

Diamond, Marion C.
1976 Anatomical brain changes induced by environment. In *Knowing, thinking and believing,* edited by L. Petrinovich and J. L. McGaugh. New York: Plenum. Pp. 215–241.

Dobkin de Rios, Marlene, and Fred Katz
1975 Some relationships between music and hallucinogenic ritual: The "jungle gym" in consciousness. *Ethos* **3**(1), 64–76.

Dobzhansky, Theodosius, Francis Ayala, George L. Stebbins, and James W. Valentine
1977 *Evolution.* San Francisco, California: Freeman.

Eggan, Fred
1954 Social anthropology and the method of controlled comparison. *American Anthropologist* **56,** 743–763.

Eliade, Mircea
1963 *Myth and reality.* New York: Harper.
1963 *Shamanism.* Princeton, New Jersey: Princeton Univ. Press.

Ellul, Jacques
1964 *The technological society.* New York: Random House.

Faris, James
1972 *Nuba personal art.* Toronto: Univ. of Toronto Press.

Fernandez, James
1977 The performance of ritual metaphors. In *The social use of metaphor*, edited by J. D. Sapir and J. C. Crocker. Philadephia: Univ. of Pennsylvania Press. Pp. 100–131.

Fillmore, Charles J.
1968 The case for case. In *Universals in linguistic theory*, edited by E. Bach and R. Harms. New York: Holt. Pp. 1–88.
1976 Frame semantics and the nature of language. In *Origins and evolution of language and speech*, edited by S. R. Harnad, H. D. Steklis, and J. Lancaster. *Annals of the New York Academy of Sciences* **280**, 20–32.

Firth, Raymond
1967 *Tikopia ritual and belief*. Boston: Beacon Press.

Flavell, John
1970 Developmental studies of mediated memory. In *Advances in child development and behaviour*. Vol. 5, edited by H. W. Reese and L. P. Lipsitt. New York: Academic Press.

Foster, Michael
1974 *From the earth to beyond the sky: An ethnographic approach to four longhouse Iroquois speech events*. Canadian Ethnology Service Paper, no. 20. Ottawa: National Museum of Man Mercury Series.

Furth, Hans G.
1977 The operative and figurative aspects of knowledge in Piaget's theory. In *Piaget and knowing*, edited by B. Gerber. London: Routledge and Kegan Paul. Pp. 65–81.

Fynn
1977 *Mister God this is Anna*. London: Fontana/Collins.

Gellhorn, Ernest and Walter F. Kiely
1972 Mystical states of consciousness: Neurophysiological and clinical aspects. *Journal of Nervous and Mental Disease* **154**, 399–405.

Gluckman, Max
1963 *Order and rebellion in tribal Africa*. New York: Free Press.

Goffman, Erving
1971 *Relations in public*. New York: Harper.

Greenberg, Joseph H.
1963 Some universals of grammar with particular reference to the order of meaningful elements. In *Universals of language*, edited by J. H. Greenberg. Cambridge, Massachusetts: MIT Press.

Halpin, Marjorie
n.d. Mask as metaphors. Unpublished manuscript.

Harrison, Bernard
1972 *Meaning and structure*. New York: Harper.

Harvey, O. J., David E. Hunt, and Harold M. Schroder
1961 *Conceptual systems and personality organization*. New York: Wiley.

Hebb, Donald O.
1949 *The organization of behavior*. New York: Wiley.
1951 The role of neurological ideas in psychology. *Journal of Personality* **20**, 39–55.
1968 Concerning imagery. *Psychological Review* **75**(6), 466–477.
1972 *Textbook of psychology*. Toronto: W. B. Saunders.

Higgs, Eric (ed.)
1975 *Palaeoeconomy*. Cambridge, England: Cambridge Univ. Press.

Hocart, Arthur M.
1954 *Social origins*. London: Watts.
1970 *Kings and Councillors* (originally published in 1934). Chicago: Univ. of Chicago Press.

Humphrey, Caroline
1971 Some ideas of Saussure applied to Buryat magical drawings. In *Social anthropology and language,* edited by E. Ardener. London: Tavistock. Pp. 271–290

Hutchinson, George E.
1957 Concluding remarks. *Cold Spring Harbor symposium. Quantitative Biology* **22,** 415–427.
1965 The niche: An abstractly inhabited hypervolume. In *The ecological theatre and the evolutionary play,* edited by G. E. Hutchinson. New Haven, Connecticut: Yale Univ. Press. Pp. 26–78.

Inhelder, Barbel, Hermine Sinclair, and Magali Bovet
1974 *Learning and the development of cognition.* Cambridge, Massachusetts: Harvard Univ. Press.

Isaac, Glynn
1976 Stages of cultural elaboration in the Pleistocene: Possible archaeological indicators of the development of language capabilities. In *Origins and evolution of language and speech,* edited by S. R. Harnad, H. D. Steklis, and J. Lancaster. *Annals of New York Academy of Sciences* **280,** 275–278.

Jacobi, Roger, and Christopher D. Stephens
n.d. Before, during and after the Alleröd: A potential economic strategy. Unpublished manuscript.

Jakobson, Roman
1960 Linguistics and poetics. In *Style and language,* edited by T. A. Sebeok. Cambridge, Massachusetts: MIT Press. Pp. 350–377.

Janov, Arthur
1970 *The primal scream.* New York: Dell.
1977 *The feeling child.* London: Abacus/Sphere.

Jochim, Michael
1976 *Hunter-gatherer subsistence and settlement. A predictive model.* New York: Academic Press.

Jorgenson, Joseph
1974 *The sun dance religion.* Chicago: Univ. of Chicago Press.

Kemnitzer, Lewis S.
1971 A "grammar discovery procedure" for the study of a Dakota healing ritual. Paper presented at annual meeting, American Anthropological Association, November, 1971.

Koestler, Arthur
1970 *The act of creation* (2nd ed.). London: Pan.

Korzybski, Alfred
1958 *Science and Sanity,* 4th ed . Lakeville: International Non-Aristotelian Library.

Lakatos, Imre
1970 Falsification and the methodology of scientific research programmes. In *Criticism and the growth of knowledge,* edited by I. Lakatos and A. Musgrave. Cambridge, England: Cambridge Univ. Press. Pp. 91–195.

Laughlin, Charles D.
1974 Deprivation and reciprocity. *Man* **9**(3), 380–396.

Laughlin, Charles D., and Eugene G. d'Aquili
1974 *Biogenetic structuralism.* New York: Columbia Univ. Press.
n.d. Myth, language and the brain: The evolutionary importance of vicarious experience. Unpublished manuscript.
1978 Ritual and stress. In *The spectrum of ritual,* edited by E. G. d'Aquili, C. D. Laughlin, and J. McManus. New York: Columbia Univ. Press. Pp. 280–317.

Laughlin, Charles D., and Ivan A. Brady
1978 Introducion: Diaphasis and change in human populations. In *Extinction and survival*

in human populations, edited by C. D. Laughlin and I. A. Brady. New York: Columbia Univ. Press. Pp. 1–48.

Laughlin, Charles D., and John McManus
1978 Mammalian ritual. In *The spectrum of ritual,* edited by E. G. d'Aquili, C. D. Laughlin, and J. McManus. New York: Columbia Univ. Press. Pp. 80–116.

Laughlin, Charles D., John McManus, and E. G. d'Aquili.
1978 Introduction. In *The spectrum of ritual,* edited by E. G. d'Aquili, C. D. Laughlin, and J. McManus. New York: Columbia Univ. Press. Pp. 1–50.

Laughlin, Charles D., John McManus, and Christopher D. Stephens
in press A model of brain and symbol. *Semiotica.*
n.d. Knowledge and neural development. Unpublished manuscript.

Leach, Edmund
1966 Ritualization in man in relation to conceptual and social development. *Philosophical Transactions of the Royal Society of London* **251**, 403–408.
1973 Structuralism in social anthropology. In *Structuralism: An introduction,* edited by D. Robey. Oxford: Oxford Univ. Press (Clarendon).
1976 *Culture and communication.* Cambridge, England: Cambridge Univ. Press.

Leboyer, Frederick
1975a Birth without violence: An evening with Dr. Leboyer. *Journal of Primal Therapy* **2**, 289–300.
1975b *Birth without violence.* New York: Alfred Knopf.

Lévi-Strauss, Claude
1963 *Structural anthropology.* Boston: Beacon Press.
1966 *The savage mind.* Chicago: Univ. of Chicago Press.
1969 *The elementary structures of kinship* (originally published in 1949). Boston: Beacon Press.
1969 *The raw and the cooked.* New York: Harper.
1971 *L'homme nu.* Paris: Plon.
1972 Structuralism and ecology. *Social Science Information* **12**(1), 7–23.

Lewis, Clive S.
1965 *Screwtape proposes a toast.* London: Fontana Books.

Lewis, Ioan M.
1966 Spirit possession and deprivation cults. *Man* (n.s.) **1**, 307–329.

Lex, Barbara
1978 The neurobiology of ritual trance. In *The spectrum of ritual,* edited by E. G. d'Aquili, C. D. Laughlin, and J. McManus. New York: Columbia Univ. Press. Pp. 117–151.

Liben, Lynn
1977 Memory in the context of cognitive development: The Piagetian approach. In *Perspectives on the development of memory and cognition,* edited by R. V. Kail, Jr., and J. Hagen. Hillsdale, New Jersey: Lawrence Erlbaum. Pp. 149–203.

Lorenz, Konrad
1966 *On aggression.* New York: Bantam Books.

Lukes, Steven
1973 On the social determination of truth. In *Modes of thought,* edited by R. Horton and R. Finnegan. London: Faber and Faber. Pp. 230–248.

Luria, Alexander R.
1976 *The neuropsychology of memory.* New York: Wiley.

MacFarlane, Aidan
1977 *The psychology of childbirth.* Cambridge, Mass.: Harvard Univ. Press.

Malinowski, Bronislav
1948 *Magic, science and religion.* New York: The Free Press.
1961 *The dynamics of culture change.* New Haven, Connecticut: Yale Univ. Press.

Maranda, Eli K., and Pierre Maranda
1971 *Structural models in folklore and transformational essays.* The Hague: Mouton.
Marshack, Alexander
1976 Implications of the Palaeolithic symbolic evidence for the origin of language. *American Scientist* **64**(2), 136–145.
McManus, John
1978a Ritual and ontogenetic development. In *The spectrum of ritual,* edited by E. G. d'Aquili, C. D. Laughlin, and J. McManus. New York: Columbia Univ. Press. Pp. 183–215.
1978b Ritual and social cognition. In *The spectrum of ritual,* edited by E. G. d'Aquili, C. D. Laughlin, and J. McManus. New York: Columbia Univ. Press. Pp. 216–248.
Meyerhoff, Barbara
1974 *Peyote hunt: The sacred journey of the Huichol Indians.* Ithaca, New York: Cornell Univ. Press.
Miller, George
1971 Linguistic communication as a biological process. In *Biology and the human sciences,* edited by J. Pringle. Oxford: Oxford Univ. Press (Clarendon). Pp. 70–94.
Miller, George A., Eugene H. Galanter and Karl H. Pribram
1960 *Plans and the structure of behavior.* New York: Holt.
Munn, Nancy
1973a The spatial presentation of cosmic order in Walbiri iconography. In *Primitive art and society,* edited by A. Forge. London: Oxford Univ. Press.
1973b *Walbiri iconography.* Ithaca, New York: Cornell Univ. Press.
Murphy, George R.
1978 A ceremonial ritual: The mass. In *The spectrum of ritual,* edited by E. G. d'Aquili, C. D. Laughlin, and J. McManus. New York: Columbia Univ. Press. Pp. 318–341.
Needham, Rodney
1962 *Structure and sentiment.* Chicago: The Univ. of Chicago Press.
Neisser, Ulric
1967 *Cognitive psychology.* New York: Appleton.
Ortner, Shirley
1973 On key symbols. *American Anthropologist* **75**(5), 1338–1346.
Parsons, Talcott
1966 *Societies.* Englewood Cliffs, New Jersey: Prentice-Hall.
Piaget, Jean
1952 *The origins of intelligence in the child.* New York: International Universities Press.
1960 *The Child's conception of physical causality.* Totowa, New Jersey: Littlefield, Adams and Co.
1971 *Biology and knowledge.* Chicago: Univ. of Chicago Press.
1976 *The grasp of consciousness.* Cambridge, Massachusetts: Harvard Univ. Press.
1977 The role of action in the development of thinking. In *Knowledge and development,* edited by W. F. Overton and J. M. Gallagher. New York: Plenum. Pp. 2–16.
Piaget, J., and B. Inhelder
1969 *The psychology of the child.* New York: Basic Books.
1973 *Memory and intelligence.* New York: Basic Books.
Powers, William T.
1973a Feedback: Beyond behaviorism. *Science* **179**, 351–356.
1973b *Behavior: The control of perception.* Chicago: Aldine.
Pribram, Karl
1971 *Languages of the brain.* Englewood Cliffs, New Jersey: Prentice-Hall.
Pribram, Karl H., and Diane McGuiness
1975 Arousal, activation, and effort in the control of attention. *Psychological Review* **82**(2), 116–149.

Radcliffe-Brown, Arthur R.
  1924 The mother's brother in South Africa. *South African Journal of Science* **21**, 542–555.
  1940 On social structure. *The Journal of the Royal Anthropological Institute* **70**, 1–12.
Radin, Paul
  1957a *Primitive religion.* New York: Dover.
  1957b *Primitive man as philosopher.* New York: Dover.
  1972 *The trickster. A study in American Indian mythology* (originally published in 1956). New York: Schocken Books.
Rappaport, Roy A.
  1968 *Pigs for the ancestors.* New Haven, Connecticut: Yale Univ. Press.
Reichel-Dolmatoff, Gerardo
  1971 *Amazonian cosmos.* Chicago: Univ. of Chicago Press.
  1976 Cosmology as ecological analysis: A view from the rain forest. *Man* (ns.) **11**, 307–318.
Ricoeur, Paul
  1962 The hermeneutics of symbols and philosophical reflections. *Philosophical Quarterly* **2**, 191–218.
Ridington, Robin
  1978a Sequence and hierarchy in cultural experience. Paper presented at annual meeting, Canadian Ethnological Society, London, Canada.
  1978b Monsters and the anthropologist's reality. Paper presented at "Sasquatch and Other Phenomena: An Inquiry into the Structure of Knowledge." Vancouver, Canada.
  n.d. Our myth, their reality. Unpublished manuscript.
Rosenfeld, Albert
  1977 "When man becomes as god: The biological present." *Saturday Review* (December 12), Pp. 15–20.
Rossi, Ino
  1974 Structuralism as scientific method. In *The unconscious in culture*, edited by Ino Rossi. New York: Dutton. Pp. 60–106.
Rosenzweig, Mark R., and Edward L. Bennett
  1976 Enriched environments: Facts, factors and fantasies. In *Knowing, thinking and believing*, edited by L. Petrinovich and J. L. McGaugh. New York: Plenum. Pp. 179–213.
Rosenzweig, Mark R., Edward, L. Bennett, and Marion C. Diamond
  1972 Brain changes in response to experience. *Scientific American* **226**(2), 22–29.
Sarnat, Harvey B., and Martin G. Netsky
  1974 *Evolution of the nervous system.* New York: Oxford Univ. Press.
Schank, Roger
  1973 Identification of conceptualizations underlying natural language. In *Computer models of thought and language*, edited by R. C. Schank and K. M. Colby. San Francisco: Freeman. Pp. 187–247.
Schank, Roger, and Robert Abelson
  1977 *Scripts, plans, goals and understanding.* Hillsdale, New Jersey: Lawrence Erlbaum.
Schiffer, Michael
  1976 *Behavioral archaeology.* New York: Academic Press.
Schneider, David
  1968 *American kinship: A cultural account.* Englewood Cliffs, New Jersey: Prentice-Hall.
Service, Elman R.
  1975 *Origins of the state and civilization.* New York: W. W. Norton.
Shearer, Jon, Charles D. Laughlin, and John McManus
  1977 A biogenetic structural model of phenomenological phases. Unpublished manuscript.
Silverstein, Michael
  1976 Shifters, linguistic categories and cultural description. In *Meaning in anthropology*, edited by K. H. Basso and H. A. Selby. Albuquerque: Univ. of New Mexico Press. Pp. 11–55.

Simmons, R.
  1973 Semantic networks: Their computation and use for understanding English sentences. In *Computer models of thought and language,* edited by R. C. Schank and K. M. Colby. San Francisco, California: Freeman.
Smith, W. John
  1977 *The behavior of communicating.* Cambridge, Massachusetts: Harvard Univ. Press.
  1978 Ritual and the ethology of communicating. In *The spectrum of ritual,* edited by E. G. d'Aquili, C. D. Laughlin, and J. McManus. New York: Columbia Univ. Press. Pp. 51–79.
Sokolov, Evgenii
  1977 Brain functions: Neuronal mechanisms of learning and memory. *Annual Review of Psychology* **28,** 85–112.
Sperber, Dan
  1975 *Rethinking symbolism.* Cambridge, England: Cambridge Univ. Press.
Stephens, Christopher D.
  n.d. a *A palaeolithic scenario.* Unpublished manuscript.
  n.d. b Archaeology and understanding. Unpublished manuscript.
Stephens, C. D., and C. D. Laughlin
  n.d. c Artifacts of knowledge. Unpublished manuscript.
Stephens, Margaret K.
  1978 Childbirth—whose baby? The history and sexual politics of delivery. Unpublished manuscript.
Tillich, Paul
  1951 *Systematic theory.* Chicago: Univ. of Chicago Press.
Tinbergen, Niko
  1951 *The study of instinct.* London: Oxford Univ. Press.
Turner, Victor W.
  1967 *The forest of symbols.* Ithaca, New York: Cornell Univ. Press.
  1973 Symbols in African ritual. *Science* **179,** 1100–1105.
Valentine, James W.
  1969 Patterns of taxonomic and ecological structure of the shelf benthos during Phanerozoic time. *Paleontology* **12,** 684–709.
Vogt, Evon
  1978 On the symbolic meaning of percussion in Zinacanteco ritual. *Journal of Anthropological Research* **33**(3), 231–243.
Waddell, Eric
  1975 How the Enga cope with frost: Responses to climatic perturbations in the central highlands of New Guinea. *Human Ecology* **3**(4), 249–273.
Waddington, Conrad H.
  1957 *The strategy of the genes.* London: Allen and Unwin.
Wall, Carol
  1974 *Predication: A study of its development.* The Hague: Mouton.
Wallace, Anthony F. C.
  1966 *Religion: An anthropological view.* New York: Random House.
Welker, Wallace
  1976 Brain evolution in mammals: A review of concepts, problems, and methods. In *Evolution of brain and behavior in vertebrates,* edited by R. B. Masteron. Hillsdale, New Jersey: Lawrence Erlbaum.
Wertheimer, Martin
  1961 Psychomotor coordination of auditory-visual space at birth. *Science* **134:**1692.
Whitehead, Alfred N.
  1929 *Process and reality.* New York: Macmillan.

Wilson, Colin
   1956   *The outsider*. Boston: Houghton.
   1976   (ed.) *Men of mystery*. London: W. H. Allen and Co.
Wynne-Edwards, Vero C.
   1962   *Animal dispersion*. New York: Hofner.

VI
SYMBOLIC
UNIVERSALS

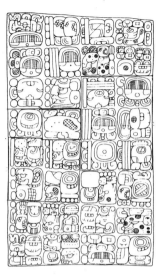

21
Introduction

MARY LeCRON FOSTER
STANLEY H. BRANDES

It seems appropriate in this section to conclude our effort to make sense of symbols with a chapter that attempts some kind of a summary of symbolic universals as they are reflected in behavior. The author is well aware of the provisional nature of this summary, but it is at least a beginning and gives some notion of the enormous complexity of the symbolic function as it is revealed through human products and as it has been variously analyzed by contributors to this book. The chapter is also useful in that it illustrates symbolic functions with data supplied by the other chapters in this volume.

To some scholars, it might seem trivial to distinguish between the paradigmatic and the syntagmatic aspects of language, as analyzed in this concluding selection, since any activity might be construed as an event in time (s-structure, in Ardener's terms) within which, at various points, alternative items (from paradigms) might potentially be realized. This is, of course, true, and the Chomskyan generative–transformational approach to language description does away with the distinction to focus entirely on its syntagmatic aspect. However, Foster considers this a major defect in that theory of language, which otherwise has much to recommend it. It is precisely at the paradigmatic level that intentionality enters language through the process of selection. Componential analysis in anthropology has shown some kinds of systematic relationships that are built into lexical paradigms, and there is no reason why paradigms of other symbolic systems cannot be analyzed as fruitfully. Studies of the distribution of semantic components are in their infancy. Bowerman's analysis of the development of semantic constructs in the course of first language learning shows how individual symbols undergo subtle shifts en route to conventionalization. The theoretical potential of Ardener's p-structures, as discussed both by him and by Laughlin and Stephens, for understanding the semantics of culture change and resistance to change, needs to be explored in depth in many cultural contexts.

Another issue that is related to this one is the degree to which referential and figurative paradigms are similarly composed. Ardener's p-structures are especially relevant here. These are not definable on the basis of paradigmatic realization in s-structures—or are they? Ardener says that paradigmatic specification (i.e., selection from a paradigm) is generated "live" in syntagmata, but that this is not true of social paradigms, of which p-structures are representative, because no one "utters" society. P-structures are templates for events but are not, themselves, realized in the event. It would seem that metal roofs and deep-sea wharfs are elements of one symbolic paradigm in the Bakweri p-structure used illustratively by Ardener, and Frenchmen and zombie-masters are elements of another. Unlike a referential system, a connotative system generates its paradigm members on an ad hoc basis. The p-structure does not "contain" members of one or the other set; it simply sets up the defining conditions for them. In this, a p-structure, while paradigmatic, is a paradigmatic abstraction based on a syntagmatic sequence, and as such seems at first glance to be little different from Chomsky's deep structure, which is itself syntagmatically organized but unrealized as syntax (Chomsky, 1965). However, as a figurative rather than a denotative representation, its paradigmatic components (i.e., those capable of direct realization rather than abstractions from them) are circumstantially dictated. It is precisely here that the creativity of event shows itself. It is triggered not by rule nor selected from among items capable of some kind of dictionary listing, but triggered by circumstance and selected from among anything in the environment that seems appropriate both to that circumstance and to the triggered p-structure.

Another way in which p-structure differs in kind from Chomsky's *deep structure* is that Chomsky claims for the latter some kind of universality (Chomsky, 1965:118), which Ardener certainly does not intend for p-structures; it is precisely the difference between the p-structure of different cultures that guides their social events into different channels.

Foster's paradigms and Ardener's p-structures, however, differ in kind. Ardener's p-structures are not concrete and include only the *conditions* for inclusion of such items as zombie-masters and Frenchmen or metal roofs and deep-sea wharfs, while Foster's paradigms are made up of them. Kuhn's (1962) paradigm and Ardener's p-structure both condition strings of events that can be realized in any number of ways; their meaning relationships have a determining influence on the direction that events will take, but environmental circumstances provide the material from which (Foster's) paradigmatic choices will be made. Turner's (1974) use of the term *paradigm* is close to Ardener's *p*-structure, but seems to have some major differences that are worth exploring in some other context. In view of the many differences in the way that the term *paradigm* has been used, we believe that Ardener is correct to reject it for the kind of underlying interrelational meanings that he wishes to describe.

Since Foster's research on primordial language provides the most significant new data that she has generated as input to this volume, and since relationships between phylogeny and ontogeny are controversial (see Part III), she would like here to call attention to the high degree of similarity between the meanings that are built into the earliest learned words and oppositions of language-learning children as described by Bowerman and the sound-meaning units that she herself has uncovered in primordial roots. Both are much concerned with spatial relationships, whether as shape as such (Eva's "moon"), as moving parts in contact (Eva's "kick"), as relational shape such as horizontality (Christy's "night night"), or relational interaction such as joining–separating (both children's "on/off"). Movement in space seems to have as much semantic saliency for small children as for primordial man. The capacity to relate metaphorically grows, in both cases, from these concrete beginnings into the capacity to make elaborate metaphorical abstractions. Thus the polysemic nature of reference seems to be primordial, contravening the conventional linguistic assumption derived from Saussure's definition of the linguistic sign, that it consists of a primary signifier–signified relationship to which additional meanings may be added through metaphoric extension.

Most authors who discuss language origins as gestural, stress pointing as associated with *naming* (see, for example, Marshack, 1976:281). Studies such as Foster's and Bowerman's (for ontogenetic symbolic similarities) indicate that it is not referential *names* that are primary but deictic relationships in space. In fact, Bowerman's prototypical model suggests that reference is very far from *naming* in any way that that term can be defined.

This prototypical paradigmatic multivalence has interesting implications both from the standpoint of detecting the first, faint homologous possibilities for symbolism in lower species and for understanding its biological functioning in the human brain. It is to be hoped that these points and others will increase the possibility for fruitful dialogue between the biological and the human behavioral sciences.

Adaptation is defined for *Homo sapiens sapiens* requires an infinitely more sophisticated model than that developed to account for it in lower species (e.g., sociobiological models such as that developed by Wilson, 1975). Washburn (1977) has argued cogently to this effect from a physical anthropological standpoint, and Sahlins (1976) from a sociocultural anthropological standpoint. An ethologist, Chalmers (this volume) takes a similar stance. While each argues from within a different discipline, their reasons for rejecting the simplistic sociobiological model for man are similar. To begin to understand the reasons for man's extraordinary evolutionary success one must start with the symbolic function in all of its complex manifestations. Such understanding requires massive effort, and all that we can say at this point is that small beginnings are being made, with this volume and elsewhere. Making sense of symbols in all of their ramifications is probably both the most difficult and most rewarding task to which man can set himself, and, as Laughlin and Stephens conclude, one that is probably necessary if human culture is to survive the technological explosion of our scientific age.

References

Chomsky, Noam
    1965   *Aspects of the theory of syntax*. Cambridge, Massachusetts: MIT Press.
Kuhn, Thomas S.
    1962   *The structure of scientific revolutions*. Illinois: Univ. of Chicago Press.
Marshack, Alexander
    1976   Some implications of the paleolithic symbolic evidence for the origin of language. *Current Anthropology* **17** (2), 274–282.
Sahlins, Marshall
    1976   *The use and abuse of biology*. Ann Arbor: Univ. of Michigan Press.
Turner, Victor
    1974   *Dramas, fields, and metaphors: Symbolic action in human society*. Ithaca, New York: Cornell Univ. Press.
Washburn, Sherwood L.
    1977   Human behavior and the behavior of other animals. Address given at the meeting of the American Psychological Association, San Francisco, August, 1977.
Wilson, Edward O.
    1975   *Sociobiology: The new synthesis*. Cambridge, Massachusetts: Harvard Univ. Press (Belknap).

are describing and that are not always recognizable to their informants. This may be a danger in the attempt to assign covert meaning, but it is a risk worth taking since theoretical validity will ultimately rest on the degree to which the anthropologist's abstractions generate new insights, supported either by new data or new looks at old.

Symbolic Modes

On the overt, or behavioral, level, symbolic relationships have a temporal dimension. This is called the *syntagmatic* dimension or mode. It is lineal in the sense that within it symbols must be arranged in terms of *before* and *after*. Lying behind this mode is the *paradigmatic*[1] dimension of symbolism. Paradigms are virtual rather than realized. Their members are interrelated through partial likeness: a sharing of semantic features. A member of a paradigmatic class may become realized by virtue of selection to occupy a before or after slot in an actualized syntagmatic sequence. Only one member of a class may be thus realized. However, the class itself may consist of a string that is syntagmatically realized. Generalizations from syntagmatic strings, such as grammatical statements that a sentence may consist of a noun plus a verb, or that lunch follows breakfast and precedes dinner, are symbolic rules constructed of paradigmatic abstractions from particular realizations, such as that *noun* may be represented by "man," "John, " or that breakfast consists of "toast and coffee," "orange juice and boiled eggs." All activities have a syntagmatic dimension, but the paradigmatic counterpart is fully developed only in human behavioral systems. Without it there would be no symbolism. Its complexity accounts for the complexity of human culture.

A paradigm implies realizable members of the paradigmatic class, which may be relatively open-ended or relatively restricted. A paradigmatic construct, called by Ardener (this volume) a *p*-structure, is an abstract organizing principle, incapable of actualization but generative of *s*-structures: realized syntagmatic sequences. It is useful to separate the two paradigmatic concepts, as Ardener has done, and this terminological distinction will be followed here.

The paradigmatic mode is organized around metaphor: a relationship of partial likeness. Syntagmatic relationships are organized around selection from paradigms to serve function. Syntagmata have a dynamism lacking in both paradigms and *p*-structures that is, at least in part, a factor of the interrelational potential that *p*-structures permit.

Culture and its subsystem, language, are open-ended, both because met-

---

[1] Use of the terms *syntagmatic* and *paradigmatic* as both linguistic and nonlinguistic modes is borrowed from Hjelmslev (1953:24).

aphor creates the possibility of virtually infinite paradigmatic addition and because temporal change forces continual syntagmatic readaptation through p-structural transformation. Thus, symbolism in culture has both potential for elaboration and for systematic checks on random proliferation. Some examples of readaptation and organizational restraint are found in the chapters of this volume by Cherry, Conkey, Kitahara-Frisch, and Ardener.

In the syntagmatic mode, problem-solving is paramount. Choices are geared to individual survival. If adaptive, they will also promote survival and well-being of the social group. In human groups, conflicts over such choices involve the imbalance of seriation. Seriation may depend either on value sequences, as from "best" to "worst," from more to less effective, or on dominance or control, through force or some other, more subtle, generation of power. Paradigmatic alternatives may be selected because they are semantically toward the top rather than the bottom of such scales. Conflict may then threaten from the bottom, and social equilibrium come to be in jeopardy. New choices are made, disrupting the existing p-structure, which must readjust to accommodate changed social circumstances. A linguistic example comes to mind. Liberated woman has recently come to object to being classified as *man* in accordance with standard, taxonomic usage. *Human* or *person* is being substituted for *man* in many anthopological texts: a conscious, syntagmatic choice of a different member of a paradigm. In address forms, women object to semantic labeling by marital status, since men are not thus designated. A new address term—*Ms.*—was devised to replace both *Miss* and *Mrs.*, expanding the paradigm for the time being, but potentially reducing it if the replacement proves successful.

At an earlier stage, *Master* balanced *Miss* as a form of address for the unmarried. Since full social maturity for men did not depend, as it did for women, on marriage, use of *Master* dwindled until it has virtually disappeared. Table 1 shows three stages in a historical paradigmatic progression from symmetry to assymmetry to possible future symmetry.

In this paradigm there is a polarization of distinctive features according to two semantic dimensions: gender and marital status. New social choices are at present reducing the value of marital status, canceling out this dimension. Thus, the governing p-structure is in process of change. Whether

TABLE 1
Changing Paradigm of Title Forms

	Male	Female	
Former	Mr.	Mrs.	Married
	Master	Miss	Unmarried
Present	Mr.	Mrs.	Married
		Miss	Unmarried
Evolving	Mr.	Ms.	

this will bring an equalization of the value attached to gender is a question. In all human societies, polarization seems to imply a hierarchy of values. Cultural reversals are sometimes devised that counteract, or temporarily adjust, the imbalance, as will be discussed later in this chapter. Here I am concerned only to present a model that will indicate the dynamic interrelationships between the two modes. Paradigms tend toward symmetry, and seem because of this to exert an unconscious constraint on the change potential. Asymmetries are corrected, often bringing new asymmetries in their train.

Componential analysis in anthropology has focused analytic attention on generic aspects of meaning, and has been criticized (see, for example, Dolgin *et al.,* 1977) for having little dynamism. This is, in fact, unavoidable since the paradigm itself lacks the dynamism of social interaction. As only one side of the symbolic coin, it is less than "real" because paradigms are, *in toto,* unrealizable since only one member can be actualized in a given syntagmatic sequence. Nevertheless, focus on this "unreal" organization of paradigms abstracted from their syntagmatic matrix has brought to light many hitherto unsuspected interrelationships in the cultural code (i.e., language) that have both *s-* and *p-*structural implications.

Kay (1971) outlines the dimensions of inclusion in paradigms and, in so doing, at least implies the repetitive formation of like paradigmatic systems, each starting from a *unique beginner,* or all-inclusive taxon of taxons (a taxon is a class), and progressing through a sequence of less inclusive taxa to terminal taxa, which classify the most specific entities that the system admits. A taxon such as the English unique beginner *plant* progresses more or less symmetrically through a succession of less inclusive taxa, such as *tree, vine, grass,* and so on, each with a similar spread of terminal taxa. This system is, in turn, replicated in other domains; for example, *animal* as unique beginner progressing through less inclusive categories such as *cat, dog, horse* to respective terminal taxa such as *Siamese, Manx; Airedale, Fox terrier; Arabian, Palomino.* Not all terminal taxa are on the same level (Kay, 1971:872), so the symmetry is never completely achieved, although it is always suggested. For example, generic *cat* moves to *tiger, lion, (domestic) cat,* and *then* to terminal taxa (*Siamese,* etc.), whereas generic *dog* moves directly to *Airedale,* and so on, omitting the intermediate stage.

Language provided man with a powerful tool for classification, but classification is expressed in many symbolic ways other than language. National flags are symbols that are understood all over the nonprimitive world. The strength of any such symbol lies in its power to classify, or subsume. I, as an American, am represented by my flag. Christians are represented by the Cross and Jews by the Star of David. These symbols are unique beginners even though visual rather than verbal. Less study has been made of nonlinguistic than of linguistic taxonomies, but analysis of the latter is itself recent and will be useful as a model for such enterprises.

What Ortner (1973) calls *key symbols* can perhaps be equated with Kay's *unique beginners*. Symbols can probably be classified into a hierarchy of more or less inclusive cultural representations, just as occurs with linguistic labels. Ortner's analysis is a useful start toward developing such a cultural paradigm. She separates key symbols into two major types: summarizing and elaborating symbols, and adds ritual as a third, but indeterminate, type, unintegrated into her asymmetrical model.

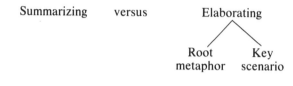

Summarizing symbols, such as flag or cross in the Western world, are items that imply whole congeries of emotion-laden concepts, while elaborating symbols are used to illustrate various aspects of culture through shared relational or qualitative meanings. Because of these likenesses, Ortner calls them *root metaphors*, and leaves summarizing symbols semantically undesignated. Cows, for the Dinka, are cited as a root metaphor, providing "an almost endless set of categories for conceptualizing and responding to the subtleties of experience " (Ortner 1975:1342). Key scenarios are idealized formulae for human action, such as the Horatio Alger plot scheme, apparently an ideal sort of *p*-structure, never realized in *s*-structure. However, in my opinion, Ortner overlooks the most important differentiation between the two symbolic types: meanings of both are connotative, but, in summarizing symbols, connotative features seem to be covert, while in elaborating symbols they are overt. The latter *equates* with simile, for the likeness is expressed, whereas in the former, a *substitution* of one thing for something similar takes place; in other words, it is the summarizing type that is a *root metaphor* and not the elaborating type, which is, instead, a root *simile*. The meaning of likeness is made explicit and is exploited for ideological purposes. In Ortner's example, Dinka social ideology is explicitly likened to the behavior of cattle. Summarizing symbols are *interpretive* of moral values, whereas elaborating symbols are expressive of them. Although they do not specify this, it is obviously the reason that Dolgin *et al.* (1977:24) say that the functions of the two are different and that a summarizing symbol is stripped of its elaborating uses and may be used (*appropriated*) by an individual or group for its own ends. It remains to be explored whether summarizing symbols ever actually derive from elaborating symbols, as such *stripping* would seem to imply.

In Ortner's model, a *key scenario* is idealized action—culturally sanctioned action *par excellence*: how an ideal character would behave under certain social conditions. This explicit, ideal model corresponds on a conscious level to scenarios of myth and ritual on an unconscious. Modified to include this, the model becomes symmetrical.

Although the meanings of both symbol types are connotative, the semantic arrangements that underlie them differ. Both use relational similarity, but those of summarizing symbols are highly condensed, whereas those of elaborating symbols are specified separately. This condensation is identical with that described by Freud (1931) as characteristic of dream symbols. Just as in dream analysis, the meanings can be made clear if abstract–relational concepts are substituted for the concrete–relational meanings of the symbol. For example, the concreteness of a clogged toilet in a dream may mean that the patient feels that he is not "getting through" to the analyst. A similarly simple cultural example may be taken from the figures portrayed on Mayan stelae, as described by Durbin (this volume), where the metaphoric symbol is examined for abstracted possibilities of resemblance to concrete features condensed in the totality of the image. The personage portrayed is of stone (enduring), is large (important), has phallus-shaped implements and attributes including weapons (male aggression or power). One figure, like another, occurs on a phallus-shaped, upright stone (male potency, replicability) and is accompanied by calendrical signs (cyclical recurrence). The hieroglyphic message is an elaborating, idealized scenario explicitly describing good birth, lineage, marriage alliance, conquest, rule, and so on. This elaborating simile (i.e. explicit) scenario accompanies the highly stylized summarizing symbol to provide idealized, specific common function, whose realization rules allow expression only of activities that are highly valued. (This is reminiscent of the highly idealized messages found on mimeographed American Christmas cards today where only the most highly valued activities of family members are described.)

We may contrast this simile scenario with a metaphor scenario as described by Brandes (this volume). In this type of scenario (often occurring as ritual [as in Brandes's example], as myth, or as artistic creation), condensation is so important that it sometimes seems as if an entire paradigm were being squeezed into a single syntagmatic slot, just as in a root metaphor (e.g., the elaborately ornamented male personage on the Mayan stele), except that there is a sequential progression in which temporal slots are themselves meaningful.

Condensation eliminates the need for a syntagmatic "build-up" since antecedents, as a total semantic "given," are compressed so that they can be represented within the single event. For example, in the ritual described by Brandes (this volume), a cannon shoots toys and sweets from an elevated position on the town hall into the town square where children scramble for the goodies. This shooting is the analogic equivalent of male (phallic cannon), ruling (town hall), adult dominance (height of canon *in* the town hall), of the young and female adolescent (the crowd below in the square) by placating them with items that they value (toys and sweets) but that are associated with childishness and triviality. The social irresponsibility of the Bighead clowns is, at the same time, contrasted effectively with the transcendent serenity of the parental figures (Giants).

There is little (perhaps nothing) in this ritual that is truly referential. The message is carried solely through connotation, thus heightening its evocative power. This contrasts with the message of the Mayan stelae, which is partially referential and partially connotative (see Durbin, this volume), effectively combining the factual reason of historical description (syntagmatic) with the idealistic condensed fantasy (paradigmatic) of the phallicized bas-relief figures. Together, the highly selective historical data and the carefully chosen artistic symbols are generated by a single, overarching p-structure.

While linguistic analysis has always relied more heavily on syntagmatic than on paradigmatic relationships, Chomsky (1957) introduces a potentially paradigmatic dimension with the notions of *deep structure* and transformation, the latter a question of the reordering of underlying structures by reversals, additions, and deletion, effecting a reorganizing of syntagmata through paradigmatic readjustment. The principle of transformation and its relationship to p-structure will be considered in greater depth in the fifth section of this chapter.

Characterization of human thought as comprising two distinct modes has a long epistemological history. What Lévi-Strauss (1966) called *concrete thinking,* Freud (1953) called *primary process,* and Piaget (1962) called *symbolic thought* depend upon analogy for their operation. Opposed to this are Lévi-Strauss's *rational* or *logical* thought—Freud's *secondary process,* Piaget's *operational thought*—that is goal-oriented and geared to temporal sequentiality and cause–effect relationships. All of these writers quite clearly believe that analogical thought is ontogenetically and phylogenetically prior to *rational* thought and less characteristic of *civilized* than of *primitive* man (see Sperber, this volume, for an opposing view).

The cognitive operational versus analogical bifurcation seems to relate to the syntagmatic versus paradigmatic dimensions of symbolization. Atemporal likeness is an organizational principle in both analogical thinking and paradigms, while temporality characterizes both rational thinking and syntagmata. In Western culture, with its strong scientific tradition, the temporal, goal-oriented dimension is favored, which, very probably, accounts for the widespread "intuitive" tendency to consider temporally deficient analogic thought the more primitive mode. It also may account for the emphasis in linguistic analysis on syntax and the relatively weaker attention given to semantic organization with its heavy dependency on metaphor. As a differential evaluation of polarities, this can be seen to correspond to a universal human cognitive characteristic already mentioned.

Whitehead (1927) called the two cognitive modes *causal efficacy* and *presentational immediacy*. Although lower animals classify to a certain extent, and use these classifications for survival (if only differentiating between classes *edible* and *nonedible* or *dangerous* and *nondangerous*), their presentational immediacy as a potential for analogic elaboration is far less developed than in humans, giving their causal efficacy far less scope. A basic difference between human and nonhuman mammalian species seems to be the discrimination by the latter of only concrete qualities of denotation as a classificatory principle; use of relational qualities by humans is the reason that to some their sign systems have been considered arbitrary (see the example of Rommel's army as ashtray on page 126). To others (for example, Sperber, this volume), figurative symbols seem arbitrary. Whitehead emphasizes the heavier emotional load that is carried by presentational immediacy as well as its timelessness, and that it requires causal efficacy regulation lest it run wild. He also sees that there is cultural danger in loss of analogical motivation, for if meaning becomes only reflex, the power of emotional renewal is lost.

This is in marked contrast to Freud, who, while doing more than any other scholar before or since to demonstrate the force, and even the inevitability, of primary process thinking, considered it essentially pathological because covert, hence almost inevitably out of control. Emphasis on the value of *conscious* thought is so strong in Western epistemology that through analogical elaboration it exerts *unconscious* pressure on Western thinkers to suppress all reference to what is covert. Positivism as the dominant scientific tradition (see Ardener, 1971) is a response to such pressure, as well as Chomsky's (1965) insistence on the syntactic organization of *deep structure*. By the same token, Freud's symbolic theories have had less influence on Western scholarship than his syntagmatically oriented developmental theories.

In extrapolating ontogenetic stages from instances of childhood behavior, Piaget (1962) considers the advent of *symbolic thought,* between the ages of 18 and 24 months, as a major developmental watershed. This stage (number 6) is characterized by play, and especially motor-sensory games, that provide a make-believe means of representing previous experience. Although Piaget believes that *symbolic* behavior continues to some degree throughout life, he sees it as waning in importance after about age 4, when play comes to approximate real experience more closely, and operational thought replaces *symbolism.*

He seems to ignore the fact that adults *play at* roles as much as children, often never revealing their true feelings (i.e., behaving as themselves) because the *role* seems to demand something quite other. (For vivid examples of adult *play,* see the chapters by Bloch and Brandes, this volume.) Gardner (1973:305–307) feels that the Piagetian model also leaves out artistic development, to which operational thought is not vital and may even be inimical. Mastery of symbol systems does not end with childhood, and its continuance is characteristic of all accomplished artists.

Far from terminating or tapering off with the passage of childhood as is largely the case with all other mammals (see Chalmers, this volume), human play continues throughout adult life. Bateson (1955) feels that play is not separable from any communicative mode in which a paradox is present because the message *this is play* establishes a paradoxical frame. He maintains that play is not primary process because the discrimination between play and nonplay is a function of secondary process, or *ego.* (For Bateson, the rituals described by Bloch and Brandes would obviously not qualify as *play.*) "In primary process, map and territory are equated; in secondary process, they can be discriminated. In play, they are both equated and discriminated" [Bateson, 1955:45]. For Norbeck (1971), play transcends ordinary behavior, and human play differs uniquely from the play of other species. He includes as play all kinds of sports and games, dancing, singing, wit, humor, dramas, comedies, theatrical performances and other forms of mimicry, art, music, and other aesthetic endeavors, and drug-induced states of psychological transcendence. Rites of reversal exemplify play in religion.

Chalmers (this volume) seems to be entirely correct in his judgment that play is a poorly defined concept—a sort of catch-all term under which a wide variety of behaviors are subsumed. According to his analysis, during ontogeny nonhuman primates carry behavioral sequences over from one set of triggering circumstances to another, even to the extent of replacing the first set entirely by the second. It is clear that analogy is used as a basis for action if certain items are reacted to as *food, danger,* and the like. Analogical operations in lower mammals, including chimpanzees learning "language", seem to be largely referential or denotative. Connotation seems to play a much lesser role if, in fact, it is present at all. If we consider this in connection with the Laughlin and Stephens (this volume, p. 331) evolutionary progression away from stimulus-boundedness: symbol→**symbol** → sign → formal sign, then it would seem that what the human investigators of chimpanzee "language" insert as a sign is interpreted by the animal as a symbol since for her it does not participate in a greater **symbol** system or plan (see Laughlin and Stephens p. 333) as it must for the human trainer.[2]

In contrast with the behavior of lower mammals, which is largely operational, with denotative comprehension almost entirely motivated by tangible reward (thus, only by immediate reward do chimpanzees apparently

---

[2] In my own usage *symbol* does not have the meaning it has for these authors. I prefer to reserve the term for units of culture. I would, then, consider the chimpanzee usage to be a denotative signal, since for the chimpanzee it does not participate in a paradigmatic system governed by a *p*-structural component.

learn "**language**"), human behavior is easily motivated by either very distant or fantasy reward. In religion the unknown is reacted to as if it were known and just as efficacious for the accomplishment of human goals as a scientifically or observationally attested prerequisite. It thus blends primary and secondary process, as Bateson (1955) claims, and therefore is not play.

Most of the ritualized activities of culture, religious and nonreligious, are not, in fact, *consciously* operational. Since neither their causes nor their goals are consciously recognized, they are neither play nor logical responses to "real" stimuli. If there are only two basic modes of thought and it is quite clear that that of ritual is not secondary process, then it must be primary process, operating through extensive use of analogy, carried over from one referential domain to another. If analogy is the motivating factor, then analogy to what? If ritual is representational, what does it represent? Where Saussure (1959) assumed that the denotative system *par excellence* was not analogically motivated, i.e., was arbitrary, Sperber (this volume) has also claimed arbitrariness for ritual, at least on a cultural (as contrasted with an individual) level, and has greatly clarified the crucial difference between denotative and connotative symbolism. The issue of connotative arbitrariness, raised by Sperber seems to be the most crucial question facing those who would analyze symbolism. In the next section we will, therefore, be concerned with the nonreferential meaning of cultural symbolism.

Culture as Symbolism

In order to explore the extent to which *culture* is symbolic—that is, complexly representational—we will need to look first at the way in which individual schemata are formed or old schemata reinforced and adapted to new circumstances. In order to understand the latter, we can do no better than to turn to a familiar and vivid example from the writings of Proust (1934).

The narrator describes an incident in his adult life when he was visiting his mother and taking tea with her. She sent out to a local bakery for a little cake, called a *petit madeleine*.

> And soon, mechanically, weary after a dull day with the prospect of a depressing morrow, I raised to my lips a spoonful of the tea in which I had soaked a morsel of the cake. No sooner had the warm liquid, and the crumbs with it, touched my palate than a shudder ran through my whole body, and I stopped, intent upon the extraordinary changes that were taking place. An exquisite pleasure had invaded my senses, but individual, detached, with no suggestion of its origin [pp. 34–35].

He struggled to bring to memory the association from the past which he felt had changed his mood. "And suddenly the memory returns. The taste was that of the crumb of madeleine which on Sunday mornings at Combray . . . when I went to say good day to her in her bedroom, my Aunt Léonie used to give me, dipping it first in her own cup of real or of lime-flower tea'' (p. 36).

Translated into the terms of our theory, what had happened was that a new syntagmatic stretch, the present event, became grafted emotionally to an old, the tea-ritual with Aunt Léonie, through the operation of analogy: the paradigmatic function. Past was covertly projected forward into the present, inducing an abrupt change in mood, which was not easily accounted for by the person undergoing the change.

It is not just recreation of the old experience that is at issue, but recreation of an *affective* experience. Since the book begins with a description of the narrator as a child in bed but unable to sleep because of longing for expressions of love from his elusive mother, one can safely assume that the indulgence of Tante Léonie, associated with the feeding of the madeleine, had unconsciously evoked in the child an earlier period in which his mother had ministered with undivided attention to his need for nurture. It may well have been as much the fact that his mother was now once again providing nourishment for him that evoked the memory of Tante Léonie, as the taste of the little cake itself. Events are linked through time by means of analogy combined with affect. This metaphoric linkage of events is the key to the symbolic mode. It is the law of semantic, as Langer (1942:119) has so cogently stated. Without it, there would be no motivation except on the immediate, gratificational level of lower mammals. It explains why humans are able to respond with feelings to very abstract concepts, as well as how culture avoids becoming a sterile reflex, in Whitehead's sense.

The reason that aesthetic experiences, religion, and play are particularly evocative of emotion is now apparent; they are more directly and specifically analogical than the ordinary experiences of everyday life. Everyday ritual may also be fiercely adhered to and defended, however, because also evocative of past affective experience.

Music is peculiarly effective as a communicative mode because it can represent the tempo of life, with its pauses, emphases, uncertainties, experiments, and resolution (also see Bolinger, this volume, on intonation in language). It becomes representative for all hearers because it is not tied to a specific experience. This suggests why painting that attempts faithful representation is less successful than that which has at least some degree of ambiguity. Just as the hearer of a musical composition must supply his own scenario, so must the viewer of a painting provide it with his own, internal analogue. Art is ''good'' to the extent that it admits a variety of symbolic interpretations. By the same token, myth and ritual are ''good'' precisely because they are analogically ambiguous (i.e., perception of relationships is an individual experience).

Freud (1931) provided us with a useful guide to symbolic organization in his discussion of dreams. He did not say so, but there is every reason to suppose, and none to doubt, that dream symbolism bears a strong structural relationship to that of the waking state. The syntagmatic dimension is present in the temporal organization of dream events as they are remembered by the dreamer after awakening. Prior relational conditions are condensed into simultaneous concrete images. For Freud, dream-displacement and dream-condensation provide the structure of the dream (1931:199). Condensation allows a short dream to describe a complex situation by means of relational juxtaposition of elements. Displacement simply means that the dream represents something that does not itself occur in the dream. Since it is true of all symbolisms that they represent in a different mode something that is basic to another, there is nothing in dream-displacement to surprise us. The displaced dream elements are juxtaposed through condensation so as to create a set of relational metaphors for something similar. An element is selected because of the common ground of meaning that it shares with whatever it represents. (This is much like an ingenious game of charades in which objects are juxtaposed to suggest rather than state a meaning, only that dreams are regularly far more clever in discovering shared relationships than the most skilled charade players.) Just as dreamed objects represent, so do dreamed actors, who should never be taken at face value and may as easily represent a trait as a whole person. Since bodily functions in dreams are just as much the result of displacement as any other dream topic, it must be assumed that they, too, represent something quite other than themselves. If dreams, at the latent (deepest) level, represent bodily function, as Freud believed, this does not necessarily mean that bodily elements in dreams are themselves factual statements. Latency simply means that each individual builds forward from his earliest analogies, successively deriving new models from new and more sophisticated analogues.

Applying the symbolic model outlined above to Freud's interpretation of dreams, we discover something of utmost importance to symbol interpretation: Simultaneity is paradigmatic. There is timelessness in events that are juxtaposed. They are the ground against which the temporal sequence is enacted, the "given" of the situation in terms of which the resolution must occur. Such a given expresses something timeless and universal having to do with biological certainties such as sexual characteristics or familial role.

We find the same kind of symbolic condensation in the setting and artifacts of ritual. Elements are juxtaposed to one another in static ways. At Christmas the evergreen wreath is at window or door, while the lighted tree stands within the house. Mistletoe is also inside but overhead in some central area such that it is impossible at some point not to walk beneath it.

If instead of searching syntagmatically for a historical (i.e., causal or *rational*) explanation of Christmas (e.g., the Druids used greens as a symbol of fertility; we inherited the custom), we search paradigmatically, we come first of all to the Biblical myth of miraculous impregnation culminating in birth of a miraculous child. Impregnation and birth normally imply a male and a female element that are juxtaposed in such a way that male phallus is placed within the female genital enclosure. This is a union which bears fruit. What more appropriate, as representation of impregnation and gestation, than evergreen (eternal) circle at the entrance, phallic evergreen tree inside with candles or lights (male fertility translated into energy) and mistletoe, also eternally green, with white (pure) berries as the result of union (represented by the kiss) accomplished through the appearence of the fetus within the womb, the promise of the child to come. These relationships are established through analogy rather than through historical causality. The fireplace with burning log also represents the fertilized womb. Santa Claus, the young-old child is born down the chimney and into the home, bringing promise of eternal felicity in the gifts he bears. Santa Claus is the most condensed Christmas symbol of all: at the same time bearded, supernatural male, pregnant female (round little belly, bag full of toys), and child who miraculously appears in the home, with promise for the future. In America Santa Claus is a summarizing symbol (see Ortner, 1973; Foster, n.d.). Santa Claus is fantasy, but his role is faithfully carried out by family members, usually parents, while his implied presence is felt by young and old.

Symbolic messages tend to be redundant. Something implicit in the paradigmatic setting, the timeless matrix, is acted out (in dream, fantasy, or actual movement) temporally. The implication is that this is the solution for the individuals involved, as against the universal potential implied by the setting.

To return to the Christmas story, the setting with wreath, tree, mistletoe, fireplace, and empty stockings provides a paradigmatic, condensed background for the syntagmatic fantasy enactment—the descent of Santa through chimney and fireplace to fill the waiting stockings from his bulging bag. Santa is the birth and the hope, condensing all of humanity and the ages in his person and providing concrete evidence of future joy through the gifts that he brings.

Notice that in ritual as in dreams, I consider the culmination of the action a solution, as Jung did, rather than a wish, as did Freud. A culmination is always a transformation, based on the materials in which the conflict is grounded, but transcending the original situation by using old materials in new ways. The oldest materials are those of early individual experience, either in the life cycle of the individual, or in the primal days of cultural symbolic organization. The two are not dissimilar since biology must have loomed as large in the consciousness of primal man as in that of the neonate.

The procreation–birth sequence found in Christmas myth and ritual is of major symbolic importance in every culture. Van Gennep (1960) first called attention to ritual enclosure and disclosure as a major feature of many transitional rites involving change of status. Death ritual also involves enclosure (burial) and (implied) disclosure (emergence into afterlife). Many other types of ritual event use this pattern. Human beings disguised behind masks are revealed to initiates, packages are ritually wrapped, and their contents subsequently disclosed. Food is universally consumed as a ritual necessity. It might be pointed out that, as a model, there are two kinds of enclosure in procreation. The first is partial, in the male–female sexual encounter. The second is total, in the deposit of the semen and the generation of the child, the ultimate disclosure. The sacredness of the enclosure vehicle itself is everywhere apparent, as church, temple, or sacred vessel. What is introduced is fire, water, or both, as the insemination essences. This is always accompanied by movement: ringing of bells, beating of drums, swinging of a censor, dancing or other rhythmic activity. At some point in the ceremony there is always ingestion. The purpose of such ceremonies is always the health and well-being (rebirth) of the individual or the community.

In many cultures analogy and ritualized analogues are consciously recognized as just as important for adults as for children, and biology is frankly admitted as the template for religious ceremonialism. The Dogon, as described by Griaule (1965), explicitly derive all of their economic, social, political, religious, and artistic forms from analogy to the human procreative process. The Ndembu (Turner, 1967) liken the forms of plant life used in ritual to human forms and products involved in procreation and nurture. In both cultures, at least some aspects of ritual are simile rather than metaphor scenarios since they are explicit rather than implicit.

Repression, considered by psychoanalytic theory to be the cause of primary process behavior produced through the dynamic unconscious (for discussion, see Cohen, this volume), is obviously differentially activated in these cultures than in our own. We may, perhaps, be justified in assuming that is is greater in Western culture because of the higher value put on scientific causality that creates a desire, unconscious and unsuccessful, to suppress primary process thinking out of existence.

Ontological Models and Phylogenetic Stages

My strategy in analyzing the growth of symbolism is first to postulate rules governing the systems and structures of modern symbolism and then to compare these to simpler (i.e., earlier) stages in the attempt to discover the earliest periods at which some rudiments of these rules can be said to exist. For data on developmental sequences in the maturation of the human child, the most completely documented account is that of Piaget, who has been concerned to discover the ways in which successive stages of learning are integrated within the life history.

Piaget (1970:13) considers that the most fruitful approach to the reconstitution of genetic stages in the rational organization of knowledge would lie in analysis of prehistory, but this is forever impossible because the psychology of early man cannot be recovered, but ontogenesis can serve as a substitute (see Lamendella, this volume, on this point). It is true that we cannot observe prehistoric man in action, nor test his ability to perform logical operations, but we do have evidence of his representative capabilities in the more durable products remaining to us in the archaeological record. These can be surprisingly revealing as Kitahara-Frisch, Conkey, and Durbin (this volume) show.

Fortunately for recovery of stages in symbolic evolution, symbolism is representation, and representation often leaves behind a palpable product. Study of material culture, once an important part of anthropology, but long in decline, must surely be revived if artifacts are to be studied for the light that they throw on cognitive function (see Cherry, this volume, for a non-archaeological analysis of artifactual symbolism). They may be just as revealing of this as are behavioral sequences, and have the advantage of greater durability, something that Piaget seems not to have considered.

Isaac (1976) has provided a sequence for the development of tool types from the Oldowan period through the Upper Paleolithic. Control over basic stone fracture progressed slowly, and by comparing tools from one stage to the next, it is possible to discover something about sensory-motor organization in the representative process. Shape was gross and unplanned for around 500,000 years, at which point, during the Lower Pleistocene, perhaps 1½ million years ago, symmetrical or mirror organization was introduced and elaborated during the Middle Pleistocene. Forms were few, and there was little regional variation. Containers probably also came in between 1 and 2 million years ago. During this period, cranial capacity doubled. One can assume that it was correlated with the discovery of binarism and especially of two important binary relationships that still prevail in modern symbolic structures: the mirroring of opposites (tool blades), and the assymetrical congruity of forms (use of containers, hafting), the foundations of paradigms and syntagmata, or analogical and logical thinking, respectively.

According to Piaget (1962:7–52), mimicry begins almost immediately after birth with imitation of noises similar to those made spontaneously by the neonate, followed later by imitation of gestures that the infant has himself first spontaneously made and can see, then by imitation of movements that he has made but cannot see, and finally by gestural imitation of movements he has not himself produced earlier and of the movement of objects that have some but not total likeness to his own movements. While this sequence is taking place, the infant is spontaneously rehearsing a whole range of articulatory sounds, ultimately learning to match his sounds to those made by an adult. By 12 to 15 months, he is able to replicate gestures that he has not previously made and to discover new tools through actual experimentation rather than imitation, and is beginning to imitate the words of adult speech.

If one compares this to the developmental sequences of the Pleistocene, one sees a similar beginning in gross imitation and a progression through mirroring to the capacity to experiment and to copy previously unknown models (see Kitahara-Frisch, this volume).

At around 18 to 24 months, the child begins the sixth, or *symbolic,* stage with the beginnings of analogical representation. Analogical representation in vocalization and gesture has already been present but not in differentiation of the symbol and what is symbolized. Early play is largely sensory-motor imitation of objects in motion. Later representations, after about age 4, more closely approximate reality. (Gardner [this volume] discusses two early styles of organizing play. His *patterners* seem paradigm-oriented and his *dramatists* syntagma-oriented.)

While ontological stages of cognitive organization are well attested in the work of Piaget and others, the method of cognitive acquisition is less well understood. However, psycholinguistic exploration of first language learning is doing much to bridge this gap. The prototype model described by Bowerman (this volume), and explored and refined through analysis of contextually embedded examples of the early word-use of her own children, will undoubtedly find application to other symbolic systems as well as language.

Semantic prototypes are, roughly, what would be the first, or *par excellence* referential meaning for a word provided in a dictionary. While adults tend to model these standardized meanings to children, the child's cognitive input to the learning situation derives operationally from spatial–relational recurrences that the child has observed and that he must attempt to bring into phase with the culturally symbolic system that he is to master. Thus, the child makes and tests assumptions about word meaning that are sometimes not in accord with conventional usage—in other words he establishes his own, individualized prototype. A difference (but one that is perhaps not as great as it seems at first glance) is that the child's usage is globally metaphoric in such a way that its underlying, defining categories are not immediately clear. Reference and metaphor are not sharply delineated, as they tend to be in adult speech. One shades into the other because of the looser way that analogical matching is applied. Evolutionary analysis of language and other symbolic systems show that phylogenetic parallels to the ontogenetic prototype exist.

In the Mousterian period, perhaps 50,000 years ago, the first burials, grave offerings, and traces of cult appear, as well as the first engraved artistic squiggles. Since the child's early symbolic play involves delayed imitation by means of object representation of what has been observed but not assimilated, it seems similar to the symbolic activities of the Mousterian epoch. Burial is a mirror representation of birth, with return of the body to enclosure, and Mousterian cults are connected with burial practices. Death is apparently seen to be in some sense like birth, and the earth, in which bodies are interred, becomes the relational mirror image of the mother. Pointed weapons are used for killing, an analogy of the male sexual penetration that leads to life. Death of an animal, like the procreative act, brings life to the hunter and his family. Containers come to be associated with oral containment of food and the contained gestation of the female. Thus, womblike food containers and generative food preparation become the proper analogical role models for females, and phallic-aggressive hunting and warfare those designated for men. All of these analogies have persisted virtually unchanged until the present day when they are suddenly being questioned by Western women. Since emotion accrues to paradigmatic analogues, it is certain that those with such antiquity will not easily be foresworn. Yet the fact that they are being questioned may lead to an important transformation.

Paradigmatic analysis has been slow to gain currency, so it is not surprising that studies of paradigmatic change are not far advanced. Pioneering work is being done especially by Berlin and Kay (1969) on the evolution of color terminology (Berlin and Berlin, 1977; Kay, 1975) and by Berlin (Berlin *et al.*, 1973) on that of classification in folk biology. These studies indicate that a universal progression from generic—at least binarily inclusive—terms to those of greater specificity has occurred. This conclusion tallies well with the phylogenetic development from gross to more specialized tool types and the ontogenetic development from gross to more refined instruments of pretend play. (See also Bowerman, this volume, for ontogenetic stages of language learning.)

Another study of paradigmatic evolutionary development is my own reconstruction of a hypothetical paradigm of prehistoric sound–meaning correspondences (Foster, 1978), based on cross-linguistic comparison of languages hitherto considered to have no common ancestry. The study began with the chance discovery that certain sound sequences were associated with certain similar meanings in languages with no known interconnection. For example, a global meaning of *outward extension or spread* underlies words containing a verbal root of the form (or something very like) [p. . .1] (vowel absent or interposed) in all of the world's languages that I have examined to date. In English, this meaning and its phonological expression (English [fl] derives from Proto-Indo-European *pl) occurs in words such as *flood, fly, flow, flat, full, field*. The root morpheme in these words correlated with that in, e.g., the following:

Finnish: *pelto* 'field,' *paljo-* 'much, many,' *palkki* 'beam, balk,' *pallero* 'chubby child,' etc.[3]; Nyanja (Bantu): *pala* 'coming out of; in great quantity or numbers,' *pala* 'to scrape, plane; go to seek; soft or loose,' etc.; Hanunoo (Malayo-Polynesian): *palpas* 'releasing, freeing, letting go,' *pulud* 'piece, section, cut off portion,' *palkas* 'shooting with bow and arrow,' etc.; Tamil (Dravidian): *pala* 'many, several, diverse,' pulam 'arable land, rice field,

---

[3] "etc." indicates that this does not exhaust the list of cognates.

region,' etc.; Yurok (Algonquian-Ritwan): *peloy* 'to be big (of human beings, animals, birds, tools, trees, etc.),' *plohp-* 'to be in spate, to flood,' *plol-* 'to be wide,' *pul* 'downriver,' etc.

Any given simple, two-consonant root almost invariably occurs in more than one word in each language and may be modified in each by the addition of an affix or affixes. The passage of time may erase some but not all of these words from the vocabulary, but since the root occurs in others it will probably not be lost entirely. Thus, roots are less likely than words to erode over time. Both sounds and meanings also undergo changes, but these changes tend to preserve some partial likeness. For example, Proto-Indo-European *p becomes English [f], which is like [p] in voiceless and bilabial articulation, and unlike it in substituting fricative for stop articulation. Sound change is also regular in such a way that we can predict from what occurs in one language what will occur in the same position in another that is genetically related to it. Thus, *p in Latin *pleo* 'fill' corresponds to [f] in English *fill* just as *p in Latin *pater* corresponds to [f] in English *father*. It is also *systematic*, so that in father the *t remaining in Latin as [t], corresponds to English [th] in voicelessness and point of articulation, but differs in substituting a fricative for a stop, just as was the case in the English change from *p to [f].

The meanings of recoverable roots are largely motional–relational, with implications of shape that derive from the direction in which the motion occurs, or as a result of the motion. While the words derived (by affixation) from these roots may represent objects (i.e., ''name'' objects), the original meaning of the root seems to have been more global and based on observed variations in movement rather than on object differentiation (note the similarity to early stages of language acquisition as described by Bowerman, this volume). When such a root is compared to another with one same and one different consonant, we discover that each consonant (here inferred by using one consonant as constant, the other as variable) has an associated meaning, so that the joining of the two was an early syntactic operation adding articulation to articulation, meaning to meaning.

The relationship of sound and meaning was one of analogy, in which the point and manner of articulation constituted distinctive features of the sound that were like the distinctive features of meaning. Thus, a projection of the two lips together provides the meaning of forewardness or projection for [p], while the pulling away of the tongue from the alveolar ridge in articulation of [l] constitutes a meaning of disjunction. The two, in combination then, provide a meaning of outward extension with separation, appropriate to the flow of water, the splitting off of a board, the separation of a field, or the distinctiveness of objects in a large group—all found in the various meanings of words with underlying *pl in the example.

Since, at the earliest stages of language, represented by this reconstruction, sound and meaning were undifferentiated (and the sound–meaning equation was not yet arbitrary) the reconstructed units cannot be said to be *phonemes,* I labeled them phememes, "a rarely used cover term for the smallest lexical and/or grammatical unit. Lexically, it is the *phoneme,* gramatically the *taxeme*" [Pei and Gaynor, 1969, pp.166].

Since, according to my analysis, these elements seem to exist in all of the world's languages, together they must make up the paradigmatic stock of the ancestral language from which presentday languages derived through a regular but differential process of sound and meaning change. The systematic organization of the complex analogical relationships between orally produced sound and spatially oriented movements shows that full development of this first language was predicated on a fairly sophisticated symbolic usage and, therefore, could hardly have occurred before the Upper Paleolithic, in which archaelogical remnants show that the necessary symbolic mechanisms existed (see Conkey, this volume; also Lamendella, this volume, for ontogenetic parallels). Language, like all but very simple technology, became a tool for symbolic representation from perhaps 30,000 to 40,000 years ago, and as in the use of any reliable tool, the operational mechanisms have retreated from consciousness (see Cherry, this volume). As this retreat took place, the oral tract as a topological analogue for movement in space was lost to view, and sounds and meanings were free to change quite independently of one another, further increasing the distance between the two, until, at the present time these relationships are scarcely discernible.

The 18 reconstructed sounds and their analogical meanings are reproduced in Table 2. Sounds are arranged in a triple, symmetrical series. Names are given to the meanings of these sounds and topological diagrams provided as possibly more representative of the meanings than the linguistic designations. It may tax the reader's imitational ingenuity to ascertain the degree to which the sound production (i.e., the positioning and/or movement of the articulators) is analogous to the topological relationships diagramed, but this mimicry is virtually essential to complete understanding of the system. In the later stages of the analysis I was assisted in the assignment of meaning to the more recalcitrant signs by obvious gaps in the meaning system, but the meaning system itself, the ingenuity and the multidimensional characteristics of the paradigm, came as a complete surprise to me as they began to emerge from the comparisons and charted organization of the data. Although the organization is mine, the shared features make such an organization possible.

The contention of Kitahara-Frisch (this volume) that both language and tool-making require the same basic symbolic potential and that concurrent development worked to the advantage of each is reinforced by the discovery of spatial analogy. Tools extend the use of body parts, especially hands and teeth, by expanding and exploiting the spatial relationships and their potential for action that nature had supplied. Language extended this in a different, but still analogical way, by reproducing the *meanings* of such relationships through analogy.

TABLE 2
Primordial Phememes[a,b]

	Conterminous				Lineal	
	Conjunctive			Extensive	Directional	
	Peripheral	Internal		Protractive		Peripheral
Feature organization	Protrusive (labial)	Intrusive (dental)	Obtrusive (alveolar)	Rectilineal (palatal)	Propulsive (velar)	Curvilinear (labiovelar)
Stopped	p Projective	t Intromissive	c Emissive	č Clinal	k Delative	k^w Reversive
Spirant	f Abessive	θ Juxtapositive	s Expansive	š Vertical	x Oppositive	x^w Apertive
Resonant	m Bilateral	n Interpositive	l Disjunctive	y Horizontal	r Sublative	w Circumscriptive

[a] Adapted from Foster, 1978, p. 79.

[b] *Phememe* is used here to mean a unit with a relationship between sound and meaning that is based on spatio–relational analogy.

Before the sophisticated instrument that I have described here could have become completely developed and integrated, there must have been a period of many millenia, corresponding to the bulk of the Paleolithic, in which simpler systems were successively tested and improved or discarded, just as early and simpler tools preceded the more complex Upper Paleolithic technologies.

During the Upper Paleolithic, varied symbolic representations appeared, and it would seem that the major aspects of the presentday symbolic design were developed at that time. Art and symbolic design rose to great heights. Depiction of hunted animals on cave walls and ceilings suggests that the procreation–death analogy was already well-developed. Accurate portrayal of symbolic animals suggests that fantasy was already "real," much as child fantasy develops into realism around the fourth year. Upper Paleolithic representation is both realistic and abstract.

Transformation, Rhythm, and Reversal

Anthropologists not engaged in symbolic analysis often complain that rigor in such analysis is impossible to achieve because if analogy is the basis of structure anything can come to be related to anything else, or, at the very least, the anthropologist as analyst is free to create analogies where they do not necessarily occur in the minds of informants. On this point Lévi-Strauss (1969) is often quoted as saying, "if the final aim of anthropology is to contribute to a better knowledge of objectified thought and its mechanisms, it is in the last resort immaterial whether in this book the thought processes of the South American Indians take shape through the medium of my thought, or whether mine take place through the medium of theirs" (p. 13). But he also says (1969), "Starting from ethnographic experience, I have always aimed at drawing up an inventory of mental patterns, to reduce apparently arbitrary data to some kind of order, and to attain a level at which a kind of necessity becomes apparent, underlying the illusions of liberty" (p. 10). His efforts in this direction have been pioneering and perhaps not always thoroughly convincing, but he has opened the way to the possibility of discovering principles underlying connotative representations.

Transformations operate on syntagmatically organized paradigmatic constructs (i.e., p-structures) that are probably finite in number as are the possibilities for transformation. The limitation on transformational potential derives from the nature of social relationships and seems to operate as a constraint on change. Thus some transformations seem to be based on universal p-structures. The formula that Lévi-Strauss (1963) provides for mythic transformation seems equally applicable to ritual, provided that the original paradigmatic construct contains a hierarchical social imbalance that can be reversed. (For discussion of this point, see Foster, 1974. The rituals described by Bloch and Brandes, this volume, could also be analyzed by application of this formula).

The mythic formula starts with a situation in which two individuals or groups are polarized with respect to power. The transformation works to redistribute values in such a way that the previously nondominant pole becomes dominant. In essence, what this amounts to is that the actor who lacks status before the transformation gains it through a maneuver that brings him into a productive relationship with the element that previously had provided the superior antagonist with his power. The element that is transferred is not represented directly, but by means of a symbolic equivalent, and the relationship between the two actors and the symbol differs from statement of the problem to transformational solution.

Lévi-Strauss's formula relates to systems of social interaction that Bateson (1958, 1970) discussed as leading potentially to *schismogenesis*. He postulates two types of social polarization: *complementary* and *symmetrical*. The former are hierarchically polarized, whereas the latter involve equal status. Together, the two types provide the potential for a contrapuntal symbolic alternation, the one giving way to the other if either threatens to prevail. In some societies, such as Iatmul, the corrective alternation may not occur before the prevailing mode brings about social fission or schismogenesis.

Either type, if left unchecked, is disruptive to society. Corrective mechanisms may come from external or internal pressures toward social integration. Like Iatmul, Western European and American societies are schismogenetic, with tension released climactically after a build-up of intense social interaction of one of the two types. He considers that some societies, such as Bali, lack schismogenetic modalities altogether (Bateson, 1970).

I recently proposed that at least in some societies, including Bali, the integrative mechanisms to correct fission are built into single ritual events, and that successive events tend to start with the polarization mode of the one preceding, and to end, climactically, with a reversion to the other. If the event maintains rather than reverses, a succeeding event will carry out the reversal. Thus, a ritual cycle is needed to complete the alternation between the two modes (Foster, 1979). The rituals described by Bloch and Brandes (this volume) seem also to illustrate this principle.

Alternation between the two modes through ritual reversal allows for status differentiation, which seems to be necessary to symbolic social dynamism, while at the same time maintaining stability by a process of equalization. The narcissism of the human individual prevents complete stability as the drive toward dominance comes to the fore. Reversal provides cultural means for the release of the tension generated by control of hostile impulses. Alternation between potentially schismogenetic modes provides a corrective transformational mechanism.

All cultures seem to provide some kind of culturally sanctioned reversal. It may allow for virtually complete, or only partial, license. Assumption of the dress and mannerisms of the other sex is one common manifestation, described by Bateson (1958) as an important feature of Iatmul schismogenetic rites. Sometimes whole groups become involved in the reversal behavior, as during the Balinese funeral when the mourners roll into ditches, splash one another with mud, and carry the corpse to the cremation in a disrespectful manner (Covarrubias, 1937:374). In both New and Old World cultures (see Brandes, this volume, for the latter), disguised men whip and taunt bystanders during religious festivals. In the United States a certain amount of sexual license as well as intoxication is not frowned upon on a New Year's Eve.

Leach (1961) equates such role reversal with sacred stretches of time. Turner (1969) adopts van Gennep's (1960) term *liminality,* to refer to such sacred periods, especially with reference to African initiation rites that typically exhibit features of what he calls *anti-structure.* Liminality provides an interval during which the somewhat artificial, or formalized, modes of the roles imposed by society are discarded in favor of an emotionally heightened state of *communitas* that binds together in fellowship those who have undergone the rigors of the rite. Communitas emphasizes both egalitarianism and the role-deprived state of the novitiate. As such, it is closely identified with the impoverished and those occupying the lowest rungs in the hierarchical ladder (Turner, 1974), providing an antidote to the hierarchical imbalance between those undergoing initiation and those controlling it.

Geertz (1972) also calls attention to the emotion-enhancing effect of symbolic reversal: "Any expressive form works (when it works) by disarranging semantic contexts in such a way that properties conventionally ascribed to certain things are unconventionally ascribed to others, which are then seen actually to possess them" (p. 26). This suggests that reversal, a dynamic semantic disarrangement, is not only characteristic of certain types of sacred ritual but also *must* occur if an expressive form is to have an emotional impact. That it is especially found in sacred ritual is probably a function of the social need to intensify and maintain belief in the sacred.

Reversals are also a form of play. They provide periods of licensed pretense, allowing a lack of control that is not "real" or "intended" on the workaday level. They allow a periodic return to an infantile freedom to vent emotion with no prolonged social repercussions, or to pretend to other roles without jeopardizing one's normal status in the real world. Liminal periods tend either to be cyclic in the calendrical year or in the life cycle of the individual, where they mark important changes in status. The periodicity of intensified emotional discharge may be as important to healthy psychological functioning as dreams seem to be to the sleeper (Parman, n.d.).

Reversals, in the Western world, seem to have become transferred from the sacred to the profane sphere with the decline in religious conviction and increased polarization of work and leisure. It may be that the very banality of unindividualized work, or work that does not directly, through its products, contribute to the well-being of the worker, increases the need for reversal into the fantasy world of sports, drugs, television-watching, and the like. Leisure activities have, in any event, moved to a position of prominence and primary expenditure of planning and effort that was hitherto reserved for workaday concerns.

In every culture we find the alternation of fantasy and workaday productions that would seem to indicate that for *Homo sapiens* the former, from perhaps the Mousterian onward, has become a biological necessity.

Conclusions

The crucial role of unconscious processes in the organization of culture, as described here, would seem to parallel ontogenetic organization and development of unconscious processes as the maturing individual learns to interact appropriately in his cultural environment. It would, therefore, seem to be of utmost importance to anthropology to integrate cultural and psychobiological models of development (both ontogenetic and phylogenetic) with one another and with cultural models governing social behavior. This requires an interdisciplinary rapprochement of the kind that the conference on which this volume was based, and the book that resulted from it, were designed to explore.

It is also of paramount importance that anthropologists interested in symbolism (and this should include all anthropologists, since culture is the symbolic paradigm upon which social behavior is modeled) recognize that symbolism is largely covert and extremely complex, and that adequate theories of culture cannot be based on explanations provided by, or embraced as "true" by informants. New ways of discovering meaning must be developed. Structuralism has pointed a way, but because structuralism has either geared itself only to the discovery of referential meaning, as in linguistics, or to a seemingly unrigorous postulation of connotative meaning, as in Lévi-Straussian structuralism, in which it appears possible to relate to, or derive anything from, virtually anything else (or in which ways of avoiding this problem are not made clear), a connotative structuralism seems in danger of being discredited.

To salvage and advance connotative structuralism, theorists must make explicit the ways in which unconscious meanings are related to the vehicles (symbols) by which they are conveyed and how the former can be extracted from the latter with some degree of reliability. This is not an easy task, but I am convinced that it can be done, and have tried in this chapter both to bring together and to expand upon some methodological possibilities. (For example, Ardener's p-structures contribute to more comprehensive models such as that of Laughlin and Stephens.) Symbolic anthropology has the potential to become the most integrative anthropological discipline, drawing upon the resources of all anthropological subdisciplines as well as other human sciences. The very notion of culture, as distinct from society, implies a paradigmatic approach. Progress will be made in analyzing culture in both its denotative and connotative aspects only when the two are firmly differentiated as Sperber (this volume) suggests.

Freud pointed the way toward a paradigmatic, or connotative, position, by showing how unconscious process was dynamically reflected in both dreams and in social acts. His theory suffered from being prestructural, and, by being connotative, was in conflict with the dominant syntagmatic and denotative (i.e., logical, rational, conscious) scientific tradition, which probably also inhibited his own exploration of some of his most seminal notions. It seems to me that a deliberate effort to couple structuralism with connotation might bring about an important integrational transformation that would make the unconscious both a respectable subject of inquiry and available to the scientific method. Science is already committed to a denotative structuralism, and a connotative structuralism may easily follow once the analytic premises become clear.

References

Ardener, Edwin
  1971 The new anthropology and its critics. *Man* **6**, 449–467.
Bateson, Gregory
  1955 A theory of play and fantasy. *Psychiatric Research Reports* **2**, 39–51.
  1958 *Naven.* California: Stanford Univ. Press.
  1970 The value system of a steady state. In *The traditional Balinese culture,* edited by J. Belo. New York: Columbia Univ. Press. Pp. 284–401.
Berlin, Brent, and Elois Ann Berlin
  1975 Aguaruna color categories. *American Ethnologist* **2**, 61–87.
Berlin, Brent, Dennis E. Breedlove, and Peter H. Raven
  1973 General principles of classification and nomenclature in folk biology. *American Anthropologist* **75**, 214–242.
Berlin, Brent, and Paul Kay
  1969 *Basic color terms: Their universality and evolution.* Berkeley and Los Angeles: Univ. of California Press.
Chomsky, Noam
  1957 *Syntactic structures.* The Hague: Mouton.
  1965 *Aspects of the theory of syntax.* Cambridge, Massachusetts: MIT Press.
Covarrubias, Miguel
  1937 *Island of Bali.* New York: Alfred Knopf.
Dolgin, Janet L., David S. Kemnitzer, and David M. Schneider
  1977 *Symbolic anthropology: A reader in the study of symbols and meanings.* New York: Columbia Univ. Press.
Firth, Raymond
  1973 *Symbols public and private.* Ithaca, New York: Cornell Univ. Press.
Foster, Mary LeCron
  1974 Deep structure in symbolic anthropology. *Ethos* **2**, 344–355.
  1978 The symbolic structure of primordial language. In *Perspectives in Human Evolution.* Vol. 4, edited by S. Washburn and E. R. McCown. Menlo Park, California: Benjamin/Cummings. Pp. 77–121.
  1979 Synthesis and antithesis in Balinese ritual. In *The imagination of reality: Essays in Southeast Asian symbolic systems,* edited by A. L. Becker and A. A. Yengoyan. Norwood, Jersey: Ablex.
  n.d. Deciphering Santa. Unpublished manuscript.
Freud, Sigmund
  1931 *The interpretation of dreams.* New York: Carlton House.
  1951 *Psychopathology of everyday life.* New York: Mentor.
  1953 *A general introduction to psychoanalysis.* New York: Permabooks.
Gardner, Howard
  1973 *The arts and human development.* New York: Wiley.
Geertz, Clifford
  1972 Deep play: Notes on the Balinese cockfight. *Daedalus* **101**, 1–37.
Griaule, Marcel
  1965 *Conversations with Ogotemêli.* London and New York: Oxford Univ. Press.
Hjelmslev, Louis
  1953 *Prolegomena to a theory of language.* Indiana University Publications in Anthropology and Linguistics, Memoir 7 of the *International Journal of American Linguistics.*

Isaac, Glynn
  1976   Stages of cultural elaboration in the Pleistocene: Possible archaeological indicators of
         the development of language capabilities. In *Origins and evolution of language and
         speech*, edited by R. Harnad, H. D. Steklis, and J. Lancaster. New York: Annals of
         the New York Academy of Sciences **280,** 275–288.
Kay, Paul
  1971   Taxonomy and semantic contrast. *Language* **47,** 866–887.
  1975   Synchronic variability and diachronic change in basic color terms. *Language in Society*
         4, 257–270.
Langer, Suzanne K.
  1942   *Philosophy in a new key.* New York: Mentor.
Leach, Edmund
  1961   *Rethinking anthropology.* London School of Economics, Monographs on Social An-
         thropology, no. 22. London: Athlone.
Lévi-Strauss, Claude
  1963   *Structural anthropology.* New York: Basic Books.
  1966   *The savage mind.* Illinois: Univ. of Chicago Press.
  1969   *The raw and the cooked.* New York: Harper.
Needham, Rodney (ed.)
  1973   *Right and left: Essays on dual symbolic classification.* Illinois: Univ. of Chicago Press.
Norbeck, Edward
  1974   The anthropological study of human play. *Rice University Studies* **60**(3), 1–8.
Ortner, Sherry B.
  1973   On key symbols. *American Anthropologist* **75,** 1338–1346.
Parman, Susan
  n.d.   An evolutionary theory of dreaming, with notes on play and learning. Unpublished
         manuscript.
Pei, Mario, and Frank Gaynor
  1969   *Dictionary of Linguistics.* Totowa, New Jersey: Littlefield, Adams.
Piaget, Jean
  1962   *Play, dreams and imitation in childhood.* New York: W. W. Norton.
  1970   *Genetic epistemology.* New York: Columbia Univ. Press.
Proust, Marcel
  1934   *Remembrance of things past.* New York: Random House.
Saussure, Ferdinand de
  1959   *Course in general linguistics.* New York: Philosophical Library.
Turner, Victor
  1967   *The forest of symbols.* Ithaca, New York: Cornell Univ. Press.
  1969   *The ritual process: Structure and anti-structure.* Chicago, Illinois: Aldine.
  1974   *Dramas, fields and metaphors: Symbolic action in human society.* Ithaca, New York:
         Cornell Univ. Press.
Van Gennep, Arnold
  1960   *The rites of passage.* Illinois: Univ. of Chicago Press.
Whitehead, Alfred North
  1927   *Symbolism: Its meaning and effect.* New York: Capricorn.

Name Index

Subject Index